The Self and its Shadows

Stephen Mulhall presents a series of multiply interrelated essays which together make up an original study of selfhood. He explores a variety of articulations (in philosophy, psychoanalysis, and the arts) of the idea that selfhood is best conceived as a matter of non-self-identity—for example, as becoming or self-overcoming, or as being what one is not and not being what one is, or as being doubled or divided. Philosophically, a sustained reading of the work of Nietzsche and Sartre is central to this project, although Wittgenstein is also fundamental to its concerns; Mulhall therefore draws extensively on texts usually associated with 'Continental' philosophical traditions, primarily in order to test the feasibility of a non-elitist form of moral perfectionism. Within the arts, several essays examine various films whose themes intersect with those of the philosophers under study (including Hollywood melodramas, recent spy movies such as the Bourne trilogy and the latest incarnation of James Bond, and David Fincher's 'Benjamin Button'); Wagner's Ring cycle is a recurrent concern; and the novels of Kingsley Amis, J. M. Coetzee, and David Foster Wallace are also prominent.

The Self and its Shadows

*A Book of Essays
on Individuality as Negation
in Philosophy and the Arts*

Stephen Mulhall

OXFORD
UNIVERSITY PRESS

OXFORD
UNIVERSITY PRESS

Great Clarendon Street, Oxford, OX2 6DP,
United Kingdom

Oxford University Press is a department of the University of Oxford.
It furthers the University's objective of excellence in research, scholarship,
and education by publishing worldwide. Oxford is a registered trade mark of
Oxford University Press in the UK and in certain other countries

Published in the United States of America by Oxford University Press
198 Madison Avenue, New York, NY 10016, United States of America

British Library Cataloguing in Publication Data
Data available

Library of Congress Cataloging in Publication Data
Data available

ISBN 978–0–19–966178–7 (Hbk.)
ISBN 978–0–19–874822–9 (Pbk.)

Contents

The mistake in traditional thinking is that identity is taken for the goal. The force that shatters the appearance of identity is the force of thinking...

Theodor Adorno, *Negative Dialectics*

Man is a rope...—a rope over an abyss. A dangerous going-across, a dangerous way-faring

...What is great in man is that he is a bridge and not a goal...

Friedrich Nietzsche, *Thus Spake Zarathustra*

All parts away for the progress of souls,

All religion, all solid things, arts, governments, all that was or is

Apparent upon this globe or any globe,

Falls into niches and corners

Before the procession of souls along

The grand roads of the universe.

Walt Whitman, *Leaves of Grass*

Introduction

The three epigraphs to this book are intended to amount to an orienting exchange of ideas about its topic: that of selfhood or subjectivity or personal identity, and more specifically a variety of articulations (in philosophy, psychoanalysis, and the arts) of the idea that selfhood is best conceived as a matter of non-self-identity (for example, as becoming or self-overcoming, or as being what one is not and not being what one is, or as being doubled or divided).

The work on and around this topic that is embodied in the essays to follow was initially conceived as an attempt to get clearer about the precise lineaments of Heidegger's version of this apparently paradoxical or perverse picture of selfhood—a version that I have written about elsewhere at some length,[1] and that accordingly takes the form of an almost absent presence in this context—by getting clearer about other thinkers' apparently distinct versions of the same picture, in particular those developed by Sartre (supposedly as a critique of Heidegger) and by Nietzsche (to whom Heidegger explicitly related his own thinking years before the extensive and controversial lectures he gave on Nietzsche in the 1930s).

Nietzsche's presence in this book has another proximate cause, however—namely, as a response to the fact that Stanley Cavell's and James Conant's attempts to present Nietzsche as the inheritor of a species of non-elitist or democratic moral perfectionism associated with Emerson has regularly been rejected by commentators on the grounds that the main body of textual evidence they employ to justify this characterization comes from Nietzsche's early collection of essays, *Untimely Meditations*, and so offers no basis for thinking of his putative perfectionism as anything other than an early and

---

[1] Cf. chapter 5 of my *Heidegger and* Being and Time (London: Routledge, 2005), and chapter 2 of my *Philosophical Myths of the Fall* (Oxford: Princeton University Press, 2005).

promptly-discarded concern.[2] So the set of three essays included here, on major Nietzsche texts taken from early, middle, and late phases of his intellectual career, is also intended to test just how good a case can be made for the idea that his early Emersonian perfectionism, with its hostility to any attempt to sort humanity into (superior and inferior) natural kinds, and its associated vision of the self as inherently transitional or self-overcoming, was something that his thinking never wished to overcome.

Sartre's presence is similarly over-determined. For some years, I had been contemplating the project of developing an introduction to his major work *Being and Nothingness* by focusing on its chain of striking and provocative examples (the waiter, the woman on a date, the weary walker, and so on); then Sebastian Gardner published his own introduction to that text—an illuminating account in many ways, but one prefaced by (and built upon) the claim that Sartre's text sets forth 'a metaphysical system of a traditional kind', and that any account of the text which directed our attention instead to its 'phenomenologically resonant, psychologically engaging' examples 'will leave the reader with little more than an intuitive grasp of Sartre's conceptions and the text itself will remain opaque ... The investment of time and attention required to read [*Being and Nothingness*] either in whole or in substantial part makes sense only if the aim is to understand why Sartre thinks that his vision possesses philosophical truth in the strictest sense'.[3]

One could hardly deny that Sartre's *magnum opus* presents us with a 'metaphysical system', on some understanding of that phrase, and that one cannot grasp the book without attaining some grasp of that system. What I resist are the interrelated assumptions that this system is of a traditional kind; that it contains philosophical truth 'in the strictest sense', whereas the chain of examples interwoven with it throughout the book presumably contains philosophical truth (if it does so at all) only in a loose or lax, anyway a merely intuitive, sense; and that clarifying the terms of this metaphysical system must or can be done in isolation from that chain of examples. The four essays on aspects of Sartre's text (one of which admittedly reaches beyond it, if only by a little) that are included in what follows might accordingly be thought of as the beginnings of an alternative or counter-

---

[2] Cf. chapter 1 of Cavell, *Conditions Handsome and Unhandsome* (Chicago: University of Chicago Press, 1990); and Conant, 'Nietzsche's Perfectionism: A Reading of *Schopenhauer as Educator*', in R. Schacht (ed.), *Nietzsche's Postmoralism* (Cambridge: Cambridge University Press, 2001).

[3] Sartre's *Being and Nothingness* (London: Continuum, 2009), p. ix.

introduction to *Being and Nothingness*—one written on the assumption that, in the context of the phenomenological tradition Sartre inherits from Heidegger, philosophical truth can be grasped only insofar as one grasps it as emerging from a concrete engagement with phenomenologically resonant examples, that its more systematic metaphysical or conceptual presentation ultimately amounts to an articulation of the truth of those examples, and hence that any attempt to attend to the metaphysics of the text in isolation from its examples is bound to leave that text essentially opaque.

This introduction is not, however, primarily intended to account for my book's content, but rather for its form; and although I cannot do so without relating that form to an aspect of its content, I also need to relate it more extensively and explicitly to my conception of how philosophy can and should be done (whether engaging with this particular subject matter or any other). The nature of both relations is importantly determined for me by something I began to appreciate only relatively recently—namely, that Heidegger and Wittgenstein can be seen as conversing about the idea of conversation as a fruitful model for grasping philosophy's place in human culture (hence as the best model for philosophy's relation to other branches or domains of that culture, and the relation of any branch or domain of philosophy to any other such branch or domain). Working out the details of this model in both Wittgensteinian and Heideggerian terms was the central concern of another earlier book of mine;[4] here I can only summarize the results of that work, and in particular guard against certain misunderstandings of the model's implications.

If we consider speaking in the light of the phenomenon of conversation, and so think of speakers as possible participants in conversation, and of the various ways in which non-conversational uses of language resemble and differ from, as well as having a variety of ways of bearing upon (that is, hanging together with, leading to and from) the capacity to converse, then we might begin by remarking that conversations themselves display both unity and diversity. What makes a conversation a single or continuous thing (both synchronically and diachronically) is the participants' common and sustained orientation towards a particular topic or subject matter (or a set or interlinked chain of such topics); what makes it a conversation as opposed to

---

[4] *The Conversation of Humanity* (Charlottesville and London: University of Virginia Press, 2007).

a collective monologue is the distinctive perspective that each participant brings to bear upon its subject matter. For the contribution that each speaker makes to the conversation will reflect not only the particularity of their own experience of the world, but also the distinctive array of knowledge (as well as the distinctive modes of its acquisition) that they have thereby acquired or mastered. Think, for instance, of the ways in which an employee of a logistics business, a Greenpeace member, and an Internet entrepreneur might contribute to a conversation about government efforts to shift the distribution of goods from road to rail.

Consequently, the capacity to converse hangs together with the possibility of growth in one's understanding, both of the specific subject matter and of reality more generally: one might learn not only pertinent facts of which one was previously unaware, but also come to appreciate how the various dimensions or aspects of a topic relate to one another, and thereby attain a deeper understanding of how that topic relates to other topics, and how and why one person might see those internal and external relations differently from another. Such an enhanced understanding would manifest itself, amongst other ways, in an enhanced ability to converse with others, since it would partly be constituted by a deeper grasp of how different individuals might bring their experience and competences to a particular conversation, and how one might best engage with what they have to say with a view to understanding it better and perhaps convincing them to see things otherwise. For a speaker to be a potential conversation partner is thus for them to have something to say (something genuinely responsive both to the reality of the subject matter and to the particular perspectives and concerns of one's conversation partners) and something of their own to say (something each is prepared to stand behind, to own rather than to disown—something through which each stakes and declares herself).

If, however, the logistics employee, the Greenpeace member, and the Internet entrepreneur can converse in such ways, that is in part because each of the various forms of human activity and discourse that they embody and draw upon have a potential bearing upon one another. The possibility of such an interpersonal exchange is a manifestation of the inherently dialogical structure of the language, and so of the culture or form of life, within which such conversational exchanges take place. This is perhaps most evident at what one might call the disciplinary level of culture—the level at which particular domains of human enquiry and practice are rendered systematic and reflective, and whose evolving relations to one another reflect the unity-in-diversity of conversation. On the one hand, the domains of politics, morality, religion, art, history, economics, and so on have their own distinctive (even if questionable and evolving) internal logic and purposes; on the other hand, whenever we try to understand a particular subject or topic, we find that any or all of these disciplines may have a contribution to make. My earlier imaginary conversation over a government transport policy in this sense reflects the way in which intellectual disciplines hang together with one another; and appreciating from case to concrete case the ways in which the perspective of a historian, an economist, a physicist, and a meteorologist might each bring something distinctive to a conversation amounts to deepening one's understanding of any such perspective by enhancing one's grasp of how it bears upon other such perspectives. One thereby deepens one's capacity to see how both the various distinctive modes of human understanding of our life in the world, and the various facets of that life itself, hang together.

But if our forms of life with language, and hence language itself, have a dialogical unity-in-diversity, then so must philosophy. After all, philosophy (like any other mode of systematic human enquiry) is itself internally differentiated and unified in just this way. It is part of deepening one's understanding of a topic or subject matter that initially appears to be the sole concern of one branch of philosophy to appreciate the ways in which work in other branches might always have a bearing on work in the given branch, and of course vice versa; and to appreciate that is inseparable from a deepening appreciation of the distinctive nature of philosophy itself (since it amounts to a deepening appreciation of how and why each of these diverse branches hangs together with others, hence of what gives activity in any such branch a claim to be considered part of philosophy). This internal dialogical unity is underwritten by the fact that each branch of philosophy might be thought of as emerging in response to certain kinds of questions posed by the existence and fertility of a corresponding aspect of the broader culture of which it forms a part—an implication carried by the labelling of its branches (e.g. 'philosophy of science', 'philosophy of art', 'philosophy of mind'). If each such facet of our form of life hangs together with the others, then the same will hold true of the bearing of each corresponding branch of philosophy upon the others.

At the same time, however, philosophy is itself one branch or facet of human culture, one part of the various human forms of life with language.

Hence it will itself form part of the diverse unity of that culture: its deliverances will have a bearing upon other such branches, whose deliverances in turn can have a bearing upon philosophy. In other words, philosophy is a potential partner in conversations with other disciplines, with each bringing its own resources and presuppositions to bear on an indefinitely ramifying range of topics, and all asking for acknowledgement of their distinctiveness as well as their pertinence. And just as one deepens one's understanding of philosophy by coming to appreciate the unity-in-diversity of its internal dispositions, so one further enhances that understanding by appreciating the various ways in which it can find and put itself into conversation with other disciplines.

Before we broach the question of the bearing this model might have on the form of the present volume, some words of warning are in order, all of which follow from the following reminder: the idea of regarding speech (and so language, culture, and philosophy) in the light of conversation is a matter of using conversation as 'a centre of variation', a specific phenomenon around which other related phenomena can be illuminatingly grouped or organized, an object of comparison or a lens through which certain otherwise-neglected aspects of the relevant phenomena come into clear focus (even if others may thereby go out of focus, here and now). So to deploy it is not to claim that all speech is a contribution to a conversation, or that every facet of a culture is always actually engaged in a multiplicity of productive dialogues (let alone a single, overarching dialogue) with every other facet, or that all philosophizing explicitly or necessarily includes reflecting upon the relations between any or all of the branches of that subject. Neither does the use of this model commit me to the claim that any given individual speaker or mode of human enquiry or branch of philosophy is always either making or is able to make a positive or penetrating contribution to a conversation with its corresponding others. Some conversations make no progress, others involve one party simply talking past another, and others again reveal each party's utter inability to comprehend the perspective of another; and of course, with respect to any given topic, any particular interlocutor might turn out to have nothing to say about, even to have no interest in, a topic of burning significance to another.

The point I am trying to make might come out more clearly if I were to say that the relevance of conversation as a centre of variation is proved as much by the incidence of conversations that go nowhere, break down, or never find a mutually intelligible starting point, as it is by those which fulfil the highest hopes of their participants; for it is only potential conversation partners that can become embroiled in conversations that go nowhere or break down or never get started—or, to put the point another way, only those essentially capable of successful interlocution are capable of failing to do so on any particular occasion, in any of a multitude of ways. The critical point is that dialogical intercourse is a standing possibility at these differing levels, and as clearly revealed as such in its failures as in its successes—one might call it the horizon within which our lives with language are lived. Accordingly, not to see that the question of the bearing of one party's perspective on another is always capable of being posed—that we can always ask how, if at all, one party's claims or concerns hang together with those of any other—is to fail to appreciate part of what makes speech, language, culture, and philosophy the distinctive phenomena that they are.

Something Stanley Cavell has said about the form of his first book has a bearing on the idea I'm trying to get across:

I had subtitled [*Must We Mean What We Say?*] *A Book of Essays* to register a problem about what a book of philosophy is, or . . . should look like . . . I had had fancies of putting that book out in a newspaper format, so that each essay could begin on the front page and end on the back page, with various conjunctions in between. Fortunately or not, given American publishing then, and my lack of say in such matters, nothing came of this. (*A Pitch of Philosophy*, pp. 77–8)

Cavell's fancy or fantasy trades upon a feature of American papers that their British counterparts typically exhibit to a far lesser extent: the practice of beginning a large number of stories on the first page which are then picked up at various points in the main body of the paper, and often brought to a close on the closing pages. But the aspect of culture that this journalistic practice brings out is also brought out by the more general fact that stories in one section of a newspaper are always in principle relateable (and very often actually related) to stories in other sections: events reported in the business section show up in national and international political stories; sports can invade the front page, the local news section, or the culture and media pages; and the editorial and commentary material can take up any story from any section of the paper, or make connections between developments reported in two or more distinct sections. Each new edition constitutes at once a snapshot of and a contribution to the conversations that are going on in the culture that produces it, and thereby contributes to the conversations that each reader of the paper might have with those who produce it as well as any other inhabitants of that culture.

In the case of the present book, however, its subject matter suggested an alternative to the format of the newspaper as a formal realization of the model of culture and philosophy as a conversation. For that subject matter is subjectivity or selfhood—the question of how best to envisage what is involved in being a person, an individual human being; and the book chooses to explore this subject matter from the perspective of particular representatives of the arts (in particular, the arts of literature, film, and opera) as well as from that of certain philosophical texts and traditions not always regarded as entirely worthy participants in the conversations of Anglo-American philosophy departments. It therefore seemed appropriate to envisage and shape the particular conversation that this book enacts as the outcome of contributions made primarily by a variety of entities or beings that are each possessed of a certain individuality, call them the bearers of proper names—that is, by particular authors, artists, directors, and actors, together with the real and fictional characters who (and, on occasion, the objects and settings which) populate their works, as well as the works thus populated.

In this way, the apparently extreme diversity of sources and perspectives that contribute to this investigation is held together by the various and sometimes surprising ways in which any one such individual appears in more than one such text. We see, for example, Wittgenstein incorporating the mythological objects and subjects of Wagner's *Ring* cycle into his thinking, and being in turn incorporated (as the author of *Philosophical Investigations*) into the fictions of David Foster Wallace; Wagner links Wittgenstein to Nietzsche, as Moses links him to Freud; Elizabeth Costello confronts Stella Dallas, through the good offices of Ted Hughes and Cora Diamond; Sartre moves seamlessly between Dostoevsky's gambler or Kafka's accused and his own hotel voyeur or stumbling mountain climber as the primary bearers of his thought; and Paul Greengrass and Marc Forster dispute the separability of James Bond and Jason Bourne with Ian Fleming and Doug Liman. This is why, instead of a thematic index or a contents page that displays the contribution of distinct chapters to separate parts which then contribute to an argumentative whole, this book's unity is best displayed in the list of 'Dramatis Personae' that precedes the first of its twelve essays, and that forms the basis of the index that succeeds them.

My hope is that, despite the linear presentation of those essays, readers will feel prompted to follow the vicissitudes of individual characters both backwards and forwards, as their perhaps unexpected appearance in apparently distant contexts raises the question of whether (and if so how) their identity is retained across or remade by these shifts of context and mode of engagement—matters that are potentially fateful for our sense of who exactly they are, without which we cannot (on my conception of the matter) appreciate what, if anything, they might bring to the conversation (both as individuals and as exemplars of their disciplinary or generic viewpoint).

One might of course object that such a list, with its promiscuous mixing of the real and the fictional, of the philosophical and the artistic, of the human, the non-human, and the textual, implies a highly questionable equality of (let's say) ontological status. But such an objection will only hold if the book that articulates itself around this list fails to make good on its guiding intuition that such ontological distinctions are themselves rather more questionable than is often thought (in part because they depend upon conceptions of philosophy and art that occlude the capacity of each discipline or practice to engage with its others), and are indeed specifically put in question by the ability of fictional persons and artistic works to cast essential light on the issue of what it is to be a person in the first place (and by the ability of certain philosophers to allow their work to be so illuminated).

Taking such a possibility seriously need not depend on simply assuming that the (non-)identity of a fictional being or a text is essentially indistinguishable from that of a real person, although it may depend on not simply assuming that the former matter is essentially unrelated to the latter; sharp contrasts may here be as useful as strong similarities, as long as they emerge from serious consideration of concrete cases. But the relevant illumination may also come from—say—a deeper appreciation of the ways in which a real individual's identity might be decisively determined by her own and others' willingness (and reluctance) to identify and be identified with the fictional characters that she invents or embodies or encounters in the specific (artistic or philosophical) works she devotes her life to composing. They are not her, but they are hers—hers to own or to disown, entities with which she risks being confused but in which she may find the best of herself; and one could equally well say that she is theirs—their progenitor, the one from whom their own independent or individual reality necessarily emerges and into whom it always threatens to be submerged (think of J.M. Coetzee and his protagonist Elizabeth Costello). And what might we say about the ways in which that individual's identity is altered or reconstituted, for herself and for others, by the way she is taken up in the work of others (perhaps by their taking up her work and its characters), and thereby into their sense of themselves (say, as indebted or resistant to her)? Even when the one so taken up finds herself to have been fictionalized thereby, say made over or simply made up, she may find its impact to be no less fundamental to her and our sense of who she is (recall the case of Sylvia Plath, Ted Hughes, and their contending biographers and commentators).

However that may be, the worth of my grounding intuition can in the end only be measured by evaluating the tuition that its concrete elaboration is found to engender; and it is the purpose of this book of essays to provide one such, necessarily experimental, realization of its potential—call it a trial run, or one issue of a cultural magazine under guest editorship, or an improvised play of multiple interlocution. The risk is that the project of staging such simultaneous exchanges merely theatricalizes the participants, converting them (whether fictional or real) into mere characters, making the drama of their encounters unduly melodramatic, even operatic; Nietzsche adverts to this (as we shall see) when he claims that conversations put into writing are like paintings that consist of nothing but false perspectives. The countervailing hope is that this way of realizing conversation will tap into the kind of theatre (or melodrama or opera) through which such theatricalizing is best overcome, one in which the characters find themselves to be genuinely in one another's presence. But as an art critic once said, presentness is grace.

Some of the material in the essays that follow has appeared elsewhere:

A version of the first half of 'Exemplars of Identity' appeared in *American Catholic Philosophical Quarterly* Vol 85, No. 4 (Fall, 2011), 639–60.

An edited version of 'The Promising Animal' appeared in S. May (ed.), *Nietzsche's* On the Genealogy of Morality: *A Critical Guide* (Cambridge: Cambridge University Press, 2011); the essay as it appears here also contains a version of what appeared in the *European Journal of Philosophy* Vol 17, No. 1 (March 2009) as 'Nietzsche's Style of Address: A Response to Christopher Janaway's *Beyond Selflessness*', 121–31.

A version of 'Orchestral Metaphysics' is to appear in D. Came (ed.), *Nietzsche and Art* (Cambridge: Cambridge University Press).

A version of 'Quartet' is to be published in G. Hagberg (ed.), *Fictional Characters, Real Problems: Essays on the Ethical Content of Literature*.

The essays on Sartre draw extensively but (for various reasons) implicitly on the biographical work of three authors: A. Cohen-Solal, *Sartre: A Life* (Heinemann: London, 1987); J. Frank, *Dostoevsky: A Writer in His Time*, ed. M. Petrusewicz (Princeton and Oxford: Princeton University Press, 2010); and A.C. Grayling, *Descartes: The Life of René Descartes and its Place in His Times* (London: Free Press, 2005).

For their helpful comments on earlier versions of some of the essays included here, I would like to thank: Alice Crary; Yi-Ping Ong; Robert Pippin and George Davis; Lanier Anderson, Josh Landy, and the students on the Philosophy and Literature programme at Stanford University; Joe Schear, Manuel Dries, and the other members of the Post-Kantian Research Seminar at the University of Oxford; Rupert Read, Oskari Kuusela, Catherine Osborne, and the other members of the Wittgenstein Workshop at the University of East Anglia. I would also like to thank the three anonymous readers of the book manuscript recruited by Oxford University Press, for their very helpful responses to the essays taken as a whole.

Dramatis Personae

People	Characters	Texts
Abraham	Aleksey Ivanovich	*Authority and Self-Estrangement*
Kingsley Amis	Paula Alquist	
G. E. M. Anscombe	Annie	*Being and Nothingness*
J. L. Austin	Apollo	*The Birth of Tragedy*
Ingrid Bergman	King Arthur	*The Bourne Identity*
Marshall Bosman	Lenore Stonecipher	*The Bourne Supremacy*
Martin Campbell	Beadsman	*The Bourne Ultimatum*
Stanley Cavell	James Bond	*Brief Interviews with Hideous Men*
J. M. Coetzee	Jason Bourne	
Daniel Craig	Brunnhilde	*The Broom of the System*
George Cukor	Benjamin Button	*Casino Royale*
René Descartes	Elizabeth Costello	*Contesting Tears*
Cora Diamond	Stella Dallas	*The Curious Case of Benjamin Button*
Fyodor Dostoevsky	Dionysus	
David Fincher	Excalibur	*Elizabeth Costello*
F. Scott Fitzgerald	The Fisher King	*Existentialism As A Humanism*
Ian Fleming	Franz	
Marc Forster	The Gambler	*The Gambler*
Sigmund Freud	Gramma	*Gaslight*
Paul Greengrass	The Interrogator	*On the Genealogy of Morality*
Adam Hall	John Lewis	
Ted Hughes	Joseph K	*Human, All Too Human*
Franz Kafka	The Meditator	
Immanuel Kant	Mime	*The Lives of Animals*
Soren Kierkegaard	Nothung	*Meditations*
Doug Liman	Parsifal	*Metamorphosis*
Thomas Malory	Polina Aleksandrovna	*Le Morte Darthur*
Richard Moran	Quiller	*Moses and Monotheism*
Moses	Siegfried	*Parsifal*
Friedrich Nietzsche	Sieglinde	*The Pekin Target*
Brad Pitt	Siegmund	*Philosophical Investigations*
Paul Ree	Johannes de Silentio	
Eric Roth	The Smoker	*Philosophy and Animal Life*
Jean-Paul Sartre	The Student	
Anna Gregoryevna Snitkina	The Voyeur	*A Pitch of Philosophy*
	The Waiter	*Quantum of Solace*
Socrates	The Woman on a Date	*The Ring of the Nibelung*
Barbara Stanwyck	Wotan	*Stella Dallas*
King Vidor		*That Uncertain Feeling*
Richard Wagner		*The Trial*
David Foster Wallace		*Understanding David Foster Wallace*
Ludwig Wittgenstein		*The Warsaw Document*
		The World Viewed

Exemplars of Identity

The Bearing of Proper Names in the *Philosophical Investigations*

Proper names are a recurring feature of the text of Ludwig Wittgenstein's *Philosophical Investigations*: in the first eighty-nine sections alone, we encounter Augustine, Russell, Ramsey and Frege, Socrates and Theatetus, the *Theatetus* and the *Tractatus Logico-Philosophicus*, Excalibur (or rather, Nothung), Mont Blanc and Egypt, Moses and the Israelites.[1] The presence of most of them may seem entirely unremarkable, since they may be taken to register the text's continual intercourse with other philosophical texts that constituted its author's immediate philosophical inheritance. To take Augustine's presence seriously might unsettle this sense of ordinariness to some extent—depending upon how seriously one takes the fact that he is a religious author as much as a philosopher. What, however, if one were to look at this parade of individual people, texts, and things from the perspective of what might initially appear to be its more anomalous members—Excalibur (or rather, Nothung), and Moses? After all, the book itself in these opening sections is obsessively concerned with names and naming; and our sense of what is at stake in such linguistic acts and functions may be significantly inflected by our diet of examples—by whether, for instance, one focuses primarily on the names of real people with whom its author was personally acquainted, or on the names of mythical individuals and objects, or people who belong to so distant a past that their historical status is hard to

---

[1] Trans. G.E.M. Anscombe (Blackwell: Oxford 1953)—hereafter PI. It was only with the publication of the revised fourth edition of the *Investigations* (by P.M.S. Hacker and J. Schulte) in 2009 that Anscombe's translation—which went through three prior editions—was significantly revised. Since much of this essay is concerned with a (potentially significant) detail of Anscombe's translation that was only altered in the fourth edition, my quotations from PI will be from the third edition (1967).

distinguish from that of myth or faith. This essay is an attempt to follow out the intuition that the latter perspective on the *Investigations* is something that this text not only permits but encourages.

I: Text—Nothung and Siegfried

1) Having asked himself 'What is the relation between name and thing named?' in section 37 of the *Investigations*, thereby recommencing the investigation of words, names, and ostensive definitions that has been underway since the opening section of the book, Wittgenstein goes on in section 38 to point out that 'strange to say, the word "this" has been called the only *genuine* name; so that anything else we call a name was one only in an inexact, approximate sense'. This conception of demonstratives as the only true names—which Wittgenstein later associates with the name of Russell—thus activates, and so depends upon, a contrast between genuine or authentic names, names properly so called, and those words which are ordinarily called 'names', but which only approximate to that status, and hence are not properly speaking names at all. Some words are names in name alone—their claim to that title is purely nominal; and the only words that do really merit it are typically not awarded it—their genuinely nominative essence is unacknowledged, hidden beneath another label altogether (for example, 'demonstrative'). In this way, a general conception of names as evaluable in terms of authenticity or inauthenticity, propriety or impropriety, legitimacy or illegitimacy, is applied to the very notion of a name itself: it is not just proper names (those paradigms of everyday namehood, the names of particular persons, animals, objects, countries, and so on) that should be thought of as claimed by or claiming their bearers either properly or improperly; the claim of any such name (and indeed of any word at all) to the status of 'name' is similarly open to evaluation, hence open to question. Even proper names might turn out to be not, properly speaking, worthy bearers of the name 'name' at all.

Wittgenstein is quick to tell us that this conception is queer, and that it springs from a tendency to sublime the logic of our language. But when he begins to explore its underlying motives more closely, in section 39, he deploys an example that may make us hesitate to accept these characterizations of the view under examination.

But why does it occur to one to want to make precisely this word into a name, when it evidently is *not* a name? – That is just the reason. For one is tempted to make an objection against what is ordinarily called a name. It can be put like this: *a name ought really to signify a simple*. And for this one might perhaps give the following reasons: The word 'Excalibur', say, is a proper name in the ordinary sense. The sword Excalibur consists of parts combined in a particular way. If they are combined differently Excalibur does not exist. But it is clear that the sentence 'Excalibur has a sharp blade' makes *sense* whether Excalibur is still whole or is broken up. But if 'Excalibur' is the name of an object, this object no longer exists when Excalibur is broken in pieces; and as no object would then correspond to the name it would have no meaning. But then the sentence 'Excalibur has a sharp blade' would contain a word that had no meaning, and hence the sentence would be nonsense. But it does make sense; so there must always be something corresponding to the words of which it consists. So the word 'Excalibur' must disappear when the sense is analysed and its place be taken by words which name simples. It will be reasonable to call these words the real names. (PI, 39)

One thing that most English-speaking readers of this text will know about King Arthur's sword Excalibur is that it is never broken or otherwise taken apart; Arthur receives it from an arm clothed in white samite that holds out the weapon to him above the surface of a lake, and he ensures its safe return at the end of his life to its original donor. So why should Wittgenstein reach for an example of a named object that so patently fails to fit the assumptions of his hypothetical, diagnostic chain of reasoning? But a quick check of the German original reveals that the object to which Wittgenstein actually refers at this point in his discussion is not Excalibur but Nothung—the sword that is central to Wagner's *Ring* cycle, and that is in fact shattered (by Siegmund against Wotan's spear) before being reforged (by his son Siegfried, and then, amongst other things, used by him to shatter Wotan's spear in its turn).

Should this new access of knowledge entirely assuage our concerns about Excalibur's indestructibility? Should we content ourselves instead with wondering how Wittgenstein's translator could have switched examples so carelessly? It is hard to avoid the conclusion that Anscombe did so because she did not take the full particularity of Wittgenstein's original example to be essential to the philosophical work it was being used to do. He simply needed some example or other of a proper name and its bearer, and he happened to light upon a sword whose name he could assume would be familiar to any German reader likely to pick up his book; so the same effect could be achieved for an English readership by substituting the name of Arthur's sword for that of Siegfried's. Anscombe might, then, equally legitimately have substituted the proper name of any other familiar object or person without doing essential damage to the points Wittgenstein will go on to make, which concern proper names and naming in general; but the equal availability of a well-known mythical sword in both cultures was an accident too happy for any translator to forgo its exploitation.

On this account of the matter, the name 'Excalibur' can happily go proxy for the name 'Nothung' without significant loss; indeed, any other proper name could equally happily represent 'Nothung' in these argumentative contexts, since 'Nothung' itself is nothing more than a representative of proper namehood in general—one name standing for any and all names, each of which is equally suited to this role because each is legitimately possessed of whatever is needed to merit the title or status of a name. But now let's recall Wittgenstein's immediate response to the queer, subliming conception of demonstratives as names—what he interestingly calls 'the proper' answer to it: 'we call very different things "names"; the word "name" is used to characterize many different kinds of use of a word, related to one another in many different ways;—but the kind of use that "this" has is not among them' (PI, 38). Does it help to combat the queer notion that demonstratives are names to think and act (for example, to translate) as if any name whatever (ordinarily understood) is substitutable for any other name when the nature of naming is under examination? Or does it rather produce an equal, if opposite, subliming of language—one according to which all names *qua* names are used in exactly the same way, that each *qua* name stands in the same relation to all other names (that of identity), and so that they have a single, nominative essence?

Another interpretative possibility would seem to open up by means of Wittgenstein's proper answer to Russellian subliming. Why not look and see what differences there are between the way the name of Siegfried's sword is used and the way the name of Arthur's sword is used? Not only might the web of interrelated differences and similarities confirm the legitimacy of Wittgenstein's expectation of variety rather than uniformity; in addition, the specific articulations of that web might themselves be open to more particular philosophical exploitation. They might, in fact, make all the difference to one's understanding of Wittgenstein's deeper purposes in this stretch of his text.

2) Nothung's first appearance in the *Ring* cycle is in the first Act of its second instalment, *The Valkyrie*, when Sieglinde encourages Siegmund to draw it from the trunk of the huge ash-tree around which her husband Hunding's house is built. It was first thrust into that trunk on their wedding day, by an old man, a stranger to the feast (in fact Wotan, the father of Sieglinde and Siegmund, although neither knows this about their paternity); only the strongest of men, the noblest of heroes, is capable of claiming it by drawing it from the tree. Sieglinde awaits such a man, someone for whom her disguised father has prepared the way, someone who will prove to be her saviour from a loveless, forced marriage; and Siegmund, who is facing the prospect of having to fight Hunding the next morning entirely unarmed, immediately realizes that this sword must be the weapon his absent father pledged to make available to him in his hour of need. So, once Sieglinde identifies him as not just her lover but her brother ('So now let me name you as I have loved you: Siegmund—that is your name!'), he leaps up, hurries to the trunk and grasps the sword-hilt:[2]

> Siegmund call me, and Siegmund am I!
> The proof is the sword, my hand soon shall hold it!
> Promised by Waelse in hour of need,
> Now it is found; I grasp it now!
> Holiest love in highest need,
> Yearning desire in longing and need,
> Burning bright in my breast, drives to deeds and death.
> Nothung! Nothung! So name I the sword!
> Nothung! Nothung! Bright, shining steel!
> Show me your sharpness, glorious blade!
> Come forth from the scabbard to me!
>
> (*The Valkyrie*, Act I, scene 3)

The moment at which the sword is drawn is also the moment at which it is named: for its successful extraction identifies its proper owner, who alone has the authority to name his own property. And the name he chooses for it

---

[2] All quotations from *The Valkyrie* use the translation by Andrew Porter, in Wagner, *The Valkyrie*, ed. N. John (London: Calder Publications, 1983).

('Not' is the German word for 'need') reflects the reason for its existence, the purpose for which it was created and which it will now (having been baptized with its own essence) begin to fulfil—that of redeeming both brother and sister. Hence, the naming of the sword is inseparable from the naming of the one who owns it: Siegmund's ability to draw the sword confirms his rightful claim to his own name, with which Sieglinde re-baptizes him just before he reclaims his father's gift, thereby authorizing him to do so—the true name which he has hitherto hidden beneath a variety of pseudonyms. Neither 'Wehwalt' (meaning 'woe') nor 'Friedmund' (meaning 'peace') are any longer appropriate for a man whose sorrow has turned to gladness in the light of Sieglinde's reciprocation of his love, and who is about to acquire the means to win his impending battle with Hunding and his clan; his true name is rather that of Wotan's orphaned son and Sieglinde's long-lost brother—the name of a hero ('Sieg' means 'victory' or 'triumph'). 'Siegmund' is not just what he is called but who he is; and he would not be who he is if he were not the namer, owner, and wielder of Nothung. In this sense, Siegmund is the rightful bearer of that name only insofar as he is the rightful bearer of that sword, which at once identifies him as needful and promises to satisfy that need; it embodies his destiny, and so his identity.

Suppose that we juxtapose this Wagnerian scene of multiple, interrelated naming with the terms in which Wittgenstein elaborates his initial understanding of the subliming, Russellian conception of naming at the conclusion of section 38:

This is connected with the conception of naming as, so to speak, an occult process. Naming appears as a *queer* connection of a word with an object.—And you really get such a queer connection when the philosopher tries to bring out *the* relation between name and thing by staring at an object in front of him and repeating a name or even the word 'this' innumerable times. For philosophical problems arise when language *goes on holiday*. And *here* we may indeed fancy naming to be some remarkable act of mind, as it were a baptism of an object. And we can also say the word 'this' *to* the object, as it were *address* the object as 'this' – a queer use of this word, which doubtless only occurs in doing philosophy. (PI, 38)

Wittgenstein's words conjure up a peculiar blend of the supernatural ('occult') and the religious ('baptise')—call it the realm of the holy; and they portray the philosopher as not only repeating the name of something whilst staring at it, but also as saying its name to that object, as if addressing it—speaking to the bearer of that name quite as if it were capable of speaking back, of holding converse with us, at the very least of hearing and responding to its proper name (quite as if implying that Russell's idea of knowledge by acquaintance—the direct private apprehension of a demonstrative's referent—is modelled on that of knowledge *of* acquaintances). Wagner's *Ring* patently inhabits the same kind of ground or condition; Siegmund both baptizes his sword and repeatedly addresses it—not only characterizing it as an embodiment of 'holiest love' but addressing it by name and issuing orders to it (including one which requires that it display the sharpness of its blade—the very property of Nothung that Wittgenstein later picks up for his own purposes). Against this background, one might wonder whether the connotation of 'festival' or 'holy day' still detectable in our concept of a holiday is one that Wittgenstein means to activate in his perhaps-too-familiar specification of language as philosophy's seedbed or ground. After all, it is by no means obvious that words going on holiday is a matter of their idling (like a *flâneur* or an engine), as opposed, say, to their having a dispensation to celebrate—to re-engage with aspects of their vitality (the kind that works of art, particularly the *Ring*—which Wagner entitled a 'festival play'—and also festivals of art such as those at Bayreuth, aim to exploit and fete) that everyday life may often appear to discount but could never entirely dissipate, since so much of that life continues (however deeply it may disavow the notion) to depend upon them.

The issues at stake here might be expressed as follows. Does Wittgenstein object to the very idea of naming as a matter of baptizing objects, and of names as capable of addressing their bearers; or does he rather object to the displacement of such ideas onto the domain of demonstratives, and to the philosopher's tendency to conjure up a private (and at the limit wholly interior or mental) context for such modes of christening and interlocution? Is any such conception of names and naming an indication that our words have begun to spin idly; or is it that the philosophical problems arise when we disregard the specific domains in which such conceptions are at home— call them collective festivals or modes of linguistic festivity—in favour of an uncannily solipsistic caricature?

3) In the context of Wittgenstein's discussion, Nothung is invoked in the first instance as part of an attempt to elucidate the intuition that names ought really to signify simples; and the feature of Nothung that appears most

directly relevant to this intuition is its exemplification of non-simplicity or complexity, and its consequent vulnerability to the fate of disassembly or decomposition into its constituent parts. Wittgenstein's first criticism of this mode of elucidation is to point out, in section 40, that it appears to confound the meaning of a name with the *bearer* of the name: 'When Mr N.N. dies one says that the bearer of the name dies, not that the meaning dies. And it would be nonsensical to say that, for if the name ceased to have meaning it would make no sense to say "Mr N.N. is dead".' So far, so good, one might think: but what relation does this point about the non-identity of bearer and meaning have to the idea that names ought to signify essentially non-complex bearers? That connection seems to depend on the assumption that 'if "Nothung" is the name of an object, this object no longer exists when Nothung is broken in pieces' (PI, 39); for only on that assumption would the brokenness of this sword entail the absence of anything corresponding to its name, and so the meaninglessness of that name. The key assumption here is thus that Nothung essentially consists of parts combined in a particular way (Wittgenstein addresses the parallel case of the broom, understood as essentially comprising broomstick plus brush, in section 60); only then would the disarticulation of those parts amount to its utter non-existence.

By switching in section 40 to the example of a person's name, Wittgenstein momentarily shifts attention away from his initial example (or perhaps one should rather say that he exploits the internal relation in Wagner between the name of the sword and the name of that sword's possessor); either way, he thereby asks us to consider the differences between the destruction of an object and the death of a human being. On the face of it, the equation of destruction with decomposition that arose naturally in section 39, when our focus was on a sword, does not arise so naturally when our concern is with a human being; or to put it more precisely, decomposition in this context is something that happens to the dead person's body, not to him, and it occurs after his death, rather than constituting its advent. On the other hand, one might conceive of the person as a combination or composite of soul and body, and so envisage death as the decomposition of that complex whole. If, however, the separated soul is viewed as that person's essence, and as itself essentially simple or undecomposable, then the person would survive the moment of his death and his name could retain its meaning because of the continued existence of its true bearer. On such a scenario, then, what determines that death and decomposition does not entail a person's non-existence is our acceptance of another version of the idea that a person's name really does go proxy for a simple. As we shall see, Wagner imagines things differently again.

Section 41 returns us to the original focus of section 39 by reminding us that the builders' language-game had been expanded in section 15 to include proper names for the building materials and the tools of those employing it, and by envisaging a situation in which the tool that had been given the name 'N' (by being physically marked with that sign) has been broken. Wittgenstein asks: Has this sign meaning now or not?

What is B to do when he is given [this sign by A]? We have not settled anything about this. One might ask: what *will* he do? Well, perhaps he will stand there at a loss, or show A the pieces. Here one *might* say: 'N' has become meaningless; and this expression would mean that the sign 'N' no longer had a use in our language-game (unless we gave it a new one). 'N' might also become meaningless because, for whatever reason, the tool was given another name and the sign 'N' no longer used in the language-game.–But we could also imagine a convention whereby B has to shake his head in reply if A gives him the sign belonging to a tool that is broken.—In this way the command 'N' might be said to be given a place in the language-game even when the tool no longer exists, and the sign 'N' to have meaning even when its bearer ceases to exist. (PI, 41)

It is well worth noting here Wittgenstein's willingness to refrain from decisively answering his own question one way or the other. What one is to say about the meaningfulness of 'N' is not simply to be read off from his earlier claim that the meaning of a person's name is to be distinguished from its bearer, but rather remains to be determined; and he can as easily imagine determinations which would license us to talk of the broken tool's name as having lost its meaning as he can ones which would license the opposite judgement. What shapes each determination, however, is whether or not the sign 'N' continues to have, or can be seen as continuing to have, a use or place in the builders' language-game: hence the smoothness of the transition from section 41 to section 43, in which Wittgenstein famously declares that 'For a *large* class of cases—though not for all—in which we employ the word "meaning" it can be defined thus: the meaning of a word is its use in the language' (PI, 43). And in his hands, this matter floats entirely free of the question of whether the brokenness of the tool amounts to its ceasing to exist; although for the purposes of the discussion at least, Wittgenstein shows every sign (as for example, in the final sentence of section 41) of being willing to take it for granted that in this case decomposition amounts to non-existence.

Is this because he takes it to be universally true that any object that is broken into pieces thereby ceases to exist as that object? Or is this true only of tools or pieces of equipment, with respect to which one might find it rather natural to say that a broken tool ceases to be able to do the job for which it is designed, and hence in effect ceases to exist qua tool? But suppose we think of the particular tool that Siegmund received from his father, and that he named 'N(othung)'; this piece of fighting equipment was broken by that same father's spear, and thereby ensured its bearer's lethal vulnerability to Hunding. Here, as in the local structure of Wittgenstein's discussion, the existence or non-existence of an object somehow hangs together with the existence or non-existence of the person whose property it is. In such circumstances, would we say that either Siegmund or Nothung has ceased to exist, or that 'Siegmund' or 'Nothung' continues to be meaningful?

In order to determine an answer to either question, certain aspects of the immediate narrative context of these events needs to be borne in mind. At the end of *The Valkyrie*, immediately after Hunding kills Siegmund, Brunn-hilde gathers up the pieces of his sword, gives them into the pregnant Sieglinde's safe-keeping, and sends her off into the wilderness away from Wotan's wrath; and the next instalment of the cycle (*Siegfried*) opens with its eponymous protagonist, sole offspring of Siegmund and Sieglinde, now grown to manhood and urging his foster father Mime the dwarf to reforge the sword.

Nothung, then, had plainly been broken—indeed shattered, smashed to splinters or smithereens; but this does not prevent Mime and Siegfried from discussing it. Indeed Mime, rather like Wittgenstein's B, is repeatedly forced to shake his head whenever Siegfried (like Wittgenstein's A) reiterates his command to repair it. There is thus no reason to think that 'Nothung' lacks meaning; but neither is there any reason to think that its shattering amounts to its non-existence. Certainly, no portion of it has ceased to exist; but more importantly, it is surely Nothung itself (shattered and unusable as it is) that was passed first to Sieglinde and then to her only son, in whose hands it is finally reforged, made good as new, and hence capable of fulfilling its destiny of bringing about the victory of 'holiest love in deepest need'. After all, as Mime struggles fruitlessly to reforge it himself, he addresses it as Nothung: Nothung exists, for him and for us, even if only in fragments or splinters. Decomposition does not, then, in this instance, equal non-existence.

And this stubborn continuation inflects the significance of our parallel question about Siegmund's continued existence. For if Nothung is the embodiment of Siegmund's destiny and identity, and it continues to exist even in fragments until its reforging by Siegfried, who then employs it to fulfil that destiny, in what sense can we say that Siegmund has ceased to exist in the world of Wagner's *Ring*? To be sure, in one straightforward sense of the phrase, he no longer exists: he has been killed, his individual life has come to an end. But in another sense, less straightforward but of far more importance in this context, he lives on: he lives on in his sword, and in the one who alone can reclaim it by creating it anew—his only son, Siegfried, who is the embodiment of the holiest love in deepest need for which Nothung was first created, through which it was first baptized, and which it too embodies. One might say: Siegfried is Siegmund reforged, created anew, just as he bears a name that is constructed from elements of his father's various names (the 'Sieg' from 'Siegmund', the 'Fried' from 'Friedmund'). In short: Siegmund no more ceases to exist in the world of the *Ring* than does Nothung. In this particular case, Mr N. is dead; long live Mr N.

The mode of continued existence at issue in the world of the *Ring* is not, of course, that envisaged in the quasi-Christian conception we canvassed earlier, according to which a person's name goes proxy for a disembodied, undecomposable soul. A person's or an object's identity is here figured rather differently—a difference embodied in the differences between Mime's and Siegfried's strategies for reforging Nothung. Mime has always relied upon solder—that is, he has conceived of the task of remaking Nothung as a matter of taking each splinter and shard of the sword and reconnecting it to its fellows, as if it were a broken vase or a jigsaw puzzle. On the face of it, this is a highly peculiar approach. Of course, the general idea that a sword is a complex object made of parts is perfectly intuitive; but that is because we share a sense of the identity of those parts (the handle, the hilt, the blade)—a sense that is determined by our prior grasp of the identity of the whole of which they are parts (our sense of what it is for a sword to fulfil its function). It is this mode of complexity that Wittgenstein is surely trading on when, in section 39, he remarks almost in passing that 'the sword

Nothung consists of parts combined in a particular way'. But Mime is treating the fragments into which Nothung has been shattered by Wotan's spear as if they were parts of Nothung in just the sense in which its handle, its hilt, and its blade are its parts. Nothung was not made by making or taking those shards and splinters and combining them in a particular way, as if each shard were to perform a particular function within the sword as a whole: it was rather unmade by breaking its natural or normal parts (particularly, of course, its blade) into mere fragments—bare pieces rather than parts. Not just any way of breaking up an object reduces it to its constituent parts; sheer destruction is not a mode of disarticulation or dismembering, any more than anarchy is a specific mode of social disorder.

Siegfried's reforging strategy is very different. He fixes Nothung's fragments one by one into a vice, and then files each to shreds; he then transfers the filings to a crucible, melts them down, pours that molten metal into a mould, and then works the resulting blade on the anvil into a sword strong enough to split that anvil with a single stroke. In other words, he gives the actual fragments into which Nothung was shattered no particular significance as parts. Rather than have their arbitrary geometry dictate his labours, he reduces them in turn to equally meaningless fragments, then to a molten fluid to which the very idea of a fragment, let alone a constituent part, has no application; and from that formless stuff he reconstitutes the sword in terms of the parts which its identity as a sword dictate. Nothung's recreation thus passes through a moment of utter decreation—a formless fluidity upon which the conception of a structured whole, or indeed structural complexity of any kind, can find no purchase; but what emerges from that fiery substance is indeed Nothung itself, as Siegfried's hymn of praise to it makes clear:[3]

> Nothung! Nothung! Glorious sword!
> Once more you are held in your hilt. Sundered no more:
> I forged you anew. No second stroke shall ever split you!
> My father was doomed, when you came undone;
> His living son forged you anew.
> For me now you laugh aloud; you shall joust with joy evermore!
> Nothung! Nothung! Glorious sword!
> To life again I awoke you.

[3] All quotations from *Siegfried* are taken from the translation by Rudolph Sabor, in Wagner, *Siegfried* (London: Phaidon, 1997).

Dead were you, in shattered shreds,
Now gleaming defiant and fair.
Let all offenders witness your worth!
Cut down all rascals, cut down all rogues!

(*Siegfried*, Act I, scene 3)

Just as with Siegmund's original hymn of baptism, Siegfried's rechristening speech-act involves addressing the sword as if it were itself responsive to speech—indeed, as if it were capable of laughter, joy, and defiance; for him, Nothung has been resurrected, awoken to new life after death. And because it is one and the same sword, it is as if his father has been returned to life along with it—in the sword, and in his living son who reforged it, and who greets its renewal in exactly the terms and mode of address first employed by his father. And this in turn implies that the mode of identity, and so of continued existence, exemplified by Nothung is offered to us as equally appropriate to the identity and existence of the people of Wagner's world. Siegfried both is and is not his father, just as his name both is and is not a reforging of fragments of his father's names (both true and false, or rather both timelessly true—'Sieg' as 'victory'—and momentarily false—'Fried' or 'peace'); he inherits his doom or fate from his doomed father, and so will fulfil the destiny that made Siegmund who he was and is.[4]

What Wagner is here tapping into is a characteristically mythological understanding of identity as fluid or metamorphic—its blazing, brilliant plasticity capable of undergoing the most extreme transformations without losing integrity, of suffering endless reshapings without loss of continuity. It is as if Siegmund and Siegfried are momentary concrete particulars moulded from that underlying substance, each a distinct realization of one and the same stuff, hence each identical to and distinct from the other. And just as Siegfried's identity is not graspable except as a reincarnation of his father, so it is not graspable as essentially distinct from his sister Sieglinde, or his father's father, or from Brunnhilde—no more than he experiences it as separable from that of his (father's, and so of course his father's father's)

---

[4] It is, however, worth noting that this patrilineal continuity is mediated by women, more specifically by sisters who are also lovers: it is Sieglinde who christens Siegmund, as Brunnhilde prophetically calls Siegfried into existence, even if both thereby further their father's wishes; and one might argue that the ultimate purpose of this lyric drama of intergenerational destiny is that one of those women should acquire apocalyptic wisdom.

sword, which partakes of the identity of the tree from which it was drawn, itself both a particular tree integrated into a particular house, and also an avatar of the world-tree or tree of life, from which Wotan first tore the spear that will twice confront itself in the form of a sword...Such chains of equivalence, of simultaneous identity and non-identity, constitute the world of the *Ring*, making it such fertile soil for psychoanalytic interpretation in all its varieties, through which each apparently individual person and object is read as internally related to every other as part of the structure of the human psyche as such. The molten fluid that is Nothung thus embodies the flux from which the Wagnerian universe of gods, dwarves, giants, and heroes is forged.

But Wagner's universe is no more sealed off from other mythic realms than any individual person or object within it is sealed off from any other. For of course, Siegmund and Siegfried are Wagner's reworkings of characters from other, earlier mythic tales, from the *Volsungsaga* in particular, where they go by the names of Sigmund and Sigurd—just as Nothung is there known as Gram (and in earlier German sources as Balmung). If one were to ask: 'Are Nothung and Gram two different swords, or one and the same sword?', how might one answer? Should one say that the answer is yet to be determined, or that one can say whatever one pleases? It would seem more accurate to say that the only correct answer is 'Yes and No'. For unless one sees, and so can find a way of meaningfully saying, that Nothung both is and is not Gram, and that Siegfried is and is not Sigurd, then one has not fully grasped what Nothung is or who Siegfried is. And when we distinguish the *Volsungsaga* from the *Ring of the Nibelungs* by describing the former as a source of the latter, we might want to ask exactly how one pictures the relationship between a mythical universe and its source when that source is itself a mythical universe populated by people and things whose relation to people and things in the universe it helped engender seems far from external. Is the retelling of a tale another tale altogether? What makes one imagined world distinct from another?

4) The bearing of these mythological matters on Wittgenstein's discussion of names and naming may become clearer if we recall that his discussion is itself structured in terms of identifying sources—the sources of a Russellian subliming of language. For first, section 39 tells us that the idea of treating demonstratives as the only genuine names derives from the thought that a name ought really to signify a simple; and in section 46,

Wittgenstein then enquires into the origin or source of that thought. More specifically, he asks: what lies behind it?—or otherwise translated: what's the story behind it? The specific story he then offers is taken from Socrates in the *Theatetus* (a tale told by a person in a text named after a person); he reports other unnamed people as subscribing to the existence of what the English translation of a German translation of Plato's Greek calls 'the primary elements out of which we and everything else are composed'— elements that exist in their own right, *an und für sich*, of which no account could be given, for each of which nothing is possible but a bare name; its name is all it has. We are plainly on mythic ground here: Socrates is recounting a mythology of the world as composed of essentially unchanging and indestructible ur-elements—call them simples.

Is there any relation between this mythic tale of the world and that recounted in the *Ring?* Taken one way, it would not be unnatural to regard the world of the *Ring* as having primary or primal elements out of which it has been composed—a sword, a ring, a helmet; gods, giants, dwarves; the tree of life, and the genealogical roots, trunk and branches of the Volsungs. In Wagnerian rather than Socratic myth, however, the nature and hence the mode of composition of those elements differs quite significantly. More precisely, it is not so much a matter of composition—of combining or soldering parts—as one of blending, mixing, inflecting, or infusing types or archetypes. If, in the terms of the *Theatetus* myth, people are thought of on the model of objects (as constituted out of pre-given parts), in the terms of the *Ring* myth, objects are thought of on the model of people (as playing a part, occupying pre-given roles, and confronting a fate that both makes them the object they are and weaves them into the repeating pattern of an endlessly unfolding metaphysical fabric).

Taken another way, however, the myth of the *Ring* might rather be thought of as entirely rejecting the compositional model invoked by that of the *Theatetus*. For if my reading of Nothung's vicissitudes is accepted, what Siegfried's reforging of that sword appears to adumbrate is a world in which questions of existence and identity cannot ultimately be approached in terms of parts and wholes at all; they are simply not conceivable as a matter of which elements in which combination comprise the given thing. Such a compositional vision is inflexible and shut-ended; it makes creation a fundamentally mechanical process that can only result in a finite number of possibilities that are fundamentally predictable from an acquaintance with the basic, indestructible, and unalterable pieces of which reality consists— elements whose possibilities of combination are predetermined, written into their nature. In the myth of the Ring, creation is a matter of moulding and remoulding white-hot fluid—an essentially plastic substance which no sooner coalesces into a concrete particular than it dissolves, only to realize itself in another concrete particular. The possible range of such realizations is neither predetermined nor wholly unconstrained; identity is essentially malleable, its metamorphoses allowing for creativity whilst always presupposing continuity at a fundamental level.

A striking aspect of Wittgenstein's critical discussion of the *Theatetus* myth is that it not only focuses on the presuppositions of its compositional model of identity, but also criticizes it in a way which pushes us in the direction of the Wagnerian myth. For the key point that Wittgenstein makes against the idea of simples is that 'it makes no sense at all to speak absolutely of the "simple parts of a chair"' (PI, 47). The term 'simple' simply means 'non-composite'; and there is no single, compulsory, absolute or context-independent way of identifying the parts of which any given thing might be said to be composed.

If I tell someone without any further explanation: 'What I see before me now is composite', he will have the right to ask; 'What do you mean by "composite"? For there are all sorts of things that that can mean!'—The question 'Is what you see composite' makes good sense if it is already established what kind of complexity – that is, which particular use of the word – is in question. If it had been laid down that the visual image of a tree was to be called 'composite' if one saw not just a single trunk, but also branches, then the question 'Is the visual image of this tree simple or composite?' and the question 'What are its simple component parts?' would have a clear sense – a clear use. And of course the answer to the second question is not 'The branches' (that would be an answer to the *grammatical* question; 'What are here called "simple component parts"?') but rather a description of the individual branches. (PI, 47)

Perhaps I am alone in thinking of this tree as an avatar of Hunding's house-tree, Nothung's living scabbard, and so of the archetypical tree of life (although if one can take this possibility seriously, one might be led to wonder whether the red apples purchased in the first section of the book are de-divinized incarnations of the golden apples belonging to Freia, with whose disappearance the tale of the *Ring* effectively commences; whether the builders who dominate the succeeding sections might be versions of the two giants whose construction of Valhalla initiates the tale of the *Ring*; whether his imagined language consisting of orders and reports in battle might perfectly suit the Wagnerian context of endlessly renewed warfare; and even whether Wittgenstein's chair invokes the Valhallan throne from which Wotan, surrounded by the fragments of his spear, watches the end of his world in *Gotterdammerung*). But whatever the merits of that intuition, the force of Wittgenstein's use of the example is clear: there is no single, absolute pre-given articulation of things into simple elements from which all other things must be composed; there is rather a variety of ways in which language-users can articulate things into simple and complex, component and whole, in terms of which they can then go on to describe whatever they encounter. Wittgenstein's moral is thus not solely that this mythological intuition about the absolutely simple, hence immortal, foundations of the world is a displaced recognition of the need for what one might call grammatical elements (for example, samples) if certain language-games are to be played ('What looks as if it *had* to exist is part of the language' [PI, 50]); his point is also that no particular language-game, with its given elements, needs to be played—that there is a variety of such forms of language, and that that variety is limited only by the limits of one's creative imagination as that plays itself out in the domain of grammar and the world.

This has two implications that reconnect Wittgenstein's investigation to its initiating example—Nothung. First, it entails that the way in which I earlier suggested that the world of the *Ring* might be decomposed into primary elements is just as legitimate as any other grammatical matrix of parts and wholes that might be legitimately applied to other domains of human life (as when building a great hall, or naming the parts of a weapon). The idea that names are mere interchangeable labels for things may have its home in such contexts; but the idea that names may penetrate to the essence of things (both objects and persons), and so either capture or distort the truth of those things, is no more and no less possessed of a *Heimat* elsewhere in our everyday lives. If something only has a name in the context of a language-game and its grammatical dispositions (cf. PI, 49), what it is for something to be a name will depend upon what kind of thing (grammatically speaking) it names.

Hence, second, no single way of articulating any given domain into elements is itself beyond question or supplementation. I earlier tried to name the primary elements of the *Ring* in terms of its narrative content and sources; but I could equally well talk of its basic musical elements (the famous themes and motifs that contribute as much to our sense of the identity of its numinous objects and characters as do their actions and passions), its theatrical elements (the famous individual singers and specific stagings that indelibly marked our sense of the opera's significance), and their various interactions in the overall context to which Wagner gave the name '*Gesamtkunstwerk*'. In each case, these assignments of names would have a point only insofar as they prepare the way for descriptions and analyses of the work that are themselves worth advancing; and each engenders criteria of identity and existence that are specific to the elements concerned.

Accordingly, if one wanted a mythological counter to the mechanical fixity of the *Theatetus* myth of reality and its inherent structure or articulation, one could hardly do better than that of the *Ring*; for its pivotal image of Siegfried's reforging of Nothung—call it a primal scene of the opera cycle— precisely embodies an understanding of human beings as not needing to allow the given articulations and disarticulations of the world to dictate their modes of response to it, but rather as capable of reforging reality in such a way as to reconstitute its modes of being without ever being able to recreate it *ex nihilo*. The thought that there is no one way in which the world is always already arrayed, and the thought that even the most imaginative reforging of the world must acknowledge its resistances (which might be the result of prior modes of its articulation), meet and merge under the blows of Siegfried's hammer. And insofar as Nothung goes proxy for its bearer, then it provides a similarly cross-grained mythology of personal identity, according to which selfhood is neither fabricated from pre-given parts nor utterly unconstrained by contexts of family, culture, and purpose, but rather endlessly reforges itself from the shattered fragments of its earlier states and conditions. To put this Wagnerian matter in Nietzschean terms: selfhood is a matter of Being repeatedly re-coalescing out of a molten core of Becoming.

One might think of this way of working through Wittgenstein's words as an attempt to renew or recreate our understanding of the primary elements of the *Philosophical Investigations*—to invite us to consider whether or not the essential nature of this text might be more penetratingly displayed if its apparently glancing and accidental choices of example were rather conceived of as aspects of its overall structure and philosophical motivation that are at least as determinative as its more evident articulation into numbered sections and paragraphs. If I am convinced that no examples or cited artworks or allusions to marginalized thinkers could be primary elements in any genuinely philosophical text, since I know in advance that they are the argumentative equivalent of grey rags and dust, then investigating the text in those terms will perhaps seem superfluous. But if I am rather inclined to think it at least possible to make an engine for philosophical progress out of such festive or celebratory aspects of our lives with words, then I ought at least to attempt to forge a reading of it in such terms. But what is it that opposes any such examination of textual details in philosophy?

II: Translation—Excalibur and Arthur

5) If Nothung's distinctive identity can be thought to have been productively on Wittgenstein's mind during the composition of these stretches of text, then it may seem simply empty to consider the possibility that the name his translator chose to substitute for the Wagnerian original throughout might have any bearing upon that composition. But there are reasons for hesitating over this dismissal. The first reason is, let's say, purely scholarly: Baker and Hacker tell us that Wittgenstein himself substituted the name 'Excalibur' for the first occurrence of that of 'Nothung' in an earlier typescript version of section 39, in which this fateful example is first introduced.[5] The second reason is more, let's say, mythological: it is no more obvious that the two names are entirely distinct than it is that the swords they denote, and the owners for which they stand, are participants in two essentially distinct mythological narratives. After all, according to Malory's highly influential version of the tale, Arthur's conception is far from orthodox (although neither adulterous nor incestuous); he too proves his claim to kingship by drawing a sword from its resting place (in this case, an anvil set into a stone rather than a tree); and the continuing presence and active reality of Excalibur as a weapon is integral to his ability to found his fellowship of knights,

---

[5] Cf. volume 1, part II, p. 116 of their *Wittgenstein: Understanding and Meaning*, 2nd edition (Oxford: Blackwell, 2005).

maintain order in his kingdom, and see off rebellion. Incest (in the form of his illegitimate son, Mordred, conceived upon his sister) is a key element in Arthur's ultimate defeat; and his mysterious passing is conjoined with the equally mysterious reclamation of Excalibur by the arm that rises from the Lake.[6]

Such marked similarities with the life of Siegfried certainly furnish grounds for regarding Anscombe's substitution of Excalibur for Nothung less as the selection of an arbitrary alternative and more as the deployment of a genuine representative of or proxy for the original. And those similarities are hardly surprising, given that the sources upon which Wagner was drawing for his operatic cycle form part of the same sea or soup of Northern European narrative archetypes through which Malory received and reconceived his own account (even if Malory's proximate sources have a distinctively French rather than Scandinavian inflection). But given that background commonality, the specific differences that each author retained and introduced between Nothung and Excalibur, Siegfried and Arthur, take on a certain salience; and they might thereby draw into the foreground certain aspects of the Wagnerian context that might otherwise be overlooked.

A fundamental part of the atmosphere or mood of the *Ring* is the idea of a world coming to an end. *Götterdämmerung* represents the termination of Wotan's rule over the earth: Brunnhilde's sacrificial immolation of herself in Siegfried's funeral pyre redeems the ring and so the foundation of that old order only by bringing it down in ruins, and the final image of that final opera is the distant vision of Valhalla, in whose burning interior Wotan himself waits quietly for whatever the future may bring. Arthur's death also represents the end of a world; but its termination is no more decisive than is his death. For in Malory's recounting of it, the mortally wounded Arthur is taken from Sir Bedivere's sight by three queens, on a barge across the Lake into which Excalibur has already vanished, declaring that he will withdraw to the vale of Avilion whilst his wounds are tended; and the next morning, Sir Bedivere comes across a newly-dug grave attended by a hermit who tells of being asked to bury a fresh corpse by a group of noble women. But

---

[6] I have used the edition of Malory's *Le Morte Darthur* edited by Helen Cooper for the 'Oxford World's Classics' series (Oxford: Oxford University Press, 1998), hereafter MD.

Malory himself makes it clear that there is no certainty that the body buried in this grave was that of Arthur; and more specifically, he tells us that

Some men say in many parts of England that King Arthur is not dead, but had by the will of our Lord Jesu into another place; and men say that he shall come again, and he shall win the Holy Cross. Yet I will not say that it shall be so; but rather would I say, here in this world he changed his life. But many men say that there is written upon the tomb thus: Hic iacet Arthurus, rex quondam rexque futurus [Here lies Arthur, the once and future King]. (MD, 516)

Here, the return of Excalibur to the Lake without suffering destruction or even damage figures the hoped-for indestructibility of its wielder, and of the kingdom he forged by its ability to destroy all other weapons used against it (hence the etymology of its name—'Excalibur' means 'cut-steel'). The Arthurian myth is thus unwilling to contemplate the reduction of its central object either to fragments or to an underlying plasticity: it withdraws into the fathomless depths of a lake, but it does so intact and with no hint that its watery resting place might dissolve its integrity.

This ultimate resistance to decay or decomposition is patently connected to the pervasively Christian cast of Malory's recasting of his sources: the internal relation between Arthur and Christ is affirmed at his end, by the way in which Sir Bedivere twice betrays his commission to throw the sword back into the Lake before finally carrying it out (thus invoking Peter's denials of Christ), as it was at the beginning when the stone from which the kingly sword must be drawn is said to have materialized against the high altar of the greatest church in London. Seen against the backdrop of the Christian promise of resurrection, even certainty that the grave in the hermit-guarded chapel hid Arthur's mortal remains would not exclude the possibility of his future resurrection— of the corruptible putting on incorruptibility. For any future rule of his would have to involve his second coming, both body and soul.

Wagner's recasting of his sources is resolutely pagan. It is willing to contemplate the complete overthrow of the old order whose passing it represents and mourns; Wotan's spear lies shattered at the end of the cycle, and even if Siegfried's and Brunnhilde's funeral pyre does hold open the possibility of the birth of a new order, no confidence in its realization—let alone any conception of its internal ordering—is presented to us (except insofar as we follow Nietzsche in seeing the Wagnerian representation of Wotan's overthrow as itself the refounding of a new, non-Christian culture that might run counter to the philistinism of contemporary Germany by reconnecting Europe to its sources in Greek culture, and in particular to its tragic drama). Arthur's life and reign, however, are in Malory's hands resolutely associated with the central images of Christianity—from the idea of his fellowship as united in search of the Grail onwards; and in so doing, Malory gives a very particular inflection to the conception of Britain as the realm of which Arthur is the once and future king.

This is the second salient point of difference between Arthurian and Wagnerian myth: the former is a myth of Britishness, and one that is historically constructed (and repeatedly reconstructed) in opposition to the very aspects of Northern European culture upon which Wagner bases the world of the *Ring* and with which he proposes to reconstruct German life and values. More precisely, according to recent scholarship, the ideological backdrop to Arthur's genesis in Latin texts of the ninth and tenth centuries is an insular elite's interest in constructing a British identity out of the remains of the Roman occupation.[7] Arthur thus appears in a proto-historical context as the last and finest representative and defender of Britishness as opposed to Englishness: Britishness is understood as importantly constituted by a certain inheritance of the Christianized later Roman empire, hence as possessed of a providential dimension, and as bitterly contesting the subsequent influx of Angles and Saxons—what we might now think of as the progenitors of Englishness, but whose origins lie in continental Europe and whose presence amounted to another successful process of invasion, colonization, and reconstitution that these texts strove to represent as a traumatic intermission in divine protection.

What Arthur, and so Excalibur, thereby represents from the outset is a conception of national identity that represses certain aspects of its own origins in order to serve certain recurrent contemporary political and cultural needs. Britishness is deliberately presented as indigenous and deep-rooted when compared to the relatively later imposition of Anglo-Saxon culture, despite its being in fact essentially defined by the (religiously-inflected) impositions of a prior wave of invasion and colonization. The Britishness for which Arthur stands is thus both hypostasized and fluid: his withdrawal to Avilion registers a sense of its indissoluble integrity, even if hidden beneath centuries of Anglo-Saxon rule; but his ultimate roots in a

---

[7] Cf. N.J. Higham, *King Arthur: Myth-Making and History* (London: Routledge, 2002)—especially ch. II.

faintly-discernable late representative of Roman rule (one Lucius Artorius Castus—'Arthur' being a version of a Roman name) registers the awareness that this identity is always already forged by external influx. What provides the resistance to new others is the internalized residue of earlier otherness; and a fundamental purpose of telling and repeatedly retelling this tale in the centuries leading up to Malory (a purpose that is repeatedly recovered in the centuries succeeding him) is to reinforce this sense of national identity as always beleaguered but essentially indestructible at times when that identity is threatened anew from without (whether that new other is Saxon, Norman, or Nazi).

Anscombe's translation-by-proxy thereby provides us with a version of the fluid, metamorphic model of identity we discerned in the *Ring*, but in the Arthurian myth, its primary application is to a country or nation; and although this myth of national identity does not exactly overturn the Wagnerian vision of selfhood as constituted by an endless movement of self-overcoming, it undeniably expresses a certain anxiety about it, insofar as its central object and individual appear to insist upon an indissoluble integrity in the face of its own future, and in denial of its own past. Continuity, understood as a construct in which one moves on from prior states of oneself by means of the incorporation or internalization of otherness, is seen as inadequate for genuine self-identity; radical renewal or rebirth represent a mortal threat, rather than being finitude's way of warding off a death-dealing fixation or rigidity. Seen in this light, the example of Excalibur embodies a certain anxiety about change or mutability—about the kinds of decomposition or reforging to which individual and collective particulars are heir—that lies hidden beneath the *Theatetus* myth, and against which the myth of the *Ring* so firmly sets its face.

There is, accordingly, a certain irony in the fact that Excalibur fails to constitute a purely British equivalent to Nothung in one further respect. For whereas the sword Wotan buries to the hilt in Hunding's house-tree is the one that Siegmund withdraws and that Siegfried reforges, the sword that Arthur draws from the stone-embedded anvil is not the sword that his proxy returns to the Lake. The sword drawn from the stone has no particular name in Malory's account of its disclosure and extraction; Excalibur is the name of the sword Arthur first acquires after his anointing as king, with the magical help of Merlin, who first directs him to the Lake from which that sword emerges when Arthur receives it as a gift from its Lady, Nineve. In other words, Excalibur is not the sword in the stone: the embodiment of Arthur's kingdom is not the ground of his kingship. One might say that questions of origin or authorization and questions of continuity or authority are in fact two different questions in Arthurian myth, even though those familiar with it (including Malory himself, who, despite recognizing the difference between the two swords, at one point inadvertently names the first 'Excalibur') tend to run them together. In this sense, one might say that the myth's inheritors tend to exceed even the myth's excessive embodiment of anxiety about the absoluteness of identity: for they (I mean we) are prone to use a single name to denote two different swords, or otherwise put, to use the solder of memory to make one textual and mythic element out of two. If we retell the tale to ourselves often enough in those terms, who is to say whether or when we will have succeeded in re-articulating it in the image of our fantasy? And since that fantasy is one the original tale both inhabits and articulates, then who is to say that we are not thereby more true to its underlying character than was Malory?

III: Intertext—Moses and Freud

6) One might then say that Anscombe's translation strategy does fit into the fields of force set up by Wittgenstein's examples, even if it reverses the key polarities. One might even go further: for in thereby explicitly foregrounding the identity of peoples as well as of people, the relation of the mythical to the historical, and the way in which two distinct things might come to be denoted by a single proper name, Anscombe's work rather neatly prepares the ground for Wittgenstein's imminent choice of Moses as an example to advance his discussion of vagueness and determinacy of sense at two closely related points.

Consider this example. If one says 'Moses did not exist', this may mean various things. It may mean: the Israelites did not have a *single* leader when they withdrew from Egypt—or: their leader was not called Moses—or: there cannot have been anyone who accomplished all that the Bible relates of Moses—or: etc. etc.—We may say, following Russell: the name 'Moses' can be defined by means of various descriptions. For example, as 'the man who led the Israelites through the wilderness', 'the man who lived at that time and place and was then called "Moses"', 'the man who as a child was taken out of the Nile by Pharaoh's daughter', and so on. And according as we assume one definition or another the proposition 'Moses did not exist' acquires a different sense, and so does every other proposition about Moses.—And if we are told 'N did not exist', we do ask: 'What do you mean? Do you want to say . . . or . . . etc?'

But when I make a statement about Moses, – am I always ready to substitute some *one* of these descriptions for 'Moses'? I shall perhaps say: By 'Moses' I understand the man who did what the Bible relates of Moses, or at any rate a good deal of it. But how much? Have I decided how much must be proved false for me to give up my proposition as false? Has the name Moses got a fixed and unequivocal use for me in all possible cases?—Is it not the case that I have, so to speak, a whole series of props in readiness, and am ready to lean on one if another should be taken from under me and vice versa?—Consider another case. When I say 'N. is dead', then something like the following may hold for the meaning of the name 'N': I believe that a human being has lived whom I (1) have seen in such-and-such places, who (2) looked like this (pictures), (3) has done such-and-such things, and (4) bore the name 'N' in social life.—Asked what I understand by 'N', I should enumerate all or some of these points, and different ones on different occasions. So my definition of 'N' would perhaps be 'the man of whom all this is true'.—But if some point now proves false?—Shall I be prepared to declare the proposition 'N is dead' false – even if it is only something which strikes me as incidental that has turned out false? But where are the bounds of the incidental?—If I had given a definition of the name in such a case, I should now be ready to alter it.

And this can be expressed like this: I use the name 'N' without a *fixed* meaning. (But that detracts as little from its usefulness, as it detracts from that of a table that it stands on four legs instead of three and so sometimes wobbles.)

Should it be said that I am using a word whose meaning I don't know, and so am talking nonsense?—Say what you choose, so long as it does not prevent you from seeing the facts. (And when you see them there is a good deal that you will not say.) (The fluctuation of scientific definitions: what today counts as an observed concomitant of a phenomenon will tomorrow be used to define it.) [PI, 79]

Suppose I give this explanation: 'I take "Moses" to mean the man, if there was such a man, who led the Israelites out of Egypt, whatever he was called then and whatever he may or may not have done besides.'—But similar doubts to those about 'Moses' are possible about the words of this explanation (what are you calling 'Egypt', whom the 'Israelites' etc.?). Nor would these questions come to an end when we got down to words like 'red', 'dark', 'sweet'.—'But then how does an explanation help me to understand, if after all it is not the final one? In that case the explanation is never completed; so I still don't understand what he means, and never shall!'—As though an explanation as it were hung in the air unless supported by another one. Whereas an explanation may indeed rest on another one that has been given; but none stands in need of another—unless *we* require it to prevent a misunderstanding. One might say: an explanation serves to remove or to avert a misunderstanding—one, that is, that would occur but for the explanation; not every one that I can imagine.

It may easily look as if every doubt merely *revealed* an existing gap in the foundations; so that secure understanding is only possible if we first doubt everything that *can* be doubted, and then remove all these doubts.

The sign-post is in order—if, under normal circumstances, it fulfils its purpose. (PI, 87)

During the same decade in which Wittgenstein was reworking the details and shifting the contexts of these two passages, Freud was writing the three essays that were published on the threshold of the Second World War under the title *Moses and Monotheism*.[8] Since Wittgenstein first decided to centre his discussion around Moses at the very beginning of the 1930s, his choice can hardly be understood as a deliberate reference to Freud's essays— although his sustained and extensive interest in Freud is well known, and he would certainly have been acquainted with Freud's 1913 text on religion, *Totem and Taboo*, upon which much of the reasoning in the later essays is explicitly based. Nevertheless, the points of contact between these two discussions of Moses are not hard to find, to the point at which one might come to think of Wittgenstein as having prepared a place for Freud's reflections in his own discussion—first, insofar as he envisages someone disputing the joint applicability of certain familiar descriptions of Moses to one and the same person, to the point of questioning whether the Israelites had a *single* leader at all; and second, in his acknowledgement of the ways in which doubts about the identity of Moses may hang together with doubts about the identity of Egypt and of the Jewish people. One might, then, envisage Freud as someone who made actual a ground for doubting the existence or identity of Moses that Wittgenstein seems to have been able to imagine in advance, even if only to emphasize the very different significance attaching to real doubts as opposed to merely imaginable ones. The question that arises once Freud's words are brought into conversation with Wittgenstein's is: what

---

[8] I have used the Strachey translation of this text—hereafter MM—as reprinted in Vol. 13 of the Penguin Freud Library, *The Origins of Religion* (London: Penguin, 1985).

follows once such an imaginary ground for doubt is actually enunciated, and thereby modulates from the merely possible to the real?

Freud's contention is that the name 'Moses' is used in the Bible to refer to two different historical individuals: first, the person who led the Israelites out of Egyptian slavery and into the desert, and second, the person who founded the religion of Yahweh around which the tribes who emerged from their wanderings in the desert reconstituted their identity as Israelites. The first Moses was a prince of Egypt, hence an Egyptian (and so not an Israelite foundling who was brought up as an Egyptian); he was a follower of Aten, a quasi-monotheistic Egyptian sun god whose worship had briefly supplanted the popular polytheistic forms of Egyptian worship under the reign of Akhenaten, before being repressed in its turn. The second Moses was a shepherd in the region of Midian and Kadesh; he adapted the local worship of Yahweh, a volcano God, into a form of monotheism around which the Israelites went on to define themselves as a people. On Freud's account, then, we have two people called Moses, two monotheistic forms of religious worship (that of Aten and that of Yahweh), hence an internal diremption or doubleness within the people of Egypt and the people of Israel (insofar as each is identified with a characteristic mode of religious practice). But this historical duplexity has been systematically repressed or covered over, and a pattern of false identity (between the Egyptian prince and the Midianite shepherd) and false difference (between Aten and Yahweh, hence between Egypt and Israel, and so between the Egyptian prince and the Midianite shepherd) imposed, in order to deny the fact that the Israelites wandering in the desert murdered the first Moses—unable any longer to bear the burden of his imperious, intransigent leadership and his equally demanding religion. They atoned for this community-constituting parricide by ultimately accepting their identification with an anti-polytheistic religion in the region in which they proposed to settle, and by presenting their current form of life and their current leader as essentially continuous with that which they first adopted and then abandoned in their flight from Egypt (whilst maintaining an absolute denial of any taint of Egyptian influence). The true Exodus narrative thus repeats what Freud takes to be the founding narrative and myth of every human community; and it operates according to a logic of repression, latency, and return that is the communal analogue of intrapsychic mechanisms of the kind deemed central to individual identity by the theory and practice of psychoanalysis.

Throughout his extravagantly radical recounting of this pivotal episode in the defining account of Jewish origins, Freud is scrupulously attentive not only to the details of the Biblical account of Moses, but also to the best available scholarship concerning Egyptian and Jewish religious rituals and history, archaeology, and anthropology. He does not, any more than his religious interlocutors, exhibit any doubt that there is a historical reality underlying these scriptures, a factual point of origin for their ethnic and religious visions. But the historical evidence is so scanty that he cannot make its scraps cohere into an intelligible whole except by utilizing the logic of psychoanalytic interpretation—which means regarding the misleading surface significance of the Biblical text and the Jewish self-understanding it enables as constructed in accordance with the logic of the unconscious, according to which negation is unrepresentable, identity conceals difference as often as difference conceals identity, and significance is always already displaced or transposed. Such uncanny chains of signification can in turn be credited only on the assumption that the patent identity of the individual psyche conceals a latent assemblage of interacting and conflicting parts or forces, in which the history of the person and the prehistory of the human race repeatedly play themselves out with decisive effect, and through which the person's ancestors (both immediate and distant) persist in determining the patterns of thought and behaviour that constitute their identity.

From a psychoanalytic point of view, then, issues of personal and ethnic identity (whether in the distant past or the immediate present) are no more absolute or unconditioned than they are either in Wagnerian mythology or in the history underlying Arthurian counter-mythology. One might say that, in the tuition they derive from such intuitions about the porousness of boundaries and the internalization of otherness, the logic of myth and the logic of the life of the mind here open upon one another. Supposing for a moment that one is willing to take such articulations of sense seriously, how might Freud's way of meaning the claim that 'Moses did not exist' bear upon Wittgenstein's way of envisaging its reception?

Wittgenstein wants to emphasize two points. First, he claims that we use such names as 'Moses' without a fixed (better, without a rigid) meaning. That is, the various descriptions we might offer of Moses and what he said and did across a variety of specific contexts do indeed amount to a series of props that I have (and am obliged to have) in readiness should the significance or truth of my claims about Moses be questioned; but which props we actually help ourselves to, when and where is not in fact settled in advance (and hence not something that must be so determined on pain of my utterances about him lacking any sense). Meaning, so understood, is more of a building site than a building—or rather, not so much a musical score to be followed as a basis for improvisation. Hence, second, whenever a particular prop or set of props is actually subject to challenge, I must make a determination of the significance of that challenge by determining the significance of that prop or set of props to my continued willingness to accept the reality of the bearer of the given name. And this second responsibility primarily involves assessing whether or not the prop under challenge is marginal or central to that sense of conviction; what Wittgenstein calls 'the bounds of the incidental' thus are at issue, and their nature and extent is not something that is or could be predetermined by rules.

Suppose, then, that we imagine a believer in Moses as a father and (re)founder of the Jewish people confronted with Freud's particular challenge to their faith. Would accepting that Moses was an Egyptian rather than a Jewish foundling alter anything essential to his religious belief? He might think that it was more central to his sense of the significance of the Jews as a chosen people that Moses led the Israelites out of Egyptian slavery than that he was a member of the people he liberated (this would be a version of the position of Wittgenstein's imagined believer in section 87). But he might rather see the idea of a slave-master presenting himself as the liberator of slaves (an inflection of Nietzsche's notorious genealogical account of the role of the priests in the slave revolt that founds the Judaeo-Christian faith) as more deeply damaging than it at first appears—for example, in suggesting an unacceptably sadomasochistic dimension to the Israelites' (admittedly grumbling) acceptance and subsequent veneration of Moses' undeniably dominating authority during the Exodus and beyond. Likewise, would the possibility that Yahweh shares many characteristics with Aten do serious damage to our believer's sense of the distinctive nature of the God whose activity picked out the Israelites amongst all human tribes for the renewal of his covenant? Or would something akin to Simone Weil's interpretative strategy in her *Intimations of Christianity among the Greeks* be an acceptable way of accommodating such family resemblances?

There seems to be more or less easily imaginable room for either reaction to these particular Freudian claims to be made out, and so for the issue to appear as a matter over which two members of this religious tradition might reasonably disagree. But it is hard to imagine *any* members of such a tradition happily accommodating themselves to the suggestion that the Israelites murdered the man who led them out of Egypt; it will certainly be essential to our believer's faith in Moses that this ground for doubt be rejected once it is raised—and not hard to envisage the weaknesses in Freud's case that might be central to making a case for that rejection. Of course, that does not show that there always already *was* such a vulnerable gap in the religious believer's structure of thought and conviction that ought to have been closed off in advance; it shows only that a counter-explanation is now needed in order to avert a (potentially very serious) misunderstanding.

But perhaps it also shows that the possibility of having to confront actual doubts arising from essentially unpredictable sceptical perspectives is an ineliminable aspect of the responsibilities one takes on when making any claims about Moses, just as anyone competent to tell a chair from a cheese-board may nevertheless find herself confronted with the question of whether an unpredictably dematerializing and rematerializing chair really does count as a chair (section 80). The underlying moral would seem to be that, for anyone possessed of the capacity to speak, and so to tell one thing from another, the responsibility to keep on making determinations of significance will never come to an end. And if this is true of our sense of the significance of other persons (of which characterizations go to the essence of their identity and which are, or have proven to be, of merely incidental relevance), why should we think that matters are any different with respect to our sense of ourselves? Which self-descriptions do we feel that we must regard as self-defining, as demanding our allegiance; and which will come to seem incidental or superficial, even false to our conception of who we are? How might this change over time, and what interplay of first-person and third-person judgements serves to chart and challenge such shifting determinations?

One might say: words whose meaning is not rigidly fixed may nevertheless be usable; but the convictions they articulate can never place themselves beyond openness to unforeseeable grounds for doubt, and so to further unforeseeable determinations of what lies at the core of such convictions and what lies outside the heart of the matter. In this sense, Freud's critique of Moses might highlight the particular value of what one might call a realistic spirit in religion. For religious faith is very often tempted to imagine formulations of doctrine and dogma that might be specified in such a way as to obviate all ambiguity or indeterminacy; and it is equally liable to imagine that acceptance of the literal meaning of a scriptural text will determine in advance exactly how that text is to be understood and applied. Call these temptations forms of fundamentalism. If Wittgenstein's treatment of Moses is right in, as it were, anticipating the ineliminable possibility of something like a Freudian critique of the relevant Biblical texts, then the case of Moses shows that not even religious uses of words can be everywhere bounded in advance by rules—that there is no such thing as a game with words 'whose rules never let a doubt creep in, but stop up all the cracks where it might' (PI, 83).

7) Suppose we accept, then, that Freud's critique exploits a possibility to which the descriptive props and textual contexts constitutive of the use of a proper name such as 'Moses' is necessarily heir, but which those actually using that name may be reluctant to acknowledge. It doesn't follow from this that Freud himself is as sharply distinguishable from the religious traditions he criticizes as he appears to think, or that he is free of fantasies about the nature and function of proper names of exactly the kind to which Wittgenstein is giving systematic attention in his deployment of the example of Moses, as well as that of Nothung. To see more clearly how things stand with Freud in these fundamental respects, we first need to consider more closely the form of his critical text.

Moses and Monotheism consists of three essays: 'Moses an Egyptian', 'If Moses was an Egyptian . . . ', and 'Moses, his People and Monotheist Religion'. Each succeeding essay is far longer than its predecessor (the first runs to ten pages, the second forty, and the last closer to ninety, in the Standard Edition). This progressive expansion is partly explained by the fact that although, as the title of the second essay implies, each essay builds argumentatively upon its predecessors (with *Totem and Taboo* discernible in the background throughout), each was originally published independently. A certain degree of repetition of previous material in later instalments was thus initially inevitable; but one might well have expected it to disappear, or at least to undergo radical reduction, once all three were combined to form a single, book-length work. And Freud himself is far from insensitive to this fact: indeed, he devotes no less than three separate prefaces appended to the third essay (two before its first Part begins, and the third at the beginning of its second and final Part) to the task of apologizing for this, and attempting to account for it.

The first pair of prefatory notes identifies the obstacles (both external and internal) that stood in the way of Freud's publishing the third and longest portion of his study of Moses. Indeed, the shift in locations in which they were composed indicates both the external obstacle and its overcoming. The first was written in Vienna, hence at a time when Freud himself and the practice of psychoanalysis more generally were still directly vulnerable to the Nazi regime and in need of the Catholic Church's protection, from which perspective it seemed unwise to publish another attempt to present religion as a neurosis of humanity; but the second was written in London, hence from the relative safety of exile, and in the knowledge that the Catholic Church had in fact offered no real bulwark against the Nazi threat. Even then, however, Freud tells us, the key internal difficulty remained:

I feel uncertain in the face of my own work; I lack the consciousness of unity and of belonging together which should exist between an author and his work. (MM, 299)

The third preface (entitled 'Summary and Recapitulation') begins by admitting a further cause for apology: the fact that Part II of the third essay 'is nothing other than a faithful (and often word-for-word) repetition of the first Part, abbreviated in some of its critical inquiries and augmented by additions relating to . . . the special character of the Jewish people' (MM, 349). In short, it is not just that the second and third essays recapitulate their predecessors; the third essay recapitulates itself. In attempted mitigation, Freud tells us that upon his arrival in London:

I began to revise the third part of my study to fit it on to the two parts that had already been published. This naturally involved a partial rearrangement of the material. I did not succeed, however, in including the whole of this material in my second version; on the other hand, I could not make up my mind to give up the earlier versions entirely. And so it has come about that I have adopted the expedient of attaching a whole piece of the first presentation to the second unchanged—which has brought with it the disadvantage of involving extensive repetition. (MM, 350)

The only consolation Freud can offer himself and his readers is that:

[T]he things I am treating are in any case so new and so important, apart from how far my account of them is correct, that it can be no misfortune if the public is obliged to read the same thing about them twice over. There are things that should be said more than once, and that cannot be said often enough. But the reader must decide of his own free will whether to linger over the subject or to come back to it.

He must not be surreptitiously led into having the same thing put before him twice in one book. It is a piece of clumsiness for which the author must take the blame. Unluckily an author's creative power does not always obey his will: the work proceeds as it can, and often presents itself to the author as something independent or even alien. (MM, 350)

This is a fascinatingly double-minded account of the formal peculiarities it undertakes to explain. On the one hand, the originality and importance of the subject matter engenders a range of assertions that cannot be said often enough (so that even more extensive repetition than is manifest in this book would be internally justified); but on the other, this repetition is clumsy and disadvantageous to the reader, and represents a failure of the author's creative power (so that there can only be merely external explanations of it). Freud's repetitiveness thus appears as at once obscure, even incomprehensible to its author, and as utterly and absolutely called-for by the nature of his subject matter and of the views about it that he has developed.

This internal tension in Freud's account is strongly reminiscent of the appearance of double-mindedness that Wittgenstein cultivates in his preface to the *Philosophical Investigations*:

[T]he essential thing was that the thoughts should proceed from one subject to another in a natural order and without breaks. [But] after several unsuccessful attempts to weld my results together into such a whole, I realized that I should never succeed. The best that I could write would never be more than philosophical remarks . . . And this was, of course, connected with the very nature of the investigation. For this compels us to travel over a wide field of thought criss-crossing in every direction.—The philosophical remarks in this book are, as it were, a number of sketches of landscapes which were made in the course of these long and involved journeyings . . . The same or almost the same points were always being approached afresh from different directions, and new sketches made . . . Thus this book is really only an album. (PI, ix)

Are the sketches of landscapes that constitute the numbered sections of the ensuing text (and which include the two circling around Moses) merely the best that Wittgenstein could do, and so a mode of writing that falls short of an ideal state to which it nevertheless always aspires (say, a fully-fledged portrait in oils); or is their condition as overlapping and variously interconnected sketches rather a reflection of the essential nature of the investigation and its subject matter? Is his book *only* an album of sketches, or necessarily such an album?

Even if we accept a certain commonality of concern here, however, the degree of overlap between and within Freud's conjoined essays far exceeds anything Wittgenstein's revisions of his *magnum opus* permitted. Indeed, if we attempt to characterize Freud in the terms he uses to characterize the rest of the world, *Moses and Monotheism* manifests a repetition compulsion—an ungovernable and opaque motivation to reiterate certain patterns of verbal behaviour that is symptomatic of an unaccommodated trauma, a psychic wound of some kind. But what kind?

The lingering uncertainty of which Freud himself talks pertains not to the well-groundedness of his claims, but to what he calls 'the consciousness of unity and belonging together which should exist between an author and his work'. The unity that preoccupies him is thus not a property of the work, but rather of the author's relation to the work. More precisely, Freud is accounting for a certain lack of coherence and continuity within his text by confessing to a corresponding lack of coherence and continuity between himself and that text. The implication seems to be that what assures the integrity of a text is not its achieved autonomy from the author, his willingness to untether it from his own idiosyncratic personality, but rather the author's maintenance of a sense of that text as continuous with himself—a refusal to acknowledge any sharp distinction between those ordered words and the one who ordered them. Such a myth of authorship carries clear echoes of Siegfried's relation to Nothung, and Arthur's to Excalibur.

But the very pattern of compulsive repetition for which Freud is attempting to account itself entails a certain continuity between this text and its subject matter—hence between its author and its subject matter. For Freud's analysis of the traditional Jewish understanding of Moses and the Exodus precisely depends upon identifying a number of constitutive repetitions or recurrences: the use of one proper name to denote two distinct people, the gradual recurrence of the religion of Aten within the early development of the religion of Yahweh, the repetition of a range of intra-psychic operations and effects at the collective level, and above all the repetition within the hidden narrative of the Exodus of the parricidal founding gesture of all human communities. In short, the religious impulse is pervaded by a constitutive compulsion to repeat.

Moreover, although Freud is attempting to undermine what he sees as a dogmatic or unquestioning religious insistence upon the absolute truth of every detail of the Biblical accounts, his own alternative account repeatedly veers towards reproducing exactly the same insistent stance. Where the Bible unhesitatingly recognizes one Moses, Freud equally unhesitatingly insists upon (no more and no less than) two, whose individual fates he finds it possible to divine in minute detail; and where the Bible insists upon the otherness of Egypt to Israel, Freud insists upon Yahweh's gradual but complete repossession by the essence of Aten. Although he freely admits that his contention has weaknesses as well as strengths, each return he makes to his argument, essay by essay, in order to extend its essentially speculative structures one further stage, tempts him to treat each preceding stage (which initially appeared as a hypothetical extension of a more firmly grounded premise) as if it were now itself utterly fixed and certain.

Why might such a mirroring of text and subject, in form and mood, come to such a pitch in this particular context? Or, to put it in the terms Freud's exculpations provide: what is it about this subject matter and its treatment that might be regarded as continuous with, as inherently belonging together with, the author of this text?

Part of the explanation must lie in Freud's implicit identification with Moses. For Freud too is a patriarch, or father of faith—the founder of a new intellectual tradition that offers its adherents a way of making sense of the world as a whole, call it a mythology; and Freud's experience up to the 1930s is that the continued existence (let alone the flourishing) of that tradition is threatened not only by hostile external forces, but also by internecine strife—amongst those with whom he first set out on his intellectual journeyings, and also amongst those who were its first inheritors, the best of whom seemed likely to continue with it in new directions that its founder could not comfortably accept. Freud's uncovering of the murder of the first Moses is thus also an expression of a certain anxiety about himself; and his repetition of this particular charge, his compulsion to come at it again from a variety of directions (and in the end, simply to keep on saying it) functions both as a way of articulating his fears and as a way of warding them off (by displacing them onto phenomena that appear to be more or less external to him, and by issuing a warning about the pervasiveness of such parricidal impulses that might induce a certain self-knowledge in his own intellectual siblings and offspring).

A further dimension of this identification concerns Freud's Jewishness, and hence the extent to which his analysis of Jewish self-understandings is a mode of self-analysis. To some extent, this aspect of the matter is entangled with the preceding one: after all, if Freud's claims about the founding of Jewish traditions upon parricide are correct, then the psychic threat he persistently experienced about his own intellectual leadership would be brought much closer to home. But another aspect of this matter becomes more salient if—in good psychoanalytic fashion—we put in question his own distinction between external and internal obstacles to publishing *Moses and Monotheism*. Such a distinction is likely to seem far from absolute to a psychoanalyst; and when someone insists on categorizing a matter as merely external, hence as secondary in comparison with what is genuinely internal, one need not be a psychoanalyst to suspect that he insists too much.

What Freud categorizes as an external obstacle to publication was the rise of Nazi barbarism, the threat this posed to psychoanalysis understood as a feature of genuinely advanced culture, and his consequent reluctance further to offend the Catholic Church, whom he viewed as his and his practice's best protection against this cultural primitivism. But in the course of this characterization, the key component of Nazi ideology—its anti-Semitism—is passed over in silence; by omitting any reference to it, Freud occludes a key feature of the political environment in its bearing on his project (not to mention his own Jewishness, and the common Nazi identification of psychoanalysis as a Jewish science). For it surely cannot have escaped him that the core of his treatment of Moses—its attribution of a collective Jewish responsibility for the murder of their own patriarch—would (despite its assumption that this is a specific ethnic repetition of a universal human pattern, and despite its attempts to render the boundary between Jewish and non-Jewish peoples more porous) resonate uncomfortably closely with the blunt ways in which the Nazis made use of familiar Christian charges against the Jews. In this context, the proper name of a particular people would not function as merely exemplary, as denoting no more than a particular instance of the way in which any human community is founded.

This coincidence has two deeply disturbing implications. First, publishing *Moses and Monotheism* in Central Europe in the middle of the 1930s might easily be taken as reinforcing such anti-Semitic blood libels, and so could have the most severe moral and political consequences (unless, of course, as Freud himself puts it, such fears 'are based on an over-estimation of my own personal importance' [MM, 297] and of the cultural salience of psychoanalysis). Second, it might cast new doubt on the validity of this psychoanalytic reading of Moses, by unavoidably raising the question of whether it constitutes anything more than a further expression of Jewish self-hatred—an internalization of the anti-Semitism directed at the Jews from without. It is thus hard to escape the conclusion that Freud's precisely-focused characterization of the apparently external obstacles to publishing his work in fact serves to repress (and hence to express) his awareness of where the most penetrating, and hence the most wounding, line of internal criticism of that work is to be found. His increasingly anxious, deeply ambivalent prefaces thus register the potentially fateful significance of a complex nexus at which Freud (as author of this text and originator of the practices it exemplifies) is repeatedly compelled both to invite and to resist the possibility of his internal relatedness to the Jewish people, Christian culture, and National Socialism—the possibility that his identity is partly constituted by the internalization of these particular others.

Such questions—which have their pressing analogues in the case of Wittgenstein, whose work repeatedly considers his own Jewishness, his relation to Christianity, and the threat of cultural barbarism—also bring us full-circle in another way; for they bear upon the various ways in which mythological understandings of the identity of bearers of proper names confront us with a vision of selfhood as fluid and porous, inherently open to other selves (individual and collective), objects, and the world they furnish—as more a matter of becoming and overcoming than being: call it non-self-identity. Indeed, the matter of proper names, more precisely the power of certain fantasies about them, in fact functions as the basic ground of Freud's whole, internally complex and compulsively repetitive enterprise.

As we have already seen, the second and third essays that make up *Moses and Monotheism* depend upon our willingness to accept the claim made in his first and most concise essay—namely, that (the first) Moses was an Egyptian. And in that essay, he offers two reasons for accepting this claim: first, that 'Moses' is an Egyptian name, and second, that the scriptural story of Moses' birth and exposure, if it is assumed to conform to all other such myths of heroic origin which have some basis in fact, must present the hero's real family as the one with which he grows up rather than the one from which he was taken. In other words, Freud's entire argumentative edifice ultimately depends upon assuming on the one hand that a property of a name must reflect a property of its bearer, as opposed—say—to reflecting a property of those bestowing the name, for example the person's foster family (as if names and their bearers are intrinsically or internally related);

and on the other, that any given proper name in myth is entirely substitutable by any other—that is, that there are really no essential differences between distinct legends about different heroes, even those with a basis in history, for their names are mere arbitrary placeholders for unvarying structural functions. In short, *Moses and Monotheism* rests upon two utterly opposed assumptions about proper names: that they are essentially manifestations of the essence of their bearers, and that they are essentially arbitrary labels, no more than bare denotations.

In this respect, we might say that the significance of Moses as an example in Wittgenstein's text is internally relatable to his earlier example of Nothung (and so of its English proxy, Excalibur); to this extent, then, Siegfried, Arthur, and Moses (and their various creators and commentators—Wagner, Malory, Nietzsche, and Freud) might be thought of as each making their own individual contribution to staking out and evaluating the mythological ground to which Wittgenstein's discussion of proper names seems repeatedly compelled to return. And what difference might an enhanced awareness of the bearing of such individuals upon the work of the *Philosophical Investigations* make to our sense of the identity of its author? Just who is Ludwig Wittgenstein?

Smoking in Wartime

Sartrean Scenes I
(Introduction)

The cafe isn't busy today: one or two soldiers in their field-grey or silver-and-black uniforms sit near the bright window, but many of the chairs are empty, the tables they cluster around still patiently awaiting the presence of hands eager to spoon sugar into thin black coffee, or to sip from an early glass of red wine. At least the place is warm, warmer than his own apartment—not easy nowadays to get the fuel; and he has spent so much time over the last months at the table nearest the fire, writing in long, furious bursts, that pretty much everyone regards it as his.

Now, however, he finds that the flow of words has slowed, running up against the need for a concrete example, something to bring the ramifying chains of abstract concepts back to earth. He reaches for the cigarette that he left carefully balanced on the ashtray—how long ago? But before his hand can even begin to move towards it, he sees that it has already burned down to the unfiltered nub: no sustenance or stimulation to be found there anymore. His cigarette case lies just next to his cup of cooling coffee, the battered gold surface still glowing in the last of the morning sunshine—but it's getting very close to the end of the month, and he can no longer recall just how many cigarettes it contains. The case is open in his hand almost before he realizes it, and only after the relief has spread through his nervous system does he notice the differences between its twelve remaining occupants (each rough cylinder distinctively dented or crumpled, some bent out of true, but all densely enough filled out) behind the rather frayed band that resists their resistance to regimentation, its thick containing horizontal rather like a child's hasty but decisive chalk-stroke marking the end of some carefully-tracked sequence (of days before a friend's birthday, of coins needed to buy her present, of tasks completed to earn those coins) . . .

'What are you up to?'

The question, the creak of the chair next to his, the shadow across the table-top—their simultaneous, mutually interfering and reinforcing arrival seems almost to be preceded by his response rather than eliciting it:

'I'm counting.'

The forgotten setting of the cafe and its occupants reorganizes itself around Pierre's familiar smiling face, restoring the case to its place among the familiar furnishings of his working days at this table long before he actually replaces it, there, next to the coffee cup but beyond the pile of manuscript, with the continuation of its introduction hanging on the need for an example, an example of complete absorption in something that is neverthe-less never entirely unaware of its absorption . . .

'Pierre, what do you remember about the beginning of the "Meditations"?'

The house is silent, entirely empty. Outside, people pass through the town square, huddled in their thick coats, intent on their errands; and somewhere amongst them are his daughter and her mother—perhaps down at the sea-water's edge; but in here there is only the man in the winter dressing-gown, his table drawn close to the fire, reading over the pages he has already covered in writing. Beside the pile of manuscript on the table there's a lump of wax—rather misshapen after its brief spell on the hearth, but with its cold, white solidity still carrying the faintest traces of its recent arrival from the hibernating hive in the rear garden, hints of scent and sweetness that the absorbed man no longer notices.

He is concentrating on an early portion of his manuscript:

But what shall I now say that I am, when I am supposing that there is some supremely powerful and, if it is permissible to say so, malicious deceiver, who is deliberately trying to trick me in every way he can? Can I now assert that I possess even the most insignificant of all the attributes which I have just said belong to the nature of a body? I scrutinize them, think about them, go over them again, but nothing suggests itself; it is tiresome and pointless to go through the list once more. But what about the attributes I assigned to the soul? Nutrition or movement? Since now I do not have a body, these are mere fabrications. Sense-perception? This surely does not occur without a body, and besides, when asleep I have appeared to perceive through the senses many things which I afterwards realized I did not perceive through the senses at all. Thinking? At last I have discovered it—thought; this alone is inseparable from me. I am, I exist—that is certain. But for how long? For as long as I am thinking. For it could be that were I totally to cease from thinking, I should totally cease to exist. I am, then, in the strict sense only a thing that thinks; that is, I am a mind, or intelligence, or intellect, or reason—words whose meaning I have been ignorant of until now. But for all that I am a thing which is real and which truly exists. But what kind of a thing? As I have just said—a thinking thing...a thing that doubts, understands, affirms, denies, is willing, is unwilling, and also imagines and has sensory perceptions. (M II: 82–3[1])

Suppose the man in the dressing gown is right in drawing this conclusion from his meditation: suppose that my existence *is* certain for as long as I am thinking. Even so, I can only prove or demonstrate my own existence to myself in this way—say, clearly and distinctly perceive its certainty—for a moment at a time. For the dubitability of my memory means that a recollection of having been thinking cannot permit me to be certain now that I existed in that remembered past; and even if I could attain such certainty, it could not make me certain that I exist now. For this meditator, that epistemological limit reflects the ontological fact that each moment in time is essentially independent of every other; 'the same power and action are needed to preserve anything at each individual moment of its duration as would be required to create that thing anew if it were not yet in existence' (M III: 96). But if my duration through time amounts to the miracle of my unceasing recreation, then certainty about my own existence cannot extend beyond the instant in which I demonstrate it to myself, but must rather itself be recreated in each new moment, by means of a renewed demonstration (that in each case amounts to a joyful expression of our creaturely essence as thinking things, and so to an acknowledgement of the creative power on which every moment of our existence depends—call it an autonomous declaration of our dependence, meditation as worship). Moreover, each new, self-contained moment of my thinking can make available to me a clear and distinct perception of myself as existing only on the further assumption

---

[1] R. Descartes, *Meditations on First Philosophy*, in *Descartes: Selected Philosophical Writings*, trans. J. Cottingham, R. Stoothoff, D. Murdoch (Cambridge: Cambridge University Press, 1998)—hereafter M.

that, whenever I am thinking, I know that I am. The man in the cafe refers to this as Alain's formula: 'to know is to know that one knows' (BN, xxix[2])—although here, of course, Alain knowingly reformulates a guiding assumption of our meditator; and his successor's exemplary story of himself counting cigarettes aims to reveal its invalidity.

In the grip of his anxiety about just how many cigarettes he might have left, this man's consciousness is not just directed upon the contents of his cigarette case: they occupy or colonize that consciousness. His awareness of them is not only direct, as opposed to mediated—an awareness of the cigarettes rather than of some mental representation of or surrogate for them; it is also dominated by its object, to the point at which the awareness is as nothing in comparison to that of which it is aware—quite as if that man's consciousness is nothing more than the site or clearing in which those cigarettes manifest themselves as objects of anxious concern, as if the significance of their nature and number (here and now, to a smoker under a wartime regime of strict rationing) is all-consuming, has in fact consumed the one who so desperately wants them to be there in order that he might consume them. No one would happily say that this man *doesn't* know that there are twelve cigarettes in his case; but anyone might hesitate to say, simply and without qualification, that he *does* know that there are. That would imply that he has simply acquired one more piece of information about his world, on a level with his knowledge of how many soldiers or tables there are in the cafe, as opposed to his suffering the full depth of its particular significance; his state is one of such pure receptivity that it might be more accurate to say that he *is* (nothing more than, nothing but, nothing in addition to) those twelve cigarettes. And I would certainly not hesitate to deny that he knows that he knows that there are twelve cigarettes; for his awareness of their position and significance in the world surely swamps or eclipses any awareness of his own position or stance with respect to them. One might say: what is revealed occludes the revealing of it.

And yet: the moment he is asked what his state of awareness (his particular position in relation to the world and its inhabitants) currently is, he can answer that question. His consciousness of the twelve cigarettes

---

[2] J.-P. Sartre, *Being and Nothingness*, trans. H. Barnes (London: Routledge, 1958)—hereafter BN.

instantaneously becomes a consciousness of his having been counting those twelve cigarettes; precipitated by Pierre's interrogatory intervention, his awareness turns itself inside out, smoothly transforming itself from a condition in which what is revealed eclipses the revealing of it into a condition in which the revealing eclipses what is revealed.

This kind of reflective movement resembles the one that is so beautifully captured when our meditator unleashes his imagination (although only with a view to its ultimately being reined in), and conjures up what people would ordinarily take to be an object of clear and distinct understanding:

Let us take, for example, this piece of wax. It has just been taken from the honeycomb; it has not yet quite lost the taste of the honey; it retains some of the scent of the flowers from which it was gathered; its colour, shape and size are plain to see; it is hard, cold and can be handled without difficulty; if you rap it with your knuckle it makes a sound. In short, it had everything which appears necessary to enable a body to be known as distinctly as possible. But even as I speak, I put the wax by the fire, and look: the residual taste is eliminated, the smell goes away, the colour changes, the shape is lost, the size increases; it becomes liquid and hot; you can hardly touch it, and if you strike it, it no longer makes a sound. But does the same wax remain? It must be admitted that it does; no one denies it, no one thinks otherwise. So what was it in the wax that I understood with such distinctness? Evidently none of the features which I arrived at by means of the senses; for whatever came under taste, smell, sight, touch and hearing has now altered—yet the wax remains . . . Let us concentrate, take away everything that does not belong to the wax, and see what is left: merely something extended, flexible and changeable. (M II: 84)

To begin with, we are wholly immersed in the object towards which we are directing our awareness: the intensity of the meditator's imagined perception of the wax's properties all-but-realizes the thing itself in our consciousness, as if we had become one with its fragrance, taste, and coldness, its derivation from bee and blossom. But then we reflect upon this initial state of identification with that which lies outside us, and interrogate it to the point at which we are meant to realize that, although we thought we knew the wax in opening ourselves to its manifest reality, in truth we didn't know it at all. Those perceptual modes of revealing reveal themselves to be misdirected or disoriented; and that revelation in turn reveals our own true nature—that we are essentially one with the eye of the mind.

Surely my awareness of my own self is not merely much truer and more certain than my awareness of the wax, but also much more distinct and evident. For if I judge that the wax exists from the fact that I see it, clearly this same fact entails much more evidently that I myself also exist. It is possible that what I see is not really the wax; it is possible that I do not even have eyes with which to see anything. But when I see, or think I see . . ., it is simply not possible that I who am now thinking something am not something . . . Moreover, if my perception of the wax seemed more distinct after it was established not just by sight or touch but by many other considerations, it must be admitted that I now know myself even more distinctly. This is because every consideration whatsoever which contributes to my perception of the wax, or of any other body, cannot but establish even more effectively the nature of my own mind. (M II: 86)

Whereas, in order to know the wax as it really is, we must penetrate beneath its appearances ('take the clothes off, as it were, and consider it naked' [M II: 85]), there is no such gap between appearance and reality with respect to our states of mind or consciousness: to be in any such state is to know that one is—such states are utterly transparent to those whose states they are, pure revelations of themselves to themselves. And where the wax is, in reality, malleable matter (beneath the surface nothing but fluid extension, viscous being of a kind likely to make some nauseous and to make others recollect Wagnerian mythologies of identity), the mind declares itself to be utterly transparent to itself, nothing but surface (hence immaterial), a pure depthless coincidence of seeming and being, absolutely self-identical.

But the self-identity of this meditator is, as we saw earlier, necessarily momentary—it is synchronic rather than diachronic, and so cannot view the self's duration over time as anything other than a perpetually renewed miracle of recreation. And by switching the example of an object of awareness from a piece of wax to the cigarettes in a case, the man in the cafe seeks at once to highlight this problem and to reveal that it invades even the synchronic moment. For the key point about the man's cigarettes is that he is counting them: and as Kant already underlined in his account of the conditions for the possibility of subjective knowledge of an objective world, grasping the particular number of objects before me presupposes the capacity to synthesize self-sufficient moments of consciousness as elements in a larger but unitary whole. In order that I be so much as capable of realizing that there are twelve cigarettes in the case, I need to be able to relate to each individual step in the counting process as one in which I—the self-same consciousness—am engaging over a given period of time. From which it follows that the nature and meaning of each of those individual steps of counting cannot reveal itself as such entirely in and of itself: one cannot know that that is what each step is except insofar as one relates it to the other steps in the counting.

But time does not simply disrupt what the meditator would regard as the diachronic dimension of the self's identity; it is at the heart of what he would regard as its synchronic dimension as well—the moment-by-moment coincidence of a state of awareness and a state of awareness of that state of awareness. To be sure, the meditator is right to recognize that any state of consciousness worthy of the name is necessarily capable of becoming conscious of itself—that even the most absorbed mode of awareness remains a mode of awareness, hence something obscurely but undeniably more or other than that of which it is aware, something that can itself be an object of awareness. But although all states of consciousness are necessarily capable of becoming the object of that consciousness, each such state neither is nor contains an actual or actualized consciousness of itself: its revealing of what is revealed is not itself always already revealed to it. That, after all, would initiate an endless regress: for by hypothesis, there can be no revealed (not even a revealing) that is not also itself (the object of) a revealing.

To put matters another way: if the intentional object of a state of consciousness helps to determine the identity of that state, then my consciousness of the twelve cigarettes cannot be one and the same as my consciousness of being conscious of the twelve cigarettes. Between the first state and the second, a shadow falls: time intervenes. The subject reflecting on his directed awareness of those cigarettes is no longer aware of the cigarettes but rather of his prior awareness of the cigarettes; he is attending to his immediately preceding state of awareness, to what he had just a moment ago been entirely absorbed in or consumed by. But that state is not the state he currently occupies; it is the unreflective state whose pre-reflective potential (the spectral presence that prevented his original absorption and its object from coinciding with one another) made it possible for him to realize his current reflective state (with its own spectral, pre-reflective refusal of self-identity, anticipating a future moment of reflection upon itself).

So consciousness turns out to be intrinsically incapable of self-identity: when the revealed eclipses the revealing, it all-but-dissolves into its object (that which it is not); and when the revealing eclipses the revealed, its object is itself as it was rather than as it is (that state of itself that it no longer is). Consciousness is thus always internally related to that which it is not—to the cigarettes, the counting of them, the reflection upon that counting, the reflection upon that reflection . . . Each intentional object at once makes its state of consciousness the state that it is (distinguishing it from any other such state) and fails fully to capture it (since even utterly unreflective awareness of that object is not the object, and awareness is always pre-reflective—even when that awareness is itself reflective).

But this non-identity is not so much a structure as a process, and a painful one at that. For the man counting the cigarettes embodies a mythology of consciousness as suffering a self-division it wants to deny. Absorbed in the cigarettes, it is as if he becomes them, becomes nothing more than them, in a kind of yearning for identity with them that finds clear expression in the meditator's invocation of sensory abandonment to the piece of wax, with its heavenly fragrance and angelic taste, its prelapsarian communion with nature (the blossoms and the bees). But even in the utmost depths of this loss of self, pre-reflection lurks: it might be activated by another (Pierre) or by oneself (the meditator), but once activated, it both reveals the non-identity of that absorptive state with its object, and reiterates the fantasy of self-identity, by encouraging us to think (as the meditator thinks) of reflection as wholly uniting consciousness with itself, revealing with revealed. Still, however, the pre-reflective demon waits and whispers, at once prophesying and enacting the destruction of that renewed fantasy, as well as its resurrection.

This is a creation myth of a very particular kind: the self creates itself by tearing itself away from the world, and then by tearing itself away from itself; but in so doing, it simultaneously realizes an aspect or dimension of itself that was always already there, and registers the equal profundity of its desire to deny it. The meditator imagines the self's createdness as its dependency upon an externally originating, endlessly reiterated miracle of recreation *ex nihilo*; but from the perspective of the man in the cafe, there is nothing to distinguish creation *ex nihilo* from self-creation (for if this creative force is wholly external to what it creates, no trace of its nature or reality could mark that creation). So absolute dependence and absolute autonomy dissolve into one another: they amount to only apparently different ways of denying what truly registers the self's finitude—its intentionality (its openness to what it is not) and its pre-reflectivity (its difference from itself, whether unreflective or reflective), aspects of consciousness that are ultimately themselves internally related (since intentionality without pre-reflexivity would convert openness to identity with that to which it is open). What the meditator's myth of the self's creatureliness really declares is that our desire to deny our finitude is as fundamental to us as that which it denies: the aspiration to be infinite—embodied in our sense that absolute self-sufficiency is something we have somehow lost, and might somehow recover—is finitude's fundamental mark. This interpretation does not (despite its author's apparent inclination to think otherwise) exactly deny the possibility of our being created by God: it amounts to a further specification of what would be involved in creating a genuinely finite, non-divine consciousness. Selfhood, whether created or not, could not be anything other than a matter of endlessly suffering self-creation—tearing oneself away from everything that is not oneself (including oneself).

The man in the cafe acknowledges the necessity for such tearing away to have something from which to tear itself when he conjoins his account of the self's non-self-identity with an account of that which is not self (that which is antithetical to consciousness) as essentially self-identical. What he calls Being-in-itself (as opposed to Being-for-itself) is variously described as opaque to itself, glued to itself, filled with itself, solid or indissoluble—it is itself, it is. For when the cigarette counter reflects fully upon his absorption in those twelve cigarettes, he finds himself to have been confronting in and through this particular phenomenon a second region of Being that is wholly other; and the reflective recoil that throws him brutally and unsuccessfully back upon himself only reinforces the absolute difference between his own Being and that of all other beings.

But that recoil is not, on reflection, just a consequence of this difference; it is also part of its emergence and expression—or rather, its emergence is its expression. Mythologically speaking, consciousness first becomes what it is (non-self-identical) by tearing itself away from Being-in-itself, hence by relating to itself as having torn itself away from the self-identical—as having lost something that it can never regain, but will never stop trying to regain. So this philosophical portrait of the utterly self-identical inevitably betrays the self's internal relatedness to it, and understands that internal relation as one of active suffering. In this sense, the portrait enacts what it dramatizes: it is one more expression of the essence of that which it aspires to characterize—one more manifestation of the negating process that it depicts.

What, then, of the author of this portrait? How exactly should we conceive of the relation between the book in which this mythology is elaborated and the person who created it? The man in the cafe thinks of creativity in this way:

One can conceive of a *creation* on condition that the created being recover itself, tear itself away from the creator in order to close in on itself immediately and assume its being; it is in this sense that a book exists as distinct from its author. But if the act of creation is to be continued indefinitely, if the created being is to be supported even in its inmost parts, if it does not have its own independence, if it is *in itself* only nothingness—then the creature is in no way distinguished from its creator; it is absorbed in him. We are dealing with a false transcendence, and the creator cannot have even an illusion of getting out of his subjectivity. (BN, xxiv)

There is a definite recoil here from the meditator's vision of his own creatureliness as involving both absolute self-sufficiency and moment-by-moment (re)creation; the man in the cafe thinks of this as a contradiction in terms, an attempt to have the autonomy of consciousness whilst simultaneously referring even its inmost parts to what is absolutely other to it. It can result only in something that is, in itself, nothing at all—not the kind of nothingness that involves being internally related to what one is not, but rather the kind that involves absolute absorption in its other. Such a contradiction cannot be accepted; but its desirability merely confirms the claim that denial of finitude is finitude's deepest impulse.

And yet, the alternative model of creation on offer here might, by the same token, begin to seem rather too directly or straightforwardly contrary to that of the meditator, from which the man in the cafe is plainly trying to tear himself away. For whilst he is careful to present the creation as tearing itself away from its creator in the beginning, he then envisages it as simply and straightforwardly closing in on itself and assuming its own being—as if creation were a once-for-all business, after which the created being must think of itself as essentially self-sufficient. This hardly coheres with his early remark about Proust's relation to his text: 'The genius of Proust is neither the work considered in isolation nor the subjective ability to produce it; it is the work considered as the totality of the manifestations of the person' (BN, xxii). Moreover, according to the terms of his own analysis, any such vision of self-closure will be simply one more way of succumbing to the idea of consciousness and its products as self-identical—a failure to recognize that self-creation must be a continuous process (since to be a self is to be endlessly self-creating), hence one which consists of endlessly tearing oneself away from whatever one is not (including what one has so far, or just, been). So even this anti-Cartesian image turns out to resemble that from which it so ostentatiously turns away, in that it succumbs to the same temptation as its putative opposite.

But we do not have to follow Sartre or his text in this respect: on the contrary, if we attempt to rescue what is valuable in his attempted negation of Descartes from that which reiterates the Cartesian error (if we hold on to his myth of selfhood as an endless struggle to recreate its non-self-identity), Sartre can provide us with a better way of understanding his own relation to his philosophical predecessors and his earlier philosophical self, and to his current philosophical creation—the book before us here and now, *Being and Nothingness*. For we can apply the same myth to an understanding of that book, and try thinking of it as aspiring properly to acknowledge the finitude of its creator; then we should expect it to establish and preserve its identity by persistently tearing itself away from that to which it is internally related— that without which it could not be what it is. That could only mean actively negating its relation to its author, to its sources, to its own preceding states (prior chapters, earlier characters or personae, preceding formulations and generalizations), and to its readers.

Such a text would actively invite a rather unusual array of questions. It might, for example, lead us to ask: is the man counting cigarettes Sartre, or someone Sartre imagines when first attempting to exemplify the non-self-identity of the self, or neither, or both? Is this cigarette counter one and the same person as the various other exemplars who appear in later chapters of Sartre's book or essentially different; and how are any and all of them (whether or not each explicitly emerges—as does the cigarette counter—from the authorial or narratorial first person, as embodiments of what 'I' thought or saw or felt or did) related to their author? Are the views advanced in the introduction (by means of such exemplars as the cigarette counter) taken for granted in later parts of the text, or displaced or reoriented in some other way? And how might these authorial views and exemplars be seen as at once internally related to, and actively refusing, those of this author's most promin-ent predecessors? In particular: is the meditator on the piece of wax simply an exemplar of authorial views and strategies that are straightforwardly antithetical to those embodied in the cigarette counter, or rather someone from whom insight can be achieved only by first inhabiting the perspective he instantiates before negating it? Just how (anti-)Cartesian is Sartre and all his works?

Suppose we think of these questions as provoked by a reflexive application of what our author begins his book by outlining as the principle of the phenomenological method he is employing—that of 'reducing the existent to the series of appearances which manifest it' (BN, xxi). This conception of the phenomenon as something whose essence is neither essentially distinct from, nor hidden irrecoverably behind, its appearances is presented in the first instance as a means of countering the invocation of disabling dualisms in philosophical analyses of physical objects and forces. But the principle (being one of method) must apply quite generally; and our author supplements his illustrations of its efficacy at the outset by contesting a parallel dualism (of potency and act) in our understanding of the genius of Proust (BN, xxii), so its application to human beings, their literary talents, and their textual creations is one that he positively invites.

If we take up that invitation, then grasping the essence of each individual exemplar and author this essay has invoked must require determining the boundaries of the series of textual appearances in and through which they are made manifest—discriminating one imagined 'I' from another (or denying that more than one such 'I' is involved), and asking whether and how the totality of this text's elements and operations make manifest the essence of their creator. Call this a matter of problematizing the boundaries between these various individuals (real and fictional), their various deeds and creations, and the individual elements of those creations. If, according to this creator's slightly later and further account of the matter, each individual person and text is what it is only insofar as it tears itself away from that without which it simply would not be, how could those boundaries be anything other than problematic; and how could any reader of a text that so regards them avoid taking personal responsibility for the way in which he chooses to draw them (or blur them)? It is, after all, part of Sartre's own project to resist being absorbed or subsumed within the work of any consciousness or text that is not his own—whether divine or human (whether Descartes or Heidegger); so anyone inspired to inherit Sartre must at least consider aspiring to the same relationship of intimate resistance to him.

Orchestral Metaphysics

The Birth of Tragedy between Drama, Opera, and Philosophy

Although *The Birth of Tragedy* is centrally concerned to advance the science of aesthetics by coming to grips with the essence of Attic tragedy, its author also characterizes the book (in his foreword to it) as being in constant conversation with Richard Wagner, and hence as a continuation of their joint struggle properly to grasp the true purpose and full value of Wagnerian opera, understood as aspiring to the status of a *Gesamtkunstwerk*.[1] One might say that *The Birth of Tragedy* is an attempt to make sense of the Wagner circle's habit of referring to their leader as Aeschylus—to ground Nietzsche's intuition that the work of both men embodies an enigmatic sublimity of a distinctive kind, one that can properly be individuated only by placing each in the light cast by the other. To christen Wagner as Aeschylus is to say not just that Wagnerian opera can only be rightly understood as a transfiguration of Attic tragic drama, but also that Attic tragic drama can only be rightly understood if seen as essentially capable of such transfiguration. The genealogical narrative that Nietzsche unfolds, with Aeschylus at the origin and Wagner as its present culmination, is thus a way of rendering perspicuous aspects of the essence of each body of work that might otherwise remain occluded, whilst recognizing that their distinctive sublimity would be lost if its enigmatic quality were ever (*per impossibile*) entirely dissipated.

It is not surprising that a young philologist of exceptional gifts, encountering works of art of whose excellence he is immediately convinced, but who cannot as immediately articulate the grounds of that conviction to his

---

[1] *The Birth of Tragedy*, ed. R. Geuss and R. Speirs, trans. R. Speirs (Cambridge: Cambridge University Press, 1999)—hereafter BT.

own satisfaction (any more than can the creator of those works), should turn for illumination to the unchallenged exemplars of artistic excellence with which he has been so much preoccupied. But this particular philologist was also a philosopher—someone whose formation included immersion in Schopenhauer, and thereby in Kant's world-historical transfiguration of the metaphysical impulse that first found its distinctively philosophical expression in Plato. Consequently, the conversation between Wagner and Aeschylus that informs *The Birth of Tragedy* in fact involves a third party— call him Schopenhauer as Educator, the teacher who makes it possible to read Kant as a culminating, subversive transfiguration of Socrates, the exemplary philosopher.

Suppose we regard the author of *The Birth of Tragedy* as the site or medium of this three-cornered conversation. What form of writing might he forge to embody such an exchange—one in which each contributor might retain his individuality without denying his internal relatedness to the others? Can there be a mode of discourse that makes equally essential reference to opera, tragic drama, and philosophy, tapping into the distinctive powers of each without corrupting the fruitfulness of all? Just what kind of text is *The Birth of Tragedy?*

1) The Satyr's Vision: Tragic Drama

Nietzsche's vision of Attic tragedy is crystallized in section 8 of *The Birth of Tragedy*, and the following paragraphs summarize its main elements:

Enchantment is the precondition of all dramatic art. In this enchanted state the Dionysiac enthusiast sees himself as a satyr, and *as a satyr he in turn sees the god* i.e. in his transformed state he sees a new vision which is the Apolline perfection of his state. With this new vision the drama is complete.

This insight leads us to understand Greek tragedy as a Dionysian chorus which discharges itself over and over again in an Apolline world of images. Thus the choral passages which are interwoven with the tragedy are, to a certain extent, the womb of the entire so-called dialogue i.e. of the whole world on stage, the drama proper. This primal ground of tragedy radiates, in a succession of discharges, that vision of drama which is entirely a dream-appearance, and thus epic in nature; on the other hand, as the objectification of a Dionysiac state, the vision represents not Apolline release and redemption in semblance, but rather the breaking-asunder of the individual and its becoming one with the primal being itself. Thus drama is the Apolline embodiment of Dionysiac insights and effects. (BT, 44)

The basic claim here is that the tragic chorus is the artistic imitation of a more primitive, more explicitly religious phenomenon—that of the agitated mass of Dionysus' servants shouting in jubilation as they are seized by moods and insights so powerful that they transform themselves before their own eyes, making them think that they are seeing themselves restored to what they regard as the fundamental spirit of nature—the satyrs (hybrids of the human and the equine, centaurian emblems of the omnipotent life-force). In that transfigured state, they undergo a vision of their god, Dionysus, as the underlying truth of things, a revelation of reality in comparison to which real experience is mere appearance. Following his methodological principle that origins condition essence, Nietzsche invites us to understand the chorus in Attic tragedy as an artistic reconstitution of the satyr chorus, and as itself the primal ground or heart of the tragic drama it helps constitute.

In this way, he finds aesthetic and metaphysical significance in an architectural fact about Attic tragedy—that the place of the chorus in Greek theatres was the orchestra, a semicircular area in front of the stage. The scene of their singing and dancing was thus essentially liminal with respect to both drama and spectators, internally related to both and so not exclusively identifiable with either. The chorus was Janus-faced—it was capable of engaging with the characters in the drama in ways not available to mere spectators, and yet its distinctive theatrical space makes it the innermost of the concentric circles of terraces on which those spectators sat (taking in both the drama as a whole and the cultural world of which it was the expression), inviting them not only to view but to identify with the chorus, and thereby to overcome their metaphysical distance from the drama in which that chorus is involved. The chorus' function as participant-observers thus allows the audience to experience the drama as if they too were participants in it.

The dramatic action on stage is then to be understood as a vision of the chorus, and so of the audience—a vision of their suffering, glorified master, Dionysus. As Nietzsche puts it: '[R]ight down to Euripides, Dionysus never ceased to be the tragic hero, and...all the tragic figures of the Greek stage, Prometheus, Oedipus, etc., are merely masks of that original hero, Dionysus' (BT, 51). By this, Nietzsche means (at least) that these tragic figures are not so much individuals as individualities, mythic archetypes rather than particular embodied souls; that they are no more absolutely distinguishable from the chorus and so from the audience than they are from one another or from the god they body forth; and that their vicissitudes reveal three truths: the vulnerability of our moral status to unfathomable contingency (as Oedipus is polluted by deeds whose nature and consequences exceed the reach of his intentions), the ultimate unintelligibility of reality (with Oedipus' mastery of the Sphinx's riddle being shown to be both catastrophic in consequence and yet merely apparent, since he cannot utilize his ability to define human being in general in order to comprehend himself or his human others), and the origin of human suffering as lying in the fate or condition of individuality as such rather than anything that specific individuals happen to do or suffer.

But Nietzsche's claim is that these Dionysian insights and effects (of both content and form) are given Apolline embodiment—in his terms, that the dramatic vision the chorus discharges is essentially a dream-appearance. By this he means (at least) that it discloses a divine power that is independent of those to whom it is made manifest; that the god manifests himself as a sequence of erring, striving protagonists; that those protagonists participate in a representation of release and redemption, even if not release and redemption *by* representation—by means of semblance or image-making; and that whilst the distinctions between character, chorus, and audience are problematized or weakened, they are not entirely deconstructed. In short, the womb of Dionysian ecstasy does and must discharge itself in structured, ordered words and deeds: its prodigious episodes of collectively-declaimed words interwoven with music and dance engender modes of speech that incarnate a form of aesthetic and dramatic fulfilment in the absence of dance and music, and in the mouths of recognizably individual speakers.

By thus understanding the tragic chorus as an aesthetic transfiguration of the satyr chorus, and viewing the dramatic whole of which that chorus is a part in the terms provided by his interpretation of that part, Nietzsche makes good on his opening claim—that Attic tragedy not only presents miraculous events (such as Oedipus' redemptive transfiguration at Colonus) but is itself a metaphysical miracle, a work of art that is Apolline and Dionysian in equal measure, an unprecedented pairing of two conflictual but productive artistic drives that Nietzsche names after the two Greek deities of art—Apollo standing for image-making and sculpture, and Dionysus for the imageless art of music.

Attic tragedy therefore establishes that the complementarity of Apollo and Dionysus is at least as important as their conflict. For whilst the culture which first acknowledged them initially understood them as essentially oppositional, hence as primarily revealing fundamental differences between individual art forms (as well as divisions within the impulses which give rise to artistic creation, and rifts in the underlying reality from which those creations emerge and into which they aspire to penetrate), the genealogical productivity of their mutual antagonism ultimately revealed an enigmatic but undeniable mutual dependence: a realization that each found its highest expression within the highest expression of the other. To regard each as essentially sunderable from the other would be to occlude the capacity of each to break itself asunder, overcoming its initial absolute individuality or distinctness in order to become more than it could otherwise be, and thereby more itself. And in so doing, it discloses the mysterious primal unity of being.

Nietzsche's opening, summary articulation of this central point about the pairing of Dionysus and Apollo depicts it in terms of a productive mutual provocation at once akin to and different from that of reproduction by sexual difference. First the stimulation of each by the other induces each to produce ever more vigorous offspring of its own (each being thereby the womb for its own progeny). Then an artistic form is established that is equally indebted to both—in which the Dionysian element forms the womb for the Apolline, but the Apolline perfects the Dionysian, so that its divine vision might be externalized and so rendered viewable, and a coherent embodiment for the womb which is compelled to discharge or project that vision might be engendered. This artistic progeny is thus a hybrid: it both contains and constitutes an aesthetic and metaphysical centaur.

Can one say the same of *The Birth of Tragedy* itself? Since it presents Attic tragedy as a centaur, it certainly contains one; can it also be said to constitute one? According to the account of the centaur it contains, the essence of that hybrid resides in a transfiguration of the satyr chorus, in which state or condition the Dionysiac enthusiast sees himself as a satyr, and as such suffers a vision of his god which perfects the state in which he suffers it. Can this characterization be applied to the author of that account?

Suppose we begin with that author's vision—in this case, a vision of Attic tragedy. It is certainly one which regards the constituent elements of that genre as various, internally related manifestations or masks of a divine duality, godheads engaged in a drama of conflict and redemption in which their distinctive identities are provisionally and miraculously overcome, and so in which the vicissitudes of that archetypal pairing make darkly visible the primal unity of all things. To this extent, *The Birth of Tragedy* plainly reproduces the basic structure of the phenomenon its opening sections depict.

That depiction more specifically claims that the visions with which it is concerned take the form of tragic mythical dramas; can the depiction itself be said to manifest (inflections of) the same three formal features? The broader historical narrative that contextualizes Nietzsche's account of Attic tragedy suggests an affirmative answer. The tragic dimension of that narra-tive lies in its basic structure of birth, death (or suicide), and prophesied, transfiguring rebirth. And its mythic status is reinforced by the fact that the narrative is genealogical in form: for each succeeding episode thereby appears as a further manifestation of the fate of the divine duality of Apollo and Dionysus. The key characteristic of mythic logic central to Nietzsche's reading of Attic tragedy—its conviction that apparently diverse and distinct phenomena are in truth metamorphoses of one or two timeless, underlying principles or powers—is thereby generalized, so that the whole of human history in the West is dramatized as a series of masks or manifestations of these dual divinities, each a more or less productive variation upon the original stock (an effect of their mutual excitation, whether irritable or arousing, and of exogenous shocks or graftings).

Many of Nietzsche's own remarks about myth prepare us for the thought that the remarks themselves should be seen as being as much mythological in status as exercises of historical scholarship. He defines myth as 'the most significant example', and tragic myth as 'myth which speaks of Dionysiac knowledge in symbols'—both definitions patently possessed of reflexive application, given *The Birth of Tragedy*'s deployments of Apollo and Dio-nysus as infinitely suggestive exemplars of the primal unity of being. He further associates myth with the basic structure of genealogical narrative when he attributes to myths a 'natural tendency to go on living and to throw out new shoots' (BT, 54), as well as a vulnerability to intellectual scepticism whose pressures result in the transformation of myth into a finished sum of historical events whose credibility wanes in proportion to the extent to which they are dogmatically asserted, until the myth then wilts, discolours, and finds that its blossoms and leaves are scattered to the four winds.

What, then, of the idea that *The Birth of Tragedy* exemplifies an essentially dramatic mode of vision? Nietzsche specifies the category of the dramatic, understood in comparison with that of the poetic, in the following way:

[W]hat makes a poet a poet is the fact that he sees himself surrounded by figures who live and act before him, and into whose innermost essence he gazes . . . For the genuine poet metaphor is no rhetorical figure, but an image which takes the place of something else, something he can really see before him as a substitute for a concept . . . [O]ne only has to have the ability to watch a living play continuously and to live constantly surrounded by crowds of spirits, then one is a poet; if one feels the impulse to transform oneself and to speak out of other bodies and souls, then one is a dramatist.

Dionysiac excitement is able to transmit to an entire mass of people this artistic gift of seeing themselves surrounded by just such a crowd of spirits with which they know themselves to be inwardly one. This process of the tragic chorus is the original phenomenon of *drama* – this experience of seeing oneself transformed before one's eyes and acting as if one had really entered another body, another character. (BT, 43)

The thought that, in these terms, Nietzsche envisions his own work as going beyond the poetic to the dramatic helps to account for his use of a literary technique that Silk and Stern rightly describe as pervasive in *The Birth of Tragedy*, and which they label 'metalepsis' (that is, metonymy, but of a double, complicated, or indirect kind). What they have in mind is Nietzsche's tendency to depict the character and vicissitudes of a phenomenon in terms provided by aspects or elements of the phenomenon itself—as when Apolline culture is depicted in terms appropriate to Apolline art ('the glorious Olympian figures . . . stand on the gable of this structure'), or Attic tragedy is equated with two tragic characters ('at once Antigone and Cassandra'), or the power of a myth is described in terms of the powers belonging to a mythological character ('it rises once more like a wounded hero'), or the passing of tragedy is characterized in terms of the lamented death of a mythic god ('Great Pan is dead!').[2]

Our discussion suggests a way of understanding why this technique is so appropriate and so effective: for it amounts to Nietzsche's writing not just as if the mythical figures of Greek tragic drama were living incarnations of concepts (so that his thinking is, as it were, poetic—literally figurative), but

---

[2] For a much longer list of examples, and their textual locations, see Silk and Stern, *Nietzsche on Tragedy* (Cambridge: Cambridge University Press, 1981), pp. 198–204.

as if he had really entered into their body and soul, and thereby into the view of the world that they incarnate. He sees everything through their eyes, articulating his experience in the terms they embody, as if the texture of their world has become that of his own subjectivity—as if he is possessed by them, transformed into these various manifestations of the dual godhead, one more mask for the divinities he divines everywhere.

In part, this metaleptic strategy follows from the liminal position appropriate to any author who understands himself as aspiring to occupy the orchestral position of the tragic chorus. For it enacts a provisional subversion of the supposedly absolute division between the spectator and the characters of Attic tragedy—as if Nietzsche is re-enacting his experience of utter identification with those mythic figures in order to invite his reader not only to undergo that experience with him, but also to experience Nietzsche's own transfiguration of tragic mythic drama in a similar way (by thinking and acting as if one had really entered—by way of Nietzsche's ensouled body of choric writing—into the body and soul of Nietzsche's Apollo and Dionysus). But one might equally well view metalepsis not merely as a strategy adopted within the book but also as the basic principle of its construction. For if *The Birth of Tragedy* does invite an understanding of itself as structured overall in the terms it posits for understanding the structure of one phenomenon it analyses, then that part of the book stands for (substitutes or goes proxy for, incarnates or exemplifies the living spirit of) the whole—an essentially metonymic effect.

2) Interlude: The Operatic Transfiguration of Voice, Body, and Words

I suggested earlier that another part of *The Birth of Tragedy* might have a metonymic function: the account offered in its concluding sections of Wagnerian opera. More specifically, my claim was that Nietzsche not only is as much concerned to illuminate Attic tragedy by reference to Wagner as to illuminate Wagner by reference to Attic tragedy, but also wants us to understand his own text in the terms provided by his analysis of both.

The mythic principle of genealogical substitution and displacement strongly suggests one way of envisioning Wagner's relation to Aeschylean drama: that which finds expression in the metamorphosis of the term 'orchestra' from naming the site of the chorus to that of the players of musical instruments. On Nietzsche's understanding, this linguistic displacement marks and effects both change and continuity, signifying a transfiguring recurrence or recreation: the Wagnerian orchestra is a mask of the tragic chorus, which was itself a mask of the satyr-chorus. What might this mean?

The envisaged architecture of Bayreuth emphasizes one central continuity by placing every seat in the audience at exactly the same level, thus echoing the egalitarianism implicit in the encircling terraces of the original Greek theatre. In both dispositions, matters of social distinction recede in the face of an essentially communal identification with the drama about to unfold—the expression of an existing or passionately desired sense of unity with one another, and with the truth dramatized on stage. The central discontinuity lies in the fact that the location whose liminality serves to effect this transcendence of individuation is occupied not by singing and dancing seers, and thus by words interwoven with music and action, but by makers of music alone. If the pairing of Attic tragedy and Wagnerian opera allows each to illuminate the other, this (un)masking tells us that music is the often-occluded essence of the phenomenon of Greek tragic drama, and that Wagner's way of rearticulating that aesthetic original nevertheless gives an unprecedented dominance to the role of music within the envisaged totality of the *Gesamtkunstwerk*.

The key feature of music in this context—its Dionysian essence—has primarily to do with the fact that Nietzsche views it as imageless, essentially non-representational. More precisely, the distinction between representation and that which is represented, between symbolic form and symbolic content, typically has no application to music: it refuses that mode of articulating and hence individuating its meaning, because it *is* its meaning, it means itself. Since its mode of signification is not that of semblance-making, it is particularly suited to articulating the underlying truth of things, with which we and all existing things are ultimately one.

Viewing myth and music as each other's other allows Nietzsche to see that Wagner's most recent thoughts about opera—according to which music was ultimately more important than the words and deeds dramatized on stage—provide an unprecedentedly deep acknowledgement of the extent to which the womb-like Dionysian enchantment out of which the tragic chorus speaks is an essentially musical mood or mode of attunement.

Since no one in Nietzsche's era (or indeed our own) was in a position to experience the musical element of the tragic chorus, his experience of Wagner's transfigured version of it was an indispensable means of disclosing its true significance. And to those who point out that since Nietzsche had, at the time of composing *The Birth of Tragedy*, never experienced a Wagner opera in performance, and had probably only ever heard piano reductions of their scores, his sense of the priority of the musical element in such operatic work was, to say the least of it, potentially overdetermined, Nietzsche could reply that it was precisely his ecstatic apprehension of the unrealized totality of those works by means of an experience of their scores that confirmed him in his sense of the distinctive physiognomy of both Wagnerian opera and Attic tragedy. One might say that, just as the striking presence of the musical element in Wagnerian opera revealed to Nietzsche the nature and significance of the missing element in our experience of Attic tragedy, so the striking dramatic element of Attic tragedy helped to flesh out the nature and significance of the as-yet missing element in his experience of Wagnerian opera.

But the displacement of the ancient chorus by the modern symphonic orchestra invites the question: where is that chorus displaced to? In the context of opera, the answer must surely be: fully onto the stage—to the dramatized, lyrical words and deeds of the singers. And since this displacement reshapes the distinction between the chorus and the individual protagonists of these tragic mythological dramas, the original significance of the tragic chorus will inevitably be redistributed between those two kinds of dramatic-operatic being.

One possible implication of this redistribution emerges if we pair a remark of Nietzsche's with one from Stanley Cavell's discussion of opera.[3] Nietzsche's remark comes from a scathing critique of the prevailing, non-Wagnerian forms of operatic work:

What will become of the Dionysiac and the Apolline where there is such a mixture of styles as I have shown to lie at the heart of the *stilo rappresentativo*? – where music is regarded as the servant and the libretto as master, where music is compared to the body and the words to the soul? (BT, 93)

---

[3] In *A Pitch of Philosophy* (Cambridge, MA: Harvard University Press, 1994)—hereafter PP.

Cavell's discussion recasts Nietzsche's familiar metaphor of the body from a rather different perspective, namely that of a commentary on the conjunction of opera's founding with the advent of Cartesian scepticism in modern philosophy, during which he attempts to specify opera's distinctive conception of the relation between the human being and her body:

[A] relation in which not this character and this actor are embodied in each other, but in which this voice is located in—one might say disembodied within—this figure, this double, this person, this persona, this singer, whose voice is essentially unaffected by the role.

A Cartesian intuition of the absolute metaphysical difference between mind and body, together with the twin Cartesian intuition of an undefined intimacy between just this body and only this spirit, appears to describe conditions of the possibility of opera . . .

[S]urely the operatic voice is the grandest realization of having a signature, of an abandonment to your words, hence of your mortal immortality. (PP, 137, 144)

Nietzsche wishes to revive the idea of music as the Dionysian soul and words as the Apolline body of Wagnerian opera; he thereby inverts the evaluative hierarchy written into the essentially representational style of current operatic forms, but leaves unquestioned the assumption that the relation between soul and body is inevitably both oppositional and hierarchical. Cavell transfigures the issue by considering the individual figure of the opera singer, and by viewing her as essentially individuated in that medium by her voice. Her voice is a manifestation or incarnation of her spirit or signature, rather than of her soul—or rather, the terms 'spirit' and 'signature' here substitute for or displace the term 'soul', retaining its function of referring to a person's essence or identity, but distancing themselves from the assumption that that essence is simply immortal, and so essentially opposed to its body. For the opera singer's voice is enigmatically intimate with her body, hence her mode of immortality is distinctively mortal; and her voice both realizes and is realized by an abandonment to her words, not an abandonment of them. Cavell thereby rejects the idea that words are a mere vessel for or servant of the voice—hence essentially opposed to or other than it, and so the human being who voices them. What the opera singer's voice is truly dislocated from or disembodied within is neither her words nor her body, but rather (as Cavell's prose, with its rapid sequence of terms for it—each no sooner deployed than displaced—positively enacts) her persona or mask: that is, her role as an actor in lyric drama as such, and her specific character in this particular opera (whoever it may be). Her voice thereby reveals music and words as essentially unified aspects of the identity that survives any maskings or unmaskings it undergoes—a duality whose productive conflict and complementarity reveal an underlying individuality.

Looking back on *The Birth of Tragedy* fifteen years later, Nietzsche declares that its author, this new soul, stammering in a strange tongue, 'ought to have sung...and not talked!' (BT, 7). Cavell's transfiguration of one of that author's key figures in the light of one of his key points of metonymic reference suggests that this attempt at self-criticism is not so much an external critique as a deployment of that same strange tongue, only without the stammer. At the very least, it suggests that the guidance Nietzsche hesitantly wished to take from his impressions of Wagnerian opera will be found in the specific modulations of his authorial voice; and since its capacity for song must be more dependent upon language alone than any opera to which it adverts, its signature or spirit must be realized primarily in the specific mode of Nietzsche's abandonment to words, his willingness to be ecstatically possessed by *their* individual spirit or signature, their mortal immortality.

That mortal immortality is most generally realized in the genealogical vicissitudes of words from Aeschylus' days to Wagner's and now our own, that is, by the endlessly-reconfigured orchestrations of their individual and collective histories to which *The Birth of Tragedy* is so obsessively attuned. And the specifically Wagnerian music of Nietzsche's voice is not audible outside or beside itself in opera, as if *The Birth of Tragedy* were an alternative libretto for *Tristan and Isolde* or the *Ring*. It is rather realized in that text's becoming increasingly possessed by those libretti: for its concluding sections begin to deploy the register of Wagnerian myth in the metaleptic way in which it employs Aeschylean and Sophoclean myth throughout—attempting to attune us to the initial intimations of a rebirth of tragedy out of the spirit of music by characterizing that revelatory, redemptive experience in the terms provided by its incarnations: initially the characters and events of *Tristan*, but ultimately one critical passage from the *Ring* cycle.

After first alluding (BT, 97) to the fire-magic of this music (using a phrase from *The Valkyrie*), Nietzsche then imagines a contemporary German in search of this rebirth as needing only to 'listen to the blissfully enticing call of the Dionysiac bird which is on the wing, hovering above his head, and which wants to show him the way' (BT, 111). And having thereby briefly sounded this note from *Siegfried*, a few pages later and within a page of his argument's conclusion, it resounds again with full force:

Let no one believe that the German spirit has lost its mythical home for ever, if it can still understand so clearly the voices of the birds which tell of its homeland. One day it will find itself awake, with all the morning freshness that comes from a vast sleep; then it will slay dragons, destroy the treacherous dwarfs, and awaken Brunnhilde—and not even Wotan's spear itself will be able to bar its path! (BT, 115)

This Wagnerian scene as evoked by Nietzsche interprets Dionysus as the guiding voice of nature, and more specifically as facilitating and embodying the heroic human capacity for becoming oneself, for transitionality or self-overcoming—the authentically human as a bridge or an arrow of longing. For this Dionysiac bird encounters the fearless Siegfried between his triumphant destruction of Fafner the dragon and his ecstatic discovery of Brunnhilde within her divine circle of fire: having accidentally touched and tasted the dragon's blood, Siegfried acquires the capacity to hear his foes' murderous thoughts (so that he can kill Mime before Mime poisons him), but also the ability to understand the language of the forest birds, one of whom tells him where to find his bride-to-be. So the transition Dionysus effects in Siegfried is one from annihilating that which seeks his death to pursuing that which promises new life, an as-yet-unattained state of self-exaltation; one might even say that it shows these two modes or moments to be internally related, so that genuinely Dionysian destruction is always in the name of the promise, and the fulfilment of a genuinely Dionysian promise is always destructive. We will return to this.

But if Dionysus is the bird, Siegfried is the one who attends to him. So by placing himself within this Wagnerian scene as one who is attentive to that bird, Nietzsche not only identifies himself with (and so as) one of those contemporary German searchers, and thereby with the country whose displaced Greek spirit Wagner promises to relocate; he also more specifically presents himself as if possessed by the lyric dramatic spirit of Siegfried. In other words, Nietzsche here exploits or submits to the inherent fluidity of mythological identity in such a way as to claim a miraculous capacity to understand his enemies far better than they understand him, a capacity that not only correlates with but may even be grounded in an equally miraculous apprehension of nature (and of nature's modes of apprehension), one that will make possible a remarriage between the human and the divine that is also a remarriage of philosophy and art, a union that presages the end of one cosmic order and the beginning of another. One might well wonder whether anyone willing to confess to such vaultingly melodramatic ambitions must also be tainted with Siegfried's utterly untroubled sense of his own heroic status, his capacity for absolute self-satisfaction; one might also wonder how far Nietzsche was aware that this self-identification might further express an intuition of the incestuousness (as well as the impending failure) of his intellectual union with Wagner, not to mention his later perception of himself as fated (like Siegfried in Gibichung Hall) to be stabbed in the back by those he considered his friends. Such are the risks of proposing the operatic as a mode of apprehending reality.

3) Theoretical Man: Socrates as a Mask of Apollo

Even if one accepts *The Birth of Tragedy*'s analysis of Attic tragedy and Wagnerian opera as having such metonymic significance, however, there is one specific difference between the vision analysed and the analytical vision. Whereas the tragic chorus discharges a spectacle of Dionysus alone, Nietzsche's dramatic, tragic myth of Western culture envisions a dual godhead, a conflictual partnership between Apollo and Dionysus as the primal ground of all things. This suggests that Nietzsche is as much a servant of Apollo as he is of Dionysus, or at least a worshipper of their union or pairing. After all, his more purely textual counterpoint to Aeschylean rebirth in Wagner cannot call upon music in any literal sense; it must draw more extensively and systematically upon the Apolline dimension of these creative drives. And Nietzsche's struggle to understand the enigmatic sublimity of Attic tragedy and Wagnerian opera is informed throughout by his inheritance of Schopenhauer and Kant, and so by an indebtedness (however troubled) to the tradition of philosophy. Phrased in mythic terms, this poses the question: how does the presence of both Apollo and Socrates inflect or transfigure the exemplary significance of Dionysus in the Nietzschean metaphysical vision of Western culture?

So formulated, this query makes a questionable assumption—that Apollo and Socrates are two essentially distinct figures in Nietzsche's dramatic mythology. This assumption might seem to be confirmed by Nietzsche's way of introducing Socrates to his narrative of Attic tragedy's suicidal embodiment in the work of Euripides: 'In a certain sense Euripides, too, was merely a mask; the deity who spoke out of him was not Dionysus, nor Apollo, but an altogether newborn daemon called *Socrates*' (BT, 60). But this remark will be misunderstood unless we take seriously the work of the words 'daemon' and 'mask' within it.

Talk of Socrates as a daemon is doubly metaleptic: it exploits Socrates' characterization of himself as possessed of an attendant or indwelling spirit in order to characterize the link between Euripides and Socrates, and it invokes a flavour of malignity now attending post-Christian uses of the term. But a 'daemon' is, in this context, not straightforwardly identifiable with a divinity: in Greek mythology, a daemon was a being whose nature lay somewhere between that of gods and men, hence at best a divinity of an inferior kind. The term certainly doesn't make Socrates sound like a third amongst equals in Nietzsche's theology.

Might we then consider him instead as a mask of Apollo (and so consider Euripides in the same terms)? A masking relation allows for both continuity and discontinuity: what lies beneath the mask is both distinguishable from the mask itself and yet its underlying truth. The suggestion is not that Socrates has no independent mythic significance at all; it is that this significance is ultimately to be understood as an inflection of that of Apollo— more specifically, an inflection of Apollo that aspires to repress or deny rather than to honour or even to accommodate Dionysus (in the manner that Nietzsche envisages Apollo making room for this foreign, barbarous deity upon his initial arrival on Attic shores, before their brief and passionate union in Attic tragedy). Socrates represents the aspect of Apollo which regrets that accommodation, which cannot comprehend why he entered into the marriage that resulted from it, and which desperately desires a divorce.

Nietzsche himself encapsulates Socrates' mythic significance as follows: he is the archetype of theoretical man. Theoretical man is optimistic, both morally and more generally. Morally, he believes that 'virtue is knowledge; sin is only committed out of ignorance; and the virtuous man is a happy man'; in other words, being moral is simply a matter of implementing practical reason. In the theoretical domain, optimism is equally central: here, the key Socratic belief is that reason can not only grasp the uttermost depths of being but correct it (improve it, engender progress). Hence the mythical resonance of the dying Socrates, rendered immune to the fear of death by reason and knowledge; it declares that a fully comprehended individual life is the only justifiable one, but that it is humanly available.

The moral and metaphysical content of this archetype utterly contradicts that of Oedipus or Antigone, those embodiments of the reality of moral luck and of the ultimate incomprehensibility of being. But from the Socratic perspective, nothing else should be expected from a medium and a genre that conflates illusion and reality, that addresses the chaotic and opaque energies of the emotions rather than the mind, and that gives itself over to inspiration rather than comprehensible bodies of creative principle. Theoretical man thus distinguishes art sharply from knowledge, as well as distinguishing within the realm of knowledge between science and metaphysics, which (as the name suggests) incorporates and goes beyond scientific knowledge, involving what one might call knowledge of knowledge. And as the various aspects of human engagement with reality are distinguished from one another, so a hierarchy of their value is simultaneously established, with art at the bottom and philosophy at the top.

From the perspective of the modern philosophical tradition (call it that of Kantian Enlightenment), Socratic theoretical optimism thus appears as a commitment to a multifaceted principle of autonomy. Its moral ideal for the individual is mirrored at the level of culture by a conception of its various dimensions as logically distinct and self-sufficient intellectual enterprises; at both levels, individual flourishing and fulfilment resides in a proper recognition of their autonomy in relation to their equally autonomous others.

Even this brief account suggests that the key connection between Socrates and Apollo lies in the former's hyperbolic incarnation of the latter's governing *principium individuationis*. The media of sculpture and dreams are Apolline because they are populated with sharply delineated human and divine figures, hence a kind of celebration of the individual; but the world of dream-experience, so often hard to distinguish from that of real experience, more generally exhibits 'the logical causality of line and outline, colour and grouping' (BT, 19). For if subjective experience (whether real or illusory) is to convey or represent a world, two things are required. It must present a multiplicity of discriminable entities, entities that can only be grouped or linked to one another in causal (or any other) relations if they can be recognized as distinct, individual entities; and what is thereby represented must be distinguishable from the representation of it—that is, the individual subject of the experience must be distinguishable from its objects (and of course from other subjects of experience). Genuinely cognitive representation must balance the competing demands of identity and relation, multiplicity and oneness: objects can only make a world (as opposed to a chaos or plenum) if they stand in relations with one another, and individuals can only recognize themselves as such in relation to a world of independently-existing objects with which to contrast the course of their subjective experience.

I have phrased these claims about individuation in Kantian terms precisely because Nietzsche himself is necessarily interpreting the genealogical development of theoretical man in the terms bequeathed to him from Kant via Schopenhauer. But of course, Nietzsche also reads Kant as the first philosopher to disclose the delusion at the heart of the Socratic inflection of this Apolline principle.

Whereas this optimism once believed in our ability to grasp and solve . . . all the puzzles of the universe, and treated space, time and causality as entirely unconditional laws of the most general validity, Kant showed that these things actually only served to raise mere appearance, the work of maya, to the status of the sole and supreme reality and to put this in the place of the innermost and true essence of things, thereby making it impossible really to understand this essence—to put the dreamer even more deeply to sleep. (BT, 87)

On this reading, the Socratic project is given a tragic inflection by a philosopher whose aim was to further or complete it. The critique of pure reason employs the very tools of the understanding that Socrates held to be capable of grasping the whole of reality; but when applied to the understanding itself (as they must be, given that human understanding is part of reality), they reveal it to be essentially limited, conditioned, and unsatisfiable. For Kant's Transcendental Analytic grounds the very possibility of knowledge about reality by showing that the mind's basic categories necessarily apply to the world of our experience; but it does so only on the assumption that we first receive something for those categories to synthesize—a body of intuition from whose marriage with the mind's activity a world will emerge, but whose brute givenness points to a reality that lies *ex hypothesis* beyond our categorial grasp: call it the realm of things-in-themselves. At these limits, therefore (one might think of them as the threshold of modernity), Socratic logic finally curls up around itself and bites its own tail. Kant stands for an embryonic form of tragic knowledge about knowledge—a mournful vision of the necessary disappointment to which all theoretical optimism is fated.

His work thus reveals the groundlessness of the Socratic privileging of metaphysics. To be sure that such knowledge is to be valued above all other modes of human engagement with reality, we must be sure that it is (however partial or incomplete in fact) completeable in principle—that is, capable of grasping the whole of reality. But our best attempt to achieve that certainty—to show that reality and our cognitive powers really are as if made for one another—in fact forces us to acknowledge the enigmatic existence of an aspect of reality that necessarily transcends those powers. But if we cannot coherently think of theoretical knowledge as total, then we cannot justifiably devalue artistic modes of engagement with reality by comparison with it. In this way, the Socratic project finds itself acknowledging in its own metaphysical terms the very thing that it originally criticized Attic tragedy for endorsing (and would certainly criticize Wagnerian opera for recovering) in its distinctive terms—the Dionysian idea that no account of reality is complete which does not acknowledge both its underlying affinity with, and its inherent transcendence of, the human capacity to make sense of it.

To subvert the Socratic inflection of metaphysics is thus not to condemn the metaphysical enterprise as such: on the contrary, the Kantian transfiguration or unmasking of Socratic metaphysics makes possible a mode of metaphysical thinking that is no less insightful or valuable than other forms of human engagement with reality, because it too acknowledges the essential complementarity of Apollo and Dionysus. But in thereby locating Kant's achievement as one episode in a genealogical story that pivots upon dramatic and operatic stagings of the intimate strife between Apollo and Dionysus, Nietzsche does mean to put in question the Socratic perception of an absolute distinction between metaphysics and every other mode of human culture, and in particular between metaphysics and art. The point is not to counter-claim (in the same absolutizing spirit) that there is absolutely no difference between these ways of engaging with reality. The point is rather to affirm their internal relatedness—not only by confirming Nietzsche's perception of a metaphysical dimension in Attic tragedy and Wagnerian opera, but also by inviting us to perceive the dramatic and mythological dimensions of Kantian metaphysics.

Seen through the lens of Attic tragedy, Kant's fundamental duality of concept and intuition, theoretical form and sensory content, appears as an epistemological restaging of the underlying structure of a tragic drama. The dark Dionysian womb of givenness engenders a sublime marriage of concept and intuition that discloses the world and the knowing subject as if made for one another, thereby presenting itself as if given for just such a purpose, as if fated to discharge itself in the Apolline synthetic activity it suffers; and that synthetic activity's attempts to grasp its own nature inexorably engender an intuition of a realm necessarily beyond its own grasp, an undifferentiatable, Dionysian reality from which it first emerged and towards which it endlessly, impossibly aspires. And it is to this tantalizing intuition of a unity underlying Kant's apparently binary critical system that post-Kantian philosophers from Fichte through Hegel to Schopenhauer are each, in their differing ways, responsive.

What Nietzsche also detects in the apparently abstract content of Kant's texts is the transposition into a cognitive key of the utterly primordial mythic theme of individuation as a fate or condition to which we are condemned, and which we are condemned to deny. For Kant's vision of us as finite knowers stages a crucifixion scene—portraying us as crucified by the burden of understanding (our conditioned capacity for cognizing reality necessarily sundering us from the world and our fellow-knowers of it) and as in turn crucifying that understanding (for according to the Transcendental Dialectic, human reason has an ineradicable tendency to construct ideas of total or unconditioned knowledge, and to present them to the understanding as attainable ideals rather than purely regulative incitements to endless incremental improvements in knowledge). And if this fantasy of overcoming our limits is no less a part of our rational nature than the limits themselves, then the process of succumbing to, overcoming, and then succumbing once again to that impulse to transcend our finitude promises to be unending.

As if to confirm this, Kant's own depiction of this primordial oscillation between the acceptance and rejection of finitude itself exemplifies it. On the one hand, his account of knowledge as finite or conditioned presents itself as giving us an assurance that we can have genuine knowledge of the way things are, and indeed of anything and everything knowable. On the other hand, in doing so, he projects a distinction between things as they appear to us and things in themselves, assigning the latter to a domain beyond our grasp; and he also projects an origin for the content of our concepts that precedes any of the distinctions imposed by the synthetic activity of the mind. In other words, Kant finds himself invoking a conception of reality as essentially beyond our grasp, to which the discriminations which supposedly make knowledge possible do not apply; and in so doing, he violates the very limits of knowledge that these invocations are intended to support—thereby succumbing to the very same tendency to deny our finitude that he wants to correct.

Can Nietzsche, unlike Kant, find a way of acknowledging the reality of that transgressive impulse and its intuition of beyondness, but without succumbing to it? Or must we see his deployment of the mythical duality of Apollo and Dionysus as just such a transgression, insofar as the figure of Dionysus appears to represent what—on Nietzsche's own Kantian and Schopenhauerian understanding—must be essentially beyond our representational grasp? If we are to understand Nietzsche's metaphysical vision at all, we cannot make do with Apollo alone (that way Socratic imbalance lies)— the reality and significance of Dionysus must be conveyed, and so must be represented, somehow; but any representation of him seems fated—simply by virtue of being a representation of the unrepresentable—to betray the insight it purports to convey.

There is, however, a difference between unwittingly betraying one's own insight, and a dramatic staging of that inevitable betrayal (one whose very theatricality is intended to invite acknowledgement of its nature). By recasting Schopenhauer's metaphysical vision of the world as will and representation (itself a recasting of Kant's vision of knowledge as a cursed marriage of concepts and intuitions) as a mythic drama of Apollo and Dionysus, Nietzsche underlines the non-literal status of his own discourse, and thereby problematizes the relation between such hyberbolically fictional figures and the reality they purportedly represent. He then reinforces the point by multiplying the ways in which Dionysus appears in his genealogical narrative—as if disarticulating or dismembering him: the god has so many different manifestations in *The Birth of Tragedy* that no particular one (whether religious, artistic, or metaphysical) can be taken as truly representing him. Rather, each is presented as one of his masks, and thus invites the inference that even this re-membering or re-presentation (construed as an attempt to identify what lies behind them all) can only amount to the construction of one more mask—one more inevitable failure to grasp the god himself. The book is, one might say, a mask composed of masks, or perhaps a masque of masks, the nature of whose constituent elements declares its own necessary distance from its object.

Dionysus is thus not one element in a Nietzschean master-narrative of Western culture presenting the work of Aeschylus, Wagner, Kant, and endless others as mere symptoms or instances of an underlying duality that has at last been captured in *The Birth of Tragedy*. Dionysus is primarily present in the elusive, dissonant rhythm or pulse—at once synchronic and diachronic—orchestrated by Nietzsche's animated collage or frieze of various attempts to represent him (and to deny him), a sequence which culminates in its creator's invocation of the Dionysiac as 'dissonance assuming human form' (BT, 115). Each representation is thereby disclosed as at once similar to and yet different from every other, both individual and typical, with strengths and limitations all of its own; hence each makes an indispensable contribution to the overall display, but neither any individual element nor some conjunction of them—not even their re-incorporation into the larger representation that is *The Birth of Tragedy*—can constitute a complete or total image of Dionysus. It is rather in the book's ragged edges and internal seams, its overt refusal to cohere as a single, totalizing representation and its openness to further insertions or extensions (a Frankenstein's monster of ecstatic scholarship), that its real attempt to present the god of the unrepresentable is to be found.

One might regard this as an attempt to acknowledge the centrality of the principle of individuation in any human attempt to grasp the essence of reality (given the inevitably structured, differentiating, and individuating nature of representation), whilst denying its absoluteness or self-sufficiency. The duality of Nietzsche's godhead is thus not so much the introduction of another deity into Apollo's temple, but rather an attempt to worship Apollo non-idolatrously—to acknowledge that we can only grasp reality in terms of some particular way of organizing it, but that any such way could never fuse with the reality it represents, and will inevitably be limited or conditioned by its organizing principles. So we cannot avoid committing ourselves to some such representation (or mode of representation); but we can allow that commitment to be informed by the awareness that—being possessed of limits—it will be open to supplementation, contestation, and displacement by other representations, each of which will itself be vulnerable to the same process of overcoming. And Dionysus does not lie behind any or all of these visions, but is rather dispersed between them—manifest in the recurring impulse to re-member him that generates such endlessly shifting family resemblances.

The Birth of Tragedy certainly questions the absoluteness of any principles of individuation at the disciplinary or cultural level, whilst acknowledging their necessity in some form or other. For its multiply metonymic structure problematizes prevailing conceptions of the distinctions between different art forms, between art and philosophy, and between art, politics, religion, science, and philosophy. A form of philosophical writing that thinks of itself as internally related to both Attic tragedy and Wagnerian opera, and of both these art forms as themselves internally related (as masks, displacements, or transfigurations of one another), does not deny the differences between art and philosophy. It rather questions the prevailing ways of characterizing and evaluating those differences, and suggests rather different terms in which to conceive them. It thereby invites the culture as a whole to rethink the way in which it has conceived of metaphysics, art, politics, and religion as essentially autonomous enterprises, but again without denying their differences or suggesting that they should be regarded as an undifferentiated whole.

So Nietzsche doesn't dismiss his inheritance of metaphysical aspirations or responsibilities; he rather suggests that they be shouldered in rather different ways, even by philosophers, and in particular that the metaphysical project can only benefit from exploiting the fullest possible range of representational modes, whilst acknowledging the fatedness of any representational project, even a philosophical *Gesamtkunstwerk*, to partiality (call it particularity of perspective). This is why he presents his own metaphysical vision as the present culmination of the long genealogical narrative that is its dramatic content, a narrative in which prior visions endlessly engender variously-inflected displacements or transfigurations of themselves, only to be transfigured in their turn.

The Birth of Tragedy is thus both a narrative of, and one more narrative in, an unending sequence of self-overcoming narratives, each revising the limits of its predecessors before being in turn revised, but all thereby amounting to versions of the same vision of human reality as a matter of endlessly constructing, transgressing, and reconstructing the limits of our present representations of reality. Nietzsche thereby declares the natality of his own vision (its otherness to absolute originality or self-origination), and foretells its future overcoming; and by thus indicating the conditions and limitations of his own work, as if underlining the inevitable failure of its inevitably Apolline endeavour, he hopes to conjure the absent presence of Dionysus.

This suggests an interpretation of the genealogical sequence of texts that makes up Nietzsche's own body of writing, from this text on. We might see each as a new mask of its author—one formed by critically evaluating its predecessor (call it a process of unmasking), which necessarily results in a new mask or re-masking, one which exceeds or transgresses the form or structure of its predecessor without ever distinguishing itself absolutely from it. In this sense, the Nietzsche texts that follow *The Birth of Tragedy* might be thought of as a sequence of displacements or transfigurations of its tragic, dramatic myth of Western culture; so that, for example, one might wish to explore the dialectic of slave and master in the *Genealogy of Morality* as a mask of the original duality of Apollo and Dionysus—each a metonym of the individual text that activates it and of the process of transition from each such text to the next in the unfolding sequence of Nietzsche's writing life (their mode of textual becoming).

Such an interpretation further suggests that the conflictual complementarity of Apollo and Dionysus might be thought of as Nietzsche's first attempt to represent the dynamics of self-identity as a process of endless self-overcoming. From this perspective (call it perfectionist), Apollo stands for the self's need for individuation, for a stable outline or provisional structure of values and affects, and Dionysus stands for the self's impulse endlessly to overcome any such structure, even if necessarily in the name of another, as-yet only prophetically-grasped, restructuring of itself. And if this is a point of view on *The Birth of Tragedy* that only becomes available much later in the unfolding unmaskings and re-maskings of the text by its author, and so amounts to a critical reconstruction or re-membering of it, then that is exactly what, from the point of view at issue, one would expect.

The Metaphysics of (Secret) Agency

Or: Three Ways of Not Being James Bond

1. Quiller

Quiller is not his real name—any more than Adam Hall is the real name of the author of the dramatized reports of this shadow executive's Intelligence missions on behalf of a London organization known as the Bureau, which reports directly to the prime minister and can function as it does only if its very existence is deniable ('Adam Hall' is a pseudonym of Elleston Trevor, the author of—amongst other popular novels—*The Flight of the Phoenix*). As the brief text entitled 'Identity' that prefaces the fourth of these reports (*The Warsaw Document*[1]) makes clear:

['Quiller'] is necessarily a code-name . . . During a mission, the code-name is never used, since a mission demands a cover and hence a cover-name, which is used even in signals between the executive and his Control. This name itself must sometimes be changed if the cover is blown and he is thus exposed to great and immediate hazard: a new cover must be arranged and with it a new name. The identities, therefore, of the Bureau's active staff are confined strictly to its secret files, for the purposes of administration. (WD, 6)

At no point in the nineteen novels that make up this series do we learn Quiller's real name; but it doesn't follow that his reports don't illuminate the identity of its bearer. On the contrary, by the end of the series (which concluded only upon the death of its author in 1995, exactly thirty years after the first instalment was published) we are in a very good position to

---

[1] London: Fontana, 1971—hereafter WD.

address the question 'Who is Quiller?' For we can now begin to appreciate the constitutive rather than contingent difficulties involved in trying to answer that question—difficulties engendered precisely by Quiller's fitness for his job.

What puts us in this position is, above all, the fact that these reports are dramatized in the first person: Quiller is always the narrator of his own vicissitudes, and no other perspective on his missions is made accessible to us. The claustrophobia this induces in the reader of these tales mirrors that of their teller: for Quiller's mode of existence as a shadow executive is intensely isolated and oppositional. In part, this is because he prefers to operate on his own; and whenever he cannot avoid the help of others, he aims to minimize its significance and hence the room for independent action that his collaborators can retain. In part, it is because his task necessarily places him at loggerheads with his host country's security, military, and police apparatuses, so that most of those he meets in the course of a mission are (at least potentially) hostile, or at best likely to get in his way. But it is also because his place in the functional hierarchy of the Bureau renders his relationship with many of those who are nominally his allies potentially treacherous.

This relationship is in fact contractually grounded. Quiller's executive function carries specific rights and responsibilities, which serve to determine his relations with those who perform different functions for the Bureau—in particular with his local director (who organizes the support he needs to operate in the field, and has a grasp of the broader significance of the mission that is not required for—and may even militate against—its successful completion by the executive), and with his control (the officer based in London who is primarily responsible for setting up the mission in the first place, and for choosing its director and executive). This hierarchy places the executive in a position which is both powerful and powerless—the familiar situation of those on the shop-floor vis-à-vis management, or (more accurately) the poor bloody infantryman vis-à-vis the General Staff. He alone can actually bring the mission to a successful conclusion; so the effectiveness of the Bureau as a whole ultimately rests on his practical know-how, and so on the skills and understanding of his trade that can only be acquired through direct experience of its potentially lethal strategies and tactics of infiltration, deception, confrontation, and combat—experience that his directors and controls lack. At the same time, however, the parameters of his activity, and of his understanding of its significance, are primarily determined by these non-executive functionaries; and this allows them not only to conceal its broader implications from their executive, but also to deceive him (positively to mislead him about what he is doing and why). Such strategies of deception are sometimes simply a way of ensuring that he performs his allotted task more efficiently, without unnecessary distractions; but they take on a very different significance in light of the fact that the executive's contract explicitly acknowledges that the Bureau can legitimately sacrifice the executive's well-being and even his life if the particular mission demands it, as well as requiring that the executive be prepared at all times to protect the Bureau's secrecy to the point of death. Partly as a consequence, the executive has the right to turn down any mission offered to him; but this merely makes it more likely that he will be manipulated into accepting a mission in the first place by his superiors, who may correctly judge both that he is the only executive capable of performing the requisite task, and that he would not do it if its true nature were explicitly defined at the outset.

Quiller's perspective on the Bureau is thus deeply conflicted: his employers make it both possible, and immensely more difficult, for him to ply his trade, so he thinks of them as both his fellow-professionals (as dedicated as he is to succeeding in the missions they take on) and as his worst enemy (willing to treat him as a manipulable and ultimately dispensable means to that end). But because that willingness is also an aspect of their professionalism, being solely an expression of their ruthless devotion to the collective task at hand, Quiller himself cannot dismiss it either as incompetence or as ignorance; it is in fact a manifestation of what he values most. So his entirely understandable hatred of the Bureau is also a kind of self-hatred; for it expresses a bewildered fury about his own willingness to dedicate himself to a profession in which such a self-sacrificial stance is not so much a supererogatory ideal as a contractual requirement.

What Quiller most fervently loves and hates about the Bureau is that it permits him to indulge his deepest desire—that of existing on the brink of death, committing himself to a form of life that gains its meaning for him precisely insofar as it ensures that every moment might be his last. The impulse here is not suicidal (although one aspect of his professionalism concerns his willingness to contemplate ending his own life in circumstances where that is the only alternative to betraying the Bureau): on the contrary, Quiller is prepared to throw all of his considerable intellectual and practical resources into avoiding the fate that his profession persistently conjures up for him, so his survival instinct is not only not absent—it is more finely honed and fully expressed than it could otherwise be. His situation is thus constituted as the locus of a conflict between a love of life and a love of death, between Eros and Thanatos—the Freudian opposition between the life instinct and the death instinct that Adam Hall explicitly draws upon from the outset of the series.

For this basic conflict shapes the plot of the novel in which Quiller makes his first appearance, *The Berlin Memorandum*.[2] At this early stage, the Bureau's structure and functioning have not yet taken on their mature form; but the deep structures of Quiller's perspective are already in place. His mission is to expose the plans and the location of a resurgent neo-Nazi group in West Germany (going under the name 'Phoenix'); and the key to his efforts is a relationship he establishes with Inga Lindt, a woman whose childhood had been spent in the *Fuehrerbunker*, who had subsequently been involved in Phoenix, and who is now wavering in her loyalty to it. It quickly becomes clear that Lindt's traumatic upbringing has bequeathed her an obsessive love-hate relationship with Hitler, and by extension with Phoenix and with fascism more generally; as Quiller puts it, she is 'half in love ... with the image of a dead god' (BM, 39), with a human being who was strong enough not only to dispense death on a global scale, but also to overcome it in himself (insofar as Phoenix represents his reincarnation, and indeed preserves fragments of his bones as relics), and hence has come for her to embody death in all its dark power.

Quiller is drawn into a sexual relationship with her not despite these facts about her, but because of them—because he cannot deny his own implication in her quasi-religious, sadomasochistic necrophilia: 'to each his aphrodisiac, and she knew mine. She made no secret of hers' (BM, 107). And the novel supplies him with an analogously traumatic developmental cause for this obsession. For it tells us that Quiller spent several years during the Second World War operating (without any institutional support) under cover as a concentration camp guard, as a result of which he saved the lives of dozens of Jews, but only at the cost of living in close proximity to the countless victims he could not rescue, in the guise of one of the agents of

---

[2] Later re-titled *The Quiller Memorandum* (London: Fontana, 1965)—hereafter BM.

their persecution. His efforts to subvert the extermination programme were as much dwarfed by its scale and reach as his more recent efforts (just prior to the Phoenix mission) to uncover Nazi war criminals in 1960s West Germany are dwarfed by the pervasiveness of their hidden presence throughout the supposedly purified structures of that society. And he cannot deny that a version of this moral darkness at the heart of German, hence Western, culture is also to be found, in all its seductive opacity, in his own soul.

To be sure, in Quiller's case, love of life is inseparable from this obsession with death. After all, the proximate cause of his having sex with Inge Lindt is his having recently escaped from implemented interrogation by the Phoenix group; more precisely, they deliberately led him to expect execution, and then released him (unconscious but unharmed) in the expectation that, after this incomprehensible but undeniable return to life, his libido— not so much his sexual desires but the renewed life-force that finds one expression through such desires—would drive him straight to Lindt, and thereby make it easier for Phoenix to acquire the information he has hitherto refused to disclose to them about the Bureau's knowledge of and plans for that group. Inge Lindt is thus the object upon which Quiller's own interwoven erotic and thanatotic drives converge: like the Bureau, which Quiller explicitly thinks of as 'the sacred bull', she incarnates his own worship of life-in-death and death-in-life.

This internal tension in Quiller's perspective underlies and marks every other opposition that structures his responsiveness to the world—and there are many such oppositions; or perhaps one should rather say that a single, underlying internal conflict finds a number of overlapping means of more immediate expression over the course of his career. For part of what we learn by approaching these dramatized reports from the executive's point of view is that what would appear from the outside to be an effortless mastery of the environment—an exhilarating capacity to get the job done in the face of the most daunting of obstacles, both human and material—is experienced from within as the result of an unremitting struggle between different aspects of the executive's identity. Quiller persistently presents himself as struggling (as he variously puts it) to follow brain-think rather than stomach-think, to overcome the organism's interior squeals in favour of the will's endorsement of certain intellectual goals, to manage the relation between the conscious and the subconscious mind, or to endorse the ego's wishes over those of the id or the libido. Although no one of these contrasts is precisely synonymous either with any other or with the underlying Eros–Thanatos opposition with which we began, there is an approximate alignment of human animality with the drive for life, and human intellectuality—and all its tools for dispassionate comprehension and mastery of its world, including its own body—with a drive not only to risk but to court death.

But these alignments are persistently complicated by two main factors. First, the mind's primary aim is to succeed in the mission, and in almost every case that requires that its possessor stay alive; so the organism's drive to survive is something that can help the will as well as working against it. This is why Quiller can often be found handing over control of his actions to instinct rather than reflection, as in *The Pekin Target*:[3] '[T]he conscious doesn't stand a chance against the powers of the subconscious when the living creature reaches the edge of life and makes its decisions according to the laws of survival; all the conscious mind has to do is feed the data in and keep clear and shut up' (PT, 119). And sometimes, it is only the organism that is capable of bringing back the mind from oblivion—as in the following sequence, about the immediate aftermath of a car-chase in which Quiller's vehicle has been forced into a river:

> Peace.
> Peace, and the sense of another place.
> My body weightless and at ease. So this is what it is like, and it will go on forever. *Night and silence, who is here?*
> My eyes open, watching the dark; my ears lulled by the soundless water; one hand drifting and touching but feeling nothing that has definition. So death, after all, is nothing spectacular; it is isolation, and the slow running on of the mind.
> But there was something here.
> Ignore it; there's nothing here.
> The weight of my body shifting in a slow dance, touching and coming away. Night, and easeful silence.
> Pressure of some kind, a sudden huge rising of the dark under my face, *and then no breathing*.

---

[3] London: Collins, 1981—hereafter PT.

Ignore it; the dead don't breathe.
Listen, you've got to—
Be quiet; I'm resting. Go away.
My ears covered and uncovered by the slow rising and falling of the water; my
eyes filled with dark and nothing to—
Water, yes. Do you want to drown, you bloody fool?
Leave me alone and shut up. I'm not interested in panic.
For Christ's sake you've got to—
Leave me alone and—
Got to wake up, wake up, wake up.
The huge rising of the dark again *and no breathing.*
Pressure in the lungs. Water, did you say?
Don't you know what drowning is? Don't you—
Shuddup.
But the night rose and slammed against my face and blocked off the breathing
and I moved suddenly, throwing out one arm and feeling the soft resistance of
the water.
Push yourself up. Push up.
Air, yes, and breathing.
A long time choking. This isn't death. This is dying. (PT, 121–2)

The second complication is Quiller's willingness to acknowledge a realm of
the mystical along with that of the organism and its psyche. Because of his
refusal to carry a gun, he is often involved in lethal unarmed combat; and he
is prone to experience the proximity of death—whether his own or that of
his opponent—with a kind of religious awe that at once displaces and recalls
that earlier necrophilia. In *The Pekin Target*, for example, he is operating in
south-east Asia, with whose culture he is already familiar because of his
martial arts training, and he finds himself only just able to overcome a young
opponent whose training equals his own:

There was a transition period when my body had moved for itself, and memory started
recording again only when I was flinging myself along the alley with my hands
outstretched to fend off obstacles and my feet driving me forward with the sensation
that the energy was coming from somewhere else, streaming into the organism and
leaving it galvanized and frantic for life. Footsteps filled the alley but the walls echoed
and re-echoed them in the narrow confines and they might only have been my own.
The first of them had stopped, perhaps, to check the dead body on the ground, giving

me time to get clear, as if the boy had reached out from whatever cosmic field of consciousness sustained him now, and chosen to offer me grace. (PK, 60)

The moment is carefully framed by the echoing footsteps, thus ensuring that Quiller's uncertainty about whether their apparently external source is really only a projection of his own activity is itself projected by the reader onto the perception of grace that follows; but even so its vision of the boundaries between self and enemy, and self and universe, as porous and provisional forges a link between the most primitive levels of human aggression and the most elevated of spiritual perceptions in such a way as to keep these reports open to a cosmic or mythical dimension of significance. And by recounting his own experience in a voice sufficiently flexible, polyphonous, and detached to give equal and unceasing expression to each aspect of his personality (body, psyche, and spirit) as it struggles for mastery, Quiller thereby presents himself as all, and so none, of them—so that he exists, in terms of the reader's experience, as author and audience of this interior drama of unending conflict, hence as identifiable at once with it and with what conditions and transcends it.

The elusiveness of Quiller's identity as it finds expression in his voice is reinforced by the distinctive range of narrative techniques he employs in order to give the action sequences of these novels their unique powers and pleasures (satisfactions which are entirely absent from the 1966 film of the first novel, scripted by Harold Pinter and starring Alec Guinness and George Segal, which utterly fails to find a cinematic equivalent for those techniques[4]). One involves oscillations between pure inhabitation of action and detached ratiocination: the former is represented by the deployment of long sentences constructed out of clauses conjoined only by 'and' and lacking any other kind of punctuation or logical structure, and the latter by complex analyses of the various aspects of the situation that brought about the actions so breathlessly recorded. A particularly clear example of this occurs in *The Ninth Directive*,[5] in which one chapter ends as follows: 'But they'd gone and I unlocked the door and went out and caught sight of sudden movement at the edge of the vision-field and plunged into a run that pitched me down a dozen yards from the door as the blast came and the fragments tore at my clothes and my ears were blocked by the explosion' (ND, 150). The next chapter then begins with a

---

[4] Michael Anderson (dir.), *The Quiller Memorandum*.
[5] London: Fontana, 1966—hereafter ND.

two-and-a-half page explanation of the rational processes underlying the course of action just described: it involves a breakdown of reaction-time phases, relative response speeds to different sensory stimuli, the mechanisms of visual perception, and the theoretical bases of explosive-avoidance training, including the advantages of orienting one's prone body away from the blast-site in order to use the soles of the shoes for protection. The reader thus begins with an experience of the narrator as pure actor, nothing more than a sequence of deeds; then he experiences him as pure cognizer, the informed intellectual source of those deeds; and then he is asked to imagine Quiller himself as fully present in both contradictory stances, as the impossible but real embodiment of their synthesis.

Quiller also employs jump-cuts in the narrative flow of the reports. First, he presents himself as caught in a potentially lethal trap of some kind; then (often between one chapter and the next) he jumps without explanation to a later scene in the narrative, hence one that can only have occurred if he succeeded in escaping from the trap; and it is only some pages later that he supplies us with the missing portion of narrative, in the form of a flashback. By deferring the narrative element that we're most eager to read, such A-C-B violations of chronology are a very effective means of increasing our desire to read on, as well as enhancing our admiration for the unguessable ingenuity with which Quiller has once again deployed his professional skills; but they also tell us something about Quiller himself. Precisely because his primary goal as a shadow executive is to complete his mission, the traps from which he must escape are essentially irritating obstacles to his doing so, and the fact that he got into them in the first place might even be taken as a worrying sign of less than total competence on his part. So the aspects of his narrative that most engage the reader's interest—call them the B-element—are the ones that are of least interest to him: they are digressions from the main narrative route, and would of course show up as such in the reports to London on which the narrative is supposedly based; so the more quickly they can be passed over the better from his point of view. The jump-cut editing thus in fact brings out an essential difference in the perspectives of narrator and reader: the shadow executive whose consciousness we are inhabiting is partly constituted as the person he is by an arrangement of interests and sources of pleasure that is fundamentally alien to our own.

Another narrative technique also involves depriving the reader of critical knowledge—but this time, knowledge that is governing the narrator's current actions. *The Warsaw Document* contains two outstanding examples of this technique. First, Quiller's mission involves regular contact with an Embassy employee named Merrick, who has been turned by the local security services: this fact about him is only revealed to us in the final chapters of the novel, but it is also then revealed that Quiller has known this for some time, and has been adjusting his activities accordingly. Merrick betrayed himself some seventy pages earlier, and Quiller there records both the way in which Merrick did so and his own sense of sudden shock, but without telling us what shocked him. He tells his tale as if we are as able as he is to identify these fateful implications, and thereby ensures that we experience the same shock, only much later and much more strongly; in other words, he treats us as if the convention that we inhabit our first-person narrator's perspective on the world is true, but in doing so, he exploits the underlying reality of our distance from him in such a way as to enhance our generic pleasures as readers.

The second example is smaller in scale: it occurs when Quiller has to hide in a cleaner's cupboard in a railway station washroom, to evade a manhunt. Two militia enter the room and try the cupboard door-handle (which Quiller has locked from the inside), and one of them decides to find a workman to open it up while the other remains on guard. Quiller immediately begins to manoeuvre a broom propped next to him in the cupboard, raising it as quickly as is consistent with maintaining complete silence until—when the broom head is level with his face—the handle touches the cupboard ceiling; then he lowers it again. We are given an exactingly detailed description of what is involved in doing this, but no explanation whatever of why it has to be done until, just as the workman begins his noisy operation on the lock, Quiller starts moving himself upwards by bracing his back against the rear wall and his legs against the front one—and we suddenly realize that the broom was his way of establishing that there was just enough space above the door lintel for him to conceal himself there when the door is opened. Depriving us of knowledge of his plan plainly enhances the suspense, particularly given the apparent hopelessness of Quiller's position; and it amounts to a narratival realization of his knowledge that he will only succeed in his task if he breaks it down into separate stages and concentrates intensely and exclusively on bringing each to a successful conclusion, rather than being distracted or paralysed by the inevitable but unpredictably swift arrival of the workman. But it achieves both aims by exploiting an inherent property of first-person narratives—the fact that even such a narrator can conceal aspects of himself from his readers, and thereby subvert the expectation that any action we view from the inside (as it were) will be completely transparent to us. Even though we are eavesdropping on his interior stream of consciousness, Quiller eludes our grasp.

However intriguing and original they may be, when treated in isolation these techniques may appear to be solely in the service of goals dictated by the genre of the espionage novel. But these novels persistently contextualize their distinctive ways of meeting the reader's generic requirements for excitement and narrative drive in terms deriving from the point at which psychoanalytic deconstructions of personal identity verge equally upon their mythological, metaphysical, and religious counterparts. Hall's initial creation myth for Quiller is never again referred to at any point in the series (no doubt because it would undermine his protagonist's necessary but unmentionable immunity to ageing); but it returns in the final episode, *Quiller Balalaika*, in which Quiller finally meets the fate he has feared intermittently throughout the series—that of being consigned to a Russian labour-camp, and thereby to the victimhood he first encountered in its Nazi form;[6] and an internal relation between technique and this primal trauma shapes what is perhaps the most pivotal phase of the whole sequence of novels—that in which Quiller is betrayed by the Bureau.

The singularity of the mission during which this occurs is signalled by the singularity of the title given to his report on it: *Northlight: A Quiller Mission* marks the point in the series at which its episodes begin to switch from having two-word titles denoting significant objects in the relevant mission (e.g. *The Scorpion Signal*) to having two-word titles conjoining the names of the agent and the mission (e.g. *Quiller Solitaire*).[7] This book's title names the mission, with the agent's name appearing only in the subtitle, just as the Bureau decides that the success of this mission must take priority over the life of that agent. So they place a bomb in the vehicle in which Quiller is due to drive himself and a Russian double agent to a rail-yard rendezvous, at which he thinks he will be taking delivery of documentation for their escape from Russia, but about which the Bureau have informed the KGB,

---

[6] London: Headline, 1996—hereafter QB.
[7] London: W.H. Allen, 1985—hereafter N.

as part of a deal to hand over the double agent in order to ensure that the Russians attend a critical summit meeting. The Bureau thereby appears to honour that arrangement whilst ensuring that the KGB can't acquire any vital information from interrogating the double agent: if his British rescuer dies with him, the Russians will not suspect British responsibility for their failure to get their hands on him.

Quiller detects the bomb's presence just before turning the truck's ignition key:

> It was the smell of death that I had recognized when I'd climbed behind the wheel. It's not always the same: it can come from gun oil, geraniums smoke, new rope and a hundred other things that in the harmlessness of their natural context can go unnoticed. But I was starting the final run out with the objective for the mission and my senses were fine-tuned and alert for any conceivable threat to the organism. It wasn't the smell of the bomb itself that had warned me. My instinct had triggered cognizance of enormous danger and in the instant I became afraid, and what I had recognized was the smell of my own fear as it sprang from the skin. (N, 153)

In other words, it is his body's deeply-ingrained and subconscious sensitivity to danger that saves his life: his willingness to be guided by his own animal being is here a mode of his fearful responsiveness to death, as well as an implicit indication that the ultimate source of the threat is internal rather than external, more intimate even than his own skin. Still unaware of that fact, however, he defuses the bomb and proceeds to the rendezvous, expecting to meet a Bureau courier: the relevant chapter ends as a van full of armed KGB agents appears on the scene.

Even at this point, Quiller knows only that the rendezvous has been betrayed: he doesn't know how or by whom (and neither do we, limited as we are to his viewpoint). So when the next chapter begins with the familiar Hall jump-cut to a later point in the story, we hurry on to discover exactly how Quiller got from A to C this time; and in so doing, we might very easily overlook something about the preceding chapter's end—the fact that, uniquely amongst all the books in this series, it is marked not just by whatever expanse of blank paper is required by the convention of beginning a new chapter on a new page, but by a centred line of three asterisks that is placed not immediately after the last line of text but at the very bottom of the page (just above the page number). We are thereby informed, if we're as sensitive to our textual environment as Quiller is to his, that this break in narrative continuity is somehow more significant, even more final, than any other its protagonist (in his role as narrator) has previously imposed. Something about the way those asterisks mark the page's lower limit and thereby isolate the block of text in its upper half makes it appear like the engraving on a tombstone; it has the smell of death about it.

In the first instance, of course, this is the death of the mission, of 'North-light': although Quiller manages to escape from the KGB trap, partly by using the bomb he removed from his truck, the double agent whose safe extraction was the objective of the mission is killed in the ensuing crossfire. So Quiller's subsequent sense of grief is first presented to us as an effect of anticipating that the Bureau's transcripts of this operation will end—unprecedentedly for him—with the words 'Mission Unsuccessful'. He is mourning the end of his hitherto flawless record, and with it his sense of professional infallibility. But even before that becomes clear to us, the jump-cut between chapters has taken us to the following stretch of text:

I have never been so cold.

You think you have been cold? Not like this.

Not like this.

This is the cold of the dead, when the blood itself is cold.

When the heart itself is cold.

This is the chill of death.

The cold was the worst.

I thought about it, recognizing it as something that I must try to stop, then realizing that there was nothing I could do to stop it. If I tried to stop it, I would meet death of a different kind.

The cold was the worst.

No. The dark was the worst.

It was the darkness of not existing, bringing with it the knowledge that you have arrived somewhere unfamiliar, not where it is dark but where there has never been light. Death, yes, the regions of death far beyond any knowing.

The dark was the worst.

No. The noise was the worst.

It was the noise of infinite destruction, the never-ending tumult of holocaust, bringing the irreversible death of silence, the death of peace. I knew now that there would always be this thunderous noise, this all-extinguishing darkness, this killing cold.

Spark.

I was curled in the foetal position on one side, ledged between metal beams and plates. A rivet was against my head and I moved a little, for comfort.

Comfort? You must be joking.

Another spark and in the total darkness it brought light enough to throw a reflection on the rail immediately below me, on the shining rail, so that there seemed to be two sparks. My eyes seized on it, my soul drank from it: there was light, just for this little time. All had not been extinguished, then.

Don't fall asleep.

No. That would be unwise.

Keep awake. If you don't keep awake you'll fall.

Yes. I'll fall down there onto the—

Wake up. Wake up or you'll—

What? Yes—wake up, I'm waking up now, I'm—*oh my Christ*—

Grab it, grab that beam, *come on.*

Close. That was rather close. (N, 174–5)

The first half of this passage is the most extreme of Quiller's many and various confrontations with a limbo-like condition he misidentifies as death: in this version, unlike those others, nothing about it strikes him as attractive—no weightless, peaceful silence of the kind he encountered in the submerged car in *The Pekin Target*. On the contrary, he is subjected to cold, darkness, and noise so intense that he loses faith in the very idea of warmth, silence, and light—as if he is beyond the very possibility of basic animal apprehension and security, condemned (impossibly) to undergo the extinction of everything, himself included, for ever. Then the passage pivots around his registration of a single, distinguishable stimulus, one redolent of religious myths of world-creation—a spark; and he is instantly returned to an awareness of his position in an independently existing environment, lodged in the undercarriage of a moving train in a posture indicative of rebirth. That process of recreation unfolds when a second spark is struck: the light it brings creates a reflection of itself in the rail below, as if its existence, and so existence as such, is inseparable from an apparent subjection to duality or splitting that must then itself be subject to integrative reinterpretation (as parts of a single comprehensible causal process). Quiller's return to existence follows that same pattern: at first he can barely distinguish his eyes seizing on the spark from his soul's drinking from it (so that body and consciousness fuse, and sensory and spiritual receptivity are one); then his awareness splits between the neutral plaintext of rational reflection and the italicized insistence of bodily apprehension; until finally both modes of comprehension fuse in a pair of sentences in which the narrative voice learns to modulate smoothly (although not seamlessly, given the continuing italicization) between both.

Quiller's narrative voice is thus already subliminally registering the scale of the psychic trauma that he doesn't yet know he knows that the Bureau has already inflicted on him; it takes several more chapters before that instinctively apprehended betrayal reaches the more overt regions of dialogue (both external and internal), and manifestations of not-wholly-controllable rage. And it takes another novel to chart the extent of that trauma, and the means by which it is overcome (that is, the means by which Quiller overcomes his unwillingness to acknowledge his absolute dependence on the Bureau and what it allows him to achieve).

Quiller's Run is the sequel to *Northlight*: like its predecessor, it fits neither of the two titular patterns all the other novels in the series share; and although its promotion of the agent's name into the main title presages the second of those patterns, it does so in the first instance because it does not function as a dramatized report of a Bureau mission.[8] Having managed to persuade his employers to return him to the West in exchange for completing an unforeseen further phase of the 'Northlight' mission, Quiller resigns; despite an intellectual awareness of his contractual obligation to accept being sacrificed by the Bureau should the needs of the mission demand it, his experience of its practical implementation makes him realize that it would prevent him ever trusting his director and control on future missions, and so make his work impossible. Instead he accepts a privately-arranged mission for the Thai government, which is aimed at preventing an arms dealer from inciting an East–West military confrontation in Asia. It is only at the end of the novel, when the mission has reached a critical stage, that Quiller realizes that the mission was in fact Bureau-authorized and Bureau-supported all along.

At that point, his pride compels him to refuse to continue; but it is in conflict with an equally prideful reluctance to let the present mission fail, and a less explicitly acknowledged awareness that only the Bureau's range of resources and experience can give him the kind of life on the brink of death that remains a hair's-breadth away from the straightforwardly suicidal. The

---

[8] London: W.H. Allen, 1988—hereafter QR.

conflict is resolved when his real director, Loman, offers him a face-saving solution: he declares that one of the operatives with whom Quiller has been working is missing and in grave danger, thereby allowing Quiller to offer to continue the mission if the Bureau makes every effort to save her. It is only made clear to us when she rejoins the group shortly thereafter that her absence was contrived, and that Quiller knew this all along. 'It was a lie and I knew that, *and he knew I knew*, but I went through the motions of believing it, and agreed to the deal and stayed with the mission. Treble-think, and in case you've forgotten, that's the trade we're in' (QR, 256).

I've mentioned two reasons why Quiller needs an excuse to withdraw his resignation: but there is a third, which turns on the particular nature of the mission whose unfolding leads to his official return to the Bureau that he never really left. The arms dealer he aims to bring down is a woman named Mariko Shoda: she is a profoundly damaged survivor of Khmer Rouge prison camps, paranoid, pathologically ambitious, and psychopathically violent; but most importantly, as Quiller advances through the mission he comes to understand her as an avatar of death—not just someone willing and eager to inflict it, but an embodiment of annihilation or nihilism as a cosmic principle. The moment when the lethal threat she represents takes on this metaphysical or spiritual dimension is the scene in which Quiller presents himself as making the run to which the title refers—when he confronts Shoda during the Buddhist funeral of one of her employees. On the one hand, he hopes to rely for his safety on the fact that it would be impious for her to kill someone on sacred ground; on the other, the ceremony itself (described with a degree of uncannily powerful conviction that is unique in Adam Hall's work) immerses him in a way of understanding the universe and its fundamental principles which thereafter transfigures Shoda's significance for him, to the point where his later attempts to resist her plans (and in particular her increasingly hysterical series of plans to kill him) are most deeply threatened by his sense that in doing so he is attempting to resist death itself, and to resist acknowledging its inherent seductiveness.

Quiller's transitional mission against Shoda is thus the purest expression of the necrophilia that structures his identity as a shadow executive; it reminds him of the undismissable attractiveness of what the Bureau has to offer him, which is why his rejoining its ranks is so precisely synchronized with his finding the means to confront Shoda on her own psychic wavelength—by allowing her to shoot him several times to no apparent effect (because he is wearing a concealed bullet-proof vest), a final and personal failure to kill him that convinces her that he is unkillable (an avatar of her cosmic opposite, life itself), and induces her to kill herself. It is as if, in order to reconcile himself with his continued work for the Bureau whose regard for him had so humiliatingly revealed itself to have limits, he must first externalize the underlying object of his deepest love and hatred, and then simultaneously destroy it and re-incorporate it, which means incorporating a fatally false perception of himself as invulnerable to death because even death's avatar cannot withstand him.

This is how I would explain the relative lack of success of the novels that succeed *Quiller's Run*: just as their titles give precedence to the agent over the mission, so in each mission the Bureau cedes increasing and increasingly unquestioned status to Quiller (by, for example, suddenly disclosing further reaches of internal administrative eminence from which to recruit suitable august controls for his missions, or supplying the increasingly large platoons of supporting troops to bring them off successfully—despite their supposedly being specifically suited to lone-wolf operatives). The specific nature of the institution becomes less clearly delineated, as does that of the missions it runs, and hence so too does that of their agent; Quiller's recovery from death-dealing betrayal by his sacred bull seems to have left him a shadow of his former self.

However that may be, the pivotal pair of novels that precede those later episodes make it absolutely clear that the necrophiliac consequences of Quiller's repressed origin as a shadow executive are directly (even if differently) inscribed into the narrative voice of every novel in the series, and indirectly inflect other aspects of that voice in such a way as sharply to distinguish Quiller from the protagonists of the two other British authors with whose work in this genre Adam Hall was at least initially associated— John Le Carré and Len Deighton. Like them, Hall defines his protagonist against the glamorous mixture of sex, sadism, and snobbery embodied in Ian Fleming's James Bond, soon to be cinematically incarnated in Sean Connery. However, unlike Le Carré, Hall exclusively inhabits the perspective of the foot soldier or field-agent, whose social status is unspecifically but clearly distant from that of the British establishment; and although Quiller shares his intellectual self-confidence, and social and professional insubordinateness with Deighton's Harry Palmer, he combines it with a far more abrasive line in irony and sarcasm, a far more uncompromising immersion in the brutal physical demands of overcoming enemy resistance, and a willingness to frame his experience in terms which leave downbeat social realism, however wryly and wittily delivered, decisively behind. In other words, Quiller is not only not-Bond, he is also not-Smiley and not-Leamas, and not-Palmer; his mode of being-in-the-world is very different from any of theirs.

The world according to Quiller is one in which countries have a soul—whether it be polluted (as in his view of Germany) or oppressed and desperate for liberation (as in his view of Poland). It is one in which individuals have a personality that is crystallized in one feature of their physical appearance or mode of being-in-the-world, and often associated with the nature of an animal or machine. In *The Warsaw Document*, for example, a resistance fighter's nature is embodied in the way she places her feet together, Quiller's control not only has but is his chilblains, and a Russian security official who is first introduced as silently guiding another interrogator by means of hand gestures is quickly reduced to the movements of that gesturing hand. Another resistance fighter strikes Quiller as resembling an eagle, and his every word and deed thereafter is directly described in those terms, whereas an anonymous but skilled and therefore potentially lethal member of the security forces is experienced during combat as a wolf; and Quiller thinks of himself—in this and every novel—as another kind of animal, common, unregarded but persistent: 'I'm just an operator sent into the opposite warren like a ferret' (BM, 136). Even the inanimate finds its objective correlative, as it were: for instance, the opposition project that Quiller must block appears in one of his dreams as a runaway black locomotive, and is thereafter always represented as such.

These modes of metonymy, and displacements of phenomena onto their metaphorical equivalents, might in isolation be taken as no more than drastic simplifications of character and context—as failures to create and sustain psychological and sociological complexity; and I've already acknowledged that a certain degree of etiolation does indeed set in by the later episodes in the series (certainly from *Quiller Barracuda*[9] on). On the other hand, even those later works disclose a compensating narrative power in such tropes, by increasingly presenting their plots as in effect generated by the book's opening image (as when *Quiller Barracuda* begins with Quiller describing interrogators as creatures with huge jaws wanting to eat you or swallow you up, centres around his identity being invaded by subliminal

---

[9] New York: William Morrow, 1990.

brainwashing techniques, and culminates in his having to risk being devoured by sharks in order to complete his mission). And the reading experience that these figurative strategies make possible in the earlier books is intensely dramatic rather than merely melodramatic; or rather, they create a mode of melodrama whose simplicities are in the service of a more elemental mode of understanding than that of empirical psychology or statistical science. For the characters so dramatized are rendered at once more concretely themselves, and something greater or more enduring than themselves: they register as individualities rather than individuals, as types rather than stereotypes. This narrator's mode of comprehending the world is thereby once again revealed as having an essentially mythological dimension—as if he finds the human world and its designs to involve the eternal recurrence of certain basic dispositions and constellations of meaning, so that the particular significance of any individual within it is partly dependent upon, and so importantly intensified by, their instantiation of that which transcends particularity.

An analogous revelation of the exemplary within the particular is conveyed by another aspect of Quiller's strategic and tactical perceptions of the world. For example, when seeking to escape from a particularly professional opposition surveillance cell in *The Warsaw Document*, he heads for the central railway station in search of a means of escape:

The thing was that within ten paces of the entrance where I'd come in they'd deprived me of visual cover. Their specialized field overlapped a neighbouring discipline: the observation of VIPs in public places; the two jobs had various factors in common and the chief of these was geometry: they moved to their stations as if instructed by the computed findings of compass and protractor; they knew the distance I'd have to go before the island cafeteria obscured me from points A and B, the angle subtended by the view of C and D, the sector through which I could move under observation from E, F and G before the A and B zones picked me up again.

They didn't see the cafeteria or the bookstall or the ticket-gates: they saw vectors, diagonals, tangents. It amounted to this: if each man were a spotlight I would have no shadow. (WD, 147–8)

The concluding spotlight image not only captures the extent to which the competence of the opposition agents in effect neuters Quiller's own professional purposes (for what is left of a shadow executive if he is deprived of his own shadow?), and further exemplifies his tendency to represent people as things. It also acknowledges with respect a capacity that Quiller shares with his opponents—that of seeing the particular situation as an instance of more abstract or general considerations. Here, the architecture of a domain designed for a particular kind of practical human activity becomes pure geometry; functional detail dissolves into the bare logic of shape and distance, but the reality of the situation is thereby not so much dissipated as sharpened—for after all, seeing the railway station in terms of its geometry is a way of seeing its underlying structure, of disclosing an aspect of its material reality (its resistance to certain kinds of human purpose) and thereby taming its unfamiliarity, by grasping it as a variation upon a theme.

Such representational strategies at the level of character and purpose reinforce, and are reinforced by, a related propensity for reiteration at the level of the novels' action sequences. Indeed, one of the great pleasures of the series as a whole is its author's willingness to allow his protagonist to resort more than once to the same tactic. For example, in the third dramatized report, *The Striker Portfolio*,[10] Quiller is ordered out of a car parked in a scrap yard by two armed enemy agents standing next to the vehicle:

The [Norfolk training school] handbook is written in Basic Civil Service and this chapter is headed: *Taking Leave of a Stationary Vehicle While Under Menace of Fire-Arms*. But the actual idea is sensible and can work if you're very quick so I leaned over and hit the handles of both doors at the same time and jack-knifed with my feet against the driving-door and kicked so hard that the door's inertia helped to send me backwards and out through the other side before it swung against them explosively and put them off their guard for several fractions of a second. Some people say you should leave the door shut while you go pitching out of the other one so that it makes a bullet-shield and there's a lot of point in that but for one thing they can shoot through the window and for another thing the Norfolk Instructions are based on psychological rather than physical factors and the chief of these is the use of surprise.

They'd expected me to emerge past a slowly opened door and in fact I was moving hard in the opposite direction and the door was bursting open against the hinge-stop with a lot of noise and up to a point it worked because the first two shots went into the seats and the third rang somewhere among the wreckage in front of me as I hunched over and started the zig-zag with my hands hitting out at the stuff

---

[10] London: Fontana, 1969—hereafter SP.

on each side of the alley to help the momentum while the fourth hooked at my coat and the fifth smashed some glass near my head. (SP, 32–3)

This passage—with its familiar oscillation between paratactically described pure action and reflectively savoured pure ratiocination—is itself plainly based on the same psychological factor of surprise that its protagonist deploys: as readers we too are expecting Quiller to exit from the vehicle via the driver's door, so what actually happens surprises us as much as it does the enemy agents. But the tactic is plainly designed to be usable in any similar set of circumstances, and any experienced executive would accordingly expect to use it more than once; so, finding himself in a similar position in *The Scorpion Signal* (the eighth novel of the series) Quiller duly does just that—thereby confounding our expectation that novelists working in this genre should operate solely according to the psychological principle of surprise, which would mean always inventing ingenious new ways for their protagonists to escape danger. Instead, Adam Hall invites the reader to find pleasure in repetition, insofar as his refusal to surprise here becomes a surprising means of sustaining verisimilitude—helping to convey the sense in which the individual missions of an experienced shadow executive are bound to become increasingly a matter of the recurrence of the same (with variations), as if gradually revealing the world's deeper and simpler adamantine necessities.

It is therefore fitting that the final page of the final novel in the series should provide us with an enduring image of its protagonist by means of a metonymical operation that alludes simultaneously to metaphysical, mythological, and religious registrations of a perception of personal identity as both fragile and fundamental, as always-already dispersed and ultimately undecomposable. This last mission has ended with Quiller taking shelter in an old fire station whilst outside the opposition are attacked by other Bureau operatives.

The great iron door of the fire station crashed behind me, cutting off the confusion outside as Legge's private army went into action. Behind the thick walls of the great building the sound of gunfire was muffled.

A fleck of debris hit the rusting fire-bell and left a faint note floating on the air. (QB, 278)

Composed by Adam Hall the day before he died, this final sentence presents Quiller as at once a random by-product of death and destruction, and a sustained harmonic presence: he has put out his last fire, dealt with his last emergency, but he will continue to linger behind and beyond the mythic melodrama of his narrating voice, in that cosmic field of consciousness that he earlier presented as the sole source of grace.

2. Bourne

At the beginning of the first film in the trilogy that recounts his story (*The Bourne Identity* [Doug Liman: 2002]), Jason Bourne doesn't even know that that is the name by which he is known to his CIA employees, who—as part of a black-ops programme named 'Treadstone'—had utilized sophisticated behavioural conditioning to turn him into an assassin. At the end of the second film (*The Bourne Supremacy* [Paul Greengrass: 2004]), he learns that his real name is not Jason Bourne but David Webb; and by the end of the third film (*The Bourne Ultimatum* [Paul Greengrass: 2007]), he has learnt that knowing his real name is of precisely no help in coming to know who he really is. The title of the first film is thus, in effect, also the title of the trilogy: the overarching narrative concerns Jason Bourne's attempts, first, to re-member who Jason Bourne was and is, and second, to discover how and why David Webb became Jason Bourne.

This insistent thematic focus is part of what ensures that the Jason Bourne of the films is essentially unrelated to the Jason Bourne of the Robert Ludlum novels on which those films are nominally based; it is of precisely no help in coming to know who the cinematic incarnation of Jason Bourne may be to know anything about his (utterly generic) literary namesake and origin. But given the nature of cinema, with the precedence it automatically gives to actor over character, we should not expect the question of Jason Bourne's cinematic identity to be ultimately separable from the question of Matt Damon's cinematic identity; for something about Damon's way of lending himself to the role of Jason Bourne has—as with all exemplary screen performances—undeniably brought about the redefinition of his stardom.

The Bourne Identity begins when Jason Bourne is recovered, with two bullets in his back and suffering total amnesia, from the sea south of Marseille by the crew of a fishing boat. On the one hand, he shows real physical competence, not only in the business of everyday life (reading, writing, adding and subtracting, making coffee, setting up a chessboard) but also in matters related to fishing: 'The knot's like everything else—I just found the ropes and I did it.' There is thus much that his body still knows, but his mind is a blank: having instinctively spoken in patently American English on his first return to consciousness, he later confronts himself in a mirror, first asking in French 'Do you know who I am?', then pleading in German 'Tell me who I am; If you know who I am, please stop messing around and tell me.' So the issue of self-knowledge and its failures is as insistent here as in the Quiller novels, even if differently configured. Bourne plainly regards himself as possessing the knowledge he desperately desires but cannot recover; and in seeing him thus confronting himself as another, hence as internally divided or non-self-coincidental, we are invited to wonder whether the inaccessibility of his self-knowledge is a mode of self-punishment, or a mode of self-defence, or both.

The general nature of Bourne's identity is unambiguously declared from an early stage, and by his body rather than his mind—or rather, by the particular mode of being-in-the-world that his body continues to inhabit, beneath or before any conscious appropriation of it. As well as having two bullets in his body, Bourne also had a capsule embedded in his hip containing the number of a safety deposit box in a Swiss bank. Its contents are revelatory—the upper level contains a US passport in the name of Jason Bourne, and an identity card indicating an address in Paris; the lower level contains a gun, a great deal of money, and a variety of other passports, each in a different name and a different nationality. What is implied by this lower level is explicitly confirmed both before and after Bourne opens the box, when he first disables two policemen who confront him in a Zurich park, and later evades arrest at the US embassy despite the most determined efforts by a multitude of heavily-armed civilian and military personnel. In each case, he simply sees the situation and does what he needs to do in order to master it—or more precisely, he hands over conscious reflective control of himself in favour of an intensely refined and flexible repertoire of psycho-physical instinct; left to its own devices, his body is subconsciously habituated to the use of extreme but coldly controlled violence, and his mind to the business of utilizing anything and everything in his environment as a means of evading pursuit, injury, or capture.

So we don't really need the sheaf of false passports to tell us that our protagonist is a clandestine operative, a spy of some sort, whose weddedness to the world so far exceeds our own that his ingrained ability to find a seamless path through its most threatening vicissitudes can only appear to us in disjointed glimpses, as a barely coherent collage of images. This is the first unveiling of the trilogy's trademark mode of presenting violent action (the cinematic analogue to Adam Hall's literary techniques that is so sorely missed in the sole film adaptation of his work)—something that Greengrass exactingly intensifies in the sequels, but which finds its clearest expression in this first film in the combat sequence set in Bourne's Paris apartment, when he and Marie (the woman who drives him there from Zurich) are set upon by another Treadstone operative (part of the CIA's desperate attempt to eliminate the threat to their reputation posed by Bourne's failure to carry out his most recent secret mission by eliminating Bourne himself.) These presentations rely upon a particular kind of editing: the use of a multitude of cuts of a speed and violence that match the conditioned reflexes of Bourne himself, but made against the grain of the action itself, slicing across the logically distinguishable phases of blow, parry, and counter-blow that might be detectable from a single, bird's-eye point of view. The viewer thereby experiences the flow of action in a way which simultaneously allows her to identify with Bourne *and* with his antagonists: she undergoes the latter's experience of visceral bewilderment as their world breaks up into incomprehensible but painfully impacting fragments, but she does so from a position of safety, screened by the screen on which these fragments are projected, as if inhabiting the detached perspective of Bourne's self-withdrawing consciousness as it is carried safely through the carnage by the very thing that caused it—his uncannily-enhanced embodied competences, his being-in-the-world-as-assassin.

But these periods of perfect fusion with the world—what we see as excellences of improvisatory know-how, as when Bourne uses a ballpoint pen to counter a knife-wielding antagonist in the Paris apartment—are experienced by Bourne himself as both deeply satisfying and deeply disturbing. On the one hand, they are the moments in which his agonizing self-doubt and self-obscurity ease, in which he can simply go with the habitual flow of his being; on the other, they are the perfect indication of what he fears most—that the identity he has forgotten is an identity he wanted to forget, an identity with which he passionately does not want to identify. And when he recalls the reason for his discovery in the water (he had gone aboard the boat of an African ex-dictator named Wombosi in order to kill him whilst making it appear that Wombosi's men had done it, but aborted his mission when he found the dictator with his children, and was shot whilst trying to escape), it becomes clear that his self-revulsion is not purely a result of his amnesiac self-discovery: he had already begun to distance himself from the identity that he now wishes utterly to disavow.

The ironies attending his identity are thus, by the end of the first film, multiple. He really was Jason Bourne all along, just as the documents in the safety deposit box show: he really had completed a number of assassination missions for Treadstone and the CIA before the Wombosi fiasco, and in this sense his body's incarnation of the modes of engaged understanding appropriate to such a function reveal the truth about who he is. On the other hand, much of what he did as Jason Bourne—certainly anything prior to the Wombosi mission—remains inaccessible to his memory and consciousness; and so, as certain familiar philosophical views of personal identity (associated with the name of John Locke) would imply, there is a clear sense in which he is not (is no longer, or not yet once again) Jason Bourne. And this provisional non-identity is confirmed by everything he does in the film after discovering who he is, or rather was: he commits himself to leaving Jason Bourne behind, vowing to disappear from the grid as long as his ex-employers leave him in peace. What he aspires to is a new life and identity, to be lived out with Marie; but he is only in a position to survive long enough to begin living it by virtue of the bodily competences that his earlier existence as Jason Bourne had inscribed into him beyond any possibility of conscious alteration, or willed erasure. Accordingly, as he and Marie embark on their new life together, Bourne himself is committed to denying what both his body and his memory persist in affirming: that he is Jason Bourne. In other words, whoever he is, he is (above or before all) not Jason Bourne; he is not Jason Bourne in a way that is not open to any other person in the world, even though every such person is not Jason Bourne either; for (as Sartre would have it) he exists in an intimately negating relation to just that identity—he is not-Jason-Bourne (and it is in this negating self-relation that he most clearly differs from James Bond, with his apparently untroubled inhabitation of his own skin—it is his not being who he is that makes Bourne not-Bond). Is not-Jason-Bourne someone he can be? Is not being Jason Bourne really a way of being someone in particular? Come to think of it, it sounds like a remarkably common way of individuating oneself.

The Bourne Supremacy re-affirms the interest of the series in issues of identity by depicting the first surfacings of a plot to kill Bourne after directly implicating him in the failure of a CIA operation to discover the identities of those involved in the disappearance of millions of dollars of CIA funds several years earlier, and thereby indirectly implicating him in the original theft. His corpse is meant to draw a line under both the initial disappearance and the contemporary failure, and to allow the real thieves (a rogue CIA officer in league with a Russian oil oligarch) to maintain their anonymity. In other words, the plotters aim to make Bourne responsible for crimes he didn't commit, and they can do so only by making him take responsibility once again for being someone he doesn't want to be—himself, the assassin he no longer is. Because their plans go awry, when their attempt to kill Bourne succeeds only in killing Marie, the plotters manage to convince the CIA of Bourne's involvement, but they end up inciting Bourne himself to seek vengeance. Since, however, this search requires him to tap into the identity he has tried so hard to leave behind, and in particular to acknowledge that he was in fact involved in a carefully-concealed double assassination that was integral to covering up the initial theft, they do in a way succeed in forcing him to take responsibility once more for being Jason Bourne. On the other hand, he takes up that responsibility in such a way as to avoid taking responsibility for the crimes he didn't in fact commit, by showing the real responsibility to rest with the plotters themselves. Moreover, his desire to honour Marie's memory (and in particular her wish that he not allow his fate to be determined by his past) leads him to refrain from simply executing the two plotters, as his earlier self would have done, and to atone for his lethal involvement in the original theft by finding and apologizing to the daughter of the couple he killed. We might think of this as a struggle on his part to incorporate Marie's voice into his history, or rather to find and activate the equivalent register in his own voice.

Thus by the end of the second film, Bourne's way of defining his identity as not-Jason-Bourne has modulated: he has shifted from what has been revealed as a hopeless attempt utterly to negate his past by fleeing from it altogether, to an attempt to negate it specifically, mission by mission and deed by deed. Rather than simply acting as if he and Jason Bourne were utterly unrelated, he is now pursuing a strategy of concrete moral negation—one in which he aspires to transcend his identity as Jason Bourne by repenting each specific mission he performed as Jason Bourne. This means that he can only escape being Jason Bourne by first recalling, and then taking responsibility for, having been Jason Bourne: he can only become a new person by overcoming the systematic repression of his past that had initially made it seem that he already was a new person, someone utterly unrelated to Jason Bourne—by owning, more specifically by atoning for, everything Jason Bourne ever did.

And just as the demands of this narrative of attempted redemption force its protagonist to close the gap he has created between himself and who he was, so Paul Greengrass intensifies and broadens the range of application of the cinematic techniques he inherited from Doug Liman (as he inherits the talents of Christopher Rouse as editor, promoting him from his position as assistant editor under Liman) in such a way as to further break down the boundary between Bourne and his viewers. The ultra-choppy editing for the action sequences is not only retained but speeded up, leading to some breathtakingly visceral passages—the combat sequence with the only other surviving Treadstone operative in Munich, the chase sequence involving road, elevated railway, and barge in Berlin, and the car chase in Moscow; and its implicit identification with Bourne's point of view is deliberately underlined by its being used in two other contexts. The first involves Bourne's flashbacks to his past, and in particular to the double assassination that protected the initial theft; Greengrass deploys exactly the same editing techniques for his presentation of these flashbacks, and thus emphasizes the internal relation between Bourne's mode of being in both contexts. For it is when he is immersed in action or overwhelmed by traumatic memory that Bourne is most himself, that is, most closely identified with his earlier self; and the bewildering violence of the film's presentation of both invites us to consider how far Bourne's lethal facility in combat is itself traumatic rather than an expression of at-homeness—an uncanny repetition of the past, even a psychotic break with the person he wants to be or become.

The second extension or expansion is easier to miss. A good example of it occurs when Bourne arrives in Berlin and is driven by taxi to the hotel at which the CIA team hunting him down is staying; amongst the montage of shots from Bourne's point of view through the taxi window, Greengrass places a brief glimpse of the road-and-rail bridge over the river on which the chase sequence I just mentioned will take place; and he follows it with an even briefer glimpse of some posters advertising a protest march—the very march that Bourne will later use as cover when he separates one of the CIA team (Nicolette Parsons, played by Julia Stiles—a minor member of the Treadstone operation in Paris seen in the first film) from her security team in order to interrogate her. The parallel seems clear: both glimpses indicate Bourne's attention to detail, or more specifically his ability to make use of the most apparently ordinary or insignificant aspect of his environment in order to achieve his purposes: he truly is someone on whom nothing is lost. But Greengrass is implicitly setting the same standard of visual acuity for his viewers; by making it possible to see on a second viewing (and just possible to appreciate on a first viewing) how every detail of his montages is pregnant with significance, he is inviting us to become viewers of a film upon whom nothing is lost.

Given this general willingness to load significance upon even the most arbitrary visual detail, however, it is striking that Greengrass concludes his film not with Bourne's cathartic confrontation with the daughter of his victims, but with a supplement or coda to it: a brief exchange between Bourne and Pamela Landy (Joan Allen)—the leader of the CIA hunt for Bourne who has gradually come to realize his innocence. Bourne rings her in her New York office, saying that he has heard that they are still looking for him; she thanks him for revealing the true villains, gives him an off-the-record apology, and then tells him: 'David Webb—that's your real name: you were born on 4/15/71 in Nixa, Missouri. Why don't you come in and we'll talk about it?' To which Bourne responds: 'Get some rest, Pam—you look tired.' At which point she, and we, realize that Bourne is observing her from the roof of the building opposite.

That concluding punch line echoes an earlier scene in Berlin, where Bourne talks to Landy by phone at their local base without revealing until the very end of the exchange that he has her under direct observation. That said, however, it seems to violate certain constraints that have thus far unified the films—in particular, by placing Bourne in the United States, rather than in a series of realistically-documented European (and, briefly, Asian) locations; and it suddenly introduces what seems like an entirely new piece of information—the business of his real name—in order to re-open matters that had just seemed to be neatly wrapped up through the culminating events in Moscow. Was this just a rather cynical way of signalling a firm intention to add another episode to this increasingly popular series of films?

But of course, the question of Jason Bourne's real name has been the implicit preoccupation of both films thus far; and insofar as the second film is explicitly concerned with Bourne's attempt to escape his own identity by taking responsibility for everything he did as Jason Bourne, then it is in fact entirely logical for that project to culminate in the need to take responsibility for becoming Jason Bourne in the first place. After all, the man we know as Jason Bourne existed before becoming involved in the Treadstone project; and Jason Bourne would not have existed at all if that man had not chosen to become involved in that project (a choice that he must have exercised on American soil, given the CIA's ownership of the project). Call this man 'David Webb': if our protagonist is properly to complete his project of getting beyond being Jason Bourne by taking full responsibility for being Jason Bourne, he must find a way of taking responsibility for choosing to become Jason Bourne in the first place—taking responsibility for his own origins, as it were. And that will mean finding a way of taking responsibility for being David Webb.

As if to compensate for even the appearance of unmotivated supplementation, *The Bourne Ultimatum* finds a way of binding its predecessor's coda back into the narrative fabric of the trilogy by in effect inserting itself into the space between the final episode of the main narrative of *The Bourne Supremacy* and its coda (to which no temporal coordinates had been attached)—that is, between Bourne's departure from Moscow and his conversation in New York with Landy. The fit isn't perfect: the third film begins immediately after Bourne's departure from the daughter's flat; but what was a coda in the second film is re-presented as a vital but not final step in the culminating joint attempt by Landy and Bourne to expose and derail the CIA's successor project to 'Treadstone' ('BlackBriar'—a programme that we hear being launched at the very end of *The Bourne Identity*, and which involves the use of illegal measures, ranging from extraordinary rendition to torture and assassination, against terrorist threats, even when they involve US citizens). More specifically, Landy is revealed as having encoded the location of the original Treadstone training facility (415 East 71st Street) into her erroneous recitation of Bourne's (or rather, Webb's) date of birth; so what the earlier film had presented to us as a revelation of the truth about Bourne's identity turns out to contain a falsehood designed to mislead CIA eavesdroppers—one more move in the espionage game. Consequently, the narrative of the third film in fact reaches its climax not with the phone call but with the event it makes possible—Bourne's penetration of the facility in which David Webb made his choice to become Jason Bourne.

So the relation between the second and third films is unprecedentedly complex and mysterious, certainly with respect to the domain of Hollywood sequels, and probably with respect to the construction of sequels in any artistic medium; indeed the very idea of a sequel is here being put under great pressure—one might rather see the relation between the two as one of simultaneous mutual dependence. For *The Bourne Ultimatum* could with equal justice be described as embedding itself within the narrative matrix established by *The Bourne Supremacy*, or as constructing a narrative matrix within which the coda of *The Bourne Supremacy* might be embedded. On the one hand, it sets itself the task of not only acknowledging but incorporating that earlier supplement in such a way as to make sense of its original appearance—thus presenting itself as engendered by a sense of absolute loyalty to, and so dependence upon, its predecessor; on the other hand, in order to effect this incorporation, it radically alters the significance of the scene it incorporates (transforming its seemingly relaxed and optimistic portrayal of humane conversation into a moment of desperate duplicity, with deep but obscure significance for both protagonists, the CIA and indeed America itself), and thereby retrospectively alters the significance of the earlier film as a whole. So the single scene that both films share might also be seen as a completely different narrative component in each context (an ambiguity that is registered in the fact that in *The Bourne Ultimatum* this scene, containing the same dialogue and actors, has barely a shot in common with the corresponding sequence in its predecessor). *The Bourne Ultimatum*'s way of manifesting its indebtedness to *The Bourne Supremacy* thereby ensures that the latter will no longer be viewable as entirely self-sufficient; its significance has been retrospectively but decisively inflected in such a way as to render its successor an integral part of itself, and so to make this sequel an essential part of its own conditions of possibility.[11]

The way in which *The Bourne Ultimatum* finds the space for its own realization within a minuscule and apparently insignificant gap in the structure of its predecessor mirrors at a formal level an aspect of the current condition of its protagonist—an aspect that serves to magnify the claustrophobia that he (and so his audience) are made to undergo. For the action sequences in this third film are presented in an even more violently disorienting version of the familiar hyper-choppy editorial technique, to the point where even habituated viewers are operating at the limits of their

---

[11] It's worth pointing out that the first film is also drawn into this complex matrix of dependent freedom, not only insofar as the third film's goal is to destroy the BlackBriar programme whose initiation we glimpse at the end of the first, but also because Landy's way of making contact with Bourne when he arrives in New York is to address a message to him over the airport tannoy using a false name (Gilberto do Piento) that we first saw—if we were paying very close attention—on one of the fake passports Bourne discovers in the Zurich safety deposit box in the first film. 'Waste not, want not' is obviously good advice for directors as well as spies...

capacity to make sense of what they are seeing; and this intensification is responsive to a key feature of the subject matter of these sequences—the increasingly confined or straitened circumstances in which Bourne has to exercise his capacity for surgically-applied violence.

The key action sequences in this film are: Bourne's attempt to rescue a journalist from a CIA team in Waterloo Station; his pursuit of, and fight to the death with, a BlackBriar operative seeking to kill Nicky Parsons in Tangier; and a car chase in New York. Each is a recognizable version of the templates set up in the previous two films—most obviously so in the case of the latter two; but all involve a massive reduction in the space within which Bourne is required to operate in comparison with those earlier counterparts. Waterloo Station is heaving with commuters; in Tangier, Bourne can only reach the enemy agent by cutting through a series of packed and heavily-populated apartments of the old quarter of the city (having to find aerial routes between buildings via narrow windows and slim balconies), and their culminating combat begins in a tiny, cluttered living room and ends with both men forced into one corner of an even tinier shower cubicle; in New York, the car chase can barely find room to get going in streets jammed with other traffic, and ends with the police cruiser Bourne is driving reduced to the reinforced core of its passenger shell before being crushed against a bridge support.

The point here is not just that the cramped spaces within which Bourne is forced to manoeuvre would engender exactly the impression of increased velocity and visual fragmentation that the film's intensification of its choppy editing induces in viewers; this sequence of action sequences also importantly contributes to the sense that Bourne's progress or regress towards the moment at which he became who he no longer wants to be is itself to be understood as a matter of moving further into an ever-narrowing corridor or tunnel. The closer he gets to properly grasping that moment—and hence to making sense of the flashback that first afflicts him at the beginning of this third film, before he has even managed to get out of Moscow—the more restricted his psychological and moral room for manoeuvre becomes. And this process of confinement comes to its climax when Bourne confronts the man who led the Treadstone training programme and inducted him into it—Dr Albert Hirsch (played by Albert Finney).

Dr Hirsch is not inclined to apologize either for the behavioural conditioning processes he used to train all the Treadstone operatives, or for the specific means he employed to encourage David Webb to pass the final test designed to demonstrate his readiness for active service—the execution of a hooded and bound man, without any indication offered of his identity, or of there being any particular pressing reason for his being killed. When Webb baulks at this, he is subjected to sleep deprivation and waterboarding for days on end, until he finally picks up the gun and shoots the anonymous victim. According to Hirsch, these forms of inducement do not absolve Webb himself of the ultimate responsibility for becoming Jason Bourne: for he volunteered for the programme rather than being picked by those running it, in the full knowledge of what would be asked of those who participated in it, and in particular in full awareness of the fact that the training process would ensure that he would no longer be the person he was when he began it. In other words, David Webb freely chose the course of action that ensured that he would no longer be David Webb but Jason Bourne. As Hirsch puts it: 'We didn't pick you—you picked us; you volunteered, right here, even after you were warned . . . You knew exactly what it meant for you if you chose to stay . . . You can't outrun what you did, Jason—you made yourself into who you are.'

Bourne's response is: 'I remember everything . . . I am no longer Jason Bourne.' But this hardly constitutes a denial of responsibility: on the contrary, if he remembers everything, then he remembers being the person who chose to become Jason Bourne; what he doesn't remember is why he did so. Hirsch's introductory speeches to the trainees are shown to include the claim that their missions will save American lives; but that just pushes the explanatory question one step further back—for why might any decent person view that goal as justifying the application of any means whatever, including the execution of American citizens? More particularly, why would David Webb, upon being told that the completion of the pro-gramme would bring it about that he will no longer be David Webb, reply that 'I'll be whoever you want me to be, sir'?

The only clue we have to this matter is the brief glimpse we are offered of the dog-tags Webb handed over to Hirsch 'without a blink' as he entered the training programme. These identity tags confirm that Webb (referred to in the flashbacks as 'Captain Webb') was a ranking member of the military; but the data they contain also includes his religious affiliation—and this tells us, if we are quick enough to see it, that David Webb was, or is, a Roman Catholic. One of the distinguishing doctrines of Catholicism is that of original sin—the belief that human nature has been fundamentally dis-ordered, that is, has been rendered structurally disposed to sin, by an originating individual act of human sinfulness (Adam's eating of the apple, as Genesis pictures it). In other words, it conveys a conception of human beings as non-accidentally inclined to do evil, together with an apparent attempt to explain how that inclination was first established (despite being contrary to the creator's intentions). But of course, to explain the origin of human sinfulness in terms of a sinful human act is patently to presuppose what one purports to explain; the doctrine of original sin is thus best understood not as a way of accounting for the human propensity to evil, but rather as an expression of the conviction that the deep-rootedness of evil ultimately lies beyond explanation—that it constitutes a limit at which the human capacity to comprehend ourselves runs out.

And this seems to be an accurate registration of the stance Jason Bourne finds himself taking towards himself, as he finally manages to complete his recovery of and from his identity as Jason Bourne by reclaiming his identity as David Webb. In one sense, this means that he is no longer Jason Bourne, and so is no longer burdened by the guilt of what he did as Jason Bourne; but since once again being David Webb means taking responsibility for what David Webb did, it includes taking responsibility for freely choos-ing to become Jason Bourne, and so taking responsibility for everything Jason Bourne was likely (indeed, designed) to do. Having become David Webb once more, he can identify no reason on earth why he should have made that choice—why he should freely have embraced moral unfreedom, the deliberate reconstruction of his personality into that of a lethal weapon. Jason Bourne thus ends his quest to discover who he is by discovering that he is the person who was incomprehensibly capable of the evil choice of becoming an evil-doer—of transforming himself into the very person from whom he has spent this trilogy of films attempting to distinguish himself, the person he felt himself not really to be. If 'David Webb' is his real name, then so is 'Jason Bourne'; and although the truth of this is undeniable, neither he nor we can find any way of making sense either of the condition it describes or of how that condition came about. What we are left with is simply a secular version of the story of Eden—a story that at first appears to explain how this individual became the evil-doer that he was and is by reference to an evil choice of his, but that is better understood as an expression of the conviction that human evil-doing is ultimately beyond rational explanation.

One might, in conclusion, note a certain analogy between Jason Bourne's sense of bewilderment at the unfathomable origins of his identity and the way in which Matt Damon's transformation of his persona as a star into that of a lethal weapon—an action hero of a kind that is at once indebted to predecessors such as Arnold Schwarzenegger or Bruce Willis and utterly transformative of their achievement—seems in retrospect (to Damon himself, no doubt, as well as to us) to be both fated and utterly contingent, at once the uncovering of a necessity and the unforeseeable outcome of a chance conjunction of choice, collaborators, and circumstance. Such unfathomable moments may be part of the condition of being a film actor, but their power of generating particular insight from case to case is not thereby lessened; and the illumination created by that sense of retrospective necessity in this case—its revelation of something specific about Damon's physical presence to the camera, his body both unignorably solid and undeniably cultivated or adaptable, and his cultivated intelligence long since reconciled to its occlusion by his all-American face—should not mislead us into thinking that it was bound to come out sooner or later. If, as the posters and DVD jackets proclaim, Matt Damon is Jason Bourne, the present truth of that proclamation of identity must be grasped against the background knowledge of its having become true, and only as a result of an unspecifiable array of interlinking conditions, at the core of which is the camera's uncanny ability to transform physiognomy into destiny.

3. Bond

James Bond is—so far as we know—his real name: his code-name is in fact a number (007), and from a very early stage it became more like an additional part of that real name than a means of concealing it. But the literary bearer of that name was very quickly eclipsed in the popular consciousness by his cinematic incarnation—or rather, by the various actors who took on that role in a hugely popular and lucrative franchise that has never really lost the glamour conferred by Sean Connery's original embodiment of it. Nevertheless, even before that franchise really established itself, its protagonist was generating generic projects possessed of a very different texture and purpose. In particular, the identity of both Quiller and Bourne was importantly and deliberately fixed in explicit contrast with that of Bond.

As I noted earlier, Adam Hall's novels formed part of a more general mid-1960's literary confrontation (also mounted by Le Carré and Deighton) with Fleming's ungovernably popular but increasingly fantastic series; and the sense the Bourne movies created of re-grounding the cinematic incarnation of the spy in reality is an effect that depended significantly upon Bourne's being not-Bond, upon his repudiation of expectations originating with Bond's various cinematic incarnations—the reliance upon exotic gadgetry and vehicles, the unending supply of infinitely powerful and megalomaniacal arch-criminals, the availability of beautiful but ultimately passive women, and the apparent invulnerability of the protagonist to any physical damage more severe than tousled hair.

By the end of the Pierce Brosnan era, some efforts had already been made by the holders of the Bond franchise to renew its vitality by incorporating some of these anti-Bond signifiers (more active women, villains emerging from more contemporary geo-political contexts, even subjecting Bond himself to interrogation, torture, and luxuriant facial hair (as at the opening of *Die Another Day* [Lee Tamahori: 2002])); but when even this valiant attempt ended by equipping Bond with an invisible car, and asking us to believe that he could wind-surf his way through collapsing Arctic glaciers, hopes for a genuine revival of audience interest were low. Then came Brosnan's retirement from the role, and the news that the highly-respected, but far from high-profile and undeniably blond, British actor Daniel Craig would be taking over the role. Could Daniel Craig really be James Bond, the Bond we knew and with whom we had begun to fall out of love? If he could not, would that spell the end of Bond, or a new beginning?

Casino Royale (Martin Campbell: 2006) chose to foreground this issue of assuming the identity of James Bond by taking seriously the fact that the book of this title actually introduced Bond to the reading public, and by re-imagining it so that it also gave an account of his first mission after having been awarded a '00' code-name—which signifies his license to kill, and so amounts to Bond himself becoming the James Bond we (think we) know. Accordingly, the film's black-and-white prologue depicts the two assassinations that Bond is asked to carry out in order to earn that license—one relatively civilized (gunshots in a darkened office), the other extremely violent and physically demanding (a vicious struggle in a grimy washroom);

and it withholds from Daniel Craig (and so from us) the signature line 'The name's Bond—James Bond' until the final seconds of the film, which suggests that more is required of the bearer of that name than the bare legal minimum.

The film is otherwise strikingly faithful to the basic plot of the book: the central element of Bond's mission is to beat the main villain (Le Chiffre) at a game of high-stakes poker, with a view to forcing him to tell what he knows to the British Secret Service, in exchange for protection from those whose clandestine funds he has just gambled away; and one of the film's most powerful scenes, in which Le Chiffre tortures a naked Bond by whipping his genitals, is taken directly from the novel. But the film also remains essentially faithful to the basic template of most previous films in the series—with the usual mix of exotic locations (Nassau, Venice), beautiful women (both of whom die), high-tech gadgets (Bond's Aston Martin is equipped with a heart defibrillator), and melodramatically-maimed villains (Le Chiffre weeps blood). To be sure, the action sequences are brilliantly realized; and they acquire new life in part by tapping into other cinematic modes of fight and flight (such as the free-running bomb-maker on Madagascar, who makes use of skills exploited by earlier films such as *District 13* [Pierre Morel: 2004]), in part by Daniel Craig's incarnation of Bond as more of a bulldozing force of will than Brosnan's elegantly intelligent predator. But for most of its (familiarly excessive) length, the film persists in inviting us to take up residence in a fantasy world of high living, sexual success (of which apparently even Le Chiffre's gleefully intimate attack cannot permanently deprive his victim), and unreflective killing—even if it shows an increased sensitivity to the costs of such a lifestyle, especially on the one living it.

Matters begin to change, however, in the final sequence of the film, when Bond discovers that the Treasury agent (Vesper Lynd, played by Eva Green) overseeing the funds for his poker game, with whom he has fallen in love, has been working all along for the organization behind Le Chiffre and has walked off with all the Treasury's money. His initial reaction of furious self-pity is not allayed by her subsequent death, nor by learning that she took the money in order to exchange it for Bond's life at the risk of her own, and that her initial recruitment by this organization was the result of blackmail (they kidnapped her lover and threatened to kill him unless she did as they wished). But he is willing to make use of her last gift to him—the phone number of the organization member who blackmailed her, and killed Le

Chiffre in order to protect the criminal forces behind him: Mr White. This is how *Casino Royale* is able to end with Bond shooting Mr White in the leg, and introducing himself—elegantly-clothed and armed with a machine gun—as 'Bond, James Bond'.

We might conclude from this conclusion that what finally qualifies James Bond (and so Daniel Craig) to be James Bond is his definitive loss of faith in the power of love and the faithfulness of women, even the best of whom is to be valued only to the extent that she is a means to furthering his professional goals. But we might rather be meant to conclude that he is laying claim to that name in roughly the same spirit in which he refers to Vesper in a concluding conversation with M (played by Judi Dench) by saying that 'The bitch is dead'—that is to say, as a refusal to admit the extent to which her death has deeply traumatized him, as an empty spell to treat an unhealable wound. At the very least, we are being invited to ask ourselves whether Bond is genuinely making a start on the individual life that a succession of earlier films (and books) have already marked out for him, or whether his particular way of failing to acknowledge part of his identity (in this case, that of a betrayed lover) is already forcing him to mark time.

With *Quantum of Solace* (Marc Forster: 2008), in which Bond devotes himself to the task of disrupting the organization behind Le Chiffre (known to its members as Quantum), the answer emerges; and the initial signs are not promising. The first three action sequences—a brutal car chase on the shores of Lake Garda, the pursuit of an enemy agent through the tunnels, streets, and rooftops of Siena, and disrupting Mr Green's plans for his treacherous girlfriend (Camille, played by Olga Kurilenko) in Haiti—arrive quickly, and are dense with tropes derived, wittingly or not, from *The Bourne Ultimatum* of the previous year. The vehicles in the Lake Garda car chase become savagely battered in the way the Bourne films have made familiar (and Bond even executes a version of the manoeuvre by which Bourne finishes off his FSB antagonist in the Moscow car chase in *The Bourne Supremacy*); Bond's scrambling leaps from rooftop to balcony in the cramped, dusty, paleness of Siena physically and visually recall the Bourne pursuit sequence in Tangier—a sequence in which Bourne also makes use of a motocross bike of exactly the kind Bond is riding when he finds Mr Green (played by Matthieu Amalric) in Haiti; and he kills his first target in Port au Prince in a fight whose brutal choreography and resort to ordinary objects as lethal weapons all follow in Bourne's footsteps. Furthermore, all three sequences rely heavily upon the choppy editing techniques that Greengrass and Rouse had exploited in their handling of Bourne's action sequences; but they deploy it in ways that seem finally to push its fragmentation of visual coherence beyond the capacity of the human eye to accommodate. The car chase sometimes dissolves into a montage of images whose relation to each other is a matter of pure conjecture; and I have yet to meet anyone who grasps the basic sequence of events depicted at the culmination of the chase in Siena, when Bond and the Quantum agent are fighting to the death on a rickety internal scaffold, with pulleys spinning, ropes tangling, and bodies and other objects frantically whipped through the air.

So the viewer quickly confronts the possibility that the Bond franchise has finally and definitively lost its sense of identity—that where *Casino Royale* had managed to find a way of blending Bourne-style signifiers of renewed realism with the canonical contexts and accoutrements of the material good life so central to the Bond universe and its pleasures, *Quantum of Solace* has simply reduced itself to a clumsy and insistent reproduction of the distinctive style of its most threatening, because most popular, alternative in the spy genre—and doing so in a way that lacks Greengrass' sensitivity to just how far this style (and particularly this style of editing) can be pushed without alienating the audience. At first glance, then, Daniel Craig's Bond begins to look like a poor man's Bourne.

But it is worth taking a second glance. For it is not quite right simply to say that certain key elements of the Bond universe that were present in *Casino Royale* are absent in *Quantum of Solace*; it would be more accurate to say that they are positively and systematically negated, denied to us. The closest Bond gets to fine dining is a glass of wine on the terrace with an old colleague, Mathis; he attends the opera, and so makes a brief appearance in a tuxedo, but he spends the whole time looking out from the backstage darkness at the audience rather than the performance (because the key members of Quantum are using the occasion to confer with one another); and the only luxury hotel in which he manages to spend time as a guest has a strikingly sterile, black-and-white design. Since that hotel suite is the setting for his sole episode of sexual pleasure, which is so briefly and perfunctorily presented as to seem merely dutiful, that aspect of Bond's good living seems to have lost much of its savour as well. Apart from a mobile phone, hi-tech gadgets are also conspicuous by their absence: the key tools for completing his mission include a battered working boat, a flimsy motor-bike, and a lumbering, barely air-worthy, twin-prop cargo plane (in which he has to evade a military jet). Can this person on the screen—character or actor—really be James Bond?

The exotic locations so familiar from earlier Bond films, and indeed from *Casino Royale*, also take on a very different cast in *Quantum of Solace*. Instead of the gorgeous beaches, sparkling water, and glamorous hotels of Nassau or Venice, we get the working port and the impoverished street life of Port au Prince; instead of lush Montenegran landscapes, we get the stony deserts of Bolivia. In fact, throughout the film, both culture and nature are presented as utterly arid and inhospitable: the Lake Garda car chase ends in a dust-wreathed marble quarry; the Siena pursuit throws up further clouds of dust as it weaves its way through that city's staging of the Palio, in which a horse race unfolds chaotically in a stony square cluttered by uncomprehending tourists; and the climax of the film occurs in 'La Perla de las Dunas'—a hotel mysteriously located in the middle of the Bolivian desert, rising like a vast blank terracotta wall out of the sands, and destined to be reduced to fiery rubble by the concluding struggle between Bond and Mr Green—with the latter left to wander in the stony waste, with only a can of engine oil to slake his thirst. As members of an audience who thought they had bought a ticket to the new Bond movie, we might not find it hard to identify with him.

But this vision of the world as a desiccated wilderness not only reflects and reinforces the specific maleficence of the Quantum organization—whose current project, under cover of a purported concern for general ecological well-being, is precisely to deprive Bolivia of its natural supplies of water in order to make profits from the business of later restoring and controlling those supplies under its newly-established puppet military regime; it also amounts to a projection of the inner life of Bond and his key female ally, Camille, insofar as both are utterly consumed by their thirst for revenge. Camille has spent years trying to get close enough to the Bolivian general responsible for her family's murder to murder him in turn; and Bond's pursuit of Quantum is (despite his repeated denials) essentially incidental to his need to punish those who deprived him of the woman for whose love he had been willing to sacrifice his career as a spy.

In short, this film refuses us any of the familiar pleasures of a Bond movie precisely because its protagonist is incapable of recognizing, let alone exploiting, any of those familiar pleasures; it pushes the choppy editing of its action sequences beyond our capacity to take any satisfaction in overcoming the challenge they pose to our senses in order to dramatize the extent to which Bond himself is struggling to retain his own capacity to find satisfaction in the world to which he finds himself consigned, and in particular to find sense or meaning in the extreme demands it makes upon him as secret agent. When those moments of his life (moments in which his life as such is at stake and from which that life—together with its compensatory pleasures—derives its meaning) teeter on the edge of complete incoherence, then so too does his sense of who he is, and of what it means to be James Bond, 007.

For this reason, one might say that *Quantum of Solace* both is, and is not, a sequel to *Casino Royale*. To be sure, the second film picks up immediately where the first left off—for the opening car chase occurs as Bond is trying to get the injured Mr White into MI6 hands despite the best efforts of his Quantum bodyguards—and everything else that ensues follows from the situation established in the earlier film. But precisely because it also picks up from Bond's psychological state at the end of the first film, there is a sense in which no progress is made in the second—in which nothing happens to Bond, in which time stands still for him, despite the flurry of barely-intelligible and utterly unsatisfying events into which he throws himself. For the world of *Quantum of Solace* is the world as Bond sees it, in the light of his brutalizing loss of Vesper: and that is an emotionally arid place, irrigated solely by the primitive desire for vengeance, in which the very idea of moving on from the events of the first film makes precisely no sense to its protagonist, until he manages either to slake or to get beyond that primordial thirst.

In order to dramatize this interior psychological aridity and stasis, *Quantum of Solace* deliberately presents itself as operating on a level that transcends or cuts across that of exhilarating events: what I variously called earlier (when noting its centrality to the Quiller novels and its increasing encroachment upon the Bourne films) the mythological, the melodramatic, or the metaphysical. This film first intimates its particular allegiance with the melodramatic by intercutting Bond's pursuit of the Quantum agent in Siena with the Palio—an archaic ceremony involving elaborate costumes and music, and activating deeply-entrenched feelings of regional loyalty, from which that city stills draw much of its contemporary vitality. But it declares that allegiance most explicitly by staging one of its key episodes in an opera house, during a performance of Puccini's *Tosca* (a 'melodrama' being in literal terms 'a play with songs and music'). For this particular lyric drama (about a woman forced to make a life-or-death choice between the two men she loves, betrayed by those who force the choice upon her, and ultimately compelled to kill herself as a result) allows the film to re-present Vesper's desperate situation (presented in essentially realistic terms in *Casino Royale*) in the terms of myth, as operatically archetypical of the—typically male—world's lethal refusal to acknowledge either love in general or the passionate speech and song of women in particular. It thereby invites us to register its own aspiration to find a cinematic equivalent to opera's conjoining of the individual and the elemental, one in which to explore the fate of a man whose refusal to cede to the woman he loved a voice in her own history proved death-dealing for her. *Quantum of Solace* is a melodrama that presents James Bond as someone whose previous failure to acknowledge Vesper has resulted in his becoming an unknown man—unknown to himself and so unknowable by others, reduced to a state of utter disorientation, lost not so much in a dark wood as in a desert.

In keeping with this mythic aspiration, the film organizes its narrative in terms of the four elements—the basic building blocks of existence: Earth (the marble quarry and the Siennese streets and rooftops), Water (the boat chase in Haiti), Air (the aerial duel in Bolivia), and Fire (the apocalyptic conflagration at 'La Perla de las Dunas'). And the film's coda both completes and revises this canonical metaphysical itinerary by invoking Ice—at once a form of aridity and its cure. For its concluding sequence is set in the frozen Russian wastes, where Bond at last finds Vesper's supposedly kidnapped lover (who it has been revealed was really operating with Quantum all along) and has the chance to kill him; but he refrains from so doing, and is welcomed back into his official MI6 existence by M, in an exchange that effectively repeats the one at the end of *Casino Royale*, and concludes with Bond claiming that he never really left. This claim, and the repetition of which it forms part, confirm the intuition that, by the end of *Quantum of Solace*, Bond has at best managed to return to the point at which he thought he had arrived at the end of *Casino Royale*—the point at which he can genuinely begin to live in accordance with the name to which he there lays claim. In one sense, therefore, *Quantum of Solace* has been no more than a long diversion or digression—more exactly, a dream-like or nightmarish running on the spot, in which frenetic activity in a forbiddingly hostile world results in no forward progress whatever. But in another sense, it has thwarted Bond's and our usual diet of active satisfactions in favour of an unprecedented attention to his interior landscape, and to the operatic struggle going on within it—his struggle to survive subjection to a self-consuming despair whose aridity can be alleviated only by the recognition that what he has for so long imagined would quench his thirst is in fact precisely what generates it.

Ice, then, holds the prospect of melting: but the film does not present us with reason to think that it will melt any time soon. And this, I think, is connected with the fact that Bond's way of winning through to the recognition that his desire for revenge is what has brought into being the landscape in which he suffers is a profoundly nihilistic one. After the destruction of 'La Perla de las Dunas', he tells Camille: 'I don't think the dead care about vengeance'—a remark which recalls his treatment of his old friend Mathis' corpse in La Paz: Bond tosses it into a dumpster, and when Camille protests, tells her that 'he wouldn't care'. Taken together, these remarks suggest that his reason for forsaking vengeance is that the dead, being utterly annihilated, can have no concerns about the world they left behind, and hence cannot be either propitiated or compensated by any vengeance enacted within it. In other words, Bond's recovery from the paralysis of vengeance depends upon a perception of death as being utterly or absolutely the end, and hence upon a perception of Vesper as utterly lost to him, absolutely absent—not only now, but for the whole of the rest of his life. One might be forgiven for thinking that any such way of overcoming grief will leave more than a few splinters of ice in the mourner's soul.

The Gamblers of Roulettenburg

Sartrean Scenes II
(Part One, Chapter One)

Although he'd seen the stone jutting up from the path, just where its verge
had begun to crumble into the valley below, and had fully intended to pass
carefully to one side of it, he found himself watching, horror-struck, as his
left foot landed squarely on its weather-beaten surface; his ankle buckled,
and the whole weight of his unbalanced body slowly, inexorably pulled him
closer to the edge, where the worn-away soil offered no purchase, serving
only to accelerate his graceless tumble into the airy emptiness; and as he gave
himself over to the world's sudden, unprecedented but absolute refusal of
support or resistance with a kind of relief, he heard a dim, distant ringing, its
volume increasing until it cut through the wind's whistling in his ears and he
reached blindly to silence the alarm clock on the table beside his bed.

Dream-imagery and memory battled for supremacy, merging and disen-
gaging with equal fluidity as he gradually recalled himself to his surround-
ings. This wasn't the crude cot in the climbing hut in which he had passed
the hot summer night after his Pyrenean climb, the climb that had given
him that exhilarating moment when, ensconced on a rock and master of all
he could survey, including the vertiginous, rail-less final passage he had just
traversed, he had written five crucial paragraphs for the opening chapter of
his book; this was the warm and welcoming double-bed into which he
had gratefully fallen after last night's disastrous visit to the casino. Now the
dream-stone and its dream-abyss dissolved into a hallucinatorily-sharp recollection of the multi-spoked, parti-coloured wheel around which the ball
clattered and bumped contrarily until settling into the slot whose number
dictated the re-gathering of all the table's scattered chips into the croupier's

grasp. Had he really staked the remainder of this month's cigarette money on red—despite the sincerity of his resolution to abstain from the circles within which any such prudent abstemiousness could only appear utterly alien to the real joy of life, to any genuinely vital individual existence? He no more recognized himself in the man who strove to maintain a façade of indifference as his chips were swept away than that man had recognized himself in his recollection of that earlier resolution.

As his eyes adjusted to the crepuscular light of the room, he saw the outline of his desk gradually sharpen, until the untidy pile of manuscript—abandoned much earlier the previous evening—presented its irregular, insistent profile. Almost before he realized it, he had turned away from this prospect, and fixed his gaze instead on the book he'd left next to the alarm clock, resting on top of his copy of *The Trial*. He reached across to pick it up: a volume of Dostoevsky's letters, a selection from the 1860s, the decade when his writing really began to find its ungrounded ground, its necessary imbalance and torsion, its extremity; when his intermittent but abysmal addiction to gambling was at its height; and when the death of his first wife left him free to love and even to marry again. He began to read.

Anna Grigorevna's pencils, much less sharp now after their second dictating session of the day, lay carefully aligned on top of her new portfolio; the pile of manuscript—small, but getting bigger with every October day—lay between them on the table, next to the tea-cups and other crockery. It really seemed as if they were going to meet their deadline: a new novel delivered to that criminal Stellovsky by 1st November, or else his publishing firm would have the rights to everything the author produced over the next nine years without payment of any kind. She still couldn't quite believe that her employer had agreed to this—had been willing to risk not only his livelihood but his freedom as an artist on this one roll of the dice, on his ability to conjure words out of thin air, so many words in so short a time. But then again, the agreement had been made during one of his short breaks from his frenzied tours of the gaming rooms of Europe, not long after Maria Dmitrievna's death, and in the midst of his obsessive, self-lacerating, and unavailing pursuit of Polina Suslova (that demon); so perhaps it had presented itself as just one more doomed, poetic gamble . . .

Between hasty gulps and bites, he talks of a new idea he'd had for a story—neither the briefly deferred final instalments of the murder mystery whose ferociously unforeseeable unfolding was gripping all Russia, nor the slimmer, darkly satirical episodes of expatriate life in Roulettenburg on which they were currently working. This third tale, he says, concerned a man grown old before his time, sick and debt-ridden, gloomy, suspicious; a writer who never ceased to torment himself over his persistent failure to realize his ideas in the forms of which he dreamed. At this critical point in his life, he continues, the writer meets a young girl—roughly of Anna's age, but in fact called Anya, who was gentle, wise and kind, tactful but bubbling over with life. Naturally, he says, this writer falls in love with Anya, and is tormented by whether she could possibly return his affection, and whether even if she did, it would involve her in a terrible sacrifice. Would she, Anna, consider it psychologically plausible for such a young girl to fall in love with such an elderly, troubled man?

Anna can see immediately the answer she should give, the answer that would express the full emotional force of her own longings: it hovers as an absolutely desirable future, with nothing standing between her and its realization in words, hence thereby in deeds and their consequences. She hesitates. If she is right to assume that her employer's imagined writer shadows his creator, then what is that creator declaring to her through the protagonist of the tale she is currently transcribing from his dictation—the young, cultivated and highly intelligent, frustrated and embittered noble-man named (not Fyodor Mikhailovich but) Aleksey Ivanovich, the narrator of events at Roulettenburg, and a man who declares from the outset that his destiny will be affected radically and definitively by roulette? She looks at her employer: the pupil of his right eye was now no longer dilated (the lingering aftermath of one of his epileptic attacks), and she could see the strikingly deep brown of both irises. She speaks.

Although the gambler referred to in Dostoevsky's tale of that title is Aleksey Ivanovich, currently tutor in the Zagoryansky household in Roulettenburg, in another sense, every central character in *The Gambler* is a gambler.[1] General Zagoryansky is gambling that his mother, Antonida Vasilevna Taravesicheva (known as 'Grandmother'), will die soon enough for him to pay off his debts to the Marquis de Grieux and still have enough left over to tempt the

---

[1] *Notes from Underground* and *The Gambler*, trans. J. Kentish (Oxford: Oxford University Press, 1991)—hereafter G.

gold-digging Mlle Blanche de Cominges to marry him; de Grieux is also gambling that Polina Aleksandrovna, the general's step-daughter and so someone who will also benefit from his mother's bequests, will accept his suit; Polina is gambling that Aleksey will not only make enough money in the gaming rooms for both of them to secure their independence, but will also recognize the reality of her love for him before his embittered frustrations with life in general, and with her unwillingness to accept his manically self-abasing expressions of devotion in particular, manage to destroy it altogether; and when Grandmother finally turns up in Roulettenburg, so full of life that everyone immediately realizes that all bets on her demise are off, she is herself quickly overtaken by the compulsion to gamble, to the point at which she barely escapes back to her Russian estate with enough money to rebuild the church which will thereby embody her penitence.

All of these people are gamblers, then; but their group portrait reveals various sub-categories or types that complicate the initial family resemblance, and that help contextualize or condition the character in the tale who epitomizes its titular theme—Aleksey. To begin with, the Russian gamblers differ from their French confrères, in that whereas de Grieux and de Co-minges gamble purely in order to maximize their financial gains and in strict accordance with their best estimate of the odds (how long, after all, can a seventy-five-year-old woman go on living?), the General, Polina, and Alek-sey do so in the first instance for love, and ultimately for no reason at all beyond their willingness to subject themselves to what Aleksey (along with their creator) thinks of as the poetry of life—the capacity of the human soul to become carried away by feeling, by the exhilarating prospect of challenging or insulting fate, and by the obstinate refusal to allow calculation or dispiriting experience to control their impulses. In this respect, Grandmother epitomizes the Russian difference: far and away the most humane, kind-hearted, and vital character in the tale, she nevertheless succumbs even more thoroughly than her relatives and retainers to the lure of the idea of miraculous and effortless enrichment, of the world's utter subordination to her imperious will.

Before he in turn succumbs to a version of this frenzy, Aleksey offers other ways of distinguishing sub-categories of gambler. He identifies two modes of gambling, the gentlemanly and the plebeian: the nobility are committed to viewing the game as a species of entertainment, one in which winning and losing are of equally little concern; the rabble not only declare their obsessive desire to win, but are willing to bend and even blatantly break the rules in order to do so, in ways ranging from attempting to earn commission by advising other players to claiming another's winning by identifying their stake as their own. He also distinguishes between those who calculate and those who intuit—between gamblers who observe runs of results and extrapolate patterns and rules in accordance with which they go on to bet, and gamblers who give themselves up to the momentary flow of experience, allowing their impulses to govern their actions.

It is plain from an early stage that Aleksey is not merely an instinctively Russian gambler, but also an instinctively plebeian and intuitive one: as might be expected from someone of his uncertain social status (of noble origins, but occupying a servile role in the general's household), he despises the aristocratic effort to pretend that gaming is a merely superficial pastime, and he has an admiring fascination for the honesty with which the various Poles in Roulettenburg throw all social convention to the wind in their pursuit of success at the tables. At the same time, he knows that self-interest would be far better served by at least the attempt to control his impulses, to rely on prudential calculation, and to treat the turns of the wheel as no more than an amusement; to do otherwise is to guarantee the frustration of his deepest desires and the baulking of his will—and yet, he still finds himself doing so. In other words, part of his Russianness finds expression in his feeling compelled to bring it about that the world will master and subvert his will precisely by devoting himself to a form of activity that he fantasizes as a means of imposing his will on that world. To live poetically is, he knows, ultimately a matter of living masochistically: it is to construct, maintain, and inhabit a universe of self-abasement.

This connection between gambling and sadomasochism is confirmed by a further, crucially determining aspect of Aleksey's situation—his relationship with Polina. Aleksey portrays her as an imperious mistress, unstable in her moods but unwavering in her refusal simply to declare her love for him, and her resolution to make him suffer in any way open to her; but his unreliably embittered narration does not prevent us from seeing that the primary obstacle to her declaring and enacting her love for Aleksey is in fact his way of declaring and enacting his love for her. He repeatedly declares his suspicion that she is either in love with, or at least willing to accept, de Grieux; he offends her pride and dignity by persistently assuming that his acquisition of money is a condition she requires if they are to be together; and he insists on presenting his feelings for her as if they required self-abasement on his part—thereby implying that the form taken by her love for him was one of haughty dominance, a refusal of equality or mutually-relinquished auton-omy, even a desire for his destruction. He thereby incites her to inhabit exactly that role in their relationship, and thus at once validates his self-abasing impulses and confirms his worst fears about Polina and about his destiny in the world.

This gives the centrality of gambling in the working-out of their relation-ship a very particular colouring or mood. For although Polina is the one who asks him to gamble for her, thereby introducing him to the gaming rooms that will bring about his downfall, she does so not only because she cannot resist de Grieux's advances without some money of her own, but primarily because she has been incensed by Aleksey's way of declaring his love for her:

'The last time we were on the Schlangenberg you told me you were prepared, as soon as I said the word, to throw yourself down head first, and I should think it's a thousand-foot drop there. Some day I shall say the word, simply in order to see how you settle your debts, and you can be quite sure I'll stick to my word. I loathe you, precisely because I've let you get away with so much, and I loathe you even more because I need you . . . '

And now once again I asked myself the question: do I love her? And once more I could not answer, that is to say, again, for the hundredth time, I answered that I hated her. Yes, I found her detestable. There were moments (whenever we concluded a conversation, as a matter of fact), when I would have given half my life to strangle her. I swear, if it had been possible to plunge a sharp knife slowly into her bosom, I believe I would have grabbed the chance with delight. And yet, I swear by all that is sacred that if on that fashionable peak of the Schlangenberg she really were to say to me 'throw yourself over', I would do so immediately, and even with pleasure. (G, 134–5)

Polina's demand that Aleksey win money for her by gambling is the word that she actually says in place of the word that he imagines her saying, the word that she promises that she will say some time soon, precisely because of the implication carried by his readiness to tell her that he can imagine her saying it—can imagine her testing the nature of his love, and so declaring the form of her own, by telling him to throw himself off the Schlangenberg. In their private world, articulated from the outset by Aleksey's fevered conjuration of it in terms that Polina can find no way to contradict, to engage in gambling is a merely provisional substitute for, a pale imitation of, actually enacting the fantasy that most deeply structures their relationship—that of casting oneself into an abyss at another's command, a command that at once comes from without and yet is explicitly invited or incited, brought into being, by the one to whom it applies: it is, in other words, to embrace the experience of vertigo, and thereby the horrified, horrifying perception of oneself as capable (not merely of not successfully resisting but) of embracing the world-given but not world-determined opportunity for self-destruction. For Aleksey, this is the meaning of his love, and so the meaning of his life as such; the underlying significance of existence declares itself under the sign of gambling as a modality of vertigo.

The gambler who wrote *The Gambler* was not averse to interpreting his own compulsion in terms of the categories used by Aleksey Ivanovich. Here, for example, is a passage from Fyodor Mikhailovich's letter to Varvara Dmitrievan Konstant, 20th August 1863:

There are several hundred gambling here, and, to be honest with you, only two of them really know what they're doing. They all lose heavily because they don't know how to gamble. There was a Frenchwoman and an English lord. They knew how to play . . . Please don't think that I'm bragging about the fact that I didn't lose in saying that I know the secret of not losing, but winning. I really do know the secret. It's very stupid and simple and amounts to ceaseless self-control at all stages of the game and not getting excited. That's all there is to it. That way you can't lose and are bound to win. But that's not the point. The point is whether, once you know the secret, you are capable of exploiting it.

On the one hand, nationality, nobility, and calculation combine to articulate the simple secret of successful gambling—ceaseless self-control, approaching the business as entertainment, and avoiding subjection to one's impulses. On the other hand, between the absolute guarantee of success and its realization, there stands the problem of exploiting one's knowledge of the secret—the ineliminable gap between thought and actuality, intention and action. And a passage from a letter to his brother, 8th September 1863, reveals something of what it is like to inhabit that gap:

You write to ask how I could possibly lose absolutely everything while travelling with someone I love. Misha, my friend, in Wiesbaden I invented a system, actually tried it out, and immediately won 1,000 francs. The next day I got excited and departed from the system and immediately lost. In the evening I returned to the strict letter of the system again and soon won 3,000 francs again without difficulty.

Tell me, after such an experience, how could I not get carried away and believe that if I followed my system strictly I should be sure to win? . . . [T]o cap it all I arrived in Baden, went to the tables, and *within a quarter of an hour* I won 600 francs. This whetted my appetite. Suddenly I started to lose, couldn't control myself and lost everything. After that I wrote to you from Baden, took my *last* money, and went to play. Starting with 4 napoleons I won 35 napoleons in half an hour. I was carried away by this unusual good fortune and I risked all 35 napoleons and lost them all. I had 6 napoleons d'or left to pay the landlady and for the journey. In Geneva I pawned my watch.

Here, Fyodor first recognizes that faith in a system—in an attitude of calculation, self-control, and self-distancing—is not the solution to the problem but rather a mode of being carried away: to think that one is sure to win if one acts in accordance with calculations that have been successful in the past is to confuse induction with deduction, to conflate a potentially accidental conjunction with a necessary connection, and to foreclose the future in all its openness. But failure is no less capable of carrying this gambler away than success: starting to lose is just as likely to make him throw caution to the winds as is starting to win. In other words, whatever one's experience, being carried away is the fundamental structure of the experience of gambling. This is underlined when Fyodor claims that being carried away by success was inevitable: since he has no reason to restrict this self-exculpatory moral to contexts of success, his defence amounts to a presentation of himself qua gambler as destined to be carried away, as a mere vehicle of forces beyond his control. What, then, of his earlier claim that the secret of gambling is ceaseless self-control? One response would be to resolve the apparent contradiction by discarding one of the contradict-ory claims—either by denying that being carried away is inevitable, or by denying that self-control is a real option for this (for any?) gambler. Another response would be to say that the experience of gambling is self-contradictory—that inhabiting it is a matter of simultaneously arrogating freedom, even thinking of the gaming room as an arena for its ultimate expression, and losing it. The gambler is both utterly convinced of his capacity for control (control of himself, and control of the world's vicissi-tudes, as exemplified by the fall of the cards or the trajectory of the ball), and utterly convinced of its absence: it is a vision of human existence as simultaneously omnipotent and impotent, or at least as oscillating endlessly between mastery and enslavement. It is a question of freedom.

When Jean-Paul Sartre comes to engage with these matters in the first chapter of *Being and Nothingness*, he does so by working towards the conclusion that freedom is at issue not just when that is the explicit object of our questioning, but whenever we pose a question about anything—that every question is a question of freedom; and once this theme is broached, it is precisely the notions of gambling and vertigo that turn out to be determinative for his thinking. But before confronting his way with these concepts, we must first grasp his way of preparing the ground for their appearance.

Sartre aims to transcend Heidegger's perspective on Being and human being by negating his starting point from within. Well aware that Heidegger's own enquiry finds its point of origin for properly posing the question of being by interrogating the nature of questioning as such, and thereby the nature of the being who questions, Sartre repeats that reflexive move in his own way. He begins by asking whether there is any mode of human conduct that might illuminate the general relation of human beings to the world; then he points out that in so doing, he adopts a questioning stance to the world; and then he asks himself whether this interrogative mode of conduct might not be the illuminating instance he seeks.

Reflecting on the nature of his questioning stance, he claims that it is conditioned by a threefold negation: the questioner makes manifest his state of non-knowing, he presupposes the possibility that the world will not provide the mode of conduct he seeks (since his question might equally well receive a negative as a positive answer), and he further presupposes that insofar as the world provides a positive answer, it must do so in the form of a limitation ('it is thus and not otherwise'). But these conditions are not specific to the particular question Sartre himself is posing: the ignorance of the questioner, and the simultaneous possibility of a positive and negative answer to the question posed, are presuppositions of questioning as such (whether pre-theoretical in nature, or part of a highly theoretical scientific enterprise). Hence, for Sartre, 'the permanent possibility of non-being, outside us and within, conditions our questions about being' (BN, 5).

Next, he argues that we should view this non-being as an element of reality, not merely an effect manifest in the realm of judgement alone (as if purely a result of comparing the result expected with the result obtained). Questioning may, after all, be a pre-judicative attitude: when my car engine refuses to work, I may expect something to have gone amiss with its carburettor, but this is typically not so much an explicit judgement about the carburettor as a mode of disclosure that makes it available for such judgements (for example, as being empty). And when I expect to see Pierre in the cafe, and he is not there, this is a positive intuition of absence—not the registration of all that is there in the cafe to be apprehended, supplemented by a judgement that my expectation has not been met: phenomenologically speaking, I apprehend his not being there as part of my apprehension of the cafe, hence of the world I inhabit. As Sartre puts it, the cafe as a whole appears as the ground of an expected figure; all of its constituent objects and people are apprehended primarily as the background for his appearance, more specifically as the ground for his non-appearance: his absence haunts the cafe in a doubly negating or nihilating way (he is not there, and the cafe appears as nothing more than the ground of that absence).

Nevertheless, the reality of non-being must be understood as a function of the presence of human beings in the world that exists independently of them: it may not be reducible to a function of judgement, but it is there at all only because of the way human beings can relate to that world—the way exemplified in questioning. More specifically, it presupposes the question-er's capacity to step back from that world, his refusal to be carried along by or away with the wholly determinate network of cause and effect.

[F]rom the very fact that we presume that an Existent can always be revealed as *nothing*, every question presupposes that we realize a nihilating withdrawal in relation to the given, which becomes a simple *presentation*, fluctuating between Being and Nothingness.

It is essential therefore that the questioner has the permanent possibility of dissociating himself from the causal series which constitutes being and which can produce only being. If we admitted that the question is determined in the ques-tioner by universal determinism, the question would thereby become unintelligible and even inconceivable . . . [I]nsofar as the questioner must be able to effect in relation to the questioned a kind of nihilating withdrawal, he is not subject to the causal order of the world; he detaches himself from Being . . . This disengagement is then by definition a human process. Man presents himself at least in this instance as a being who causes Nothingness to arise in the world, inasmuch as he himself is affected with non-being to this end. (BN, 23)

Since questioning involves disclosing the possible non-being of an existent, and disclosing oneself as both not-knowing and capable of coming to know (hence, capable of being other than one presently is), it presupposes the freedom of the questioner; and it thereby raises the possibility that the human being's responsibility for the arising of nothingness in the world (which would otherwise constitute a plenum, a wholly self-determining and hence self-sufficient totality) is not separable from its responsibility as such—its relating to itself as responsible or accountable for what it thinks, says, and does. In other words, it invites us to enquire into the possibility that, if nothingness arises out of human being, it is because human being as such is possessed of freedom—more precisely, that freedom is another way of characterizing human being's capacity to secrete nothingness. What, then, is human freedom if it is through it that nothingness comes into the world? And in what mode of consciousness is the nothingness of freedom most clearly manifest?

Once again, Sartre appropriates and alters Heidegger's answer to this question, by refracting the Kierkegaardian conception of angst or anguish through the prism of vertigo and gambling, understood as disclosing the human being's nihilating relation to his future and to his past respectively. In vertigo, I am afraid not of falling over the precipice but of throwing myself over: the angst is generated not by the fear that external circumstances (a crumbling path, a jutting stone) might cause me to stumble, but rather by the fear that my strategies for avoiding such dangerous features of the environment might not be realized—that there is no necessity that they be transformed from possibilities to actualities. This is because whether they are implemented or not ultimately depends on me, and I am not in this respect functioning as a cause that determines its effects: for as we have already seen, to think of oneself in such terms is to reduce oneself to the status of a causal link in the plenum of nature, and thereby to abolish oneself as human. Even the manifest dangers of the precipice, and my horror at the fate it promises, do not determine my future conduct.

Note that Sartre's claim here is not that our freedom is absolute, in the sense of being infinite or unconditioned; it is finite freedom, hence a freedom that is necessarily conditioned (by external and internal influences alike). The crucial point is that those conditions are not themselves absolutely determinant—they are not causes in relation to which our thoughts and deeds are mere effects; and insofar as there is the smallest gap or interval between conditions and outcome, then that outcome must be our responsibility, ours to own or disown. Even if the nothingness between condition and outcome is infinitesimally small, it renders our freedom ineliminable and in that sense (and only in that sense) absolute.

What vertigo reveals is that nothing can compel me either to pursue or to avoid any given form of conduct in the future; for I am not the self that I will be, the self that will either take or not take the relevant course of action (I am separated from that self by time, and nothing in me or my world can entirely close that gap by determining what I will do or be). And yet the self that I will be is nevertheless the self that I am—otherwise its possible fate would not induce horror in me, would not be horror over *my* fate. 'Thus the self which I am depends on the self which I am not yet to the exact extent that the self which I am not yet does not depend on the self which I am' (BN, 32). Nothingness thereby slips into the heart of my relation to my (future) self: I am not the self that I will nevertheless be.

If vertigo discloses our anguish over the future, gambling discloses our anguish over the past. More precisely, this mode of anguish manifests itself in the experience of a gambler who, having made a sincere decision not to gamble any more, feels all his resolution melting away as he approaches the gaming table. His resolution both is and is not his: he realizes that it is a resolution that he and no other actually made; but if it is to be effective now, it must in effect be remade by him now, must be assented to anew by the self he now is, the self whose assent or dissent is not determined by the self he was. Seen now, not gambling is no more than a possibility, one forbidden by his previous resolution, but one that is not thereby necessarily beyond realization; he realizes that nothing—certainly nothing he resolved in the past—prevents him from gambling. He both is and is not the self that he was.

Putting together the disclosures of vertigo and akratic gambling, Sartre concludes that 'consciousness confronts its past and its future as facing a self which it is in the mode of not being' (BN, 34). Between motive and action lies nothingness, non-identity—freedom is the transcendence of immanent causal determination. But it would falsify his vision to think of gambling and vertigo as each revealing a different portion or component of the self's non-identity, as if its relation to its past and to its future were two entirely separable aspects of its structure. For if that were so, one would be forced to view the nothingness that relates the self to itself in both directions as if it were itself decomposable into separate portions or components, which would amount to treating that nothingness as if it were something (something specific, with particular parts or structures). Sartre is better understood as inviting us to regard vertigo and gambling as internally related to one another by negation, as non-identical in just the way that the selfhood they disclose is non-identical. What might this mean?

On the face of it, the akratic gambler's experience of selfhood and that of the sufferer from vertigo are simply opposed to one another. Not only does one concern the present self's relation to its future and the other its relation to its past; the future-oriented experience concerns the self's capacity to overcome its physical vulnerability to the causal nexus it inhabits by asserting its own projects, whereas the past-oriented experience concerns the self's capacity to protect itself against psychic and social damage by that means. But the more closely we examine the details of these particular experiences, the less obvious their distinctness becomes. The experience of vertigo is, after all, a kind of gambling: it registers the anguish of the fact that one's most deeply-rooted instincts of self-preservation might not be enough to protect oneself against oneself, against finding oneself compelled to risk absolutely everything. And the akratic gambler experiences a kind of vertigo: he finds himself on the edge of a precipice of risk, and discovers that what is most likely to impel him over it to his utter destruction is not external factors and forces but himself. In both experiences, then, a ruinous outcome is positively courted by the one whom it will destroy: both amount to revelations of the self as not only related to that which it is not, but as related to its own annihilation (thereby returning Sartre's analysis of angst to its Heideggerian origins, in which human mortality as such turns out to be the most fitting object of anguish).

More specifically, the experience of vertigo as Sartre describes it has a peculiarly dialectical structure. It begins with the perception of features of the environment as dangerous because they function as elements in a deterministic causal system whose effects on the self, once activated, are inexorable (once I step onto the crumbling verge, the laws of physics will propel me into the abyss), and so reveal me to myself as a thing—as one more element in that system, hence the mere vehicle or transmitter of forces imposed on me from without. It is in reaction to that self-perception that I throw all of my psychological strength into the project of acting so as to obviate these dangers; but in so doing, I simply reveal that this psychic counter-thrust is not in fact equal to the task I envisage for it, because it is not truly opposed to the causal thrust it aspires to counter—it is not a kind of cause, and hence not a counter-cause but rather an upsurge of nothingness in the causal plenum that at once disrupts that causal regime and yet leaves itself ungrounded, because nothing (the nothingness that it is) entails that our project will be successfully implemented. And we only recover from that anguished self-perception (if we do) when we realize that, if nothing entails that we will avoid the abyss, equally nothing entails that we will succumb to the impulse to embrace it. Hence, what the experience of vertigo reveals is that we are (not) things, that we are things in the mode of not being things. That is, it discloses us to ourselves as undeniably and indissolubly related to the domain of thinghood, as essentially physical beings in a physical world, but as related to that world by negation, negatingly: we exist as not-merely-physical, not as physical beings who are in addition psychological beings (as if consciousness were another, supplementary kind of substance).

What, then, of the akratic gambler? He approaches the gambling table convinced that his earlier resolution to stop gambling renders him immune to its present temptations; and he discovers that, insofar as he relates to that resolution as something he has done, as something past, it offers no guarantee whatever that he will avoid gambling. In other words, he discloses his previous projects as guaranteeing nothing about his present behaviour: he cannot relate to himself as if his motives were a kind of determining cause, a way of ensuring how things will be with him—as if his consciousness were another kind of substance possessed of causal powers. And he will only recover from the anguish of this self-perception (if he does) when he realizes that, if his prior resolution offers no magic barrier to gambling, then his currently-revived temptation to gamble once more has no greater determinative power; for either motive to bring about the action that satisfies them, he must identify himself with it and thereby make it the ungrounded ground of his conduct. The gambler thus arrives at a perception of himself as not a cause, and so as not a (psychological) substance; we are undeniably and indissolubly related to the domain of consciousness, but we are related to it by negation, negatingly; the nothingness that we are intervenes between us and our psyches, rendering us non-identical with the array of desires, motives, and resolutions that we nevertheless are, hence as not-merely-our-consciousness.

On the one hand, then, the details of the two cases reveal further differences in the aspects of the self's non-identity that vertigo and gambling disclose: the former is as much about the self's non-identity with its body as with its future self, and the latter is as much about the self's non-identity with its mind as with its past self. On the other hand, both reveal exactly the same tendency on the part of those who undergo them—that of regarding themselves as akin to entities or substances, as a kind of thing (whether physical or mental); and the motive for such misinterpretation also appears to be the same in each case—namely, that of disowning one's responsibility for oneself, one's accountability for one's thoughts, words, and deeds, by imagining that one's efficacy as embodied consciousness is a matter of activating or directing a species of causal power that guarantees the realization of its effect. The anguish of freedom, so understood, is the anguish of discovering that it exists at all only if it exists as the nullity or nothingness that relates apprehension or motivation to action, in the non-identity of cause and effect in the domain of human reality.

The gambler who wrote *The Gambler* is explicitly referred to at this precise point in Sartre's portrayal of his akratic gambler, quite as if Fyodor Mikhailovich was its original; and this reference is designed to demonstrate the unreality of philosophical accounts of such akrasia in terms of a conflict between the forces of reason and the passions, as if the self were a field of psychological physics:

In reality—the letters of Dostoevsky bear witness to this—there is nothing which resembles an inner *debate* as if we had to weigh motives and incentives before deciding. The earlier resolution of 'not playing anymore' is always *there*, and in the majority of cases the gambler when in the presence of the gaming table, turns toward it as if to ask for help; for he does not wish to play, or rather having taken his resolution the day before, he thinks of himself still as not wishing to play anymore; he believes in the effectiveness of this resolution. But what he apprehends then in anguish is precisely the total inefficacy of the past resolution. It is there doubtless but fixed, ineffectual, surpassed by the very fact that I am conscious *of* it. (BN, 32–3)

This may be an accurate articulation of some portion of Dostoevsky's letters, but it is highly partial in its identification of the persistence of his gambling compulsion as manifesting a doomed desire on his part to have his past resolutions determine his current conduct. There is at least equal textual justification for understanding Dostoevsky's gambling as expressing his desire to control the future, and to be capable of risking everything in order to do so; as we have seen, on the one hand, he distinguishes between a good and a bad way of gambling (associating himself with the successful way, one which combines calculation with self-control), and on the other, he positively embraces the possibility of ruin that gambling involves, precisely because running that risk shows both the strength of his will, and the superficiality of world views that identify the essence of the human with the realm of prudential reason. But this latter motive, in which the motif of vertigo (understood as the self's horror at its compulsion to self-destruction) is surely implicit, runs exactly contrary to the aspiration Sartre identifies with gambling taken on its own—that of sloughing off present responsibility by regarding past resolutions as removing any room for it. In other words, Dostoevsky sees in gambling a desire for mastery (of the world, the future, and the self) rather than a desire for self-enslavement.

What might Sartre have thought if, instead of guiding his analysis by the gambler's letters, he had taken his bearings from *The Gambler*—itself a text that might be described as comprising letters of Dostoevsky, certainly as one containing an alter ego of his (however much he may be related to him by alterity rather than repetition, say by negation, by the nothingness that inserts itself between creator and character)? In Aleksey Ivanovich's life, gambling is never something he resolves to eschew, hence never something in relation to which he might either renew such a resolution, or regard it as possessing magical determinative powers over his present actions. It is rather something he cannot disentangle from his relationship to Polina—she first directs him towards the gaming tables for her own purposes; he later returns to them when she comes to his room, claiming that the money he will win is required to ensure their joint happiness, but in reality using the activity to avoid the invitation implicit in her scandalous overnight stay; and even at the conclusion of the tale, he envisages returning to those tables primarily 'in order to let Polina know that I can still be a man' (G, 274).

The significance of this contextualization of his gambling is encapsulated in the relation that author and characters see between Aleksey's gambling and his promise to throw himself off the Schlangenberg if Polina asked him to: this is where Sartre's companion concept of vertigo finds its inverted or negated place in the life of his gambler's gambler. Aleksey's gradual transformation into a gambler is the way in which he realizes that promise, the way in which he tries to show himself worthy of her love, and hence the way in which he understands what it means to be a worthwhile human being. His life becomes a matter of striving to be true to his past expression of the horrifying compulsion to throw himself into the void; the experience of vertigo lies in his past, invoked as part of a resolution to which he then strives to be true, precisely by renewing it (even if in transfigured form) rather than by imagining its effect to control his future merely because he invoked it in the past. His future is rather lived out under the sign of gambling, as fundamentally open or undetermined, as an arena in which everything is at stake, always vulnerable to accident or happenstance and yet potentially capable of being mastered. It is quite as if the fictional gambler imagined by the real-life gambler that Sartre re-imagines amounts to a systematic negation of the polarities and oppositions that characterize what the philosopher wanted to make of this gambler's creator.

But I want to conclude by pointing out that, in one respect at least, Sartre's re-conception of the gambler's gambler serves to bring out an important aspect of Fyodor's and Aleksey's self-understanding that might otherwise be passed over. For, having approached the nullity of human freedom through the prism of vertigo and gambling, Sartre then conjoins or interweaves their implications by invoking a particularly pertinent example of a third kind of human activity—'the act of working at this book' (BN, 36):

In the act of tracing the letters which I am writing, the whole sentence, still unachieved, is revealed as a passive exigency to be achieved. It is the very meaning of the letters which I form, and its appeal is not put into question, precisely because I cannot write the words without transcending them towards the sentence and because I discover it as the necessary condition for the meaning of the words which I am writing . . . [T]he sentence which I write is the meaning of the letters which I trace, but the whole work which I wish to produce is the meaning of the sentence. And this work is a possibility in connection with which I can feel anguish; it is truly my possibility, and I do not know whether I will continue it tomorrow; tomorrow in relation to my freedom can exercise its nihilating power. But that anguish implies the apprehension of the work as such as *my* possibility. I must place myself directly opposite it and realize my relation to it . . . On the one hand . . . I have been 'wanting to write this book', I have conceived it, I have believed that it would be interesting to write it, and I have constituted myself in such a way that it is not possible to *understand me* without taking into account the fact that this book had been my essential possibility. On the other hand . . . *nothing*, not even what I have been, can compel me to write it [and] the permanent possibility of abandoning the book is the very condition of the possibility of writing it. (BN, 36–7)

This invocation of Sartre's letters (the ones constituting the words we are currently reading) can hardly fail to remind us that the self-portrait Sartre draws on to compose his example of the akratic gambler comes from

Dostoevsky's letters—despatched to his family and friends between episodes at the gaming tables of Europe, as well as between episodes or chapters of his novels; and once it does, we might recall that the novel about gambling that he dictated in 1866 is itself a series of episodes narrated by its protagonist, Aleksey Ivanovich; more specifically, it comprises a manuscript written by him during the sequence of events he is narrating, and one from which he breaks off for at least two extended periods. The first, lasting one month, is registered at the beginning of chapter 13, before Aleksey narrates his tale's double catastrophe—Grandmother's ruinous gambling, and his own ruinous decision to gamble instead of (or as his way of) acknowledging Polina's risky visit to his hotel room; the second, lasting twenty months, is registered at the beginning of chapter 17, which records the narrator's concluding encounter with Mr Astley, Polina's authorized messenger and observer.

These breaks invite us to recognize that Aleksey is as much a writer as he is a vertigo-suffering lover and a besotted gambler: more precisely, they suggest that, for him, these categories are inter-defining, perhaps even different ways of giving expression to the nothingness that is his freedom. For both refusals to continue writing betoken points at which his life-project reaches a crisis: in the first, his relationship with Polina comes as close as it ever will to becoming real, only to be annihilated; and in the second, the reality of her love for him is revealed at just the point he is incapable of acting on that knowledge. Both therefore constitute demonstrations of the ineliminable gap between possibility and actuality, motive and act; and he finds that the experience of both prevents him from continuing his narrative, breaking off the sequence of letters, words, and sentences whose construction has occupied at least as much of his time as anything they have allowed him to record and convey. But is this because he finds it impossibly traumatic to relate the life-changing significance of the events that cause this textual interruption, so that these two crises are related to us only when they have become for him events in the relatively distant past—mere objects of his consciousness, and so registrations of the self that he is in the mode of not-being? Or is it rather that what he continues to do during these non-writing periods—namely, to gamble (first in Roulettenburg, later in towns across Europe)—somehow compensates for the missing acts of textual production, as if writing itself were a kind of gambling? In the former case, the breaks in this manuscript would represent breaks in his capacity to identify with the self he was; in the latter case, the exercise of that capacity to identify with himself is being equated with the ability to make words compose sentences that in turn compose chapters and books—but that ability is itself being figured as one of vertiginous risk-taking, as an endless sequence of moments in which one compulsively throws oneself into the void, risking nothing less than everything.

Dostoevsky's dictation of Aleksey's tale to his stenographer and wife-to-be is also a way of equating writing and gambling, since in his case only the successful completion of *The Gambler* within a month will allow him to win the gamble with his career and livelihood that he initiated when he signed his contract with Stellovsky. But as that month progressed, these dictations transformed themselves into the medium for another kind of gamble, of exactly the kind with which Aleksey had involved himself by returning to Roulettenburg—that of falling in love. But whereas Aleksey recounts his love for Polina as one of the subject matters of his tale, Dostoevsky's love for Anya Grigorevna is created and maintained by his telling of it to her. It is therefore the reverse of surprising that his actual proposal to Anya takes the form of his telling her another fictional tale whose protagonist is also its author's alter ego, whose desire to marry is precisely analogous to that of his author, but whose placing in a fictional frame allows that author to propose to his audience whilst simultaneously making manifest the extent to which her acceptance of it would constitute a gamble on her own part. Whereas Aleksey's retention of absolute control over his tale reflects his desire for absolute mastery over his relationship with Polina (even if that mastery requires his self-abasement), Dostoevsky invites Anya to become the co-author of his, and so of their, romance: whether it will continue, and in what way, depends in the end on what one might call her readerly responsiveness.

When Sartre takes up the image of writing as gambling, and as living, the text whose production he represents is the text within which he represents it, and the relation in which it involves the self of the author is essentially one with himself—more precisely, one with his past and future selves. No other seems to interrupt that narcissistic circuit, certainly no beloved other (unless that beloved is now not another but the self itself). And yet, others do invade this text, helping to interrupt and thereby reshape the broader hermeneutic horizon within which Sartre produces it. His first chapter begins by taking orientation from Hegel and Heidegger; it proceeds by reference to a chain of imagined individuals, critically including an akratic gambler; and this imaginary gambler deliberately licenses the text's invasion by another in whom reality and fictionality are unfathomably intertwined (via its avowal of the example's rootedness in the real letters of a real author and gambler one of whose most famous tales is dictated to a beloved other, and is devoted to the creation of a fictional gambler, vertigo-suffering lover and author). Sartre knows and declares that his relation to Hegel and Heidegger is both internal and negating, hence metonymic of his relation to himself; does he also know that his relation to Dostoevsky and Aleksey is a relation to two contexts in which the exemplary phenomenology of vertigo, gambling, and writing are as forcefully present as in his own text, although in very different relations to one another? And should we therefore think of that relation as both internal and negating? If so, then those others to whom Sartre stands in a relation of not-being not only extend beyond the domain of his own consciousness; they extend beyond the domain of philosophy and of reality. In short, part of what is involved in understanding Sartre ('s gambler) is understanding that and how he is (not) Dostoevsky and (not) Aleksey.

The Melodramatic Reality of Film and Literature

Or: Elizabeth Costello's Cinematic Sisters

In a recent exchange of essays, Stanley Cavell and Cora Diamond each celebrate the thought of the other by finding reason to take philosophical pleasure as well as philosophical instruction from J.M. Coetzee's decision to deliver his Tanner lectures in the form of a pair of fictional tales devoted to the celebratory occasion on which the famous Australian novelist Elizabeth Costello delivers the Gates Lecture at Appleton College—an opportunity she uses to address the moral status of non-human animals, and in particular to advance her view of the ways in which we currently organize the production of meat for food:[1]

We are surrounded by an enterprise of degradation, cruelty, and killing which rivals anything that the Third Reich was capable of, indeed dwarfs it, in that ours is an enterprise without end, self-regenerating, bringing rabbits, rats, poultry, livestock ceaselessly into the world for the purpose of killing them. (LA, 21–2)

I recently placed this three- or four-cornered conversation at the centre of a book-length study of the ways in which philosophy and literature might learn something from each other[2]—a study that I imagined as a kind of intellectual biography of Coetzee's fictional protagonist. I want now to add

---

[1] Diamond's and Cavell's essays—'The Difficulty of Reality and the Difficulty of Philosophy' and 'Companionable Thinking' respectively—are both reprinted in *Philosophy and Animal Life* (New York: Columbia University Press, 2008), hereafter PAL, to which all references to either essay will be keyed. Coetzee's Tanner Lectures, published as *The Lives of Animals* (Princeton: Princeton University Press, 1999), will be cited as 'LA'; his novel *Elizabeth Costello* (London: Secker and Warburg, 2003), in which those lectures are reprinted, will be cited as 'EC'.

[2] *The Wounded Animal* (Princeton and Oxford: Princeton University Press, 2009).

or disclose a further layer of complexity to this portrait of Elizabeth Costello by taking further a suggestion that I barely managed to articulate in that book, a suggestion prompted by the fact that Cora Diamond's original essay pairs Coetzee's Costello with Ted Hughes' poem 'Six Young Men' as her two leading examples of what it might mean to encounter a difficulty of reality.

1) Exposure to Slaughter: Diamond, Coetzee, Hughes, Cavell

What, then, does Diamond mean by a difficulty of reality?

[T]he phenomena with which I'm concerned [are] experiences in which we take something in reality to be resistant to our thinking it, or possibly to be painful in its inexplicability, difficult in that way, or perhaps awesome and astonishing in its inexplicability. *We take things so.* And the things we take so may simply not, to others, present that kind of difficulty, of being hard or impossible or agonizing to get one's mind around. (PAL, 45–6)

Coetzee's lectures exemplify this phenomenon primarily because, according to Diamond, in Elizabeth Costello they present a woman who is not so much advancing a hyperbolic or outrageous argument by analogy about the morality of factory farming as she is displaying or declaring her woundedness, her being haunted in her mind, first by what we do to animals, and second by the fact that this horror, which reduces her to a terrible rawness of nerves, is treated as if it were nothing, simply part of the accepted background of ordinary life, by most other people. Diamond sees clearly that Costello's sense of having her sanity under threat is as much a matter of the second horror as of the first—that an essential part of what is driving her mad is that what she experiences as an inexplicable horror is not so experienced by others, and that this divergence between herself and her fellow human beings is itself painfully inexplicable.

But Diamond actually opens her discussion, and thereby prepares the ground for her treatment of Coetzee and Costello, with a poem in which Ted Hughes describes his experience of looking at a photograph—a photograph of six people who were soon to die on the Western Front of the Great War. The poem ends with the following stanza:

That man's not more alive whom you confront
And shake by the hand, see hale, hear speak loud,
Than any of these six celluloid smiles are,
Nor prehistoric or fabulous beast more dead;
No thought so vivid as their smoking blood:
To regard this photograph might well dement,
Such contradictory permanent horrors here
Smile from the single exposure and shoulder out
One's own body from its instant and heat.[3]

Why this poem? In what ways might it be thought to exemplify a difficulty of reality, of the kind confronted and exemplified by Elizabeth Costello? Most obviously, because it confronts the impossibility of encompassing in thought the reality of human mortality; less obviously, because it confronts the death of six young men in war, and more specifically in a war which epitomizes (certainly for the country in whose name they died, and more generally for Western Europe) the senselessness of war, that perfectly familiar and perennial aspect of human experience that is nevertheless capable of driving us to the point of madness in attempting to encompass its reality in thought.

Beyond this, however, there is the central relevance of photography to the poet's sense of exposure. For what is threatening to drive him mad here is the simultaneous sense that no one could be more alive than these six men smiling in front of his eyes, and yet no one and nothing could be more dead; and his ability to see six dead men alive and smiling before his very eyes is possible only because he is looking at a photograph of them taken shortly before they went to war, and to their deaths. It is therefore perfectly possible to describe the situation in a way which makes it seem the very reverse of impossible or insane: what could be more familiar than the idea that the subjects of photographs might be dead? And so what could be more amenable to straightforward description and thought than the idea of dead men smiling in a photograph? Diamond imagines a young child shown a photograph of her dead grandfather, who asks, 'Why is he smiling if he's dead?', and who is then told that he was smiling when the picture was taken, which was before he died:

---

[3] From 'Six Young Men', in Ted Hughes, *Collected Poems*, ed. P. Keegan (London: Faber, 2003), pp. 45–6.

The child is being taught the language-game, being shown how her problem disappears as she comes to see how things are spoken of in the game. The point of view from which she sees a problem is not yet in the game; while that from which the horrible contradiction impresses itself on the poet-speaker is that of someone who can no longer speak from within the game. Language is shouldered out from the game, as the body from its instant and heat. (PAL, 45)

The difficulty of reality that Diamond is trying to locate here is thus inseparable from the fact of photography. The instant and heat of the rending flash that shoulders out language and thought certainly registers the worst of war (the rifle-barrel and the bomb); but it also registers the camera's reliance upon the dazzling light of a flashbulb to take its single exposure, and so marks a difficulty that might arise even when the subjects of a photograph are neither victims of war nor even dead. For what any photograph, by its very nature, exposes us to is the mysterious relation between a photograph and what it is a photograph of—between the real person, object, or environment in front of the camera when the photograph was taken and what the resulting photograph presents to its viewers. And this, as Diamond well knows, takes us to the threshold of an aspect of Stanley Cavell's work that remains implicit in her ensuing discussion of it— his substantial body of writing on film and philosophy, which finds its initial orientation in a consideration of the material basis of film, which (at least until yesterday, before avatars of the future such as *Avatar*) necessarily involved considering the relation between photographs and reality.[4]

Cavell begins those reflections by claiming that, whereas it makes perfect sense to say that a painting presents us with a likeness of something or someone, it would not be quite right to say that a photograph presents us with a likeness: what Cavell thinks we want to say is that it presents us with the thing itself. A photograph of an object is not, as a painting of it may be, a visual representation of that object (it does not stand for that object, nor form a likeness of it); it is rather a visual transcription of it. However, it does not transcribe the sight or look or appearance of an object in the way in which a recording can be said to transcribe the sound of an object; for

---

[4] Reference will be made to three volumes of this work: *The World Viewed: Expanded Edition* (Cambridge, MA: Harvard University Press, 1979)—hereafter 'WV'; *Pursuits of Happiness* (Cambridge, MA: Harvard University Press, 1981); and *Contesting Tears* (Chicago and London: Chicago University Press, 1996), hereafter 'CT'.

objects do not have or make sights in the way that objects have or make sounds. There is, one might say, no way of reproducing the 'sights' they make without reproducing them, or better, there is nothing of the right sort for a photograph to be a photograph of short of the object itself.

When we look at a photograph of Barbara Stanwyck, we see Barbara Stanwyck—the woman before the camera when the photograph was taken; we do not see a representation or reproduction or image or replica of her, we see the woman herself. And yet we know that a photograph of Barbara Stanwyck is not Barbara Stanwyck. But saying that amounts only to saying that a photograph is not a human being; who would deny it? And this reminder of what no one could reasonably be expected to have forgotten does not address the real difficulty, which is precisely that of understanding what it is for something to be a *photograph* of Barbara Stanwyck (as opposed to, say, a painting of her or a recording of her voice). The woman herself is not there; but there she is, nevertheless, in the photograph; what seems for all the world to be happening, ontologically speaking, when we look at a photograph is that we see things that are not really there. Cavell finds that he wants to say: The reality in a photograph is present to me while I am not present to it. And so the motion-picture camera can make a world present to us from which we are absent, can cause live human beings and real objects in actual spaces to appear to us when they are in fact not there.[5]

This is what leads Cavell to consider film to be a moving image of scepticism—the very theme in his work that Diamond's discussion of difficulties of reality is explicitly designed to highlight and interpret; so I take it as no coincidence that her invocation of a child and a photograph of her grandfather at once recalls and revises Cavell's reference (in his consideration of photography and reality) to the puzzlement of a male child when someone remarks, of a photograph, 'that's your grandmother' (WV, 18). Daughters and (grand)fathers, sons and (grand)mothers—shifts of gender and skips between generations: what's the difference, when mysterious origins are at issue? We shall return to this.

But in the context created by Diamond's discussion, it is worth emphasizing immediately that Cavell's formulations are designed from the outset not so much to dissipate or dissolve the aura of magic and mystery with

---

[5] For a more detailed presentation of Cavell's stance on these matters, see chapter 9 of my *Stanley Cavell: Philosophy's Recounting of the Ordinary* (Oxford: Oxford University Press, 1994).

which he takes the relation between photographs and their subjects (or objects) to be imbued, but rather to maintain themselves within it. As Cavell himself puts it:

It may be felt that I make too great a mystery of these objects. My feeling is rather that we have forgotten how mysterious these things are, and in general how *different* things are from one another, as though we had forgotten to value them. (WV, 19)

Where his interlocutors, happy to employ the concepts of a 'representation' or a 'reproduction' or a 'likeness' apart from their ordinary criteria, thereby elide important differences between sound recordings, visual representations, and photographs in such a way as to occlude the specificity of the photographic, in all its mysteriousness, it is precisely Cavell's orienting assumption that obscurities are internal to our experience of photographs and so of film, rather than something blocking our way to a transparent understanding of those phenomena. Hence:

The commitments I set myself as I wrote were, first, to allow obscurities to express themselves as clearly and fervently as I could say, and, second, to be guided by the need to organize and clarify just these obscurities and just this fervour in the progression of my book as a whole. (WV, 162)

The point is not to avoid the achievement of clarity, but to recognize that such clarity that can be achieved must be clarity about just these obscurities, hence clarity that must be the result of working through those obscurities rather than banishing them, and so may result only in making it clearer to both author and reader that obscurity is internal to the phenomenon of photography and so of film. In other words, Cavell sees in the domain of photography as such exactly the kind of difficulty of reality, the possibility of experiencing something that is perfectly everyday as constitutively enigmatic, that Diamond sees as central not only to Coetzee's writing about Costello but to ordinary human experience more generally.

2) Sisters Beneath the Skin: Costello as an Unknown Woman

That was as far as my initial articulation of this line of thought went in my book on Coetzee. I intend to take a few more steps, here and now, in attempting to clarify its specific obscurities by relating the fictional character that Diamond pairs with Hughes' poem to a certain range or type of character and star with which Cavell concerns himself in *Contesting Tears* (and which I found myself already invoking earlier in this book, when contemplating the mythic, melodramatic treatments of male unknownness in the Quiller novels, and the Bourne and Bond films). In short, I want to test the intuition that Elizabeth Costello might be a sister of the unknown women who give their name to the genre of Hollywood melodrama that Cavell has disclosed as derivable by negation from that of remarriage comedy.

In comedies of remarriage, the drive of the narrative is not to get the central pair together but rather to get them back together: the fact of marriage in these comedies is not the hoped-for culmination of a tale of young lovers striving to overcome obstacles to their union, but an attained relationship currently subject to the threat of divorce, so that a willingness to be married here appears as requiring an unending willingness to remarry. Central to these relationships is the woman's demand for an education of some kind from the man (deriving from her sense that her life asks for some transformation, a re-creation that is also a re-creation of the human), and the man's willingness to undergo an investigation of his authority to provide it; his authority is demonstrated and her transfiguration effected by means of their ability to sustain a meet and happy conversation, a mutually appreciative witty responsiveness. The melodramas, by contrast, concern women who could neither manage nor relish such relationships with men, and so must achieve genuine existence (or fail to) apart from marriage; they lack a common language with the (always inadequate and often villainous) men of their world, so that their words are pervaded with an isolating irony, often rising to arias of divorce from all around them, to which those around them react with bewildered hostility.

This melodramatic vision of the crippling loneliness of such (mis-) marriages is at the heart of Milton's sustained pleas for divorce, and it has its operatic counterpart in the universe of Wagner's *Ring*. Siegmund's attempts to prevent a woman's forced marriage are what lead him to rescue Sieglinde from her own loveless union with Hunding (even if the incestuous terms of her redemption leave us to judge whether her flight from voicelessness leads only to an equal and opposite narcissism); and that rescue leads in turn to their father Wotan's mismatched and unhappy conversations with Fricka, dramatizing a loneliness within his marriage that the *Ring* relates to a more profound isolation, call it a metaphysical narcissism—his despairing inability to find anything in his world's unfolding that does not carry the mark of his own creative labour (everything that happens in the Ring narrative happening either because of what Wotan intended should happen, or because of what he does in attempting to realize his intentions).[6] Whatever one might want to say about the men as well as the women of these operas (and indeed about the fact that such self-lacerating loneliness is not there a condition exclusive to women), the route to re-creation or recovery canvassed by the women of the melodramas involves a systematic negation of the existing world's claims upon them, in the name of a higher, unattained state of society in which alone genuine individuality is attainable for them, and apart from which that society's claims upon them are shown to lack any real authority. In this way, the self's non-self-identity and that of its society appear as internally related; and in one exemplary case (that of Bette Davis playing Charlotte Vale in *Now, Voyager* [Irving Rapper: 1942]), the general task of finding a way to accept their difference from and sameness with themselves appears in more specific terms previously encountered in our discussion of Wittgenstein's treatment of Moses—namely, Charlotte's willingness to acknowledge some given name or description as rightly applied or not, or more precisely as a willingness to question whether even rightly applied names or descriptions could in principle capture who she is.

With this exceedingly brief summary in place, let us recount the further ways in which Coetzee's presentation of Elizabeth Costello resembles not only that of Charlotte in *Now, Voyager*, but also that of Paula (Ingrid Bergman) in *Gaslight* (George Cukor: 1944), Lisa (Joan Fontaine) in *Letter From an Unknown Woman* (Max Ophuls: 1948), and Stella (Barbara Stanwyck) in *Stella Dallas* (King Vidor: 1937). Elizabeth is immensely isolated from the world around her, to the point of madness; and just as pretty much every word its inhabitants utter during her stay at Appleton irritates or bruises her (say, chagrins her), so she perfects the negation of conversation that her exchanges with them represent by declaring and ensuring that every wounding word she utters gives expression to her own woundedness: 'I am . . . an animal exhibiting, yet not exhibiting . . . a wound, which I cover up under my clothes but touch on in every word I speak' (LA, 26).

[6] Cf. Stephen Greenblatt, 'The Lonely Gods', *New York Review of Books*, 23 June 2011.

Her speech consequently takes the form of passionately judging her world: she finds it wanting, in need of radical, pervasive transformation that is no more than a step away (that is, not blocked by material or moral necessities, but essentially available, neighbouring us); but because its currently attained state is such as to render her voiceless (her horrified perception of its present dispensation inarticulable in the terms provided by the dominant conception of rationality—'the great Western discourse of . . . reason and unreason' (LA, 25)), any claim she stakes in the name of its unattained but attainable state, and so of her own unrealized but realizable capacity to exist otherwise (to transcend her current haunting of her own life), inevitably takes on the accents of insanity. What to her is a condition of absolute expressiveness is for that very reason also one of absolute inexpressiveness: because everything she says is touched by her woundedness, nothing she says can truly touch her hearers. From their viewpoint, her sense of victimization by what she knows can only appear hyperbolic, inordinate, melodramatic—an apparently excessive response to apparently banal facts or circumstances; what she thinks she knows remains utterly unknown to her interlocutors, and since the trauma of that knowledge constitutes her as the animal she is, she too remains to that extent unknown.

Although her age occludes any real possibility of dramatizing Elizabeth's relation to her parents (and so of any specifically troubled or troubling relation to her real mother), she is explicitly presented as a mother, and even a grandmother—her son John (through whom many of Coetzee's tales of Costello are mediated) has a family: but her ability to (grand)mother her offspring is strictly limited, aligning her in this respect more with Lisa than Stella amongst the sisterhood. For whereas Stella finds ways of allowing her daughter to enter the world that she wants but for which her mother has no taste, Lisa's ability to mother her child is sacrificed to her desire to take revenge on Stefan's failure to perceive her, to the point at which she withholds awareness of the child's existence from his father until it is too late for both. But the air of hyperbolic victimization around Elizabeth's mothering is both more pervasive and more explicit than that: sometimes, her daily seclusion for the purposes of her writing induced melodrama in her children ('when they felt particularly sorry for themselves, he and his sister used to slump outside the locked door and make tiny whining sounds' [EC, 4]), and sometimes it induced melodrama in her ('she . . . stormed around the house in Melbourne, hair flying in all directions, screaming at her children, "You are killing me! You are tearing the flesh from my body!" (He lay in the dark with his sister afterwards, comforting her while she sobbed; it was his first taste of fathering)' [EC, 30]).

These memories certainly exemplify the way in which, like that of her sisters, Elizabeth's past more generally is frozen and mysterious, embodying forbidden and isolating topics; but more specifically, they indicate a feature of Coetzee's staging of Elizabeth's family romance that allows for a version of the unknown woman's search for or competition with a mother. For Elizabeth's relations with the mother of her grandchildren are profoundly poisoned, quite as if she sees herself as in competition with Norma for John's love, perhaps even for his ability to parent those who are not his offspring; and the Tanner lectures end with a scene in which John accepts the invitation to mother his mother: 'He pulls the car over, switches off the engine, takes his mother in his arms. He inhales the smell of cold cream, of old flesh. "There, there" he whispers in her ear, "There, there. It will soon be over"' (LA, 69).

The same fact of Elizabeth's age might also in part account for the most obvious difference between herself and her putative sisters from the melo-dramas—there being no specific man in her life whose failure to acknow-ledge her, and thereby to hold open the possibility of her finding her voice within their current state of society, incites her rejection of its terms and conditions more generally: call it the absence of any specific negation of marriage. This difference must not, however, be exaggerated: after all, Elizabeth's fame as a writer is founded on her novel *The House on Eccles Street*, in which she liberates Molly Bloom from her husband's home and gives her a voice in such a way as to reveal the limitations of Joyce's original attempts to realize an authentic femininity. So one can regard Elizabeth's general way with words as inflected by that origin, hence as always amounting to a recovery of the woman's voice from its male counterfeits and confinements. Moreover, one can think of her Gates Lecture as an aria of vengeful divorce, comparable in its tone and range to that delivered by Paula to her husband; the difference is that Elizabeth speaks (or sings or screams) prophetically to her captive audience from out of a yet-to-be-realized world in which literature has at last divorced itself from philosophy, having transcended its oppressive subordination to philosophy's confining ideas of what reason and knowledge and experience and passionate speech might be. Whether we think of that envisioned divorce as the end of all possibility of conversation between the two spouses, or rather as a way of establishing for each the autonomy without which intercourse between them could never be genuinely productive (of surprise as much as confirmation), will depend on how absolute one understands Elizabeth's refusal of philosophy's terms of accounting to be. I have argued that that absoluteness has been much exaggerated.

However that may be, who would venture to say that pronouncing the end of this currently forced or cursed marriage between philosophy and literature is essentially unrelated to the project of emancipating the female voice (in philosophy, in literature, in Western culture)? The fact that the male voice of philosophy is, in Coetzee's staging, primarily embodied in Costello's daughter-in-law does not so much conflict with this suspicion as inflect it, by suggesting that women are no less capable of subjecting themselves to coercively masculine tones of speech and thought than men are capable of disclosing feminine registers of the human voice within their own expressions. And if one finds that Norma's utterances are convincingly masculine, and Elizabeth's convincingly feminine, then one might find grounds for cautious optimism (rather than radical pessimism) in the fact that both are articulated by a male novelist.

We might regard these connections as sufficient reason to reconsider the apparently obvious further but related difference between Elizabeth and the women I have claimed as her sisters—namely, that her primary concern is with the voicelessness of non-human animals in the history of their relations with humans, rather than with the voicelessness of human females in the history of their relations with human males. Cora Diamond touches on this matter when she finds that Coetzee and Elizabeth link knowledge with embodiment as an alternative to allowing oneself to be deflected from a difficulty of reality such as the one Elizabeth claims to confront:

Coetzee's lectures ask us to inhabit a body. But, just as, in considering what death is to an animal we may reject our own capacity to inhabit its body in imagination, so we may, in reading the lectures, reject our own capacity to inhabit in imagination the body of the woman confronting . . . the difficulty of what we do to animals . . . I am inviting you to think of what it would be not to be 'deflected' as an inhabiting of a body (one's own, or an imagined other's) in the appreciating of a difficulty of reality. This may make it sound as if philosophy is inevitably deflected from appreciation of the kind of difficulty I mean, if (that is) philosophy does not know how to inhabit a body (does not know how to treat a wounded body as anything but a fact). (PAL, 59)

This passage aligns the imaginative task of inhabiting the body of an animal with that of inhabiting the body of a woman ('just as' we may reject the former, 'so' we may reject the latter). What difference would it make if the fictional person inviting us so to inhabit the body of an animal were a man rather than a woman; or a real woman rather than a fictional one; or a fictional woman imagined by a female rather than a male author? Is a female philosopher better placed to disclose and assess these analogies and differences than a male philosopher? Do women inhabit their own bodies (and so perhaps an imagined other's body, whether that other is real or fictional, human or non-human) differently from men? Or is it rather that any human being, being embodied, has access to distinctively feminine and masculine ways of inhabiting their bodies, and so to correspondingly distinctive ways in which knowledge of animal bodies might be either 'inordinate . . . or mere or bare or pale or intellectualized or uninsistent or inattentive or distracted or filed, archived . . . or insipid or shallow' (TW[7], 84)? When men and women try to confront the issue of the companionability of human and non-human animals, and perhaps diverge in their attraction to conceiving the issue as one of 'determining the pertinence and discovery of a just and rational legal order, or, rather . . . on finding the trauma and hysteria, or say inordinateness, in acknowledging a reciprocal recognition, seeing them as our others' (TW, 96), they might understand this divergence to be a matter of choosing between a terrain of convention and culture on the one hand, and one of biology and nature on the other; but they might instead ask themselves how far that choice of terrain is itself inflected by the particular intersection of nature and culture that each of them instantiates, body and soul.

Be that as it may, on Cavell's account of the matter, the women of the melodramas participate in what Freud regards as the hysteric's distinctive capacity for conversion—'a psychophysical aptitude for transposing very large sums of excitation into the somatic innervation': that is, a capacity for modifying the body as such, rather than allowing the excitation to transpose

---

[7] Cavell, 'The Touch of Words' in W. Day and V. Krebs (eds), *Seeing Wittgenstein Anew* (Cambridge: Cambridge University Press, 2010)—hereafter 'TW'.

into consciousness or to discharge itself in practice. Elizabeth Costello cannot exactly be said to have difficulties transposing her excessive agitation into consciousness or discharging it into her linguistic practice; but as someone whose life is distinctively a life with words, perhaps one should think of her as possessing the capacity for the 'conversion of concepts' (another phenomenon with which Diamond is particularly concerned in a variety of contexts).[8] For just like Cavell's unknown women, Coetzee's Elizabeth aims to reconfigure the entire circle of our moral concepts; where they seek to create the conditions in which they might reclaim a voice in their own history and so a distinctively female voice in the conversation of humankind, Elizabeth seeks to create the conditions in which animals might speak to and through specifically human animals on behalf of the fellowship of animate being (just as Camus' grandmother's hen spoke to him and through him on behalf of all mortal beings when he campaigned to abolish the guillotine—cf. LA, 62). As Emerson almost said, around every circle of embodied knowledge, another circle always waits to be drawn; the human animal's vulnerability to experience is inherently (although not of course inveterately) inordinate—always capable of exceeding its known bounds or limits.

3) Conclusion: Flesh and Blood, Mother and Child

Such a conversion of concepts is also, of course, what Cavell attributes to the event of film as such: 'To my way of thinking, the creation of film was as if meant for philosophy—meant to reorient everything philosophy has said about reality and its representation, about art and imitation, about greatness and conventionality, about judgement and pleasure, about scepticism and transcendence, about language and expression' (CT, epigraph). I want to conclude by asking what might be disclosed if, instead of asking what is revealed by seeing Elizabeth Costello through the lens of the melodrama of the unknown woman, we ask what is revealed by seeing film as such through the lens of Elizabeth Costello's traumatic responsiveness to reality— whether sense might be made of the idea that our responsiveness to film is,

---

[8] See, for example, her essay 'Wittgenstein on Religious Belief: the gulfs between us', in D.Z. Phillips and M. von der Ruhr (eds), *Religion and Wittgenstein's Legacy* (London: Ashgate, 2005).

as such, inherently (if not inveterately) inordinate, or say melodramatic, as if the threat or the promise of an apparently excessive response to apparently banal images haunts our reception of screened images quite generally.

Three overlapping strands of Cavell's account of individual melodramas offer routes for exploration here. First, there is his account of our uncanny intimacy with Stefan, as, upon reading its eponymous letter, he undergoes an assault by a sequence of earlier images from the film in which he stars:

When the man covers his eyes . . . he is in that gesture both warding off his seeing something and warding off at the same time his being seen by something, which is to say, his own existence being known, being seen by the woman of the letter, by the mute director and his (her?) camera—say, seen by the power of art—and seen by us, which accordingly identifies us, the audience of film, as assigning ourselves the position, in its activeness and passiveness, of the source of the letter and of the film; which is to say, the position of the feminine. Then it is the man's horror of us that horrifies us—the revelation, or avoidance, of ourselves in a certain way of being feminine, a way of being human, a mutual and reflexive state, let us say, of victimization. (CT, 111)

In Cavell's reading of *Gaslight*, according to which the falling and rising gas jets by which Paula's husband at once persecutes her and betrays himself are also the light by which we see the figures on the screen, this victimization is understood to be a form of vampirism (one life the sapping of another's). And in his reading of *Stella Dallas*, Cavell interprets the window through which Stella watches her daughter's disappearance into married life as a figure for the screen on which these figures (and any others produced by photogenesis from their originals) are projected, and then he subjects this screen to a further interpretation:

Film assaults human perception at a more primitive level than the work of fetishizing suggests; film's enforcement of passiveness, or say victimization, together with its animation of the world, entertains a region not of invitation or fascination primarily to the masculine nor even, yet perhaps closer, to the feminine, but primarily to the infantile, before the establishment of human gender, that is, before the choices of identification and objectification of female and male, call them mama and papa, have settled themselves, to the extent that they will be settled.

Having come to insist on the dimension of infantilization in the viewing of film (cutting across cultures, races, genders, generations) . . . I will articulate this subject further as the search for the mother's gaze—the responsiveness of her face—in view of its loss, or of threatened separation from it. (CT, 209–10)

Each of these specific claims is of course meant, not as an individual step in a single general argument about film, but rather as partial specifications of each film's way of understanding the viewing of film as such, a way that other films in that genre (and outside it) might each contest, displace, or otherwise put in question. Even so, relocating them in the context provided by Elizabeth Costello makes it impossible to avoid at least noting two results of their possible intercourse.

The first is that, if we interpret the way of being feminine that so horrifies Stefan as that of maternality or mothering, and recollect that we are as much aligned with him as a viewer of this film's images as we are with their source, then what horrifies us about ourselves as viewers may turn out to be our capacity to mother ourselves—as if we feel victimized by the human capacity to reproduce or procreate to which our natality points us, selfhood as a matter of being with child with oneself (flesh of my flesh). Individuality thus stands revealed as existing only in the self's willingness to separate itself (rendingly, if necessary, as Sartre emphasizes) from the inordinately responsive gaze of its attained state, in its willingness to risk the loss of that responsiveness in order to find the right distance from it—the distance Stella establishes as she walks away from the window, but not exactly out of the screen on which we view her ecstatic smile, as if refusing to respond to our misplaced desire that she should utterly confine her attention to us, merging with us as we impossibly aspire to merge with her.

The second result is that, whilst the dimension of infantilization in film viewing may undercut differences of culture, race, gender, and generation, it thereby emphasizes embodiment and its commonalities. In this way, the newest medium of human artistic achievement is also the most precisely calibrated to recall us to our most nearly biological selves, our flesh and blood as it tears itself away from its own flesh and blood, our bodily nature as it is drawn into acculturation. Then our task is to derive useful tuition from this cinematic intuition of ineliminable fellowship with our fellow animals.

Fetters, Shadows, and Circles

Freedom and Form in *Human, All Too Human*

Having already experimented with (and thereby revised and revalued) the form of a scholarly monograph (*The Birth of Tragedy*) and that of a collection of essays (*Untimely Meditations*), Nietzsche's next textual venture essays a new form—one typically described by commentators as 'aphoristic', although that term is not one Nietzsche himself uses, preferring to characterize it at the outset as the provision of 'psychological maxims' in the manner of La Rochefoucauld (I: 35[1]). Part of the difficulty in assessing the significance of such formal characterizations of his work lies in the fact that its internal structure reflects a particularly complex process of extension, republication, and retrospective reflection, even by Nietzsche's restless standards.

The first volume of *Human, All Too Human* appeared in 1878: subtitled 'A Book for Free Spirits', and dedicated to Voltaire, it consisted of 638 numbered remarks, divided into nine titled sections or chapters, and concluding with an epilogue in the form of a short poem. Two further continuations of this material were then published: *Assorted Opinions and Maxims* (consisting of 408 numbered remarks, without any division into chapters) in 1879; and *The Wanderer and his Shadow* (comprising a further 350 numbered remarks, also without division into chapters, but with brief prefatory and concluding material which presents them as the result of a day-long dialogue between the eponymous wanderer and his shadow) in 1880. In 1886, Nietzsche published a second edition of *Human, all Too Human*, within

---

[1] All references to this text will be to R.J. Hollingdale's translation (Cambridge: Cambridge University Press, 1996). Citations will be to specific remarks by number, within the relevant portion of the text: Volume I will be cited as 'I', Volume II as 'II, pt 1' and 'II, pt 2', and the Prefaces as '1st pref' and '2nd pref'. Un-numbered material at the beginning and end of Volume II, part 2 will be referred to as 'prologue' and 'conclusion' respectively.

which its two supplements were combined to form what he entitled 'Volume II' of the work; that second edition contained two new prefaces—one (written in the spring of 1886) to the work as a whole, and one (written in September of the same year) to Volume II alone; but the dedication to Voltaire was removed. In the six years that lay between the composition of the main text of both volumes and the composition of those two prefaces, Nietzsche had written and published *Daybreak,* the initial version of *The Gay Science, Thus Spake Zarathustra,* and *Beyond Good and Evil*; in the immediate future lay the *Genealogy of Morality* and *Twilight of the Idols* (amongst other late works).

Some key interpretative challenges leap out from this brief compositional narrative. First: to what extent should our understanding of the material of Volume I be influenced by the material contained in its two distinct continuations or supplements? Second: to what extent should our understanding of the material in Volume I and Volume II be influenced by the two prefaces Nietzsche affixes to them in 1886? Third: to what extent should our attempts to answer the second question be influenced by the fact that Nietzsche attaches the earlier 1886 preface to the work as a whole, and the later to Volume II alone? In other words, what significance if any is there in the fact that he presents his latest, most up-to-the-minute reflections on the project as prefatory only (or primarily, or at least in the first instance) to the original project's later continuations? And fourth: to what extent should we regard the relation Nietzsche takes to the 1878–1880 material in his 1886 prefaces as determined by material he composed and published in the intervening six years—in particular by *Daybreak,* the book which appeared in 1881, and so might be taken as one more continuation of *Human, All Too Human*'s two initial continuations (although it might also be taken as effecting a decisive break with that initial project, insofar as it always maintained its own distinct existence and title)?

At the most general or abstract level, all four of these questions concern the hermeneutic value of authorial retrospection. To what extent can or should an author's later reflections on the significance of a given body of his writing be taken as useful or even as essential guidance for understanding that earlier work? And to what extent does distance in time affect the value of that guidance? Does increasing authorial distance from the moment of creation facilitate a deeper penetration into what was more inchoately or un-self-consciously at work within it, or does it progressively reduce the degree of authority such reflections might legitimately claim (with the author becoming no more than another reader, or even rather less, insofar as he is now reading his earlier writing from the position of his later authorial concerns and commitments)?

This problem of relating *Human, All Too Human* to other stages in Nietzsche's intellectual career is not solely a matter of formal hermeneutic difficulty, however; it is also a problem that the content of the book inevitably poses for us. For, together with *Daybreak*, this text is often taken to be the high-water mark of Nietzsche's love affair with natural science, and hence as part of a phase in which he reacts violently against the romantic pessimism (or pessimistic romanticism) of his previous writings—a reaction against which he soon reacts in turn, certainly by the time of *Thus Spake Zarathustra* (if not earlier). If such a developmental narrative were true, it would certainly create a real internal pressure for the later Nietzsche to account for what (by the time he was composing the two prefaces) might appear to have been a short-lived period of aberration or distraction, a temporary going off the rails. But this reason for discounting the claims of the prefaces can be no stronger than the grounds for interpreting *Human, All Too Human* as at once a love letter to natural science and a disavowal of his earlier work. So perhaps a good point of entry to the hermeneutic complexities outlined above is to ask, with respect to Volume I of this work, exactly what the nature of its relationship to science, and so to its author's earlier writings, might be.

1) Opinions, Maxims, and the Scientific Spirit

The first volume of *Human, All Too Human* is certainly full of words of praise for science, usually by way of contrast with the fantastic deliverances of metaphysics, religion, morality, and art (the matrices of deep insight in his earlier writings). In the first couple of dozen remarks in the book, for example, Nietzsche praises the sciences for their patient accumulation of unpretentious local truths (I: 3), and then proceeds to invoke a variety of such 'truths' as markers of authority in the course of his analyses—as when he attempts to explain the logic of dreams by reference to the internal agitations of the nervous system (I: 13), alludes to empirically established sympathetic resonances between strong moods and related sensations (I: 14), and analyses the most primitive form of judgement as a new, third sensation produced by two preceding single sensations (I: 18). On this level, it appears that he is beginning a campaign in which the deliverances of specific natural sciences will be deployed as ways of demystifying the airy and grandiose speculations of metaphysics, religion, morality, and art—so that the man of science appears as the representative of higher culture, the primary way in which the human race consolidates its emergence from its more or less barbaric childhood. Indeed, according to I: 27, the relevant template is a sequence of progressive transitions from religion through philosophy and then art to 'a truly liberating philosophical science'. Here is one straightforward sense in which the coiner of these remarks presents himself as a Renaissance man—the first inheritor of that cultural revolution's greatest gift, an embodiment of Enlightenment.

So understood, Nietzsche's love for science would be a love for its unrivalled capacity to uncover specific truths—to disclose how things actually are from case to case (by contrast with the empty posturings of metaphysics and religion, morality and art). But later remarks precisely undercut any such assumption that the value of science resides in its results. In I: 256, for example, he tells us that 'the value of having for a time rigorously pursued a *rigorous science* does not derive precisely from the results obtained from it: for in relation to the ocean of things worth knowing these will be a mere vanishing droplet. But there will eventuate an increase in energy, in reasoning capacity, in toughness of endurance; one will have learned how *to achieve an objective by the appropriate means.*' And later still, the point is made more generally:

[T]he procedures of science are at least as important a product of inquiry as any other outcome: for the scientific spirit rests upon an insight into the procedures, and if these were lost all the other products of science together would not suffice to prevent a restoration of superstition and folly. There are people of intelligence who can *learn* as many of the facts of science as they like, but . . . they lack the spirit of science: For them it is enough to have discovered any hypothesis at all concerning any matter, then they are at once on fire for it and believe the whole thing is accomplished. To possess an opinion is to them the same thing as to become a fanatical adherent of it, and henceforth to lay it to their heart as a conviction . . . Insofar as genius of every kind maintains the fire of convictions and awakens distrust of the modesty and circumspection of science, it is an enemy of truth, no matter how much it may believe itself to be truth's suitor. (I: 635)

Here, the truly liberating aspect of science is not its product, but its process, or more precisely the spirit in which it proceeds, and hence in which it relates to its products: the difference between superstition and science is the difference between being invigorated by certainty, and the virtue of 'cautious reserve' or 'wise moderation' (I: 631). As Nietzsche puts it: 'the pathos of *possessing* truth does now in fact count for little in comparison with that other, admittedly gentler and less noisy pathos of seeking truth that never wearies of learning and examining anew' (I: 633). In other words, the value of scientific hypotheses lies in their hypotheti-cality—their provisionality, their openness to being overturned by further scientific advance, and hence the transfiguration of potentially paralysing sceptical doubt into a productive method of unending experimentation, a technique for making progress by subjecting one's views to the sternest possible trials, a willingness to abandon what hitherto appeared well grounded.

The critical contrast is thus between convictions and opinions—no one of any passion can avoid holding opinions, but only inertia of the spirit lets them stiffen into convictions. 'He . . . whose spirit is *free* and restlessly alive can prevent this stiffening through continual change . . . redeemed from the fire, driven now by the spirit, we advance from opinion to opinion, through one part after another, as noble *traitors* to all things that can in any way be betrayed—and yet we feel no sense of guilt' (I: 637). And the connection between form and content here is, I hope, evident. By titling the first continuation of Volume I 'Assorted Opinions and Maxims', Nietzsche marks on its very first page the key reflexive moral of the concluding remarks from which it begins again—that author and reader have been, and will be, advancing from opinion to opinion without resting unques-tioningly upon or within any single one of them. To put matters in the way he favours in the second 1886 preface (which intervenes at precisely this point of transition between the 1878 and 1879 texts), what matters about these remarks is not so much their content but their spirit—of 'cheerful and inquisitive coldness', 'a *determination* to preserve an equilibrium and com-posure in the face of life', 'a repugnance towards all staying still, towards every blunt affirmation and denial . . . a dietetic and discipline designed to make it as easy as possible for the spirit to run long distances, to fly to great heights, above all again and again to fly away' (2nd pref: 1, 5). These elements of his most distant self-interpretation, at least, do no more than elaborate upon the concluding moral of the very first run of remarks that Nietzsche composed for his free spirits.

What, then, should we make of what he entitles his 'Final opinion about opinions', placed roughly midway between these earliest and latest markers of scientific intent, in the 338th remark of the 1879 text?

One should either conceal one's opinions, or conceal oneself behind one's opinions. He who does otherwise does not know the ways of the world or belongs to the order of holy foolhardiness.

Since the ways of the world are one of Nietzsche's central preoccupations in this text, in which he also repeatedly expresses his aversion to holy foolhardiness, he seems to be inviting us to view the assortment of opinions and maxims we are presently reading as a way of concealing either his opinions or himself. But in what way do they do so? Are the opinions expressed in the text not really his own? Or is it that the direct expression of one's real opinions is an excellent way of concealing oneself, because a person's opinions and her self have essentially nothing to do with one another? What, then, are we to make of the fact that this remark is, as its internal title declares, itself an opinion? Is it not Nietzsche's real opinion about opinions? Or has he somehow concealed himself behind this opinion as well?

Here it matters that Nietzsche characterizes this opinion of his about opinions as 'final'—a qualification whose apparent claim to end the text's succession of opinions is put in question by its author's already-established high opinion of the provisionality and self-questioning epitomized in the spirit of science, and in the corresponding aspects of the aphoristic genre in which all his opinions are expressed (in their multiplicity, their mutual questioning, their refusal of any total ordering or single system of subordination, their openness to future continuation). But perhaps Nietzsche's point here is precisely to demonstrate that the concept of 'finality' can be projected in two very different ways or spirits—call them the metaphysical and the empirical, or the absolute and the actual. For the formal features that give each aphorism its air of self-sufficient finality (each so cleanly separated from its neighbours by its individual number, title, and point) are possessed to an equal degree by every other aphorism in the sequence; hence none can claim absolute or unconditional finality, as if putting an end once and for all to the process of opining. Rather, each achieves finality insofar as it gives full or complete expression to the specific opinion it embodies; and hence each displays its (contextualized or concrete, call it finite) finality as equally capable of satisfying our desire to remain wedded to that opinion or of allowing us to divorce ourselves from it, its self-sufficiency facilitating our freedom to leave it behind in order to articulate a further, as-yet-unarticulated opinion (which, once it attains expression, will itself be capable either of retaining our interest or of freeing it).

If this is right, then we have reason to believe that the opinion that one's opinions either reveal oneself or conceal oneself does in fact conceal Nietzsche's real view about the matter: for it presupposes a view of the relation between opinion and self that he rejects. If the genuinely free spirit finds finality repugnant, and aspires above all again and again to fly away, then her self is neither revealed in any opinion (or assortment thereof) nor concealed behind it: it is revealed in her passage between opinions, her advance from one opinion to the next, her willingness to betray any particular opinion however passionately she has been initially moved to fix upon it.

If there is anything final in such a spirit, it is its transitionality. Since opinions, being inherently provisional, are not in fact betrayed by being overcome, and hence those who overcome them cannot intelligibly feel a traitor's guilt for so doing, the only disloyalty about which the free spirit could and should feel guilty would be disloyalty to disloyalty itself—disloyalty to the goal of relating to one's opinions as overcomeable (rather than regarding them as convictions, the unalterable ground of one's identity, hence the kind of thing one could find oneself guilty of betraying). And that is why Nietzsche's real opinion about opinions finds expression not in this opinion, and not in some other opinion that this opinion about opinions conceals, but rather in the redemptively traitorous, fruitfully self-betraying interaction between this opinion and its title, and between the words that make up that title.

If something like this account of II: 338 is properly responsive to it, and hence discloses something more generally instructive about the movement of Nietzsche's texts, why do they ask so much of us as readers, and in this particular way? Nietzsche himself poses this question at the outset of his earlier 1886 preface, hence at the outset of the second edition of *Human, All Too Human*, when he reports that:

I have been told often enough, and always with an expression of great surprise, that all my writings . . . contain snares and nets for unwary birds and in effect a persistent invitation to the overturning of habitual evaluations and valued habits. (1st pref: 1)

Since free spirits will be systematically associated in the coming texts with unfettered flight to and at great heights, to talk of a text addressed to such spirits as containing snares for unwary birds implies that its treacheries are designed to distinguish the free from the fettered spirits amongst its actual readers, or more precisely to facilitate their transition from the latter to the former condition. If one brings to the text a desire for finalities of significance, for single or absolute fixities of sense, then to that extent one's reading habits manifest one's broader submission to unfreedom—reiterating an already-too-often-satisfied desire to remain netted and ensnared in oneself. But if any such reader is willing to stay with this text, she will find that its constituent remarks no sooner invite her to fix upon an interpretative opinion than they turn traitor to it, refusing to satisfy her expectations of finality; and they thereby invite her to consider the possibility that such textual self-betrayals disclose its author as intending to communicate the more general emancipatory potential of self-betrayal by exemplifying it, so that the treacherousness of his text is internal to its point (hence, one might say, a mere appearance of treachery, an initial impression that a proper understanding of its function will allow us to overcome and so discard).

Any such invitation may, of course, be declined—in which case the reader will remain unsatisfied, taking from the text nothing more than she brought to it, apart from a settled sense of its treacherousness. Those who manage to take it up, however, can show their fidelity to that text, and so to its author, only by overcoming their impulse either to reiterate or to reject its parade of opinions in favour of re-enacting its movement between opinions, its preference for what the later 1886 preface calls 'the serpent's prudent art of changing its skin' (2nd pref: 2) over the implied alternative— the imprudent art of stunting one's potential for growth by clinging to a skin one might otherwise outgrow (let alone by clinging to another's skin, itself no sooner assumed by that other than shed, and not so that other serpents might assume it in turn). Thus might new habits of reading exemplify new habits of living.

And it is by sorting opinions with maxims that Nietzsche serves to indicate this concern for habits of living; for of course, maxims are most familiarly principles of practical conduct—say, expressions of a philosophical science of life. And just as he does with his conception of opinions, so Nietzsche devotes some remarks in the 1879 continuation of *Human, All Too Human* to the nature and significance of maxims.

The worst readers of maxims are the friends of their author when they are exercised to trace the general observation back to the particular event to which the maxim owes its origin: for through this prying they render all the author's efforts null and void, so that, instead of philosophical instruction, all they receive (and all they deserve to receive) is the satisfaction of a vulgar curiosity. (II: 129)

When a maxim straightaway impresses them with its simple truth, the inexperienced always believe it to be old and familiar, and they look askance at its author as though he has desired to steal for himself what is common property: whereas they take pleasure in spiced-up half-truths and make this fact known to the author. The latter knows how to evaluate such a hint and has no difficulty in divining from it where he has succeeded and where failed. (II: 165)

A good maxim is too hard for the teeth of time and whole millennia cannot consume it, even though it serves to nourish every age: it is thus the great paradox of literature, the imperishable in the midst of change, the food that is always in season, like salt—though, unlike salt, it never loses its savour. (II: 168)

These maxims specify successful maxims as those which avoid any taint of the merely personal—no philosophical instruction can be gained by tracing them back to their origins in the author's individual experience, or by regarding them as if their author regarded them as his private property (as if their value resided in their novelty or idiosyncrasy), or as if they were the private property of a particular era or epoch. If they are like salt, then they are not so much a food that is always in season, but rather a kind of seasoning: time's teeth cannot consume them not because they are too tough but because they are not designed to be so consumed. They are not so much a form of nourishment as a means of enhancing the flavour or savour of any such nourishment—call it a matter of (culinary) style or presentation rather than (nutritional) content. The value of maxims thus cannot reside in the ingestion or expulsion of their content—of whether or not one accedes to the view any maxim advances; it is rather a matter of what remains unchanged between shifts at the level of content, the imperishable, vital form that endures across every transition from one maxim to another—in maximhood as such, in the way each maxim succeeds and is succeeded by another, hence achieves its axiomatic status in an inherently momentary way, and so an inherently provisional and transitional form. The staying power of a Nietzschean maxim thus resides not in our affirming them as perennial truths, but in our acknowledgement of their capacity to invite and then repel endorsement, again and again, unendingly.

2) The Law of Identity and the Truth of Becoming

If we think of what is imperishable in the midst of change as precisely the potential for change and its unending activation, then these formal matters return us to the central lesson at the level of content that Nietzsche draws from his identification with the spirit of science. For the early remarks of Volume I focus unremittingly on the error that he takes to be central to metaphysical, moral, and religious thinking—the denial of becoming. This foundational theme is in fact sounded from the very beginning of the sequence:

All we require, and what can be given us only now the individual sciences have attained their present level, is a *chemistry* of the moral, religious and aesthetic conceptions and sensations, likewise of all the agitations we experience within ourselves in cultural and social intercourse, and indeed even when we are alone: what if this chemistry would end up by revealing that in this domain too the most glorious colours are derived from base, indeed from despised materials? Will there be many who desire to pursue such researches? Mankind likes to put questions of origins and beginning out of its mind: must one not be almost inhuman to detect in oneself a contrary inclination? (I: 1)

  All philosophers . . . involuntarily think of 'man' as *aeterna veritas*, as something that remains constant in the midst of all flux, as a sure measure of things . . . Lack of historical sense is the family failing of all philosophers . . . they will not learn that man has become, that the faculty of cognition has become . . . the whole of teleology is constructed by speaking of the man of the last four millennia as of an *eternal* man towards whom all things in the world have had a natural relationship from the time he began. But everything has become: there are no *eternal facts*, just as there are no absolute truths. Consequently, what is needed from now on is *historical philosophizing*, and with it the virtue of modesty. (I: 2)

Pretty much every concrete analysis of a particular psychological, physio-logical, social, and cultural phenomenon Nietzsche goes on to offer in this volume takes the form of disclosing its chemistry (the base elements from which it is compounded), which he thinks of as a way of disclosing its history—the evolutionary processes by means of which it became what it now is. Whether or not one finds the details of any particular chemical analysis or other form of evolutionary narrative entirely convincing matters to Nietzsche, of course; there is no reason to deny that he has a considerable investment in their individual plausibility, case by case. But he is plainly even more deeply invested in two more general features that these particular explanations have in common. First, he wants us to be struck by the extent to which the historical chemistry of the world as it currently presents itself to us reveals it to be built out of falsehoods—that, as he puts it, 'that which we now call the world is the outcome of a host of errors and fantasies which have gradually arisen and grown entwined with one another in the course of the overall evolution of the organic being, and are now inherited by us' (I: 16). And second, he wants us to be struck by how often understanding a phenomenon is a matter of understanding how it became what it is. At both levels, what Nietzsche wishes to achieve by means of his unremitting reiteration of techniques of historical philosophizing is an alteration in our conception of what a genuine explanation looks like, what form it should take: it is the method, or the spirit that inhabits the method, and not its individual results, that matter most to the one deploying it.

Dwelling for a moment on the first of these two more general methodo-logical morals will allow us to see that, and how, it brings about an important re-evaluation of the value of the scientific method that is its vehicle. For the moment he identifies the inheritance of error and illusion that makes up our world, Nietzsche is quick to acknowledge that it is a kind of 'treasure: for the value of our humanity depends upon it' (I: 16). In other words, to recognize the non-absoluteness and illusoriness of what religion, morality, and art have woven into our world is not to deny their offerings any value whatever—they may still enhance our lives, contribute to our vitality. And he expands upon the implications of this recognition later in Volume I:

Science bestows upon him who labours and experiments in it much satisfaction, upon him who *learns* its results very little. As all the important truths of science must gradually become common and everyday, however, even this little satisfaction will cease . . . But if science provides us with less and less pleasure, and deprives us of more and more pleasure through casting suspicion on the consolations of metaphysics, religion and art, then that mightiest source of joy to which mankind owes almost all its humanity will become impoverished. For this reason a higher culture must give to man a double-brain, as it were two brain-ventricles, one for the perceptions of science, the other for those of non-science: lying beside one another, not confused together, separable, capable of being shut off; this is a demand of health. In one domain lies the power-source, in the other the regulator: it must be heated with illusions, one-sidedness, passions, the evil and perilous consequences of overheating must be obviated with the aid of the knowledge furnished by science.—If this demand of higher culture is not met, then the future course of human evolution can be foretold almost with certainty: interest in truth will cease the less pleasure it gives: because they are associated with pleasure, illusion, error and fantasy will regain step by step the ground they formerly held: the ruination of science, a sinking back into barbarism, will be the immediate consequence. (I: 251)

As the imagery of the double-brain implies, this portrait of science in its relation to non-science is not just a blueprint for a healthy culture, but also a code of conduct for the higher individuals who can create and inhabit such a culture. On both levels, the spirit of science taken on its own is not just insufficient for genuine health, but fated to subvert its own achievements: even if it is part of adopting a scientific perspective to recognize metaphysics, religion, and art as more primitive modes of human culture and self-understanding, it is part of genuine human ennoblement to remain open to the degenerate in one's culture and in oneself.

Degenerate natures are of the highest significance wherever progress is to be effected. Every progress of the whole has to be preceded by a partial weakening. The strongest natures *preserve* the type, the weaker help it to *evolve*. (I: 224)

The primitive dimensions of our being are treasured because they are the power sources of evolution or continued becoming; the very same passion and heat that must be moderated if it is not to rigidify opinion into conviction must also be activated if we are to move on from our existing state to a further, as-yet-unrealized state—even though the power thereby unleashed also requires regulation by the application of cautious reserve, so that whatever new ideas or practices are so passionately seized upon do not themselves acquire the status of absolute conviction.

Taken as an implicit reflection on Nietzsche's current relation to his earlier condition of romantic pessimism, this figure of the two ventricles implies a continued place in his mental economy for the insights and motivations that found expression in *The Birth of Tragedy* and *Untimely Meditations*. Taken as the articulation of a maxim for personal conduct, it implies an idiosyncratic conception of individuality as structurally dual: there is the aspect of the self that plunges in, that wholeheartedly inhabits its current world, and wholeheartedly suffers the attraction of its future state, and there is the aspect that withdraws from any such immersion, relating to any current inhabitation with a productive scepticism. If the spirit of science is confused with some particular result of applying its method, then barbarism threatens no less than if we refrain from applying science at all; hence a healthy or vital self is one which is always capable of moving on from whatever passionate commitment currently absorbs it to whatever future commitment currently attracts it, rather than one which wishes to settle for some particular commitment, even a purportedly more scientific or progressive one. The spirit of science as Nietzsche conceives of it does not aspire to settle us somewhere beyond the reach of the joys that metaphysics, religion, and art can and should give us, somewhere in which we can settle instead for the joys of science alone; it rather aspires to unsettle our persistent willingness to settle for some particular version of any of those joys. The goal is not to become scientific, but rather to practise the science of becoming.

And this takes us to the second of the two more general morals I identified earlier. For Nietzsche loses very little time before contrasting his emphasis on historicality and becoming with what he introduces as one of the most fundamental laws of metaphysics—the law of identity:

When one day the history of the genesis of thought comes to be written, the following sentence by a distinguished logician will also stand revealed in a new light: 'The primary universal law of the knowing subject consists in the inner necessity of recognizing every object in itself as being in its own essence something identical with itself, thus self-existent and at bottom always the same and unchanging, in short as a substance'. This law, too, which is here called 'primary', evolved: one day it will be shown how gradually, in the lower organisms, this tendency comes into being: how the purblind mole's eyes of this organization at first never see anything but the same thing; how then, when the various pleasurable and unpleasurable stimuli become more noticeable, various different substances are gradually distinguished, but each of them with one attribute, that is to say a single relationship with such an organism ... In our primary condition, all that interests us organic beings in any thing is its relationship to us in respect of pleasure and pain. Between the moments in which we become conscious of this relationship, the states of awareness of sensation, lie those of repose, of non-sensation: then the world and everything is devoid of interest to us, we notice no alteration in it ... To the plants all things are usually in repose, eternal, everything identical with itself. It is from the period of the lower organisms that man has inherited the belief that there are *identical things* (only knowledge educated in the highest scientificality contradicts this proposition). It may even be that the original belief of everything organic was from the very beginning that all the rest of the world is one and unmoving. (I: 18)

Whatever one makes of the actual evolutionary narrative on offer here, the critical point for its author is twofold. First, it allows him to present even the most fundamental laws of logic and metaphysics as the product of a process of becoming (and even more specifically, to present a timeless law of reason, which metaphysics tells us is what timelessly distinguishes us from the animal realm, as derived precisely from, and so always marked by, the vicissitudes of organic existence); and second, it in effect aspires thereby to legitimate the replacement of the law of identity with its opposite or shadow—with what one might call the law of non-identity, or becoming. For if even the law of identity itself has a history, has become what it is, and so is not identical with what it presently is, and so is not self-identical, then it invalidates its own claim to universality, necessity, and eternality, and confronts the fate of undergoing an evolution into its obverse—of becoming what it really is by becoming its other, the law of non-identity. And if logic defines reason, and rationality defines humanity, this amounts to a redefinition of human beings as imposers of the law of non-identity, not only on all things other than themselves but also on themselves. It invites us, in other words, to characterize human beings as self-legislators of non-identity—as the self-originating source of their own incessant self-differentiation, their unending becoming.

3) Freedom of the Will and Freedom of Spirit

That this is the essential background to understanding Nietzsche's conception of human freedom is confirmed by the fact that no sooner has he outlined his critique of the law of identity than he associates it with another metaphysical error—our belief in freedom of the will:

[E]ven now, indeed, we believe at bottom that all sensations and actions are acts of free will; when the sentient individuum observes itself, it regards every sensation, every change, as something isolated, that is to say unconditioned, disconnected: it emerges out of us independently of anything earlier or later. We are hungry, but we do not think that the organism wants to sustain itself; this feeling seems to be asserting itself *without cause or purpose*, it isolates itself and considers itself *wilful*. Thus: belief in freedom of will is a primary error committed by everything organic, as old as the impulse to the logical itself; belief in unconditioned substances and in identical things is likewise a primary, ancient error committed by everything organic. (I: 18)

The law of identity facilitates and is facilitated by the conviction of freedom of the will because the latter is a way of absolutizing the self-sufficiency or autonomy of the human individual. According to Nietzsche's history of this principle of morality (I: 39), we begin by calling individual actions good or bad by virtue of their consequences; then we call actions good or bad in themselves; then we shift focus to the motives of those actions; and then in turn to the whole character or nature of the person whose motives these are. It matters to him that this is not only an error but a self-subverting one: for if we can only be held accountable for our actions if we can be held accountable for the whole nature from which they flow, and if scientific philosophizing reveals that our nature is in fact determined by preceding causes outside our control, then we cannot be held accountable for anything we do. But it matters more to him that we understand how and why we embark on the analytic regress that consigns us to such nonsensicality: and here the critical thing is our drive towards the unconditioned or absolute. Our working assumption is that if our freedom is not total, it is not freedom at all; and that is what compels us to construct a conception of ourselves as *causa sui*—utterly self-originating causes, who thereby detach themselves entirely from the actual causal flux of the world, as if we existed entirely independently of all other things, as divine beings whose every mode of activity arises from their essential nature alone. Thus does our identity appear to us to depend upon our absolute self-identity—capable of being ourselves only if we are essentially self-creating and self-recreating *ex nihilo*.

If, then, freedom of the will is a constitutive metaphysical and moral error, does it follow that human beings merely appear to themselves to be free? Since Nietzsche addresses the book in which he advances this opinion to 'free spirits', then even if he doubts the current actuality of such spirits, it is hard to believe that he aspires to deny the reality of freedom altogether— 'free spirits of this kind do not exist, did not exist . . . [but they] *could* one day exist' (1st pref: 2). Moreover, on the basis of his argument thus far, he can only claim to have shown a certain conception of freedom to be utterly self-subverting; so one can avoid the nihilistic conclusion by rejecting the premises from which it emerges. Is there, then, an alternative conception of freedom to be found in these pages—one which depends upon finding a way of making sense of the idea of individuals who live by the principle of non-self-identity, understood as a way of accepting (not that they are absolutely determined but) that their freedom is and must be non-absolute, conditioned, finite rather than final?

Nietzsche's characterization of the genuinely free spirit goes hand-in-hand with his characterization of its opposite, the fettered spirit:

The fettered spirit takes up his position, not for reasons, but out of habit—acquired habituation to spiritual principles without reasons is called faith. (I: 226)

All states and orderings within society—classes, marriage, education, law—all these derive their force and endurance solely from the faith the fettered spirits have in them. (I: 227)

Narrowness of views, through habit become instinct, conducts to what is called strength of character . . . The man of strong character lacks knowledge of how many possibilities of action there are and how many directions it can take: his intellect is unfree, fettered, because in any given case it presents to him perhaps only two possibilities . . . The environment in which he is educated seeks to make every man unfree, inasmuch as it presents to him the smallest range of possibilities. The individual is treated by his educators as though, granted he is something new, what he ought to become is a *repetition*. (I: 228)

The fettered spirit is a repetition—first of all, of the community he inhabits, and of the habits that community inculcates within him via its customs: the ideally unfree community is one which has narrowed down its range of customary ways of living to as close to one as is possible, and the ideally unfree member of that community accordingly has as close as possible to one way of life to live out. Critically, then, at both communal and individual level, there is no distinction between what one does and what one might have done: whatever one does is simply what is done, that to which no alternative is imaginable and hence for which no justification is either available or needed. Heidegger would think of it as 'das man': Nietzsche invites us to think of it as the law of identity as applied to human life—the complete coincidence of actuality and potentiality, of who one is and who one might be. It is the absolute absence of freedom.

The free or unfettered spirit is thus characterized in opposition to this vision of absolute self-identity:

He is called a free spirit who thinks differently from what, on the basis of his origin, environment, his class and profession, or on the basis of the dominant views of his age, would have been expected of him. He is the exception, the fettered spirits are the rule . . . what characterizes the free spirit is not that his opinions are the more correct but that he has liberated himself from tradition, whether the outcome has been successful or a failure. As a rule, though, he will nonetheless have truth on his side, or at least the spirit of inquiry after truth; he demands reasons, the rest demand faith. (I: 225)

The free spirit is thus non-identical with his culture or community, indeed with any larger group within which his individuality might be swallowed up in habit and repetition. Most importantly, however, he differs from himself: if he is always aware of other possibilities that he might be exploring or enacting, then even when he stays with whatever possibility with which he is currently engaged, he does so in the knowledge that who he is and who he might be do not coincide. One might say that he retains a sense of even his deepest conviction as no more than an opinion, hence questionable, hence ultimately provisional, and inherently open to alteration—an attitude towards himself that amounts to a perpetual willingness for self-overcoming, a willingness to sacrifice his present state in the name of some future, unattained but attainable, state (towards which, once attained, he will then aspire to maintain a similar reserve). Nietzsche thinks of this as one kind of traffic with one's higher self:

Everyone has his good days when he discovers his higher self; and true humanity demands that everyone be evaluated only in the light of this condition, and not in that of his working-day unfreedom and servitude. A painter, for example, should be praised and revered in the light of the highest vision he is capable of seeing and reproducing. But men themselves traffic in very various ways with this higher self of theirs and are often actors of themselves, inasmuch as they afterwards continually imitate that which they are in those moments. Many live in awe of and abasement before their ideal and would like to deny it: they are afraid of their higher self because when it speaks it speaks imperiously. It possesses, moreover, a spectral freedom to come or stay away as it wishes; on this account it is often called a gift of the gods, whereas in reality it is everything else that is a gift of the gods (of chance): this however is man himself. (I: 624)

To stand in relation to one's higher self is not something that any given person might or might not attain: it is part of what it is to be human. And discovering or disclosing the reality of that relation to oneself is no different: anyone can make that discovery, and everyone has days on which they do so (hence neither the relation nor the capacity to disclose it are the exclusive property of some subset of humanity, call them the higher or the noble, the masters as opposed to the slaves). But there are two different ways of imagining what is involved in staying true to those daylight moments. If we attempt to prolong them by reiterating the vision of some particular day, then we cover over the more fundamental matter—the imperiously critical self-relation any such vision presupposes (Emerson refers to it as the alienated majesty of genuine thought). What matters for the spectral or spiritual freedom that one's higher self embodies is not the particular vision but one's capacity at any given point to receive such a vision, and to be commanded by it—the willingness to reiterate, not some particular state or condition we have seen (which will result in our imitating ourselves, acting out our lives in sheer self-repetition), but our willingness to evaluate any and every aspiration we have thus far reproduced in the light of some further aspiration that commands us to reproduce it, and so to change ourselves, perhaps radically.

The genuinely free spirit thus engages both ventricles of his brain, with the result that no state he attains is final; his mode of living is essentially transitional, or, as Nietzsche elsewhere puts it, 'anticipatory' (I: 614)—a mode of becoming rather than being, an unending process of differentiating himself both from what he presently is and from what he might come to be, identical with neither (because constituted by his relation to both) and hence non-identical with himself. This is why in I: 272, Nietzsche aligns freedom of spirit with the power of expansion that deposits annual rings of individual culture in just the way a tree's rings mark its annual expansion:

the free spirit identifies himself not with any one ring or with their nested totality, but with the power of expansion that they make manifest—what one might call the organic imperishable in the midst of change.

4) The Wanderer and his Shadow

This last image might also provide a helpful way of picturing the convoluted structure of *Human, All-Too-Human* that I began by outlining. Each textual phase—the 1878 volume; the 1879 supplement; the 1880 supplement; and the two 1886 prefaces—might be thought of as annual rings, or (in more explicitly Emersonian terms) as each a circle drawn around the preceding one, and itself inviting the drawing of another circle around it. In this sense, every succeeding ring has built upon the preceding one in order to go beyond it, and thereby to reveal the full extent of the possibilities implicit within it, as well as the further possibilities opened up by the exploitation of the initial ones. This is why my reading of the three main circles of this text has thus far allowed itself to exploit passages and remarks from the second volume of *Human, All Too Human* only insofar as they can be shown to have their origin or root in passages and remarks from the first volume.

At the same time, however, one implication of this image is that the later, more expansive textual circles find themselves in a position to stake out new ground—to find ways of articulating the central thinking of the first volume in ways that depend upon it, but also take it in directions that it could not have attained in its own terms. So one question we must confront is: what, if anything, do the two later supplements add to the picture of spiritual or spectral freedom painted in the first volume? I want to suggest that the beginnings of an answer should be found as much in differences of structure as in differences of content, and in two such structural differences in particular. First, the initial volume is subdivided into nine chapters or sections, each with their own, quasi-aphoristic titles, whereas both supplements dispense with any such internal structure. And second, the second supplement (unlike the first supplement, but taking its bearings—as we shall see—from the end of the first volume) presents the unbroken run of its numbered remarks as standing in a very particular relation to a conversation between a wanderer and his shadow.

Nietzsche's supplementary discarding of chapter structure cannot be accounted for on the grounds that the supplements do not cover the same range of topics adumbrated by the chapter headings in volume one: on the contrary, many commentators have pointed out that one could regiment those supplementary remarks under the same general headings (religion, metaphysics, politics, art, and so on) without too much difficulty. So Nietzsche himself must believe that one of the lessons he himself has been taught by the experience of writing Volume I is that a structural principle he took to be essential to the articulation of his vision at that point has been revealed (in large part, by the process of attempting to realize it) to be a dispensable form of regimentation—a skin to be sloughed off in the process of expansion. And one can see why: for chapter divisions interrupt the run of remarks in ways that serve to occlude the message they aim to convey by embodying. The principle of succession or transitionality, as Nietzsche understands it, is not one that operates (either differently or identically) in a number of distinct domains, or in relation to a network of self-sufficient subject matters: it rather takes its unpredictable guidance from any insight into any particular issue that might be assigned to any domain of human culture, and it finds that any such insight might in turn cast emancipatory light on an unpredictable range of other particular issues. To accept prevailing understandings of what makes an opinion 'political' or 'moral' or 'religious', and to reflect them in the form of one's reflections, is precisely to accommodate and reiterate habits of cultural evaluation that it is the free spirit's particular goal to put in question. A deeper insight into the difference between free and fettered spirits thus leads Nietzsche to a vision of chapters as themselves fetters to thought—at least here and now.

The second structural difference is the framing device of the wanderer and his shadow, which has two sources in Nietzsche's own writing. The first, proximate source is the final remark in Volume I (with its title 'The Wanderer'); so using that figure to frame and so to stage the work of the final part of Volume II declares Nietzsche's sense of continuity between these phases of his project. The second source reaches much further back, to the concluding pages of *The Birth of Tragedy*, in which—as I argued earlier in this book—Nietzsche makes metaleptic use of a key transitional scene or sequence of scenes in the third opera of Wagner's *Ring* cycle, in which Siegfried kills the dragon and his foster-father Mime, before being led towards Brunnhilde by the Dionysiac bird of the forest. But whereas the earlier Nietzsche identified himself with Siegfried, here he identifies himself with a figure called 'The Wanderer', whose path weaves around that of Siegfried as he travels from the forest home in which he reforges Nothung and towards his heroic destiny within the ring of fire, and whose voluminous cloak and hat disguise the features of Wotan.

So this framing device at once implies continuity with Nietzsche's earliest writing (more specifically a persistent willingness to regard artistic, meta-physical, and mythological expressions of Romantic pessimism as fit media for achieving freedom of spirit—as if acknowledging something inelimin-ably operatic about that goal), and also a certain discontinuity—a shift of identification, and so of perceived identity. For although Wagner's Wan-derer is (qua Wotan) the ultimate source of Siegfried's weapon, purpose, and existence, and the bearer of authority of a kind that frightens away even the bird of Dionysus, he is also (qua Wanderer) an ultimately powerless commentator upon the fateful journey Siegfried is undergoing: for his actions in *Siegfried* essentially amount to exchanging riddling questions with, and issuing ineffective warnings to, Mime, Alberich, Fafner, and finally Siegfried himself. His two identities fuse in his concluding attempt to block Siegfried's access to Brunnhilde with the spear on which Nothung shattered when it was wielded by Siegmund; but this time it is the spear which is shattered, and the Wanderer who silently gathers up its fragments and departs the stage.

So should we think of Nietzsche as now identifying himself with an exhausted and impotent order of culture and cosmos, whose representative can only observe the coming of its superlatively vital successor—as if using opera to acknowledge opera's supersession by heroically quotidian science? Or is he rather identifying with the Wanderer's refusal of stasis and habita-tion, his prophetic access to the future (both the means of its birth and its nature), and with his willingness to suffer dismissal by another whose inauguration of a new order is at once beyond him and essentially an expression of his own deepest desire (the self-created solution to the problem of slipping the bonds of the contract incised on his spear)—call it his way of staying loyal to disloyalty, or of combining self-enslavement with self-mastery?

An answer to this question can emerge only by assessing the significance of the fact that Nietzsche's Wanderer (unlike Wagner's) is equipped with a shadow—an interlocutor who is and is not himself. The duo are thus in a position to provide a brief prefatory and concluding exchange that encircles the second supplement's main text, and thereby characterizes its run of numbered remarks as a kind of precipitate of their conversation—more precisely as epitomizing *what* they 'can peaceably agree upon' (II, pt 2: prologue) as opposed to *how* they came to that agreement. And each participant in the dialogue offers a reason for this formal constraint or denial. The wanderer declares: 'Heaven defend me from long-spun-out literary conversations! If Plato had taken less pleasure in spinning-out his readers would take more pleasure in Plato. A conversation that gives delight in reality is, if transformed into writing and read, a painting with nothing but false perspectives: everything is too long or too short.' And his shadow welcomes the prospect of pure product on the grounds that 'they will all recognize in it only your opinions: no one will think of the shadow' (II, pt 2: prologue).

There seems to be a certain internal tension here. On the one hand, we encounter an explicit formal or figurative acknowledgement of the dual structure of selfhood as depicted throughout this project (and hence, presumably, as instantiated in its author)—selfhood as an unending process of internal debate or dialogue between an individual whose name betokens his commitment to becoming, and his shadow, call it his spectre or spirit, the higher self that embodies his freedom. This is confirmed by the fact that the wanderer's shadow opens the dialogue by speaking, but only in order to give the wanderer someone to speak to (that is, to allow him to speak), and the wanderer hears his shadow's voice as a weaker version of his own: so the ensuing dialogue is internal to the wanderer, with his shadow voice appearing at first to be more distant or as yet not fully realized, call it the voice of his unattained self; more generally, his shadow is the manifestation of his motive to wander, since it will usually lie either before him (as an ideal to be attained) or behind him (as an ideal that has been attained and so is to be overcome). But on the other hand, the particular form or mode in which the outcome of their interaction is given expression appears to be aimed at disguising or otherwise transcending that processual origin and its structural underpinnings. The key question that immediately arises is this: if the aim of this supplementary text is to advance a conception of the self as essentially transitional and dual, why choose a mode in which to give this conception expression on the grounds that it conceals process and disguises duality?

If we take both the wanderer and his shadow as embodiments of Nietzsche, the author of the text in which they appear, and of which they claim joint authorship, we might help ourselves to see that the reasons that these two aspects of his authorial identity offer for this choice of form imply that it is ultimately dictated by Nietzsche's conception of his relation to his readers. Qua wanderer, he thinks that transcribing in written form the process that actually resulted in his aphorisms would significantly reduce the amount of pleasure his readers might take in his work; and qua shadow, he is comforted by the thought that the wanderer's preference for product over process will turn the reader's thoughts away from him. So now our question can be more precisely reformulated: why does Nietzsche want to give his readers a kind of pleasure or delight that can arise only from the occlusion of his own particular course of wandering, and hence by his apparent denial of the structural duality that makes such wandering possible?

We know that Nietzsche is very likely to conceive of his reader as being in the condition that he thinks most people in the current condition of European culture occupy—that of being a fettered spirit, capable of freedom but currently existing under the tyranny of cultural habit. Since he subtitles his text as 'a book for free spirits', we can also be confident that his primary goal is to invite his reader to exchange her fetters for freedom—to discover the structural duality that lies concealed beneath her actual self-identity, and activate the capacity for becoming that her relation to her higher self makes possible. How, in the light of this goal, should he manage his relation to his readers? How should he present himself to them as author, and thereby situate them as readers of this author?

Paradoxical as it may seem, he could not activate the reader's dormant duality simply by explicitly presenting or representing his own active duality in his writing—for example, by transcribing (à la Plato) every concrete, self-critical exchange in the dialogue that constitutes his existence. For he would then risk encouraging his reader to fixate upon the particularity of her author, and so allow her to think that her own progress depended upon reproducing the process by means of which the author himself made progress. And this would amount to the mere reproduction of author by reader—as if the author wanted above all to reiterate the content of his own vision and vicissitudes in his readers, so that they might act out his life, and thus fail to live out their own; as the wanderer puts it himself, 'I want no slaves around me' (II, pt 2: conclusion). What he needs to do is not to reproduce his own wanderer-shadow duality in the body of the text, but rather displace it onto (or embody it in) the relation between author and reader—to relate to the fettered reader in the role of her higher self, in order thereby to induce a disclosure and activation of that reader's own occluded higher self, and consequently render himself dispensable in that role—a mere transitional object in this therapeutic movement from fettered to free-spirited reading, and so from fettered to free-spirited living. But if Nietzsche is to occupy that role in relation to the reader even on a provisional basis, he has a further reason for not presenting himself as doubled or divided qua author; for the self's higher self is not itself divided or processual—it is rather a singular or unified, unremittingly self-questioning and self-critical perspective that the self takes upon itself. Its authorial proxy or exemplar must therefore manifest exactly the same critical single-mindedness.

More precisely, Nietzsche must first get his readers to recognize that their current state is fettered, and then get them to realize their freedom by taking their own higher self as their guide. So he will certainly need to advance opinions that deliberately flaunt their aversion to current cultural evaluative habits; only thus can he provoke his readers into recognizing that one can think otherwise, hence that they must take responsibility for either continuing to think in conformity with others or for refraining from doing so. But he also needs to advance them in such a way as to discourage any attempt on the reader's part simply to exchange subordination to the authority of the community for subordination to Nietzsche's authority—which would amount simply to the acquisition of new fetters. The point of the exchange or dialogue is not to get his readers to agree with his views rather than with those of the general culture; it is to get his readers to relate to themselves as responsible for their own views, and hence as always capable of changing them. In short, he needs to exemplify the reality of the reader's higher self without colonizing it.

He would not achieve this emancipatory goal if he presented the cognitive product of his own dialogical processes in the familiar, essentially impersonal form in which such claims to knowledge are typically advanced—as a series of theses, doctrines, or dogmas. For that would imply that their acceptance was a demand of pure reason, and so would encourage another version of fettered reading and thinking—inviting his readers to relate to those views as if they were the only possible view to take, hence not something for which either author or reader need take any personal responsibility, and not something from which they might ever need to move on. It would simply encourage another denial of process, and act as a reinforcement of stultifying self-identity.

If, however, Nietzsche presents himself as essentially and provocatively opinionated—if he presents his counter-cultural views as a sequence of aphorisms that carry their personal investment on their stylistic face—then he makes it possible for the reader to evaluate his opinions as genuinely personal rather than impersonal, hence as the expression of one particular individual; and in this way he makes it possible for her to recognize herself as another individual standing in relation to him, hence responsible for making her own individual judgement about the matter in hand to which they both stand in the relation of judgers. The aphoristic form to which Nietzsche resorts thus invites its readers to register something that goes beyond the content of any given opinion of his—namely, the fact that all opinions are momentary and provisional realizations of subjectivity, ways in which a particular self takes an evaluative stance to the world and so to itself within it.

The single sequence of provocative opinions that constitutes the main text can thereby legitimately aspire to effect a transition from readerly self-identity to readerly non-self-identity. Such a text actively criticizes the evaluative habits the reader unreflectively reiterates from her culture; this forces her into an active critical engagement with that author; and this alerts her to (and, aspires to activate) her capacity to criticize and overcome herself—to traffic directly rather than indirectly with the imperious voice of her higher self. It is thus precisely by emphasizing the content or substance of his views, in all their polished, sequential singularity, that Nietzsche manages to acknowledge their 'how' in a manner that might emancipate his reader. For as aphorisms, their processual origin is not so much reproduced or asserted as it is enacted, being absorbed into their form and thereby made capable of informing their interaction with the reader.

5) Foreshadowing: A Philosophy of the Morning

What, then, of the two furthest or greatest circles in this textual expansion: the two 1886 prefaces? In one sense, they can't be taken simply on those terms—as two further additions to the same nest of circles constituted by the three main texts; for the gap between the composition of *The Wanderer and his Shadow* and that of the two prefaces was sufficient to accommodate the publication of several other books—stretches of text that Nietzsche patently did not regard as part of the *Human, All Too Human* project (since he didn't present them as supplementary to it). On the other hand, his clear concern in both prefaces is to situate the three main texts of that project in relation to both his earlier and his later thought—quite as if we could and should use the same figure of nested circles to comprehend the relation between *Human, All Too Human* and the works it succeeds and precedes, as well as the relations between its constituent parts.

The first of the 1886 prefaces, appropriately placed at the beginning of *Human, All Too Human*, invites us to look backward, to that on the basis of which we find ourselves at this textual threshold. More specifically, it suggests that, from a perspective attainable only by going through the coming book, we can think of Nietzsche in that book as struggling against a certain kind of fettering of his own spirit:

One may conjecture that a spirit in whom the type 'free spirit' will one day become ripe and sweet to the point of perfection had had its decisive experience in a *great liberation* and that previously it was all the more a fettered spirit and seemed to be chained for ever to its pillar and corner. What fetters the fastest? What bonds are all but unbreakable? In the case of men of a high and select kind they will be their duties: that reverence proper to youth, that reserve and delicacy before all that is honoured and revered from of old, that gratitude for the soil out of which they have grown, for the hand which led them, for the holy place where they learned to worship—their supreme moments themselves will fetter them the fastest, lay upon them the most enduring obligation. The great liberation comes for those who are thus fettered suddenly, like the shock of an earthquake: the youthful soul is all at once convulsed, torn loose, torn away—it itself does not know what is happening. A drive and impulse rules and masters it like a command; a will and desire awakens to go off, anywhere, at any cost; a vehement dangerous curiosity for an undis-covered world flames and flickers in all its senses. 'Better to die than to go on living *here*'—thus responds the imperious voice and temptation: and this 'here', this 'at home' is everything it had hitherto loved! (1st pref: 3)

Nietzsche here characterizes *Human, All Too Human* as resulting from his sudden, uncontrollable, and imperious impulse to free himself from a situation defined by his loyalty to the soil from which he had grown, and his reverence for those who had first led him onto his path of thinking—Schopenhauer and

Wagner pre-eminently among them. To that extent, then, commentators who interpret this text as a moment of discontinuity in Nietzsche's development—as his 'anti-romantic self-treatment', his disavowal of *The Birth of Tragedy* and *Untimely Meditations*—are in agreement with the person who resulted from it, and who is now interpreting that moment retrospectively. But they fail to note Nietzsche's equal emphasis upon this reactive phase of his spectral freedom as somehow excessive—as, for example, when he notes 'how much sickness is expressed in the wild experiments and singularities through which the liberated prisoner now seeks to demonstrate his mastery over things' (1st Pref: 3). And the judgement he presents himself as ultimately making about his earlier self after his recovery from these excesses amounts to a renewed acknowledgement of the value of that against which he so violently reacted: 'You shall become master over yourself, master also over your virtues. Formerly *they* were your masters; but they must be only your instruments beside other instruments. You shall get control over your For and Against and learn how to display first one and then the other in accordance with your higher goal' (1st pref: 3).

These remarks characterize Nietzsche's youthful identification with romantic pessimism as inherently virtuous: the alteration needed to effect his freedom of spirit was not a simple inversion of that valuation—as if genuine freedom for him consisted in regarding scientific naturalism as virtuous and romantic pessimism as vicious; the key issue is rather whether those virtues relate to their possessor as masters or as (not slaves but) instruments, as means of renewing one's attraction to one's higher self. So, even from this later point of view—itself achieved only by passing through every prior stage of his development, including the first—Nietzsche regards his youthful intellectual passions as an essential part of who he is, and of the value of what he does; what he wished to leave behind was not what he learnt from Wagner and Schopenhauer, but rather the enslaved and so self-enslaving attitude he presents himself as having initially adopted in relation to them as teachers.

One might, of course, wonder whether even this rather nuanced retrospective evaluation of his earlier self is wholly trustworthy. After all, his conception of freedom of spirit as outlined in *Human, All Too Human* is a recognizable descendent of the notions of selfhood and of genuine individuality that are central to his earlier writings (where they are couched either in terms of an inner duality of Apollo and Dionysus, or in terms of the avoidance of philistinism); and one central aspect of those earlier images is their emphasis on freedom as self-reliance—which means freeing oneself from the aim of merely imitating one's teachers as opposed to replicating the self-critical self-mastery they aspire to exemplify. To this extent, it isn't obvious—from the perspective of that early work—just how traumatic and earth-shaking a shift is in fact registered in Nietzsche's embarking on his book for free spirits (something that his continued evocation of Wagnerian characters would anyway suggest). Certainly, the polished, incisive but remarkably cool tone of its aphoristic prose hardly cultivates an air of convulsive self-aversion; it seems rather closer to the 'pale, subtle happiness of light and sunshine, a feeling of bird-like freedom, bird-like altitude, bird-like exuberance . . . in which curiosity is united with a tender contempt' (1st pref: 4) that Nietzsche associates with a midway condition between sickness and health—call it convalescence. So when he portrays himself in this preface as having been 'beside himself' (1st pref: 5) during the writing of *Human, All Too Human* and its immediate successors, that self-description need not be taken as a kind of self-criticism, but as a kind of praise: for it suggests not that he was out of his mind, but that he was ecstatic in just the way that the structural duality of selfhood (making us, and him, always already beside ourselves in a sane sense) requires. He thereby, however unconsciously, characterizes himself even in 1878–1880 as existing in the very condition of becoming and self-overcoming that he aspires towards in texts that are both earlier and later than this one.

The later 1886 Preface represents this enduring image of self-overcoming in a marginally revised version of an image that first surfaces in the earlier Preface—that of free-spiritedness as 'the son of tomorrow and the next day' (1st pref: 2), or 'the health of tomorrow and the day after' (2nd pref: 5). As Stanley Cavell has pointed out,[2] the German phrase common to both formulations is 'morgen und übermorgen', which puts in play exactly the prefix by means of which Nietzsche distinguishes men from after- or over- or super-men; if so, then 'the day after tomorrow' is the day reconceived or transfigured by the over-man, the essentially transitional or self-overcoming man, the genuinely free spirit: it is the overcoming of the day, the day as non-self-identical, because always inviting its own transcendence. In this way, both prefaces employ a phrase about openness to futurity to turn us to

---

[2] Cf. 'Old and New in Emerson and Nietzsche', in Cavell, *Emerson's Transcendental Etudes*, ed. D.J. Hodge (Stanford, CA: Stanford University Press, 2003).

the future, by importing into our experience of this early text a constellation of ideas that come to dominate the later writings, for the moment at which—in *Beyond Good and Evil*—Nietzsche characterizes the philosopher as a man of tomorrow and the day after tomorrow. But perhaps 'importation' is exactly the wrong word here: perhaps Nietzsche's emphasis on this phrase in just these prefaces is designed rather as an acknowledgement that the ideas it embodies were originally exported from this particular text, hence from this phase of his thinking (and so from the earlier phase of his thinking to which this one is indebted).

Here is how the first volume of this text ends, at the conclusion of a remark entitled 'The Wanderer':

[T]here will come the joyful mornings of other days and climes, when [the wanderer] shall see, even before the light has broken, the Muses come dancing by him in the mist of the mountains, when afterwards, if he relaxes quietly beneath the trees in the equanimity of his soul at morning, good and bright things will be thrown down to him from their tops and leafy hiding-places, the gifts of all those free spirits who are at home in mountain, wood and solitude and who, like him, are in their now joyful, now thoughtful way, wanderers and philosophers. Born out of the mysteries of dawn, they ponder on how, between the tenth and the twelfth stroke of the clock, the day could present a face so pure, so light-filled, so cheerful and transfigured:— they seek the *philosophy of the morning*. (I: 638)

It is this final remark that the second supplement at once identifies as its point of origin and overcomes or transfigures by inducing its protagonist to bifurcate, dramatizing its wanderer as in discourse with his shadow—that aspect of himself that is extinguished by the night and reborn out of the mysteries of the dawn. Shadows are inhabitants of daylight: as the wanderer's shadow puts it, 'when man shuns the light, we shun man' (II, pt 2: conclusion). But what happens to the wanderer's shadow in the forenoon, between the tenth and twelfth stroke of the clock? If that phrase refers, not to the period between ten a.m. and twelve noon, but to the moment of the penultimate stroke of a clock announcing noon, then his shadow is about to vanish: with the sun directly overhead, the wanderer's feet will eclipse or mask it. So the immediate forenoon foreshadows the moment at which the wanderer and his shadow will merge or coincide—at which he succeeds in realizing his unattained higher self; and the earlier preface presents such a moment of self-realization as permitting him to 'draw near to life' once more, 'as if his eyes are only now open to what is near at hand' (1st pref: 5)—which is why this is also the moment at which the day (and everything it reveals, call it the everyday, the near) presents so pure and transfigured, so enlightened, a face. The wanderer's morning is thus the period when his shadow creeps closer and closer to him; whereas in the afternoon and evening it elongates, extending the distance between it and him. At the dawn of each new day, the sun opens that gap to its maximum extent once more, and thereby sets him the task of closing it again by walking into the future, which means cultivating a willingness to keep on walking, from one attained state to the next, unattained but attainable state that inevitably opens up before him—a willingness to wander that is also a willingness to seek. Such is Nietzsche's philosophy of the morning.

The Trials of Desire

Sartrean Scenes III
(Part One, Chapter one; Part Two, Chapter One;
Part Three, Chapter One)

1. Someone must have been telling lies about Annie, for, without having done anything wrong, she was arrested one fine morning. Before she could properly grasp what was happening to her, she found herself on a crowded platform at one end of a large room; she had been stationed beside a table behind which sat a small, fat, wheezing man. He had been laughing and whispering to another man, who now came out from behind the table and stood a few yards away from Annie; he was short and stocky, with dark hair brushed back across his skull, and through a pair of thick-rimmed glasses he peered at the pages of a rather battered notebook. The sight of this book seemed familiar to Annie, but before she could retrieve the relevant memory, its owner looked quickly around at the people huddled in front of the platform, as well as those squashed into the cramped environs of the gallery, before addressing Annie directly:

'You were at the Croix de la Paix cafe yesterday evening, were you not?'

And now she had it: she'd seen this little man at the cafe many times before, but certainly last night, when he appeared to be dividing his time between furiously scribbling in this notebook and gazing directly at her table—gazing directly at her, in fact, and so intently that when someone (obviously a friend of his) had pulled back a chair to join him at his table, he had blushed furiously, quite as if he'd been caught with his eye to a keyhole. And hadn't one of her fellow-students at the university once told her that he was a philosopher?

'Since you saw me there yourself, I can't see the point of asking me that question.'

'These matters have to be established to the satisfaction of the Interrogation Court, and in particular to its Examining Magistrate'—here her interrogator gestured with rather excessive politeness to the fat man behind the table.

'Then I am more than happy to confirm that I was there; but I don't see how anything that went on there could justify my being arrested, let alone interrogated.'

'No doubt, no doubt: but that ignorance of yours in itself helps to confirm the accuracy of the charges that have been laid against you.'

'What charges?'

'The charge of self-deception, or as some would have it, bad faith.'

'I really have no idea what you're talking about'.

'And of course, that is exactly what one would expect someone in bad faith to say, and indeed to say in good faith.'

Annie began to see the difficulty of her situation more clearly—even its danger. So she resolved to adopt a different strategy with respect to her rather self-satisfied interlocutor: to make it clear that she was more than willing to meet him on the intellectual ground he occupied with such an infuriating assumption of exclusive access.

'Perhaps you would be so kind as to inform me of your grounds for arraigning me on this charge.'

'It would be my pleasure. At the cafe yesterday evening, you shared a table with a man—rather a good-looking man, it seemed to me. The two of you appeared to be enjoying yourselves: the wine and the conversation flowed freely, and at one point, your companion moved to cover your right hand, which had hitherto been resting on the table, with both of his.'

Here, the interrogator paused, as if conscious that he was now approaching the crux of the matter, and that every care had to be taken to prepare the ground properly for his central claim.

'Would you deny that the two of you were on a date—in other words, that the evening was understood by both of you to have a romantic inflection?'

Annie was puzzled.

'You've lost me, I'm afraid. Pierre and I went to the cafe because we'd both been working hard in the philosophy library that day, and needed to relax.'

The interrogator seemed almost pleased by this response; he looked around at the crowd, then gestured towards the table.

'I won't bother to read into the record Pierre's own account of the evening, which offers a rather different perspective on the matter, because whatever you might have initially assumed about the nature of this social occasion, you must surely have been aware of the meaning of your companion's gesture midway through the meal—the way in which it made explicit something that had been implicitly informing the occasion from the moment that it was proposed and agreed to?'

'What meaning?'

'Its meaning as an expression of desire—of his desire for you.'

Annie laughed.

'Now I can see where you've gone wrong. Of course, things may have looked that way to an ignorant observer—if you'll pardon the expression; but the truth of the matter is that I don't even recall Pierre making that gesture, because for most of the evening we were deeply engaged in conversation—in *intellectual* intercourse of a kind that you, with your philosophical interests, ought to be able to recognize, and to appreciate. I don't deny that Pierre admires and esteems me greatly, as I do him. But our relationship is, to employ a term that I'm sure will be familiar to you, Platonic; it's based on a respect for one another as rational beings.'

These words produced a rather unpleasantly sceptical murmur from the (almost entirely male) crowd in the Chamber; but far more unpleasant was Annie's awareness that as she spoke them a deep flush had gradually begun to suffuse her neck and cheeks. She put her hand up to her face, both to confirm the existence of the blush and to conceal it; but the interrogator was far too quick for her.

'Your body seems to betray you now, just as it betrayed you yesterday evening. For that blush only confirms what was evident to me, even from some distance away, catching glimpses of you both through brief gaps in the crowd—namely that your response to your companion's gesture took the form of making no response at all. Your hand neither resisted his, nor reciprocated; instead it continued to lie on the table, as inert as the wine-glass and the dinner-plate between which it was placed. It was quite as if you had disowned your own hand—as if you aspired to transcend it, and indeed your whole bodily reality, altogether; as if you wished to deny that your body was yours at all.'

Annie was now utterly bewildered, and increasingly angry.

'You couldn't be more wrong, Monsieur. My hand was not unresponsive to the meaning of Pierre's gesture, because Pierre's gesture—if he really did make it, and I genuinely don't remember him doing so—could not have had a meaning of that kind. And I'm blushing now simply because this extremely—masculine—audience, not to mention the uniformly male officers of the Law in the platform with me, seem determined to deny that a woman and a man might have a relationship that isn't sexual, or rather one in which Eros has been refocused on the beauty of the soul.'

Her interrogator smiled, but only fleetingly.

'I have no doubt that you mean every Platonic word you're saying; that is, I don't question your sincerity for an instant. My claim is rather that your sincerity is here simply a further expression of what I earlier called bad faith.'

Annie had begun to recover her self-possession after the unfortunate incident of the blush; with the nature of the charge against her now clear, and its sexist inflection all-but-undeniable, she took the opportunity to go on the attack.

'So now honesty is simply a further expression of bad faith, is it? And speaking without any intention to deceive is simply a more complex way of engaging in deception. If your idea of philosophical clarity is this kind of equation of opposing concepts, then it's little wonder that its achievements are hard to distinguish from those of the sophists.'

The interrogator smiled again, this time rather more indulgently.

'I believe, madam, that a perfect exemplification of the coherence of my analysis of sincerity was to be found in the cafe last night, and was indeed encountered there by both of us. Do you recollect the waiter who served you and your companion (and indeed myself)?'

Annie paused: and as she did so, an image invaded her consciousness—an image of a tray of cups and glasses floating through the smoke-filled air, perpetually threatening to topple onto the heads and tables beneath as it slid abruptly sideways between the pillars and shifting crowds, kept in a metastable equilibrium by that annoyingly adept waiter who had taken their order just a little too solicitously when he arrived, and who was now heading their way once more. The contrast between his smoothly flexible arm and hand, and the almost martial stiffness of the rest of his body, as he delivered her coffee without spilling a single drop, was almost enough to deprive him of the tip his performance all-too-clearly demanded.

'Yes—I remember him. What of it?'

'There, I would say, is a man who is whole-heartedly (might we not say sincerely?) committed to being a waiter; someone who has thrown himself body and soul into the realization of his role. And yet, I think you will agree, he succeeds only in performing or playing at being a waiter; for the very completeness with which he devotes himself to getting up at five o'clock, sweeping the cafe floor, starting to brew the coffee, only confirms the extent to which his doing so is a function of his having chosen to value this array of activities above any other role he might inhabit, and hence the extent to which he cannot simply be identified with this choice—the extent to which he is always more or other than the content of any particular choice, or sequence of them.'

Annie uneasily recalled her own uneasiness when that same waiter materialized next to her and Pierre that evening, bending over them just a little too eagerly, inserting himself all the more forcefully into their inter-course precisely because his attempt to avoid doing so was so patently sincere. And then all of a sudden she *did* remember Pierre's hands jumping away from hers, as if abashed, to reach for the menu or his wallet, whilst her own remained inert, as if taking pride in being as little affected by its liberation as by its prior imprisonment.

She could feel her confidence in the meaning of that evening's events beginning to drain away, as if the interrogator had the power not only to redefine them from a perspective essentially inaccessible to her, but also to induce her to accept that redefinition (and thereby accept herself as equally beholden to both perspectives, the one she still occupied and the one she could never occupy). Quickly, she shifted her ground.

'I don't deny that sincerity might itself sometimes be a performance, without always being such a performance; but let that pass. For the real problem with your levelling a charge of self-deception at me (or indeed, at anyone else unlucky enough to find themselves within reach of your gaze) lies in the contradictory nature of the concept itself. Deceiving another person is one thing; but with self-deception, the primary target of the deceit is also the deceiver: bad faith is, after all, on your account a mode in which the self lies to itself. But the very idea of such a thing is surely incoherent;

how can a self deceive itself, since it can be deceived only if it lacks access to the knowledge possessed by the deceiver?'

'Perhaps this is the appropriate moment to call upon Herr Freud as an expert witness, M. Interrogator?' The suggestion came from the Examining Magistrate; and in response, there was a flurry in the crowd to the right of the platform, as an elderly, bearded man smoking a large cigar pulled himself to his feet. But before he could rise to his full height, the interrogator moved towards the magistrate, shaking his head vigorously.

'Much though I welcome your willingness to facilitate my examination of the accused, I'm sorry to say that Herr Freud's ideas simply can't help us here. His notion of repression does not so much account for self-deception as reiterate the apparent difficulty it poses; for the idea of repression presupposes that the one subject to repression is also the one imposing that repression, and so must apprehend that which is purportedly being held beyond its own apprehension. So, either the same problem recurs, or we drop the notion of a censoring function or authority altogether, in which case the Freudian idea of the unconscious becomes a tool for facilitating exactly the kind of bad faith it claims to explain; for the very idea of the id as distinct from the ego severs consciousness from itself, making itself absolutely other to itself, just as Annie over there was trying (without success) to separate herself from her body, and thereby from the man so interested in it.'

The elderly gentleman cried out in fury, and attempted to make his way to the platform nevertheless, before being restrained by court officers at the magistrate's order; and as the disorder was contained, Annie's retreating blush returned with full force, this time fuelled by anger, and facilitated by a deepening recollection of the kind of philosophy that her interrogator had been described as advocating when he had first been pointed out to her in the cafe—the cafe she was beginning to wish she had never visited.

'So the articulations of psychotherapy are bad faith in conceptual form, are they? What about your own conceptual articulation of the self—as that which is not what it is, and is what it is not? Isn't that a prime example of such a contradictory concept, one which unites in itself an idea and its negation, and thereby facilitates the necessary slippage from one to the other?'

'But, if it please the court, the slippage that facilitates bad faith is precisely the one that my formulation tries to resist. I just pointed out that, for Annie,

her companion's gesture with his hand was all facticity and no transcendence—mere matter in motion; and he himself was all transcendence, to be
addressed as pure personality rather than a necessarily embodied soul. As for
her own hand, and her embodiedness more generally: that she relates to
as simply not her, essentially unrelated to her consciousness. Recall the
waiter: for him, his role as a waiter is the project with which he identifies
himself, despite the fact that he is not identical with it; his choosing to
devote himself entirely to being a waiter precisely implies that he could
have done otherwise, and so declares his non-identity with waiting at
tables. Both of them stake their lives on understanding the non-identity
of consciousness as if its facticity and its transcendence were either utterly
synonymous or absolutely unrelated—so that the one might either entirely dissolve into the other (facticity as essentially nothing other than
transcendence, and vice versa) or entirely fail to (facticity as essentially
other than transcendence, and vice versa). Whereas my formulation is
meant to emphasize that facticity and transcendence are essentially related
to one another, even if negatingly—that the facticity of the self is its
transcendence negated, and its transcendence is its facticity negated: it's
not so much that each is not the other, as that each is not-the-other, each
is the other's other (hence, each would not be at all except as not-the-
other). And that formulation prevents what Annie is trying to do: it
refuses to allow facticity or transcendence either simply to be, or simply
not to be, the other. But of course, it is only because facticity and
transcendence are related negatingly that people like Annie can attempt
to deny or surpass them: she can only deny her body because it is hers,
the body that her consciousness is not; and she can only identify herself
with her consciousness because it is hers, the consciousness that her body
is not.'

Annie couldn't help herself; this adversarial parody or negation of a
conversation had reached such a plane of speculative abstraction that it
had somehow recovered a genuine engagement with its subject matter, and
she found herself absolutely invested in contributing to it.

'It's rather worse than that, though, isn't it? It's not just that the non-
identity of selfhood makes bad faith possible (including theoretical accounts
of the non-identity of selfhood made in bad faith); it's also that this non-
identity makes it possible for us to continue in bad faith—makes bad faith a
stable, self-maintaining mode of being non-identical with oneself.'

Her interrogator looked a little startled at his interlocutor's willingness to react as if her current difficulties with the Law simply didn't exist; but he happily made use of the invitation her comments embodied.

'I'm inclined to say that putting oneself in bad faith is like putting oneself to sleep, and that being in bad faith is like dreaming. Once this mode of being has been realized, it is as difficult to get out of it as it is to wake oneself up; for dreaming isn't just a series of episodes but a way of being in the world—a self-sustaining alternative to waking life, a parallel world. On the one hand, anything that reality might contain can be reproduced in a dream (as Descartes was so eager to emphasize); on the other hand, everything we encounter in a dream differs from anything we might encounter in reality (being, so to say, inherently unreal, non-existent). Dreaming differs from reality not in some particulars, but in every particular (given that existence is not a predicate); hence, it is as capable of sustaining itself as is waking life, even if it does so otherwise. Bad faith engenders and inhabits a dream of the self's non-self-identity: perhaps one should rather say a bad dream, even a nightmare. It doesn't deny the reality of selfhood—it caricatures or distorts it, making either too much or too little of distinctions that are real but relational; but of course, this means that we can learn much about the reality of selfhood from the kind of distortion that results from what Herr Freud'— here bowing courteously to the still muttering would-be expert witness in the crowd—'might want us to call the dreamwork of bad faith.'

2. Joseph K. must have been telling lies about him to someone, for, without having done anything wrong, Warden Franz was arrested one fine morning. Before he could properly grasp what was happening to him, he found himself on the Examining Magistrate's crowded platform at one end of the Interrogation Chamber; the magistrate had been laughing and whispering to another man standing next to him, who now came out from behind the table and stood a few yards away from Franz. He was short and stocky, with dark hair brushed back across his skull, and through a pair of thick-rimmed glasses he peered at the pages of a rather battered notebook, before raising his head:

'You were present at the arrest of Joseph K. yesterday morning, were you not?'

Although distinctly disoriented by suddenly being allotted the role of the accused, Franz was not at all unfamiliar with the role of witness at such proceedings; so he found it fatally easy to enter into this kind of interrogative dialogue with the man who appeared to be his accuser.

'Strictly speaking, sir, Warden Willem and I were both there; or rather, we went together with the Inspector assigned to that particular case to Monsieur K.'s lodgings.' Franz looked around the crowded Chamber. 'Isn't Willem here, sir? You should certainly talk to him as well as me; in fact, you should probably talk to him rather than me—he is the older, more experienced man, someone I've always looked up to as a teacher and a leader. He was really the one in charge.'

'Please let us determine to whom we talk; after all, who said that warden Willem has been accused of anything?'

Franz's unease increased; how could he be the only person accused of something, when he never did anything without Willem? What was he accused of, anyway?

'To return to the matter at hand: it was your task to alert Joseph K. to his new legal status?'

'That's right, sir; and to prepare him for initial interrogation by the Inspector.'

Franz's interrogator took a pace or two away from him, and then returned.

'Please tell us exactly how you went about your duties that day.'

Franz strove to recall the morning at issue, which he had never previously regarded as anything out of the ordinary.

'We arrived early, sir; it's always best to make sure that the bird hasn't flown to work, or on a trip. In fact, we were there at seven o'clock; and the landlady—a Madame Grubach—let us in straight away. But we ended up cooling our heels for the most part of an hour; Mme. Grubach warned us that Joseph K. never had his breakfast before eight o'clock, and was usually fast asleep until she knocked on the door with his tray. But I found this hard to believe; so I took the liberty of looking through the keyhole of the door to his room, a little before eight o'clock, and sure enough I saw him lying in bed, wide awake. In fact, he seemed to be staring through his window, which looked out on to the apartment block next door; and when I took a quick look through the corresponding window in the room in which Willem and I were waiting, I saw that Joseph's gaze was being returned with interest by an old lady in the apartment opposite. Her gaze really was remarkably intense, full of a hungry curiosity; and then I realized that she had probably noticed our own earlier arrival and was no doubt eager to enjoy whatever damaging consequences might flow from it for her supposedly respectable neighbour. By the time I returned to the keyhole, something about this exchange of glances had disturbed Joseph to the point of moving him to ring for his breakfast. But before the bell began to sound, I straightened up, knocked on the door, and informed him of his new legal status.'

'How did he react to this news?'

'Not very well, sir: but then very few people do, and I've learnt not to expect otherwise. He was rather abusive; he waved various identity documents in our faces, as if the legal system in this country ever produces cases of mistaken identity; and he seemed to want to meet our Inspector in his nightgown—a rather shocking breach of decorum for an employee of a respectable bank.'

'We shall return to the matter of the nightgown, warden; but before we do, I want to clarify the issue of Joseph K.'s breakfast. What exactly did he have to eat that morning?'

Franz was more than a little puzzled by the direction of the questioning, but his habits as a professional witness overrode any self-protective instincts.

'During one of his rather petulant retreats to his room, I again applied myself to the keyhole, and I observed him eating an apple that he picked up from the washstand—a good choice, I thought: food and drink in one.' He omitted to mention the degree of self-consciousness induced in him as he went down on his knees before the door a second time, aware as he was that the old lady across the way had moved so as to make use of a direct line of sight into the room he and Willem were occupying, and had been joined by an even older man. Why should he be ashamed of having done his duty?

'But what happened to the breakfast that Mme. Grubach had prepared for him, as she always did, and as she confirms doing on the day in question'— here, the interrogator brandished a document taken from the magistrate's table—'in this witness statement?'

Franz began to sense treacherous ground underfoot.

'It arrived when he was searching in his room for those pointless identity documents; and since he showed no sign of re-emerging, and the breakfast—which looked quite delicious—was getting cold, Willem and I decided to eat it ourselves. Or at least, Willem decided that we should;

he certainly ate the lion's share of it.' And once again, Franz looked around the crowded courtroom for his erstwhile partner.

'So whilst you both gorge yourselves upon milk, bread, and honey, as if newly-arrived inhabitants of the Promised Land, your ward and charge is reduced to a meal whose constituents might have come directly from the Garden of Eden—one not just primitive but primal, one might say.'

Franz remained silent. Primal? What on earth was this man talking about? The interrogator savoured his puzzlement, and turned with a rather self-satisfied expression to the crowd before saying:

'Surely you recall that the Bible associates the eating of an apple with the acquisition of knowledge of good and evil? You and your fellow-warder had no need of it, knowing as (you thought) you did all about Joseph's guilt, and taking that knowledge to license your impertinent plundering of his means of sustenance; whereas his ignorance of what had rendered his hitherto-comfortable life so pervasively and absolutely persecutory led him to fall back upon the most basic of foodstuffs, at once seeking the simple comfort of satisfied bodily desire and acting out the hoped-for acquisition of the knowledge he lacked.'

Franz hoped that his expression did not betray the full extent of his incomprehension.

'But of course, Warden, the knowledge of good and evil that the eating of the Edenic apple bestows is knowledge arrogated to God alone; hence, this staging of the human impulse to satisfy bodily desire is ultimately allegorical of the human desire to be as God—to be God. After all, the need to eat and drink in order to live is the defining mark of the finitude of the human animal; our embodiedness makes us dependent on the world outside us for our continued existence, insofar as that body must ingest its environment in order to replenish itself, endlessly remaking itself out of what is not itself, interiorizing the exterior by negating its constituents. Each individual desire might be satisfied, each particular lack made good (even if others take the food that is properly ours); but no negation of a particular desire can negate desire as such, which will always return in the form of some new desire, thereby teaching us that the human mode of being as such takes the form of lack, dependence, non-self-sufficiency, and so engenders our most fundamental desire—namely, to be not subject to desire, to transcend (that aspect of) our finitude. And since it is definitive of our idea of God that he lack any such lack, any kind of dependence on what He is not, being essentially non-finite, it follows that our desire not to desire is, in effect, a desire to be God.'

The interrogator paused, then turned back to Franz with an almost apologetic air.

'But you don't really want a lecture on the human condition as one of desiring the impossible—desiring to be both human and not-human, both individual consciousness and absolutely self-sufficient embodiment of all reality: being human as desiring to be both what one is not and what one is. What directly concerns us here and now is one particular desire that you and your fellow-warden seem to have become gripped by during your encounter with Joseph K., a desire whose specific mode of satisfaction also has its Edenic aspect, being an arrogation of divine rather than legal power. I mean, of course, your interest in Joseph K.'s clothes and underclothes.'

Suddenly, Franz realized what must have happened: Joseph K. had complained about this aspect of their treatment of him.

'Now I begin to see why I am being interrogated; but I can assure you that this is all based on a misunderstanding. The initial problem arose because Joseph K. proposed to meet the Inspector wearing only his nightgown. So we simply pointed out that this would be unacceptably informal, and encouraged him to change into more appropriate clothing.'

'Did you not suggest to him that he hand over his underclothes to you before meeting your Inspector?'

'We did indeed, sir; but as we explained to him then, that was simply because if he handed them over at the depot, they were very likely to be stolen, and even if they weren't, they could only be repurchased at very extortionate prices. We were only trying to be helpful, sir.'

'But, Warden, why on earth should Joseph K. have to hand over any articles of his clothing at the police depot? It is true that he was under arrest, but as you both very well knew—and as Joseph K. himself was about to discover from your Inspector—his arrest not only did not involve his going to jail, it didn't even involve his being confined to his own lodgings. So if he was entirely free to go about his everyday business, why should he need to be deprived of his clothing?'

Franz was dumbstruck. He remembered with absolute clarity how unconvincing and weak Joseph K.'s blustering had sounded, beneath the forbidding gaze of the Inspector (and indeed, now he came to think of it, beneath the hungry gaze of Joseph's neighbours, a group whose number had swelled to three as they repositioned themselves to observe his initial interrogation). And all the time, he had been taking careful note of everything they had said and done in private, feeling the very reverse of gratitude for their remarkably tolerant treatment of his initial shock and anger, and now—even when he was probably himself being dragged even further into this vast machine of interrogation and judgement—he had reached back and delivered a potentially fatal counter-blow. How could the meaning of that perfectly everyday situation have turned so decisively, and threateningly, against him? It was as if the whole of his world had instantly reshaped itself, so that all its possibilities of feeling and action were now aligned against him. Franz tried feebly to summon up his defences.

'But sir, it's a tradition that body-linen is the warder's perquisite; and I have plans to be married; and of course, Willem—who was certainly the moving spirit behind all our actions—has a family to feed.'

'So now, not content with bringing your service into disrepute by your own actions and by your slanderous remarks about corruption in the depot, you defend yourself by further blackening the reputation of the legal system you represent. Now you tell us that corruption is not just a matter of individual failings, but a proud tradition of the service—something inherent in the very idea of wardenship.'

'M. Magistrate, I rest my case.'

As the interrogator moved away, the magistrate looked directly at Franz for a long while, then—without shifting his gaze—he bellowed:

'Law-Court Attendant, summon the whipper.'

Out of the corner of his eye, Franz saw a man push through the crowd towards the platform; he was wearing a tight-fitting dark leather garment, which nevertheless left his throat, much of his chest and the whole of both arms bare; and he was carrying a rod. Franz took a step backwards, his eyes searching frantically around the Chamber:

'Where is Willem? He was at least as guilty as me; in fact, he was the ringleader. Is he not to be punished as well?'

3. Someone must have been telling the truth about the interrogator, for one fine morning he was arrested. Before he could properly grasp what was happening to him, he found himself on the platform in the Examining Magistrate's Interrogation Chamber; but this time he occupied the place of the accused, and in his own familiar place behind the magistrate's table was

an elderly, bearded man, smoking a large cigar and dressed in the robes of an Advocate. Before the interrogator had time to call out his name, the Advocate had moved over to him and whispered in his ear:

'Don't worry. Even if my line of questioning seems particularly risky or self-incriminating, trust me: this is the only way in which we might be able to acquit you of the charges.'

'What charges?'

But it was too late: the magistrate had called for silence, and the Advocate began.

'Monsieur S., could you please tell the court where you were yesterday evening?'

The interrogator hesitated; but the Advocate looked meaningfully at him and said:

'I can assure you, Monsieur, that telling the truth is all that is needed to set you free.'

'I spent the early part of the evening in the Croix de la Paix cafe, at my usual table. I think I left after a couple of hours.'

'Did you leave alone?' The Advocate paused: 'Perhaps I should rephrase that; did anyone else leave at the same time you did?'

The interrogator took a deep breath, as if contemplating a leap into a freezing sea.

'I left when Annie left, in the company of a gentleman with whom she had spent the evening.'

'You followed them, then?'

'Yes.'

'Could you please tell us why?'

'Jealousy, curiosity, perversity: any of these, all of these.'

'I see. And where did the couple lead you?'

'To an apartment block not far away from the cafe. The man had a key to the front door, and I managed to slip through it before it closed; the lift doors had just shut, so I noted the floor on which it stopped, and then raced up the stairs just in time to see them enter an apartment at the end of the corridor, closing the door behind them.'

'What did you do then?'

'I walked up the corridor to the apartment, knelt down and looked through the keyhole.'

'And what did you see?'

What should he say that he had seen? The dimly-lit tableau he had been expecting, in which the man Annie called Franz had taken off his jacket, stripped the dress from Annie's shivering body, and begun to ply the whip he had taken from the chest-of-drawers in the bedroom? Or a scene of a very different kind, in which the two people sat across the kitchen table arguing with one another, occasionally moving into the study to locate a book from which some decisive passage was to be read aloud? But he was supposed to be telling the truth.

'I'm not sure that I could tell you exactly what they were doing, but even if I could and did, I wouldn't really be responding truthfully to your question; because the truth is that I didn't care what they were doing, I simply wanted to observe them (doing whatever they happened to be doing) whilst being unobserved myself. I wanted to enslave them without their even knowing that they had been enslaved, to reshape the meaning of what they were doing without them even knowing that it had been reshaped. I wanted to insert myself like a shadow between them, invisibly but decisively remaking the significance of their relationship.'

'But why?'

Why indeed? Because he wanted to be (their) God, the unobserved observer of human reality, the uncreated creator of its meaning? Because, when Annie had noticed him observing them in the cafe, she had turned the tables on him simply by virtue of gazing back at him, transforming him into nothing more than a mildly contemptible violator of their privacy; so that he had felt a sudden imperative to free himself from the role into which he had been thrown, to re-establish mastery over his own identity by mastering hers?

'Is the Law interested in motives, or in deeds?'

At this sign of resistance, however polite, the Advocate gave the interrogator a warning glance; but he seemed to accept the implicit admonition.

'How long did you spend observing whatever was to be seen behind the apartment door?'

'I had no sooner applied my eye to the keyhole than I heard footsteps in the hall behind me; so before I could become properly absorbed in what I was observing, before I could even register the significance of what I heard, I found myself gripped body and soul by shame. For my observer, whoever he was, had instantly reduced my being to that of a voyeur; the transcendence which sustained and hence surpassed my factical realization of myself as a voyeur was itself transcended—if not utterly annihilated then certainly alienated from me. For now I found myself forced to interpret myself as that other saw me, and to interpret the world as the other saw me within it—a world in which I no sooner apprehended the dark nearby corner of the corridor next to me as a hiding place than I rejected recourse to it because of the risk that the other had a flashlight, or some other means of illuminating it should he wish to do so. His mere presence had remade the world in accordance with his own projection of its possibilities, and remade me along with it; more precisely, he revealed the gaze of the other as something always already internal to my consciousness, insofar as that consciousness is embodied, even if it relates negatingly to its embodiment. My paralysis was not simply induced by his pinning me onto the role of voyeur; it was more fundamentally induced by the realization that my being is such that it is always already vulnerable to being so pinned—hence, always secreting a perspective upon myself that I can never myself occupy, and thereby disclosing my life as caught up in a more comprehensive dimension of significance that I can neither deny nor grasp. I felt myself enslaved to a wholly other source of judgement that was nevertheless a condition of my being; my transcendence stood revealed as masterable just at the moment at which I was attempting silently to master Annie's transcendence. In short, my shame lay bare my being-visible, and all the dangers inherent in such utter defencelessness before a freedom that is not my own.'

The Advocate paused again, this time to give the interrogator's remarks a chance of being at least partially absorbed by the rather restless crowd—no doubt less wholly committed to the life of the mind than either Annie or Monsieur S.

'How did you react to being discovered before the keyhole?'

The interrogator took a deep, ragged breath, before composing himself sufficiently to reply.

'When I had composed myself sufficiently to turn around, I immediately recognized the man in the corridor as Joseph K.: my work in the Interrogation Chamber had made me more than familiar with the case against him, and with his reactions to it. Unfortunately, this meant that he recognized me no less speedily; and I could see my world of possibilities being reshaped once more as he contemplated the use to which he might put the—shall we say—discrepancy between my official role and my current preoccupation.

But the situation turned out to have a painful dimension for him as well; for he had entered the building in order to visit the very apartment into which I had been attempting to gain a view, because Annie was his girlfriend. So when he pushed me aside and knocked at the door, then opened it with his own key, to find Annie with another man—let alone with the man who had recently been assigned as his warder—his initial confusion was almost as great as my own. He slammed the door in their faces, then dragged me away, out of the building and back to the Croix de la Paix cafe, where—he told me—he needed time to think.'

'And what was the result of his cogitation?'

'Blackmail. He said that if I didn't abuse my powers as an officer of the court in order to bring both Annie and Franz into difficulties with the Law, he would reveal my own humiliating proclivities, and thereby destroy my career, my livelihood, and my life. So I did exactly as he asked; as the magistrate himself can confirm.'

The Advocate nodded.

'I'm sure that your explanation will limit the damage that this revelation might otherwise have done to your career.' The magistrate looked far less certain of this than the interrogator could have wished; but the Advocate moved quickly on.

'The nature of my interest in your case is, however, rather different. When you first came to see me, declaring your firm intention to confess to the authorities rather than to permit Joseph K. to continue to use his knowledge of your vice to enslave you, I was happy to do so. But I cannot refrain from doing everything in my power to strengthen the defence that your confession both requires and provides; for—despite your rather jejune objections to my methods, not to mention your equally embarrassing public recitation of them in this very hall whilst in thrall to Joseph K.'s wishes—I believe that they might be used to reinforce your claim to be understood and pardoned rather than condemned for your wrongdoing.

'You told me once, I believe, that you always experienced the gaze of another as an attempt to obtain mastery over you—that you could not even visit the park and observe another man seated on a bench with a book, without suddenly experiencing the vertiginous sense that the structure of the world you inhabit was being sucked away from you and towards him, as if he constituted a black hole for the world's being—an unoccupiable and

incomprehensible perspective upon that world which nevertheless pene-
trated you with a sense of your own powerlessness to retain mastery of your
own possibilities, let alone of the field of their potential deployment. It was as
if you had no more reality for him than the dogs being taken for a walk by
their owners—as if you were just one more enslaved animal. I think you even
claimed that this was the truth that Kafka's art attempts to describe in *The
Trial*.'

The interrogator fought the blush that threatened to rise into his cheeks;
but he didn't deny the Advocate's testimony.

'You will know that many of my patients suffer from what I call "paranoia"—they complain that all their thoughts are known and their actions
watched and supervised; in my view, their complaint is not exactly false.
There is a power of this kind, and it afflicts or informs every human being;
but it is normally internal—the result of introjecting a parental imago,
constructing an ego ideal, and deputing the voice of conscience as its
watchman. The paranoiac is pathological only insofar as he takes this
voice to come from outside; his problem is that the internal split inherent
in all properly functioning human beings is experienced in so radical or
exaggerated a way that it creates an aspect of the self that that self cannot but
regard as not his, as not him but another, a wholly external locus of
judgement by which he is continuously threatened. What you have done
is build a picture of the human condition according to which this pathological state is normal; so that a person's sense of the gaze of the other as
persecutory and enslaving is straightforwardly sane.'[1]

'I'm tempted to say that even paranoiacs can have real enemies, metaphysically as well as empirically. To be more precise: I don't deny that the
locus or voice of judgement is internal, or is experienced as always already
within us; I claim only that this interior split is an effect or register of our
vulnerability to the other and his ability to place us within his world, and
thereby to displace ourselves from our world and its structures of meaning.'

'And displacement is precisely the issue I wish to raise. For the experiences you describe sound to me remarkably like the experience of the first
child when a second child comes along—the dislocating realization that one
is not after all the centre of the universe; the realization that the world exists

---

[1] Cf. chapter four of Nancy Bauer, *Simone de Beauvoir, Philosophy and Feminism* (New York:
Columbia University Press, 2001).

independently of any single inhabitant of it, and that that independence is partly constituted by its capacity to provide an environment for multiple consciousnesses, each of which must acknowledge the reality of other centres of consciousness in the world if it is fully to acknowledge the world's independent reality, and thereby to acknowledge its own independent reality within that world.'

'That makes it sound as if recognizing one's own non-centrality is a developmental stage that normal people manage with flying colours. But any authentic description of the social world and its ways would demonstrate that a refusal to recognize any such thing is in fact the normal human condition. Of course, many of us deny it, and cleave to myths and ideologies that deny it: human solidarity, an ethics of compassion, the idea of full mutual acknowledgement that is encoded in our visions of revolutionary socialism and romantic love. But these are not attempts to recover the underlying reality of human social life from its peculiarly pervasive misprisions and failures of realization; they are just further exercises in bad faith, refusals to recognize that our relations to others no more involve coincidence or synthesis than do our relations with ourselves. If we exist only insofar as we relate negatingly to ourselves, then the same must be true of our being-for-others.'

'Just think for a moment about the myth of romantic love, according to which each lover aspires to be the absolutely satisfying object of the other's desire whilst simultaneously being the absolutely satisfied desirer of that other. To satisfy the first aspiration, one would have to be nothing but one's body, whereas to satisfy the second, one would have to be absolutely not one's body; hence, to satisfy both aspirations at once, one would have to be simultaneously absolute facticity and absolute transcendence, purely in-itself and purely for-itself—in other words, one would have to be God in relation to one's lover. The myth of the beloved lover is simply a displacement of the myth of God: it re-incarnates that impossible object of human desire, which is to be at once utterly human and utterly non-human, to be pure freedom and pure self-sufficiency. And whenever we attempt to realize this fantasy, we find ourselves enacting an endless oscillation between sadistic mastery of the other (impossibly aspiring to reduce her to an object) and masochistic enslavement to that other (impossibly aspiring to be a mere object for her), as the necessary failure of each aspiration forces us to adopt its equally incoherent opposite.'

That's why it really didn't matter to me whether Annie and Franz were having sexual or intellectual intercourse behind that apartment door, the interrogator realized; the desire manifest in either kind of conversation is essentially the same, and essentially hopeless.

He paused for a moment, as if trying to calculate just how risky it really was to continue resisting his Advocate's strategy for ensuring his acquittal; but, with a shrug of his shoulders, he went on.

'This kind of bad faith is in fact just as prevalent in philosophy as in the everyday life it aspires to delineate and diagnose. Even Heidegger, who committed himself more extensively and originally than anyone else in the history of the subject to just those aspirations, ended up developing an intuition of interpersonal relations as approximating to the experience of a crew rather than of conflict—being-with-others rather than being-for-them. To read him, you'd think that human reality disclosed itself most deeply in an encounter with others as fellow-workers in a collective task, with all sharing a single goal and being willing to subordinate themselves to it. To be sure, he later allows for the way such projects might be disrupted or unhinged by the relation of each individual involved in them to his own mortality, by each person's being-towards-death; but he never seemed to realize that the nullity or nothingness or non-self-identity of mortal individuality is most concretely encountered in each individual's encounter with others, with their capacity to strip your world of everything that made it yours, and so to strip you of yourself. Death is other people.'

The interrogator paused, and looked almost apologetically at his Advocate; but in doing so, he encountered a gaze in which compassion and dispassion were so intimately mingled that he couldn't tell whether his self-indulgent outburst had definitively broken the relations of trust between them or had rather decisively confirmed them. After a long moment, the Advocate turned to the magistrate:

'Your honour, I have no further questions. Instead, I move that the court dismiss this case out of hand, on the grounds of the mental incapacity of the accused.'

4. The interrogator had been sitting silently in his darkened room for hours when the knock came on his door. He had been released on bail several days ago, when the magistrate reserved judgement on the Advocate's motion for dismissal; neither sacked nor employable, neither under arrest nor free of

legal supervision, he saw no reason to go anywhere or do anything. So when he opened the door, and recognized the two people on his doorstep, he acceded to the implicit significance of their presence without any discernible resistance.

Before he quite recognized what was happening to him, he found himself standing with his two escorts in a quarry on the edge of town, overlooked by a single house. As they removed his overcoat and arranged him ceremoniously on a large, uneven boulder, he saw a window in the house open, and a woman leaned out from it, as if to get a better view of what was happening below; was it Annie, or a much older woman? Her arms were outstretched, although whether in order to condone or condemn what was taking place was obscure—as obscure as her identity. Either way, her gazing presence made no difference to events in the quarry.

One of the two escorts produced a long, thin, double-edged butcher's knife, allowing the moonlight to gleam on the blade before passing it to his companion across the interrogator's half-bare chest. The weapon was passed to and fro several times, before returning to the grasp of the one who had brought it; and all the time, the interrogator waited dumbly. Then suddenly, the other escort's hands were at his throat, whilst the first thrust the knife into his heart and turned it there twice. With failing eyes, the interrogator could still see the two of them, Franz and Joseph K., cheek leaning against cheek, immediately before his face, watching the final act. 'Like a dog!' he said: it was as if he meant the shame of it to outlive him.

Countering the Ballad of Co-Dependency

The Realistic Spirit of David Fincher's *The Curious Case of Benjamin Button*

The Curious Case of Benjamin Button (2008; director: David Fincher; writer: Eric Roth) went into the Oscars with no less than thirteen nominations (including ones in the categories of 'Best Director', 'Best Film', and 'Best Actor'), and came away with just three statuettes—those for 'Art Direction', 'Make-Up', and 'Visual Effects'. That precipitous falling-off between initial evaluation and eventual reward not only approximates rather closely to the degree of contrast between the generally excited audience anticipation of this long-gestating film, and the essentially dismissive immediate critical reaction to its actuality; it also hints at the reasons for it, by implying that the film's claims on our attention turned out to be merely technical—more precisely, a matter of perfectly arranged surfaces concealing an absence of genuinely substantial human or artistic interest. And Fincher's decision to work with a screenplay by Eric Roth seemed to confirm this implication; at the very least, it invited his critics to interpret *Benjamin Button* in the light of Roth's most famous earlier film—*Forrest Gump* (1994; dir. Robert Zemeckis), the technological wizardry of which seemed to function solely as a delivery vehicle for chocolate-box sentiments such as, 'Life is like a box of chocolates'—as if acknowledging the humanity of its protagonist required assuming the limitations of his mind.

We should, however, resist implication and invitation alike; for the digital wizardries of *Benjamin Button* are not only in the service of artistic and human concerns of real moment—concerns that have been central to Fincher's work from its troubled beginnings on the set of *Alien³*—but are themselves an important thematic preoccupation of the film itself. Indeed, it is precisely his desire to pursue those long-standing concerns further that leads Fincher not only to deploy computer-based digital motion-capture technology in his film, but to make that film a study of one way in which such technology might disclose itself as a medium of artistic exploration.

In making this argument, I will be taking for granted two general, orienting assumptions that I hope to have established elsewhere. The first is arrived at in the chapter I devote to Fincher's work in the second edition of *On Film*[1]—a chapter which focuses on his contribution to the 'Alien' series, but also devotes much attention to *Se7en*, as well as canvassing briefer characterizations of the ways in which his subsequent films (from *The Game* to *Zodiac*) elaborate upon the thematic matrix established by his earlier work. I argue there that Fincher is obsessively interested in the human body as both the source and the subverter of meaning in human life, and with structures of meaning as at once the condition for the possibility of genuinely human existence and its most threatening contemporary danger (because of the inveterate tendency of such structures to disguise the material reality of our being, typically by proliferating to the point of suffocating excess). One expression of this interest, most evident in *Alien*[3] and *Zodiac* but traceable elsewhere, is Fincher's persistent desire to frustrate or refuse our generic expectations (as when he voids his first film of suspense by realizing Ripley's worst nightmare before the opening titles of *Alien*[3] are completed, or when he tracks the ways in which the reality of the Zodiac case resists our search for narrative closure, clear motivation, and decisive revelations of guilt or innocence). Another is his willingness to declare and explore the conditions of the medium of film as such—that which makes cinematic significance possible. An exemplary instance is the virtuoso extended tracking shot in the middle of *Panic Room*, in which the camera repeatedly violates the constraints of material reality in the town-house (passing through the handle of a coffee jug and two solid ceilings) in order to render maximally perspicuous the state of play between its inhabitants and the criminal intruders; this shot declares the discontinuity of narrative space and the space of the camera, whilst simultaneously declaring the camera's mastery by the demands of narrative, and so suggests that the

---

[1] London: Routledge, 2008.

cost of our voyeuristic intimacy with his protagonists is our inability to help them (to cross from our space to theirs).

This incorporation of an impossible visual trajectory into a film that otherwise rigorously observes the conventions of its genre and the physical limits of its narrative setting—this synthesis of impossibility and actuality—takes us to the second of my orienting assumptions. Here, the earlier work I'm drawing on is *The Wounded Animal*, which focuses on J.M. Coetzee and his troubling reconceptualizations of the relation between philosophy and literature. Part of my account of that part of his writing which concerns the novelist Elizabeth Costello depends upon identifying in both writers a commitment to what I there call 'modernist realism'—a term derived from the following exchange between Costello and her son, who queries his mother's right to describe not only herself but Kafka, and in particular his famous story 'Report to an Academy' (in which a 'civilized' ape called Red Peter tells the story of his life to a learned society), as exemplary of realism:

'When I think of realism', he goes on, 'I think of peasants frozen in blocks of ice. I think of Norwegians in smelly underwear...people picking their noses. You don't write about that kind of thing. Kafka didn't write about it.'

'No, Kafka didn't write about people picking their noses. But Kafka had time to wonder where and how his poor educated ape was going to find a mate. And what it was going to be like when he was left in the dark with the bewildered, half-tamed female that his keepers eventually produced for his use. Kafka's ape is embedded in life. It is the embeddedness that is important, not the life itself... That ape is followed through to the end, to the bitter, unsayable end, whether or not there are traces left on the page. Kafka stays awake during the gaps when we are sleeping, that is where Kafka fits in.' (EC, 32[2])

Kafka's ape is not in a realistic situation; no real ape has been, or (we think) could possibly be educated to the cultural level of an average European. Nevertheless, having fantastically embedded his ape in European culture, Kafka develops its consequences with a rigorous attention to the real nature of the ape and of the culture he (impossibly) inhabits. A real ape will have sexual and emotional needs; real human beings would try to satisfy them, in order to maintain their profits, and would care little about the sanity of the mate they procure, or the potentially monstrous consequences of their

---

[2] *Elizabeth Costello* (London: Secker and Warburg, 2003).

congress. The fictional reality that its author has constructed thus results from his unrelenting immersion in the reality upon which he is drawing to do so; and the same technique is fairly obviously at work in other Kafka stories—for example, 'Metamorphosis', which begins with a man having turned into an insect. Thus, even narratives which take their starting point from a sheer impossibility (beyond anything to be encountered in reality) might nevertheless count as a contribution to the project of realism, insofar as the development of those narratives can be seen as a logically and emotionally rigorous unfolding of the consequences of that unintelligible origin—as unsentimental articulations of what the impossible embedding of one reality into another might reveal about both. And in comparison with Red Peter and Gregor Samsa, the impossible condition in which Benjamin Button finds himself might seem almost mundane.

1) Counter-Romantic Realism: The Clock and the Ballad

We can begin moving closer to the cinematic Benjamin Button (Brad Pitt) by taking guidance from two signposts that Fincher himself has erected for that purpose—one internal to the film, and one external. The internal signpost is to be found in its complex opening, which frames the main story it is about to tell in a highly specific and multilayered way: we are introduced to Benjamin's friend and lover Daisy Fuller (Cate Blanchett) on her deathbed, as she prepares belatedly to bequeath Benjamin's diary-cum-scrapbook (what he calls his last will and testament) to her daughter, Caroline (Julia Ormond). The film to come presents itself as creating a visual transcription of that text as Caroline reads it to her mother, with each new episode in Benjamin's story prefaced by a moment in which Caroline's voice modulates into that of Benjamin as it speaks over the events on which it comments.

This basic framing device already amounts to the anticipatory invocation of a literary reference point—although here, the author at issue is not Kafka but Kipling, and in particular one of his 'Just So' stories: the tale of how Old Man Kangaroo got his hind legs. This tale appears twice in the film to come—once when Daisy's grandmother reads it to Daisy and a twelve-year-old Benjamin at the beginning of their life-defining relationship, and again when Daisy in her seventies reads the same story from her grand-mother's book to Benjamin five years before his death. It thereby relates the film's story to the territory of a creation myth, in which the apparently unaccountable origins of a creature's apparently peculiar bodily inheritance are shown to be in reality both intelligible and fitting, and in which everything hangs on the timeliness of its creator's act of endowment (both projected recitings of the tale include its final sentence, 'This is the picture of Old Man Kangaroo at five in the afternoon, when he got his beautiful hind legs, just as Big God Ngong had promised'). And, as we will quickly learn, in directing her daughter to the diary, Daisy is indeed giving Caroline an account of her own hitherto-unknown origins: for its rough assemblage of words and images will reveal that Benjamin is Caroline's real father, a revelation that at once requires and provides an account of why he aban-doned them both, which in turn means recounting the peculiar relation in which he stood to his own body, and that determined the course of his life.

Caroline's recitation of the diary to Daisy is thus simultaneously Daisy's way of reciting its tale to her; so this framing device condenses or inter-weaves both of Daisy's previous relations to the telling of the Kipling tale (first as auditor, then as reader); but the connection with Kipling is strengthened by the way in which Fincher frames his own framing device—that is, by Daisy's way of preparing the ground or setting the tone for that textual bequest (and so for its recitation and reception). For before directing Caroline to the diary, she tells her a story that her own father told her, about how the railway station in New Orleans, newly built in 1918, acquired a very peculiar clock: and this fable is not only a 'Just So' story if ever there was one, but one in which time, timing, and timeliness are very much at issue.

According to Daisy's (father's) account, the clock was made by Mr Gateaux—a genius at his trade, a blind man married to a Creole woman, a father whose son joined up at the end of the First World War and died on the Western Front. Driven by grief, Mr Gateaux constructs and installs a clock which runs backwards, and introduces it to the assembled crowd: 'I made it this way so that perhaps the boys who were lost in the war might stand and go home again, home to farm, to work, have children, to live long, full lives; perhaps my own son might come home again. I'm sorry if I offended anybody. I hope you enjoy my clock.' And as he says these words, we are shown two sequences of images: one of the battlefield, with one American soldier amongst a horde of others rising from the earth, his body expelling bullets, and running jerkily backwards to safety, as showers of mud contract into the ground from which shells extract themselves before departing harmlessly into the distance; and one of Mr Gateaux's son jumping backwards from a slowing train, turning 180 degrees, then clumsily stumbling back into his parents' embrace. The first of these sequences is new to us, but the second is identical to one we have already seen—in which Mr and Mrs Gateaux bade farewell to their son as he departed for the Front.

Out of respect for its maker and his feelings, the clock is left to function as Mr Gateaux intended; and the film notes that Benjamin's birth roughly coincides with the inauguration of the clock, regularly cuts to its continued functioning as Benjamin's life unfolds, records its retirement (in favour of a digital timepiece) just before his death, and finally (in its last frames) shows the 2005 floodwaters overwhelming it. In this way, an alignment between clock, protagonist, and medium is carefully established and maintained, and an array of issues that will be of central concern to the coming film is given a preliminary articulation.

Most directly, we are invited to compare the diremption between the clock and its hands with the diremption between Benjamin and his body; for the outer movements of the clock's hands run backwards, whilst its inner mechanism follows the standard horological course, just as Benjamin's body will age backwards while his inner, psychic development follows the standard human course (we shall return to this). But Mr Gateaux fantasizes an equivalence between the reversed hand-movements of his clock and the reversed direction of time: he constructs the former in order to conjure the latter (out of grief, out of love). But a clock whose hands move counter-clockwise around its face is not in fact running backwards: we need only imagine reversing the order of the numbers on the face around which those hands sweep in order to see that, if the clock's inner mechanism still functions normally and is connected in the normal way to those hands, they can just as accurately track the passage of time, and so it can just as fittingly be used to measure its passage, as if its hands were moving in a clockwise direction. So there is no necessity to interpret the apparently counter-temporal trajectory of Benjamin's body as an indication that his relation to time is any different from that of all other human beings (we shall return to this, also).

By showing (in the battle sequence) how easily film is capable of appearing to realize Mr Gateaux's fantasy of time-reversal, Fincher declares the facility with which cinema (particularly in its current state of techno-logical revolution) can fall in with such refusals to accept the reality of human finitude—encouraging us to take comfort from the illusion that they might be transcended. But by pairing his time-reversed reunion of the Gateaux family with its original, he also shows that it is possible for film to diagnose and criticize such fantasies; for that pairing amounts to a vision of the original event being negated, and so reveals that Mr Gateaux's true desire (as his words all-but-declare) is not that time be reversed, but that the actual course of events be other than it was—so that it did not include his son's death on the battlefield, or his enlistment in the army that led to that death. His grief and love thus misunderstand their own object: he does not want his son to live his life backwards; he wants his son's life to have unfolded differently—so that other, equally possible intersections of inci-dent and accident would have occupied the space of the actual than those with which he finds it so hard to reconcile himself.

In other words, within the mood of love-infused mourning and melan-cholia that Daisy's 'Just So' story establishes for everything that is to come, Fincher is already indicating that the true concern of his film is not to embody a fantasy about reversing time but to refuse it, and in so doing to give an account of its apparently unaccountable origins, which will turn out to lie in an inability to accept that any individual human life consists of a sequence of events that amount to no more than the accumulation of what happened to happen.

There is another, more external signpost from which this interpretation of Fincher's mode of presentation of Benjamin Button takes its bearings. In various interviews and discussions surrounding the film's theatrical release, its director characterized his initial interest in Roth's script as deriving from its refusal to be the story of a romance:

We talked initially about the notion of what I call the ballad of co-dependency, which is what all romance has been since Shakespeare, which is '*I can't live without you.*' *Romeo and Juliet* was about teenagers, and that's been adopted by almost every art form since then, and has become the de facto way that people deal with romance, which is absurd. In *Button* they were both sexually active, they weren't waiting for each other, which I liked in the script. And he had these characters who got on with their lives and then met up again, and then got on with their lives and went other places and did other things and then met up again. I really liked that and I said I wanted to strip back anything that's part of the ballad of co-dependency.

I loved that the kernel, the meat of the thing, was really about something that was very, very sad. The nougat was about that and yet the chocolate-caramel envelope it was in was this love story, which I thought was a very interesting act of sedition. I loved the fact that you could literally be talking about the same piece of material and one person saw it as a love story and I saw it as something so much more profound. (CCBB[3], 27)

The relationship between Benjamin and Daisy is undeniably central to the film; but a major part of the dissatisfaction with which its audience initially responded to it surely lies in the refusal of that relationship to satisfy our generic expectations of romance. Benjamin and Daisy are of unique significance in one another's lives—indeed, Benjamin introduces Daisy to us as 'the person who changed my life forever', the person who was the first fully to appreciate who he was. But the sequence of subsequent events that makes the nature of that life-altering significance manifest is not one in which two souls overcome initial disparities and obstacles (both internal and external) in order to attain romantic union (in marriage, and the founding of a family) of a kind that sustains itself unchangingly, thus amounting to the end of narrative sequence altogether in favour of an earthly inhabitation of eternal life, a fated fusion of two people in the absence of which neither would be capable of truly being himself or herself, whole and entire.

On the contrary, each is shown to be more than capable of surviving the other's absence. Benjamin's time as a crew-member on the tugboat *Chelsea* is one in which he experiences love for the first time (with Elizabeth Abbott [Tilda Swinton]) and in which Daisy begins to realize her vocation as a dancer; he refuses (or at least does not respond to) her post-war attempt to seduce him, and is in turn refused when he appears expectantly, first in New York, and then at her hospital bedside in Paris; when they do finally get 'married', their co-habitation lasts only a handful of years, involves a serious disagreement about the desirability of parenthood, and ends with Benjamin leaving after his daughter Caroline's first

---

[3] *The Curious Case of Benjamin Button: The Making of a Film* (New York: Rizzoli International Publications, 2008).

birthday; and although Benjamin dies in Daisy's arms, he does so as an infant whose calm acceptance of unconsciousness neither supports nor undermines Daisy's heartbreaking conviction that he knew whose arms they were.

For each refusal, disagreement, or departure, a reason is evident, and each can accept its sufficiency for the one who acts upon it (without necessarily accepting it for himself or herself); and no particular refusal spells the end or the mislaying of their significance for each other, hence the breaking of their relationship (even temporarily). In short, their story instantiates Benjamin's characterization of human life in general—as 'a series of intersecting lives and incidents out of anyone's control'. Their relationship is no more the working out of fate and destiny than it is the mere aggregation of happenstance—neither a romance nor the meaningless sequence of accidents that we might be tempted to think is the only alternative to the denial of romance, but rather an utterly unexceptional example of the ways in which human beings can sustain a meaningful relationship in a world which neither requires nor prohibits that possibility.

The film emphasizes this generic refusal by presenting other versions of non-co-dependent relationships: Queenie and Tizzy; Benjamin and Elizabeth; Daisy and her boyfriend David; Daisy and her second husband Robert. And the various versions of what one might call the romance of the family on display here are no less resistant to our desire for the conventional: the original Button family, Benjamin's adopted family (both primary and extended) in the Nolan foundation care home, Daisy Fuller's troubled childhood (with unfaithful parents, and a grandmother for a mother), and the family she recreates after Benjamin's departure—all exhibit deviations from the nuclear norm (absent or unknown or misperceived fathers, absent or dead mothers, uncertified betrothals, the unforeseeable intermixing of kinship and kindness) that are at once individual, extreme, and utterly everyday. Each is what it is, with its specific admixtures of pain and pleasure, deep-reaching flaws and flights of imaginative transcendence; but none are simply conventional, and the individuals involved in these relationships each find that (for all their variousness, mutability, and transience) they are nevertheless capable of flourishing within them—neither destined to do so nor fated to fail.

2) The (Mis-)Marriage of Body and Soul: Benjamin Button's Condition—Cinematic and Literary

Suppose, then, that we try to bring together the guidance of the clock and the ballad, and ask how we should understand the relationship that lies at the heart of this film's unintelligible point of origin—that between Benjamin Button and his body. For just as Benjamin's relationship with Daisy has been persistently misunderstood, so his relationship with his body as the film presents it has been mischaracterized, from the film studios' pre-publicity onwards. This film's Benjamin Button is not someone who 'ages backwards' during the course of the film's narrative: he begins life in 1918 as an infant, then undergoes childhood, adolescence, maturity, and old age before dying at the age of eighty-five. In other words, he ages in just the way we all age—he learns how to speak, count, and read in the first five years after his birth, yearns to mix with other children and play with toy soldiers, attains sexual potency a decade thereafter, makes his way in the world in the late 1930s, confronts the death of his parents and the onset of parenthood in the years after the Second World War, and dies (having suffered early-onset dementia for more than a decade) in 2003. It is Benjamin's body that begins with the debilities of a normal eighty-five-year-old human being and ends in the condition of a normal human infant: he is born with cataracts, deafness, and crippling arthritis, gradually gains muscle tone, hair, and perceptual acuity to the point at which his adult physical potential is fully realized, and then equally gradually but irreversibly falls away from that state, shrinking in size, then losing his motor skills and capacity for speech before dying with the unformed, unmarked features and physique of a baby.

We can appreciate the distinctiveness of the predicament that Fincher's Benjamin confronts by contrasting it with that created by the author of the short story from which Roth adapted his screenplay. When we first meet F. Scott Fitzgerald's Benjamin Button, he is 'partially crammed into one of the [maternity ward] cribs' (CC[4], 4) because his body is not only afflicted with the ailments of old age, but also has the usual physical proportions of the elderly human body; and more importantly, he exhibits all the character and behaviour traits of a seventy-year-old man (he wants a rocking chair to

---

[4] *The Curious Case of Benjamin Button and Six Other Stories* (London: Penguin, 2008).

sit in, violently rejects a bottle of milk, asks for a cane, has a taste for cigars and no taste for playing with rattles or trains). As Fitzgerald puts it: 'He was as puzzled as everyone else at the apparently advanced age of *his mind* and body at birth' (CC, 10—my italics). And the longer he lives, the younger his mind and his body become. The older he gets, the more he seeks out the company of the young, the more he desires to sample their pleasures, and the less compatible he becomes with his ageing wife; during his time at Harvard in the latter years of his life, he becomes progressively distanced from those in his peer-group, as he finds their worldliness increasingly shocking and their workload increasingly challenging; then he retreats further and further into a world of childlike fantasies and pleasures, until—as he takes up residence in the family nursery—all the events of his past 'faded like unsubstantial dreams from his mind as though they had never been' (CC, 27). When he dies, his world has contracted to light and dark, hunger and repletion, and the dim faces of his carers as they hover over his crib.

Fincher's Benjamin's body describes exactly the same anti-entropic or counter-ontogenic arc as that of Fitzgerald's Benjamin, but with one significant exception—although his body at birth is afflicted with typical ailments of the elderly, its size or scale is that of a normal newborn baby. That exception is significant, because it provides an initial cue to the critical fact that, whereas for Fitzgerald's Benjamin the trajectory of mind and body are precisely aligned with one another (in the 'reverse' direction), the trajectory of Benjamin's psychological or psychic or personal development—call it the journey of his soul—stands in an inverse relation to that of his body: it is entirely normal. That is why, whereas both Fincher and Fitzgerald conceive of Benjamin's final years as involving an increasingly radical contraction or infantilization of his consciousness, the film explains this as the effect of a disability to which the elderly are prone, whereas the short story presents it as the culmination of his inverted but coordinated 'progression' towards childhood.

Fincher's Benjamin is thus related to Fitzgerald's in just the way that the former's body and soul are related to one another: this is adaptation by negation or inversion of the original. But the nature of that Rothian operation entails that, if either of these Benjamins can be described as ageing backwards, it is Fitzgerald's rather than Fincher's. That is why Fitzgerald's Benjamin is presented not as gaining experience but as shedding it; and that is why all of Fitzgerald's technical skills have to be brought to bear on the beginning of his tale, in which he chooses Benjamin's father as our point of view upon his son's arrival and early years in the world, in order to finesse the fact that his Benjamin has to possess the character and tastes of an old man without his having had any experience through which to have developed them, and hence without his having any memory of doing so (or indeed of doing anything whatever). By contrast, Fincher's Benjamin acquires experience and memories in the usual human way. He doesn't begin with the character and tastes of an old man, but with those of an infant; and as he gets older, he finds it more difficult to respond to the spontaneity of Daisy's mind and heart: scarred by his time at war, he is paralysed by her seduction of him in the gazebo, then rather too inclined simply to accept that her New York boyfriend is an immoveable presence in her life, and—despite finding it possible to reconnect with her for a few years in the 1960s—he not only resists the idea of having a child, but it is as much his lack of the psychological flexibility needed to act as a father to Caroline as his fear of her reaction to his accelerating physical youthfulness that leads him to abandon his family, or at least to try to—since he keeps on circling back to them as the years progress, unable to break those habitual links.

Fincher's Benjamin is thus not someone who ages backwards; it would be more correct to say that he is someone whose body ages backwards, and thereby resists his normal psychic development—in the expression of his childhood curiosity and liveliness, in the management of his adolescent energies, and in the enjoyment of his later ventures into the human world of family relationships. It would not be quite right to think of this as a matter of his being afflicted by a malady or a disease, one that is physical rather than psychological or emotional in nature. For such illnesses are afflictions of the body, afflictions that someone's body has or suffers—specific infirmities, or deviations from the physical human norm; whereas (one wants to say) Benjamin's affliction *is* his body. But this way of putting it isn't quite right either: for (unless we mean that merely having a body—embodiment as such—is an affliction), this form of words implies that Benjamin's body is intrinsically abnormal in some specific way. And yet no state or phase of Benjamin's bodily development, let alone any particular feature of his physical or bodily being in any one of those states or phases, is in that sense out of the ordinary; all of us in time suffer exactly the same specific blends of opportunities and limitations inherent in infant, adolescent, mature, and elderly bodies of the distinctively human kind that Benjamin undergoes. It is rather their sequence or order that causes the problem: not some way in which their order alters the order *of* time, but something about their order *in* time, or rather, the relationship between their temporal ordering and that of the states or phases of his mind (not excluding his heart and spirit).

In Fitzgerald's Benjamin, one might say, body and soul are co-dependent: when Fitzgerald invites himself to create a human being who instantiates the idea of 'ageing backwards', he tells the tale of someone whose soul and body undergo the passage of time in perfect harmony, exhibiting a lifelong marriage (even if in the reverse direction). It's as if Fitzgerald shares the perceptual habits and conceptual assumptions of most of those who en-counter Fincher's Benjamin: a man who is manifestly old and feeble must be old and feeble in spirit, just as one who is manifestly young and vigorous must be young and vigorous of heart. Is this what it must mean to say (with Wittgenstein): the human body is the best picture of the human soul? But in Fincher's narrative, no such ballad of co-dependence is sung or shown or acted out: for most of their earthly career, his Benjamin's body and soul are out of synchronization, with the former persistently depicting the latter as what it is not. This might suggest that, whereas Fitzgerald eschews a dualistic picture of soul and body by refusing to allow the two to desyn-chronize, Fincher projects things in such a way as to suggest that body and soul can become essentially unrelated, as if each inhabited its own parallel but essentially independent world, as if it were simply a happy accident that the expressions and actions of a human body typically declare or depict the states of its soul, anyway no more than a matter of fact (something that might be otherwise).

And yet, the film also depicts the body and soul of Fincher's Benjamin as having to make the best of their relationship, despite the obstacles uninten-tionally but undeniably created for each by the other's independent and autonomously developing nature; it depicts that relationship as indissol-uble. We might think of this as Fincher's counter-reading of Wittgenstein's aphorism: anything that can picture something else can also depict it wrongly—hence the impossible possibility of Benjamin's unharmonious marriage between soul and body; but in order for depiction (right or wrong) to be so much as possible, that which depicts and that which is depicted must share something—they must be internally related. So, if the human soul *is* essentially picturable by the human body, that is because the soul is always embodied, always the soul of some particular body or other. Divorce is thus out of the question, metaphysically speaking; but it doesn't follow that the marriage of soul and body must take co-dependent form—that of eternal fusion or mutual absorption, with neither partner able to survive the other's refusal to be their perfect mirror or proxy. It may rather be possible to discover ways of managing lifelong, non-harmonic cohabitation—ways of living together that satisfy both parties without demanding their submergence in one another. If we can no more choose which bodies we have than we can choose whether or not to be embodied, then Benjamin's task is indistinguishable from that of his fellow human beings: it is to make his body his own, to own it as the field of his (soul's) expression rather than disowning it (whether by absolutely denying its relevance or by enforcing its absolute subordination).

The simultaneous specificity and universality of Benjamin's condition (the sense in which it individuates him, but also relates him to every other human being) emerges in part by the way in which the film narrative juxtaposes his struggle with that of Daisy. From the moment we first see her until Benjamin arrives by her hospital bed in Paris, she appears to fulfil the Fitzgerald fantasy of body and soul as co-dependent: Daisy is not only someone who dances, but someone for whom dancing is a vocation, her mode of being-in-the-world. Her body has become such a finely-tuned instrument, such a perfect means for realizing her every thought and feeling, that it is as if no gap or division exists between it and her—her soul no more embodied than her body is ensouled. But their flawless mutual information does not make Daisy any less a part of the wider world, of the various dialectical intersections of culture and nature (home, care home, ballet schools, theatre companies, cities) that make up the essential contexts of her evolving life; for to be embodied is to inherit a necessarily worldly mode of being, and thus—as her street accident in Paris shows—an inherent vulnerability to the slings and arrows that world might direct at her.

Fincher's virtuosic representation of Benjamin's intensely emotional envisaging of the immediate causal context of that accident—with its grievously calm attribution of equal weight to the real world and its equally conceivable, infinitely preferable, but undeniably non-actual counterpart—at once recalls and renders explicit the lesson of his earlier, equally binocular realization of Mr Gateaux's fantasy about his dead son's impossible resurrection. The routes taken by various individual people and things in that particular city on that specific morning so as to bring about Daisy's collision with a taxi might so easily not have happened in exactly the way they did—it wasn't fated or destined: it was no more than happenstance, but by the same token, it was no less than that—it was something well within the compass of the everyday, which is in the end no more than what happens to happen. To have perfect control of one's body does not negate one's vulnerability to the actual: if anything, it heightens it, since the world's ability to wound thereby acquires maximally injurious power. Daisy's entire conception of the course and meaning of her life, and hence her deepest self-conception, is shattered by the shattering of her leg; precisely because she had so absolutely subordinated her body to her soul, she had rendered herself absolutely vulnerable to the insubordinate world.

By sheer accident, the moment at which Daisy's body turns the tables on her is also the moment at which Benjamin reaches the brief phase of his life in which the opposing trajectories of his body and his soul intersect—at which his physical and his psychic development undergo a honeymoon period of harmony, each arriving at the height of their maturity. If Daisy had not suffered her accident, she and Benjamin would most likely have entered their own honeymoon period: each perfected, hence each perfect in the other's eyes, as if this were the phase of their very differently incarnate lives in which they were fated to become everything to one another, to fulfil their shared romantic destiny. Instead, Daisy's suddenly-acquired physical imperfection renders Benjamin's physical perfection repulsive: and Benjamin thereby learns that the possibility of perfect harmony between body and soul—something he imagines himself to be deprived of in any extended way by his body—would be no guarantee of the perfect satisfaction of his embodied desires. Having the trajectory of body and soul normally aligned does not guarantee its maintenance; and even when it is attained, its ultimate significance (the meaning it can have for others and for oneself) is deeply and ineluctably determined by what goes on in the wider world that is every embodied being's field of inhabitation—that series of intersecting lives and incidents out of anyone's control.

But the film does not share Daisy's initial assumption that the world's disruption of her relationship with her body amounts to the end of her (meaningful) life; on the contrary, it shows us that she will find ways of continuing to make room for dancing in her life (as a teacher), as well as a way of consummating her relationship with Benjamin—even if only briefly, and with the knowledge that its inevitable end can only hold the threat of devastation. More specifically, even though it shows her to be well aware in advance of what might happen if she becomes pregnant with Benjamin's child (given his inclination towards flight), it also shows that Benjamin's inevitable end need not take the form one might expect. For his body's gradual transition into childhood and infancy is prefaced by his mind's sudden collapse into dementia: so instead of experiencing the gradual retreat of his soul behind or beyond his contracting physical capacities, as if losing touch with the untouched man himself before losing him altogether, Daisy finds herself first confronting an adolescent whose soul is already all-but-lost, then taking care of a child whose mind is as unformed as his body. But it's still Benjamin—not because his mind remains, even if beyond her reach; but because his one and only body, the sole field of expression of his singular soul, survives to die in her embrace.

That is why our brief late glimpse of Daisy as an old woman, walking in the grounds of the Nolan house with a toddler, and pausing to stoop to receive a kiss from him, acquires such resonant emotional power: for it shows us that even within this last extremity of dislocation and mismatch into which their embodied souls have thrown them, they have managed to maintain the loving significance of their relationship, even if in unpreced-ented form. So when we are then shown the infant Benjamin closing his eyes for the last time in Daisy's arms, we see primordial, embodied human need being met with a soulful love that is spousal, maternal, and grand-maternal all at once—as if embodying every loving soul in Benjamin's life (each recalled in the film's concluding sheaf of portraits), and thereby bearing witness to the fact that bodily separateness need not undercut the true marriage of souls, but rather makes possible every incarnate inflection of such internal relatedness.

3) The Digital (Mis-)Marriage of Actor and Character: Benjamin Button and Brad Pitt

Where Daisy struggles, first to achieve a perfect marriage between body and soul, and then to survive the divorce that the world inflicts upon it, Benjamin's character is formed primarily by the general mis-marriage between his body and his soul. And what his body's persistent but various ways of resisting and frustrating the developing desires of his soul engender is a person whose *forte* is observation rather than action: unable to expect his body's powers and capacities to give untroubled expression to his will, he settles instead for allowing the world and everything within it to make an impression on him—or, as he puts it, 'to make a dent on your life'. That is not to say that he does not act; but every notable action he takes (following Mr Oti into town, taking Daisy onto Captain Mike's tug, transforming his appearance for Mrs Abbott, and so on) clearly has the status of a reaction (to Mr Oti's perceptive invitation, to Daisy's inviting construction of a den beneath the dining table, to Mrs Abbott's deliberate self-adornment); and for the most part, Benjamin simply goes with the flow of his experiences. In this sense, the inexplicably but profoundly hilarious reminiscences of Mr Daws (which recall six of the seven occasions on which he was struck by lightning in his life) constitute a fantastically extreme incarnation of the mode of being of the only person to whom each one of those recountings is directed, and for whom they constitute lightning strokes of experience in themselves—the person upon whom other people make a dent rather than a scratch, the man upon whom nothing is lost. It is as if Benjamin's life as a whole is a displaced substitute for Mr Daw's missing seventh memory; for his bodily condition makes him a long-term lightning rod for the world's electrifying, incandescent reality.

If this is an affliction, it is one that is at least internally related to the condition of the people upon whom the creators of this film themselves hope to make an impression—its audience, seated in the dark before these projected images, viewers of a world that is present to them but to which they cannot make themselves present, and upon or within which they cannot act. Does this condition of present absence before absent presence prevent our access to the word's reality, or does it rather render that reality unprecedentedly incandescent, purely electric?

It seems undeniable that Fincher means us to consider the impression made upon us by the fact that the actor who plays Benjamin Button is Brad Pitt—an incandescently attractive screen presence if ever there was one. But does Brad Pitt actually play Benjamin Button? Is that character played by that actor, in the way in which—say—Brad Pitt played Detective Mills in *Se7en*, or Ted Manson plays Mr Daws? The cast list for *Benjamin Button* in fact aligns the name of its eponymous character with that of seven different actors (three playing Benjamin in the years 1928–1931, 1932–1934, and 1935–1937, another three playing him when his bodily age is 12, 8, and 6, with Brad Pitt playing him in the period between). But this does not signal Fincher's employment of a familiar cinematic technique for presenting the whole of an individual's life—that of using different actors to play the same character at different ages; on the contrary, Fincher has said that Brad Pitt would have refused to take on the role at all unless a way had been found to allow him to play Benjamin throughout his life. Accordingly, at every stage of that life that is enacted by someone other than Brad Pitt, Benjamin's face is in fact a digitally-altered version of Brad Pitt's face; more specifically, Fincher's technical wizards used digital motion-capture technology to map the bone structure, contours, and expressive repertoire of Pitt's actual face, remodelled them in accordance with their best estimates of how such a face would alter with the passage of given amounts of time, and seamlessly conjoined what resulted with the bodies of each of those six other actors.

Consequently, this film confronts us with four interrelated dependencies, all of which are involved in film-making quite generally, but each of which is differently inflected when its realization depends primarily upon digital rather than photographic resources: that between Brad Pitt and Benjamin Button, that between Brad Pitt and other actors, that between Brad Pitt and his screened projection, and that between Brad Pitt and his body. It is only the use of digital resources that allows this actor to play this character throughout that character's life, and thereby to ensure that he (Brad Pitt) embodies or incarnates Benjamin at every stage of his screened existence rather than entirely ceding that task to others at certain biographical points. But that gain in actorly autonomy (call it an enhancement of the screen actor's traditional, photographically-facilitated priority over the character) itself presupposes the acceptance of a different, unprecedented kind of dependence on other actors: for Pitt's digitally-altered features require six other bodies on which they might be grafted, so that in the relevant phases of Benjamin's life, his screen incarnation is (neither a single individual actor nor a sequence of such individuals, but) a hybrid of Pitt's facial physiognomy and the bodily carriage of some particular, older or younger, other (a diremption within the field of the actorly body rather than between that body and its soul). No doubt future technical developments might allow an actor to dispense with this dependence (perhaps by using motion capture technology to capture the physiognomic signature of his whole body); but even in this hybrid case, face trumps body—no viewer is likely to be left dissatisfied by even a subliminal apprehension of the divergent registers of face and body, because the various digital realizations of Pitt's face compel our recognition of his singular presence before us, from the very beginning of the film on, more strongly than anything that those other bodies can mobilize or manifest.

Is this a reassuring perception for an actor, particularly one whose stardom has hitherto depended at least as much on his physical beauty as on his acting talent? On the one hand, it suggests that his physiognomic signature retains its singularity through the full range of physical changes to which time is likely to subject his body; on the other hand, the digital technology that demonstrates this can do so only because his body's signature is in fact reproducible, and in an unprecedented way. Photographic cinema always required the actor's presence before the camera in order to reproduce it on the screen; digital cinema (insofar as it is dependent on motion capture technology) cannot do without the actor's presence before a camera at some initial point, but thereafter it can produce his presence on screen without any further need for his presence before a camera, and furthermore can present him to us as he was or will be rather than as he is (now) or was (when originally captured).

Brad Pitt the actor does not have the kind of body that Benjamin Button was born with; but his screen incarnation (for the existence of which the actor's physical body currently remains a precondition) can now age backwards or forwards within the context of any particular film, entirely independently of anything the actor himself does or does not do before a camera here and now. Does this expand the actor's range of bodily expression, or render it essentially inexpressive (as if his body is no longer his own)? Can he continue to believe that, with respect to his stardom, physiognomy is destiny, or does the sheer existence of *Benjamin Button* demonstrate that its vision of life as inherently something that could be otherwise is also a prophecy about the future of stardom in the domain of the digital? Perhaps the absolute mutability of his screen presence—the overcoming of its absolute dependence on his real bodily presence—will seem a price worth paying, if it allows him to escape his subjection to the gaze of the camera (and so his body's absolute dependence upon that camera's violently transfigurative powers). Call this digital cinema's counter to this particular traditional ballad of cinematic co-dependence. It is nevertheless worth remembering that if a clock starts thinking of its hands as mere conveniences, essentially for others, then it is likely to start thinking of itself as existing essentially for others' convenience. And if its hands were suddenly to become movable by those others, in any direction and at any speed those others might choose, without reference to the functioning of its inner mechanism, this would not enhance its usefulness to them as a guide through the sublunary world of space and time, so much as annihilate it altogether.

The Promising Animal

The Art of Reading *On the Genealogy of Morality* as Testimony

1) Getting Underway

We are unknown to ourselves, we knowers, we ourselves, to ourselves, and there is a good reason for this. We have never looked for ourselves – so how are we ever supposed to *find* ourselves? How right is the saying: 'Where your treasure is, there will your heart be also'; *our* treasure is where the hives of our knowledge are. As born winged-insects and intellectual honey-gatherers we are constantly underway towards them, concerned at heart with only one thing—to 'bring something home' . . .

We remain necessarily strangers to ourselves, we do not understand ourselves, we *must* confusedly mistake who we are, the motto 'everyone is furthest from himself' applies to us forever—we are not 'knowers' when it comes to ourselves. (GM[1], P. 1)

Why are we knowers not only unknown to ourselves (as Nietzsche begins by claiming) but necessarily so self-estranged (as he finds himself insisting by the end of this opening section of his preface)? Why *must* we be confused or mistaken over who we are? If the problem were just that we have never hitherto looked for ourselves, then it would be easily solved: we could simply start looking, and thereby overcome our ignorance of ourselves. But how would born intellectual honey-gatherers go about such a task? They

---

[1] F. Nietzsche, *On the Genealogy of Morality*, trans. C. Diethe, ed. K. Ansell-Pearson (Cambridge: Cambridge University Press, 1994)—hereafter GM: translation modified on occasion. All citations will be by essay and section number (e.g. 2.1) or to the preface (e.g. P. 1).

would think of it—as they think of all knowledge—as something that is to be gathered or collected, something to be brought home. But then seeking to know ourselves would require us to regard ourselves as essentially capable of being brought home, hence as presently (and perhaps forever) not-at-home to ourselves; to gather knowledge of ourselves, we must first be willing to conceive of ourselves as necessarily self-estranged or self-distanced.

So if Nietzsche thinks that we knowers are condemned to misunderstand ourselves, that must be because he thinks we are condemned to resist any understanding of ourselves as in need of gathering or collection, hence as dispersed or disseminated or internally differentiated, call it non-self-identical. What makes it impossible for us to achieve self-knowledge is thus the depth of our commitment to a conception of ourselves as always already at home to ourselves—as self-identical, hence essentially transparent to ourselves (both from moment to moment—no sooner thinking something than knowing that we do—and with respect to our essence, which is of course thinking). We are essentially unknown to ourselves because we persist in regarding ourselves as essentially known; we will never look for ourselves because we think we have always already found ourselves, and have done so without ever really having to look. For when all is said and done, what there is to know about ourselves—the full depth and extent of our nature—is that we are knowers, essentially cognitive creatures, born collectors.

And yet the very conditions of our lives as intellectual honey-gatherers declare the underlying truth of our condition to be otherwise—to be in fact exactly as our conception of (self-)knowledge as gatherable would expect. For as such gatherers, we are constantly making towards the hives of our knowledge, hence always returning from journeying away from those homes, and so never actually residing in them: we are, in short, always on the way to or from home but never at home—always not-at-home. And if knowledge is a phenomenon of the hive, to which we make one essential contribution (even if not the one Nietzsche's words attribute to us, since what foraging bees gather is not honey but pollen, honey's raw material), then the honey of knowledge is not merely essentially collectable; its emergence or creation is also essentially collective—an achievement of the group and its dynamic hierarchies and divisions of labour. And the point of this shared enterprise is not the piling up of treasure as an end in itself, but the production of something useful to the survival and reproduction of the group. So if our treasure really is where our heart is, and our heart is with the hive, then our heart is itself dispersed or disseminated, residing essentially outside ourselves, something in relation to which we are always either no longer or not yet there.

One might, however, ask whether the hearts of such intellectual honey-gatherers really can be in the hive; more precisely, one might ask exactly what it is that such honey-gatherers really treasure. Is it the knowledge, or the gathering of it, that they value most—the collection or the collecting? If these winged creatures of cognition really treasured the collection above the collecting, why would they never stay with the collection but rather dedicate themselves to the unending task of enhancing it, which inevitably means maintaining their distance from it in order to look for (more of) it? Such a creature is either mistaking the means for the end, and so mislocating her treasure and her heart; or else she truly prefers seeking knowledge to having it, and so treasures being underway above being home. More exactly, her form of life suggests that her true home is to be found, is indeed a matter of her being, underway—that her creaturely essence lies in seeking or voyaging. She is, after all, a winged thing.

This does not exactly mean that we are wrong to think of ourselves as knowers (since the term captures the process of collecting as naturally as it does the product). Perhaps one should rather say that it reveals us as not really understanding what it means to say this of ourselves—that the true significance of that self-description is not something we have as yet brought home to ourselves, or allowed ourselves to be struck by, something we have not yet properly experienced. And indeed, in the portion of the first section of his preface that we have so far passed over (the sentences connecting the two paragraphs I began by quoting), Nietzsche connects our confusion about knowing to a certain estrangement from our own experiences:

As far as the rest of life is concerned, the so-called 'experiences'—who of us ever has enough seriousness for them? or enough time? I fear we have never really been 'with it' in such matters, our heart is simply not in it—and not even our ear! On the contrary, like somebody divinely absent-minded and sunk in his own thoughts who, the twelve strokes of midday having just boomed into his ears, wakes with a start and wonders, 'What hour struck?', sometimes we, too, *afterwards* rub our ears and ask, astonished, taken aback, 'What did we actually experience then?' or even 'Who *are* we, in fact?' and afterwards, as I said, we count all twelve reverberating strokes of our experience, of our life, of our being—oh! And lose count. (GM, P.1)

It is the human being immersed in his own thoughts, apparently at one with his mind, who is in truth absent-minded, because he is in fact lost to his experiences, incapable of being struck by them even when they boom into his ear. If one is seriously to experience each reverberating stroke of the world's impact, one must count them or rather recount them—think of this as taking the time to provide a recounting. So being present to my experiences is a matter of first suffering their impress, and then offering an account of them: the fulfilment of any impression lies in its expression, and thus requires a capacity and willingness on my part to make that impression other to me, to actively distance myself from it in time and thereby allow it to reverberate—that is, to reappear in verbal form, to find words for it for which I am willing to be accountable, and thereby to take responsibility for my own experiences, in the absence of which my experiences, and so my life and my being, will remain absent or lost to me, something in which I am simply immersed or sunk.

Properly recounting our conception of 'experience' thus reveals two things about ourselves as beings possessed of an inner world or interior life as well as a place in nature, call it genuine subjectivity: we are necessarily capable of distancing ourselves from ourselves—of taking a perspective on our experience; and this capacity is inseparable from a capacity to articulate our experiences—which means both finding words for them and taking responsibility for doing so in the sight (or rather the hearing) of others, contributing to the collectivity of speech. It follows that properly to know ourselves as knowers—no longer being simply immersed or sunk in my being as a knower but genuinely experiencing what it means to be a man or woman of knowledge—will involve distancing ourselves from that state, getting underway on a journey or transition from it to whatever state lying beyond it allows us to gain perspective on it by providing a recounting of it. Only those who no longer wholly inhabit that mode of being can properly bring it home to themselves as it really is, or rather was.

Those who are (still, presently) knowers cannot, therefore, seriously understand themselves as such—they cannot mean or take responsibility for describing themselves as 'knowers' (since they are confused about what it means to do so); and they would also (equally mistakenly) reject any description of themselves as knowers who are unknown to themselves. Conversely, anyone who is in a position not only to say but to mean (to be genuinely accountable for saying) that she is a knower who is unknown to herself will not say so, for she must no longer be (purely or simply or wholly) a knower, and hence would, in so describing herself, misdescribe her current self in terms appropriate to her past self, the self from which she has departed.

From what perspective, then, could anyone advance the claim that 'We are unknown to ourselves, we knowers'? The problem here is one of time, or say tense: using the present tense seriously in such a self-description appears to be either beyond us or behind us, depending on whether we truly remain self-unknown knowers or have gone beyond that state or condition. Or one might say that it is a problem of pronouns or persons: someone who is no longer a self-ignorant knower might coherently describe those who remain so in such terms, but then the third-person or the second-person would be the appropriate mode of address—and yet this speaker talks not of 'they' or 'you' but of 'we' (that is, him and us, the author and his readers) being knowers who are unknown to ourselves. But if either he or we really were unknown knowers, then he would not say so—because he would regard it as either false, or not worth making (since anyone to whom it applied would reject it, as if it were mere booming in their ears).

Suppose, however, that our author has therapeutic designs on us; then it might be essential to his purpose to speak as if from an impossible perspective or subject position. For what he says presupposes that we are simultaneously both self-ignorant knowers, and beings who no longer inhabit that mode of being; and that presupposition would in a sense be valid if we were underway from the former state to the latter—that is, inherently between states, transitional, becoming, but also inherently between just those two states, beings whose aspiration to go beyond the condition of self-ignorant knowing was engendered and oriented by some aspect of that condition. If that were the case, then we would be in (an internal relation to) both states: we would be moving away from the first and towards the second, and the latter precisely because of the former. And what, after all, is more calculated to stimulate a knower's energies than the insinuation that her knowledge is not only somehow deficient, but is so with respect to the one domain of her knowledge that she has hitherto assumed to be beyond doubt—her knowledge of herself?

The real point of saying something to us whose apparent point presupposes that we are simultaneously both self-ignorant and becoming otherwise is thus not that Nietzsche thinks that that presupposition currently holds true of us, his readers; it is that he hopes thereby to encourage us to *make* it true. For if our commitment to knowing does drive us to figure out this presupposition of Nietzsche's address, then in so doing we will come to realize not only that he apparently believes that our relation to ourselves might be other than it currently is, but also that only someone who was already underway in just that sense—already effecting this transformation in his own case—could have attained the perspective from which to offer such encouragement. If Nietzsche can do it, and if, having done it, he addresses us in a way which identifies himself with us, quite as if—as far as he can see—he is essentially indistinguishable from us in the relevant respects, then why can't we? And then we might find ourselves realizing that simply to be so encouraged is in fact already to go beyond our initial condition of self-ignorant knowing, because it involves at least imagining things to be otherwise than they appear to be, realizing that what seems necessary may not in fact be so. And we might further appreciate that the willingness to offer such encouragement constitutes one way in which another might take responsibility for their own experience of self-overcoming, by finding words for it which he can give to those most in need of them—his fellow intellectual honey-gatherers whose winged nature is currently unknown but nevertheless essentially knowable to them, if they can only find the time and the seriousness properly to bring their current mode of being home to themselves.

2) The Kingfisher and the Fisher King

As if to confirm his claim to be underway or transitional, the remainder of Nietzsche's preface presents a select autobiography of his writing life as first on the way to knowing, and then on the way beyond it—strokes of the pen recounting strokes of the clock. The two most distant markers of this process are his adolescent suspicions of God's relation to evil, and his adult interrogations of Schopenhauer's nihilistic morality of compassion (begun at least by the time of *Untimely Meditations*, and renewed in every text thereafter, but still apparently in need of re-enactment). It is perhaps particularly worth noting the ways in which Nietzsche takes the first of these ventures as prophetic with respect to his current one, as having sounded notes to which his later ear simply becomes more thoroughly attuned. For his thirteen-year-old self was concerned with the origin of evil, and 'gave God the credit for it, making him the *father* of evil' (GM, P.3). And that last phrase not only assigns to God one of the traditional titles of the Devil; it also puts into play the fateful image of God as creditor to which the second essay will return, as well as (via the idea of metaphysical paternity) giving a material or literal inflection to the notion of genealogical descent to which all three of his present essays give a cultural and historical inflection, just as they transpose his ontological query about evil into a linguistic or etymological one (about the origin of 'evil'). The implication seems clear: a deeper understanding of what is at stake in these issues requires no shift of focus, but rather a transfiguration of method—from the material mode to that of language and form of life, the medium in which (as the first section of the preface suggests) the distinctively human animal fundamentally finds itself, and loses itself.

Two other such signposts are, however, both more proximate and more immediately significant. The first is the 1878 edition of *Human, All Too Human*, which coincided with Nietzsche's brief perception of Paul Rée (and his work on *The Origin of Moral Sentiments*) as a companion free spirit (a member of the company to which *Human, All Too Human* dedicates itself in its subtitle). Some commentators have been sceptical of Nietzsche's claim that, even then, his views and Rée's were significantly divergent; and one could certainly have hoped to see a more nuanced presentation of Rée's book than as straightforwardly 'contradictory and antithetical' to Nietzsche's own 1878 text (cf. GM, P.4). But as I argued earlier, *Human, All Too Human* is itself far less straightforward an endorsement of the merits of scientific naturalism than many commentators assume; so Nietzsche's claim that the essays of the *Genealogy* ought to be viewed as expressing 'mainly the same thoughts' as *Human, All Too Human*, only 'riper, brighter, stronger and more perfect' (GM, P.2), posits a degree of continuity between these two stages of his career that is worth taking seriously.

Doing so need involve no discounting of the weight Nietzsche also assigns to the degree of discontinuity—most clearly when he talks of 'a *fundamental will* to knowledge deep inside me which took control, speaking more and more clearly and making ever clearer demands' (GM, P.2). This description of himself as a man of knowledge, so swiftly after identifying such men as his current target of critical evaluation, hardly suggests an unwillingness for self-criticism. So when he takes Rée to task for being an

English genealogist, it is worth remembering that he also presents the process of saying 'no' to each of Rée's propositions as not only internal to the composition of *Human, All Too Human*, but also as his way of 'bringing to the light of day those hypotheses on descent to which these essays are devoted' (GM, P.4); in this sense, Rée's apparently absolute otherness was and is internal to Nietzsche's own progress, a way of being a man of knowledge which Nietzsche insists upon rejecting precisely because remaining within it was a live option for him. Perhaps this is why, whereas in *Human, All Too Human* the wandering free spirit is figured in conclusion as suspended between the tenth and twelfth strokes of the midday clock, the critic of knowledge is envisaged at the outset of his labours as being challenged to awaken to all twelve strokes. Each is listening to the same clock at the onset of midday (and thus is to be distinguished from the likes of Justice Shallow, whose recollection of the chimes at midnight expresses a nostalgia for gaiety long lost); but the genealogist is—shall we say—fractionally more advanced or untimely, being in a position to recount additional strokes of time's passage through the forenoon.

The second, even more proximate, signpost appears only in the final section of the Preface, when Nietzsche is attempting to account for the difficulty of understanding his present book:

With regard to my *Zarathustra*, for example, I do not acknowledge anyone as an expert on it if he has not, at some time, been both profoundly wounded and profoundly delighted by it, for only then may he enjoy the privilege of sharing, with due reverence, the halcyon element from which the book was born and its sunny brightness, spaciousness, breadth and certainty. In other cases, the aphoristic form causes difficulty: this is because this form is *not taken seriously enough these days*. An aphorism properly stamped and moulded [coined and cast], has not been 'deciphered' just because it has been read through; on the contrary, this is just the beginning of its proper *interpretation*, and for this, an art of interpretation is needed. In the third essay of this book I have given an example of what I mean by 'interpretation' in such a case:—this treatise is a commentary on the aphorism that precedes it. I admit that you need one thing above all in order to practise the requisite *art* of reading, a thing which today people have been so good at forgetting—and so it will be some time before my writings are 'readable'—,you almost need to be a cow for this one thing and certainly *not* a 'modern man': it is *rumination*. (GM, P.8)

Although Nietzsche here appears to distinguish the case of *Thus Spake Zarathustra* (completed two years earlier) from those 'other cases' in which the aphoristic form of his writing is the source of its difficulty, he also conjoins the two, by choosing as his epigraph to the third essay a sentence from *Zarathustra* which is not only aphoristic in form but derives from a section of that book that (like most of its other transcriptions of Zarathustra's discourses) is composed almost wholly of aphorisms, and furthermore is entitled 'Of Reading and Writing':

Carefree, scornful, outrageous – that is how wisdom wants us to be; she is a woman, and never loves anyone but a warrior. (TSZ[2], 68)

No doubt in part because of this conjunction, many commentators have tended to assume that this epigraph is the preceding aphorism upon which the third essay is a commentary. More recently, it has been argued that the relevant aphorism is rather to be found in (or consists of) the first section of that essay, which was in fact added to the essay at the last moment, at which point Nietzsche also added to his Preface the final section that explicitly adverts to it:

What do ascetic ideals mean? – With artists, nothing or too many different things; with philosophers and scholars, something like a nose and sense for the most favourable conditions of higher intellectuality; with women, at most, one *more* seductive charm, a little *morbidezza* on fair flesh, the angelic expression on a pretty, plump animal; with physiological causalities and the disgruntled (with the *majority* of mortals), an attempt to see themselves as 'too good' for this world, a saintly form of debauchery, their chief weapon in the battle against long-drawn-out pain and boredom; with priests, the actual priestly faith, their best instrument of power; with saints, an excuse to hibernate at last, their *novissima gloriae cupido*, their rest in nothingness ('God'), their form of madness. *That* the ascetic ideal has meant so much to man reveals a basic fact of human will, its *horror vacui; it needs an aim*—, and it prefers to will *nothingness* rather than *not* will.—Do I make myself understood? . . . Have I made myself understood? . . . '*Absolutely not, sir!*'—So let us start at the beginning. (GM, 3.1)

Christopher Janaway has made perhaps the most extensive and convincing case for taking the climactic remark that we 'prefer to will nothingness rather than not will' as the aphorism Nietzsche really had in mind, with the preceding list of domains in which the ascetic ideal shows up functioning as, in effect, a contents list for the long and involved essay that follows, with

---

[2] Nietzsche, *Thus Spake Zarathustra*, trans. R. Hollingdale (London: Penguin, 1969)—hereafter TSZ.

each item on that list being ruminated upon—chewed over long and hard, swallowed and multiply digested—by some specific subsequent section or sequence of sections.[3] And he is careful to point out that accepting his hypothesis need not prevent us from cleaving to the thought that relating the epigraph to the essay remains relevant to the business of the latter's proper interpretation: 'It is conventional for such epigraphs to be pregnant and oracular, putting the reader temporarily off balance, gesturing away from the work they preface, creating a tension within it, or providing an indefinitely large space for associations' (BS, 177–8). More specifically, for instance, Janaway points out that the epigraph lies immediately adjacent to the concluding gesture of the second essay, which silences its own invocation of a man to come who might redeem us from the ascetic ideal, on the grounds that it risks appropriating to itself something 'to which Zarathustra alone is entitled' (GM, 2.25). Such connections can be recognized and exploited, Janaway suggests, 'without forcing the [essay] into the uncomfortable mould of "commentary" upon it' (BS, 180).

My concern is to exploit the associative field between epigraph and essay by relating both to the specific ways in which the final section of the preface first invokes Zarathustra. So doing will not, then, bring this reading into conflict with Janaway's general interpretative claims: indeed, it will allow us to identify certain important tensions between epigraph and essay that become more rather than less apparent if we accept Janaway's picture of its first section as listing the essay's forthcoming sequence of particular cases.

We are told in the preface that only someone who has been profoundly wounded and profoundly delighted by Zarathustra can share the halcyon element from which the book was born, and thereby claim expertise in relation to it. 'Halcyon' is originally a name for the kingfisher, a bird said by the ancients to breed in a nest floating on the sea around the time of the winter solstice, and to charm the wind and waves so that the sea was calm for this purpose: hence, by extension, the phrase 'halcyon days' refers to a period of calm weather, idyllic happiness, or prosperity. This already gives us good reason to prefer Hollingdale's translation of the epigraph's third specification of how wisdom wants us to be as 'outrageous' rather than (as, say, Diethe has it) 'violent'. More importantly, it entails that Nietzsche's reference to Zarathustra as having been born is no accident: the halcyon element

---

[3] C. Janaway, *Beyond Selflessness* (Oxford: Oxford University Press, 2007)—hereafter BS; chapter 10.

is that of breeding and birth, and more specifically (given its affinity for the winter solstice, and its capacity to calm the waves) of a birth that amounts to an alternative incarnation of divinity.

If the kingfisher represents Christ, then the fisher king is not far away—the last in the mythological line of guardians of the Holy Grail, the ruler whose wounded groin not only immobilizes him but figures the decline of his realm into sterility, until both he and it are healed by one of Arthur's knights, Sir Percival, and the grail recovered. Little wonder, then, that Nietzsche's discussion of the ascetic ideal in art focuses on Wagner's late opera *Parsifal*, which recounts exactly this Christian story, but in accents of utter seriousness that lead Nietzsche to wish that its creator meant it to be a parody of tragic religiosity, rather than an exemplary incarnation of the ascetic wasteland in which Nietzsche himself now wanders, fishing for vitality and finding only ruination, seeking a warrior to heal life's pervasive woundedness, a kingfisher for the true descendent of the fisher king.

This intimate contestation of the example of *Parsifal* underlines Nietzsche's continuing sense of opera in general, and Wagnerian opera in particular, as sufficiently inward with his concerns to require radical contestation; but the shift of focus from the *Ring* cycle to *Parsifal* suggests a certain revision of Nietzsche's sense of his relation to Christianity. As we saw much earlier in this book in the context of Wittgenstein's invocation of Nothung, Wagnerian mythology as it finds expression in the *Ring* seems to define itself in opposition to the Christianized universe of the Arthurian tales. Here, however, just as Wagner's late work seems to find (if not common, then at least) cultivatable ground with that Arthurian world, so Nietzsche's declaration of disgust with what he presents as Wagner's relapse acts to occlude his own late willingness to turn a symbol of Christ to his own purposes (hence to find his own way by working through Christian resources, however radically revised). As the Dionysian bird of the forest invoked in *The Birth of Tragedy* is transfigured into a Christian kingfisher, what matters more: the bird's transfiguration, or Nietzsche's continued identification with it?

This invocation of *Parsifal* also confirms what the preface already declares—namely that on Nietzsche's understanding of the redemptive matter it brings into focus, the cure for woundedness lies in woundedness. More specifically, just as the fisher king's recovery of a world in which enjoyment might once again be taken is effected by a spear's insertion into the wound it aspires to heal, so rebirth from the wound of asceticism involves suffering a more profound wounding from which comes the taking of a more profound delight—undergoing the enjoyable injury of Zarathustra's words.

If Zarathustra's readers are thus fisher kings to his Sir Percival, then Nietzsche's citation of Zarathustra's words on reading and writing as at once displacing and propelling his own (as a mode of utterance to which the second essay reaches out only for the third essay to reach beyond) suggests that he has internalized their thrust. His current writing appears as the outcome of his reading even his most proximate earlier writing as if it had been composed by another, thereby becoming the Sir Percival to his own fisher king—once again taking his bearings from his prior state or condition. Revitalizing this wasteland will thus involve overcoming the wasteland in oneself by going through it, intensifying the wound in order that it might fructify, transcending asceticism by means of asceticism. The first step in so doing is coming to see that one's current circumstances really have been laid waste by such asceticism—in fields and in ways that one might never have suspected of harbouring such sterility; and the second is to admit the extent to which that sterility is constitutive of one's own present state.

This is why Nietzsche stresses in the first section of the third essay that the ascetic ideal has 'meant so much to man': by this he certainly means that its meaning has gone deep with us, but he equally certainly means that it has taken on so many different guises and inflections—not only in religion and ethics, but in art, in science, and in philosophy. The ascetic ideal is most clearly recognizable as a morality of compassion and pity, of self-sacrifice and self-denial, of life denial and self-hatred; but it turns out to be not so much an ethics as an ethos—a mode of evaluation that is equally capable of structuring one's impressions and articulations of art and the artist (as in Wagner's late, decadent turn towards Christianity), of science (with its practitioners' willingness to sacrifice themselves to the pursuit of the underlying truth about reality, and thereby to the diremption of the world of appearance, perception, and affect from that of a reality comprehensible only by means of the timeless categories of mathematics), and of philosophy (with its association of knowledge with virtue, its commitment to the ultimate intelligibility of the real, its preference for Being over Becoming, and its own version of our all-consuming love for truth). To understand the will to truth as an expression of the ascetic ideal is to understand that morality is never just a matter of moral evaluation: there is no corner of human culture whose form and content cannot incarnate an ethical stance and system of values. Morality is thus not so much a sector of human life as a dimension of it. The Enlightenment vision of the autonomy of morality from religion, politics, science, and art in fact functions as a way of occluding the moral dimension of art and science, and thus of overlooking the true reach of the religious values it aspired to transcend.

More specifically, however, acknowledging the ascetic roots of the will to truth means recognizing the ascetic dimension of philosophy; it means recognizing the extent to which that wound is carried even by one who aspires to wage war against it—precisely because the banner under which that war is waged is the desire to discover the truth about morality, and so about its offshoot the will to truth. Nietzsche incarnates the will to truth's ultimate perversion—its turning upon itself; the truth about truth includes acknowledging that men and women of knowledge are ignorant of the extent to which their own enterprise, and hence their own identity, is marked by the ascetic ideal itself. Fully to diagnose the problem involves seeing that the diagnosticians constitute part of that problem; any serious polemic against asceticism must accordingly become a form of self-criticism—it must commit one to suffering an intensification of one's woundedness, by making that woundedness into the instrument of its own deepening. It is not just a matter of becoming the Sir Percival to one's own fisher king; it is also a matter of recognizing this Sir Percival as the fisher king's progeny, as another mask or manifestation of the king himself.

What, however, of the delight that is supposed to go together with this woundedness? It can only derive from the hope that the self-wounding turn of our inner woundedness will take us beyond that mode of self-injury. But the term 'delight' turns a particular facet of its meaning towards the light, in the context in which Nietzsche here sets it—a context in which the preface's halcyon element symbolizes birth, the epigraph of the third essay specifies a warrior's way of satisfying wisdom's womanly desires, and the first section of the third essay talks of the seductive charm of fair female flesh. The deeper organizing idea here is that of 'woman', and so of 'delight' understood as female 'delectation, allure, charm'. One should certainly not take Nietzsche's detection of a 'little *morbidezza*' on that fair flesh to be expressive solely of scornfulness or contempt: as a term of art, *morbidezza* originally referred to ways of painting human flesh so as to capture its lifelike delicacy, before it acquired connotations of sickliness and decay; and we have anyway already established that healing and new life are to be found in injury, in the vulnerability of living flesh, if they are to be found at all. What is rather more striking is the way in which these prefatory and epigraphic registrations of Zarathustra's inwardness with femaleness highlight the presence of 'woman' in the third essay's initial list of contents; for in truth, that item is the only one of the seven types that Janaway distinguishes to receive next to no detailed, ruminative analysis in the essay itself. Janaway refers us to section 14, alone amongst the subsequent twenty-seven sections, as having any bearing on that type; but that section contains just two sentences in which women are invoked—more precisely, two sentences in which the sick woman is presented as a tyrannical extreme version of another general type, that of modern human weakness or debility. Since every other type or category announced in the first section receives extended and elaborate consideration, why is that of 'woman' barely registered?

My intuition is that 'woman' is nowhere to be found in the essay because she is everywhere in it; but such omnipresence might be realized in two different ways. The first possibility is that the category of 'woman' is given no specific analysis because each category that is so analysed can be regarded as an inflection of it. The implication of Nietzsche's omission would then be that the ascetic formations of morality, religion, art, science, scholarship, and philosophy are individual variations on the angelic expression that the plump, well-fed human animal likes to adopt for itself, each one way of giving vulnerable, bovine, self-interested flesh a tint of delicacy, a species of seductive charm, and ultimately the possibility of overcoming the perversity it incarnates through a certain, generative radicalization of that very perversity. But there is also a second possibility: that the category of 'woman' is given no specific analysis because every specific analysis in that essay is conducted from a female point of view—from the viewpoint of a self-aware wisdom who actively encourages the outrageousness of the warrior she recognizes as her intimate other, her twin self, desirous above all of the impulse to exceed oneself, to go beyond, to be extravagant that the word 'outrage' connotes (and that Zarathustra's imaginative inhabitation of a perspective in which he can 'see myself under myself' [TSZ, 69] prophesies).

Such intercourse between male and female allows wisdom to combine woundedness with delight in a manner that promises to bear new fruit, of a kind that might charm waves into placidity and infuse the wasteland with bright, breeding light. This would (in turns of phrase at work in Zarathustra's discourse 'On Reading and Writing') be the divine birth of a writer who writes in blood (say, out of, and about, genealogy), and whose relation to his readers goes beyond merely knowing them to embodying the desire to stimulate their desire to exalt themselves (as wisdom seeks to stimulate her warrior self). He does so by declaring that, although he is currently looking down at them, in so doing he sees himself under himself; in other words, their current lack of exaltation is one he previously shared, and he attained his current exaltation solely by a process of self-mastery or self-overcoming—first aspiring to something higher, and then ascending to it on the stepping stone(s) of his earlier self, through a self-abasement that disclosed and emancipated a divine, dancing wisdom that was always already within him.

3) Giving Names and Making Words

If the structure of the third essay is explicitly declared to exemplify the correct, ruminative way to read a Nietzschean aphoristic text, it might be worth taking seriously the possibility that the other two essays that make up the *Genealogy* exemplify the same structure, and hence aspire to suffer the same interpretative practice, the same art of reading. If so, we should expect to find each to begin with (if not an aphoristic remark then) a claim that initially poses some kind of challenge to the understanding, and the remainder of the essay to constitute an elaborate unfolding of the significance it incarnates. And insofar as each preceding essay contributes to our understanding of the nature of the wound that the ascetic ideal has delivered to the human animal, then each thereby enhances our understanding of what it means for Nietzsche to identify all knowers, and hence himself, as animals whose essence derives from their ways of bearing that wound.

Suppose we approach the first essay, 'Good and Evil, Good and Bad', on the basis of that assumption. Then we find ourselves presented in its first section with what is not so much an aphorism as a riddle in human form:

—These English psychologists, who have to be thanked for having made the only attempts so far to write a history of the emergence of morality—provide us with a small riddle in the form of themselves; in fact, I admit that as living riddles they have a significant advantage over their books—*they are actually interesting!* These English psychologists—just what do they want? You always find them at the same task, whether they want to or not, pushing the *partie honteuse* of our inner world to the foreground, and looking for what is really effective, guiding and decisive for our development where man's intellectual pride would least wish to find it (for example, in the *vis inertia* of habit, or in forgetfulness, or in a blind and random coupling of ideas, or in something purely passive, automatic, reflexive, molecular and thoroughly stupid)—what is it that actually drives these psychologists in precisely *this* direction all the time? (GM, 1.1)

Nietzsche canvasses two possible solutions to his riddle: either these psychologists manifest some combination of malicious anti-humanism, disillusioned idealism, anti-Christianity, and a lewd need for the thrill of self-debasement; or they manifest the bravery of 'generous and proud animals, who know how to control their own pleasure and pain and have been taught to sacrifice desirability to truth . . . even a plain, bitter, ugly, foul, unchristian, immoral truth . . . Because there are such truths' (GM, 1.1). Nietzsche declares that, although he has been told that they are, in reality, 'old, cold, boring frogs' who have transformed the inner life of man into a swamp simply because that is the element in which they are most at home, he is not only resistant to hearing this, he refuses to believe it: 'if it is permissible to wish where it is impossible to know, I sincerely hope that the reverse is true' (GM, 1.1). In other words, he wants to respect these analysts holding a microscope to the human soul, by thinking of them as possessed of a presiding good spirit—the spirit of scientific endeavour.

Even if we aren't yet in a position to recognize that good spirit as the will to truth, and thus as an extreme expression of the ascetic ideal, the related ironies at work in this passage are hard to miss. To begin with, the first solution to his riddle assigns to the English psychologists exactly the range of predicates which his own, coming genealogical analysis will invite from its initially resistant readers; so by presenting himself as rejecting that first solution in favour of interpreting these English psychologists in the apparently more flattering terms offered by the second (terms that he will later claim for his own work), Nietzsche enacts a certain kind of identification with the riddling object of his interest. They are, he hopes, no more frogs than he is; they are, he would like to believe, animals as brave, generous, and proud as he takes himself to be: this is why such hoping is also the fulfilment of a wish. But if it is barely permissible to have these hopes for others (whose real motivation is presented as somehow beyond his knowledge, presumably because the riddle their existence poses finds no expression in their essentially uninteresting texts), is it more or less permissible to hope as much for one's own project? Is it a realistic hope, or mere wish-fulfilment? And is it in the end permissible to substitute hoping and wishing for knowing—quite as if pure or mere cognition articulates itself on ground to which the claims of desire and the projections of hope also stake a claim (so that truth is entangled with goodness, and the present with the future, and the former pair with the latter)?

We will have to return to this last question; but the earlier ones are here more pressing. One might at first think that knowing one's own motives and attitudes cannot be a challenge (at least not in the way that knowing the motives of another may be), and so conclude that such hopes are rather better grounded in one's own case—except that the preface has just told us that knowers are unknown to themselves, and Nietzsche is articulating these displaced hopes at the very outset of his project, when it is (surely?) impossible to know its fruits (whether immediate or ultimate), and hence its nature.

One might, accordingly, conclude that, when Nietzsche asks, 'What do these English psychologists want?', he is also asking (and so inviting us to ask), 'What do I want?' (thereby reinforcing, for those of his current readers familiar with Freud's analogous and [in]famous question, the idea of his identification with the female perspective). He is expressing an anxiety about what will turn out to be the correct solution to the riddle posed by his own existence; and in so doing, he declares at once an indebtedness to the English psychologists and a desire to resist a possible fate or threat that they also embody. He thereby presents his own project as one in which a certain mode of knowing aspires to overcome itself from within, to find a way of inheriting its current realization otherwise; and the first step in that process appears to be a willingness to think the best of that current realization—to make an effort to find cheer and inspiration in what might otherwise represent the expiration of heat, vitality, and interest.

Such a conclusion is not undermined, but rather underlined, by recalling the role played by that (ironically) exemplary English psychologist, Paul Rée, in the preface to the *Genealogy*—about whose book, *The Origin of Moral Sentiments*, Nietzsche there has the following to say: 'I have, perhaps, never read anything to which I said "no", sentence by sentence and deduction by deduction, as I did to this book; but completely without annoyance or impatience' (GM, P.4). This mood of calmness and patience is enough on its own to qualify the gesture of negation; but even Nietzsche's way of articulating that gesture takes on a rather different cast when recounted together with the way he shapes the contrast between masters and slaves in a later section of this first essay:

Whereas all noble morality grows out of a triumphant saying 'yes' to itself, slave morality says 'no' on principle to everything that is 'outside', 'other', 'non-self': and *this* 'no' is its creative deed. This reversal of the evaluating glance—this *inevitable* orientation to the outside instead of back onto itself—is a feature of *ressentiment*: in order to come about, slave morality first has to have an opposing, external world, it needs, physiologically speaking, external stimuli in order to act at all—its action is basically a reaction. The opposite is the case with the noble method of evaluation: this acts and grows spontaneously, seeking out its opposite only so that it can say 'yes' to itself even more thankfully and exultantly,—its negative concept 'low', 'common', 'bad', is only a pale contrast created after the event compared to its positive basic concept, saturated with life and passion, 'We the noble, the good, the beautiful and the happy!' (GM, 1.10)

Against the background of this account, Nietzsche's prefatory dramatization of his relation to Rée as that of systematic nay saying to an author whose way of putting things was 'back-to-front and perverse' (GM, P.4) in relation to his own—this portrait of Rée as his absolute other or non-self—would amount to an indictment of Nietzsche himself as belonging to the party of the slaves. Little wonder, then, that the beginning of the first essay not only manifests real uncertainty about the border between the English psychologists and himself, but also looks for a way of making this internal relatedness to that which he most deeply resists somehow productive or vital rather than cause for self-hatred and despair.

And sure enough, in the second section of the essay, some cause for overcoming that despair is indeed found, even if it lurks only in parenthesis. For at this point, Nietzsche declares his difference from the English psychologists as one in which he maintains their presiding spirit whilst infusing it with an essentially historical philosophical practice—one which overcomes the 'idiocy' of their moral genealogies by contesting their essentially unhistorical assumption that unegoistic acts have always and everywhere been called 'good':

Now for me, it is obvious that the real breeding-ground for the concept 'good' has been sought and located in the wrong place by this theory: the judgement 'good' does *not* emanate from those to whom goodness is shown! Instead, it has been 'the good' themselves, meaning the noble, the mighty, the high-placed and the high-minded, who saw and judged themselves and their actions as good, I mean first-rate, in contrast to everything lowly, low-minded, common and plebeian. It was from this *pathos of distance* that they first claimed the right to create values and give these values names . . .

(The seigneurial privilege of giving names even allows us to conceive of the origin of language itself as a manifestation of the power of the rulers: they say 'this is so-and-so', they set their seal on everything and every occurrence with a sound and thereby take possession of it, as it were) . . . It is only with a *decline* of aristocratic value-judgements that this whole antithesis between 'egoistic' and 'unegoistic' forces itself more and more on man's conscience,—it is, to use my language, the *herd instinct* which, with that, finally gets its word in (and makes *words*). (GM, 1.2)

On the one hand, Nietzsche commits himself not only to the claim that master morality precedes slave morality, but also to the hypothesis that the first expression of master morality is also the origin of language as such—a seigneurial privilege indeed; he thereby reconceives evaluative judgement as not merely one domain of language use but rather as its originating medium, so that language as such, in all its more specific formations and deformations, must be conceived of as inherently possessed of an evaluative dimension (a point upon which the third essay will fatefully elaborate). On the other hand, there is something unsettlingly biblical or Judaic about the terms in which Nietzsche presents this vision of the masterly origin of language. His masters' first words declare the goodness of their actions and their consequences (and so their own goodness), just like God's first words in response to His acts of creation *ex nihilo* (according to the book of Genesis); and his account further assumes that language begins with acts of naming that are also expressions of power or mastery—thereby following the basic structure of the Genesis narrative of language's primordial human use (in which Adam is invited to take up his stewardship of creation by assigning names to all its creatures). Perhaps Nietzsche would regard this predecessor narrative as one further, unwitting philological trace of the moral reality that preceded the form of life that Genesis aspires to under-write; but I can't be the only reader to recall here that the same trace is activated when Wittgenstein opens his later investigation of language by citing Augustine's memories of his own acquisition of language, according to which 'grown-ups name some object and at the same time turned towards it . . . [indicating] the affections of the soul when it desires or clings to, or rejects or recoils from, something'.[4] And this conjunction of naming with the expression of a desire for possession (or dispossession—call it owning or disowning) is isolated for particular exploration by Wittgenstein, in important part by contrasting it with an imagined shopping trip in which words appear more variously equipped and desire more domesticated or at home in the world, so that speaking remains internally related to desire without desire as such necessarily being expressive of setting one's personal seal on creation, as if to be human were to be desirous of mastering the universe as such, making ourselves its centre.

The extent of Nietzsche's uncritical commitment to such a vision of language is, however, put in question by the partly parenthetical remark which concludes the passage I cited: 'it is, to use my language, the *herd instinct* which, with that, finally gets its word in (and makes *words*)'. The thought that slave morality sets its seal on our thinking and living by enforcing the connection between goodness and altruism is familiar; what is less familiar is Nietzsche's association of slave morality's forging of this particular linguistic connection with the making of words as such—quite as if whatever the masters had achieved by their initial, powerful, evaluative naming of things, these names were not (not yet, not quite) *words*—not until the slaves got their word in. Why not?

A world in which creatures do nothing but apply 'names' to things in accordance with their settled attraction or aversion to them is one in which utterances are closer to sound than to speech, because insofar as these acts of possessing the world are purely expressive of their utterers' unchanging character and its spontaneous, undeviating manifestations, they will be purely repetitive—utterly invariant, hence essentially unchanging and essentially unresponsive to any change in their environments. 'Words' which are essentially incapable of such responsiveness—call it projection into new circumstances which elicit new possibilities of sense—are not really words at all, any more than a parrot's acquisition of a small menu of

---

[4] Cf. L. Wittgenstein, *Philosophical Investigations*, revised 4th edition, trans. P.M.S. Hacker and J. Schulte (Oxford: Blackwell, 2009), section 1.

sounds keyed to a small menu of phenomena amounts to the mastery of a vocabulary, a set of ways of saying something.

Words must be capable of iteration; but words that are never used in anything other than the elemental or original ways in which they were first used are not capable of constituting a language, and so are not capable of constituting their users as users of language. Anyone whose affective responses to the world are such that they can find adequate expression in unending reapplications of the same evaluative name to the same things are not creatures capable of speech—because they are not capable of distancing themselves from themselves, by putting their responses in question or otherwise indicating that things might be named (which here means evaluated) otherwise, hence that the way they name them is their way, theirs to own, for which they can be held accountable. Such creatures could not speak because they would have nothing of their own to say; in Heidegger's terms, such a 'language' would lack the possibility of mineness: others might prefer to say that in such circumstances the first-person pronoun (and so its second- and third-person analogues, whether singular or plural) would lack purchase or point.

Slave morality's getting its word in amounts to making words out of the masters' 'words' because the slaves' use of them involves, and so introduces (in the terms of section 10), reversal, opposition, and reaction against the static iterations of the masters' essentially self-involved and self-reinforcing self-expressions; as Sartre would put it, they introduce negation. They initiate an 'orientation [of language and its users] to the outside rather than back onto itself' (GM, 1.10) which introduces the possibility of a genuine reaction to the external world, because it involves the capacity to recognize stimuli as genuinely external, hence not absolutely within the utterer's possession but other to him (as the master is other to him). The connection that slave morality makes between goodness and altruism may be resentful, but it is genuinely original—it remakes the world, together with everyone in it; and even if it amounts to the expression of a herd instinct, it thereby at least acknowledges the collective nature of genuine speech.

Insofar, then, as Nietzsche's gestures (in the preface, and in the first section of the first essay) put into play the possibility of a certain identification with the English psychologists specifically and the ascetic ideal more generally, they align him *with* rather than against those who first embody a genuine use of language (as he acknowledges when he describes his making of the point about slave morality making words as something he does in *his* language, language that is genuinely his own—just as his recognition that the collective nature of language is inherently vulnerable to failures of individuality finds expression in his coining a new phrase for that failure—'herd instinct'—thereby enacting the other possibility that words, collectively owned, open up). Finding his own way with words does not mean jettisoning the idea that words as such express evaluations (that concepts are expressions of our interests) and so register desire; but it does mean acknowledging that creativity here and now, in the aftermath of the slave revolt, will mean tapping into the creativity of that revolt, and so will require a reflexive employment of the capacity of words to invert, reverse, and oppose—a turning or conversion of the key concepts of our form of life against themselves, in the name of a hoped-for future. And the first indications as to what that might involve are laid out in the concluding sections of the first essay.

4) The Eye of the Cave and the Ear of the City

Section 14 begins with the book's narrative voice suddenly asking whether anyone would like to go down and take a look into the secret of how they fabricate ideals on earth. The volunteer is addressed as 'mein Herr Vorwitz und Wagehals'—a name variously rendered by translators as Mr Rash and Curious, Mr Nosy Daredevil, Mr Daredevil Curiosity, or Mr Wanton-Curiosity and Daredevil. Janaway, the sole commentator to find any real significance in this curious scene, summarizes the subsequent course of events as follows:

The narrator affects to send this member of the public down into a fetid, cavernous workshop, reminiscent of Wagner's Nibelheim, where morality is cobbled together by shadowy, stunted creatures brimming with *ressentiment*. The authorial voice receives reports from the front-line emissary as if from the safety of surface daylight, goading him on until what he witnesses becomes unbearable and he demands to be returned to the open air. (BS, 102)

What does Nietzsche achieve by casting section 14 in this vivid, dramatic form? According to Janaway, his emotive rhetoric aims at harnessing the reader's own disquiet over the untrammelled exercise of power by the overtly powerful in order to convert it into a still greater disquiet over the covert desire to exercise power that Mr Rash and Curious reports as motivating the fabrication of Christian and post-Christian moral ideals. For what he discovers is that the covert basis for our current aversion to the nobles' treatment of the weak and helpless is itself essentially indistinguishable from the overt basis of the nobles' system of values; the only difference between them is that the fabricators of slave morality have lied about its true ground (in the powerful drives of their self-interest, their hatred of strength and life, and their self-disgust). As Janaway puts it:

Nietzsche enacts disgust on the reader's behalf, but it is a disgust with a specific and complex object: *that a system of values which exists to fulfil (in imagination) the drive towards power should falsely pass itself off as in opposition to the drive towards power.* At this point Mr Rash and Curious shouts 'Enough! Enough!' Nietzsche perhaps hoped that evoking this disgust might be enough to break the reader's allegiance to judging things good or evil, preparing the way one day for new combinations of affects for and against that he would regard as healthier. (BS, 105–6)

The general plausibility of this interpretative model seems to me to be undeniable; but Janaway's interpretation of Mr Rash and Curious is rather less close and detailed, rather less precisely responsive, than his approach seems not only to license but to require—quite as if he has not entirely succeeded in sloughing off or working through a certain embarrassment about the (certainly unpleasant, probably anti-Semitic) rhetorical register of this section: exactly the kind of embarrassment that Janaway imputes to other commentators. Of course, this embarrassment not only must not be denied; it must be suffered. The question is whether, by undergoing or going through it, we gain access to anything of significance.

To begin with, Janaway shows no interest in the question of why it is one Mr Rash and Curious who responds to the narrator's opening question. Why someone of that name—given this essay's association of naming with both power and evaluation? If, as Janaway suggests, this member of the public can plausibly be identified as 'the representative of you and me, the present readers of Nietzsche's text' (BS, 104), Nietzsche's naming of him at the very least implies a certain conception of the identity or situation of his readers—call it a diagnosis of our willingness to stay with this text, even to this point or kind of unpleasantness. Curiosity is, after all, exactly what one might expect from knowers; so the narrator's willingness to christen his volunteer with this term constitutes a reminder that Nietzsche takes his audience to be primarily representatives of the will to knowledge and truth, the philosophers pre-eminent among them. To characterize such curiosity as rash or daring—even, in this context, dangerous—further suggests that his volunteer's descent into the 'dark workshop' will not merely satisfy his curiosity about morality, but will also begin to threaten his unknownness to himself; for in confronting these disgusting fabricators, he is confronting the creators of his own identity as a valuer of truth.

The sense that Nietzsche is specifically addressing himself to a philosophical readership is further strengthened by the aversive relationship between this tale of a gloomy subterranean cavern in which our everyday reality is constructed out of illusions from which the philosopher alone can emancipate us, and one of philosophy's founding myths about its own origin, nature, and status—Socrates' cave. And once this general similarity is recognized, the specific differences between Nietzsche's and Socrates' imaginings take on a deeper significance.

Janaway points out that there is an emphasis in Nietzsche's version on 'what can be immediately detected by the senses' (BS, 104); but this is not quite right, or rather insufficiently specific. For whereas Socrates' cave is a space of primarily visual illusions (he does mention in passing the construction—by echo or reflection—of a soundtrack that synchronizes with the shadows on the wall, but the prisoners thereby hear the noises that the objects behind them really make, misperceiving only their point of origin), in Nietzsche's cave, Mr Rash and Curious remains throughout incapable of seeing anything. Despite acceding to the narrator's suggestion that he wait for his eyes to adjust to what the narrator calls 'this false, shimmering light', he quickly declares that he 'cannot see anything but can hear all the better'; and what he reports thereafter is restricted primarily to aural matters— rumour-mongering whispers from every nook and cranny.

Two other senses are also invoked in Nietzsche's version: Mr Rash and Curious repeatedly complains about the smell, the bad air (not surprisingly, given that another word for wanton curiosity might be 'nosiness'); and he once describes the impression made on him by the lies of the cave-dwellers in terms of their 'sugary mildness', quite as if tasting their deceptive sweetness. But vision has no role to play at all, let alone the canonical Platonic one (as is perhaps registered in Mr Rash and Curious' noting that the cave-dwellers have to huddle together for warmth, presumably because they have no fire, hence no way of seeing the illusions it might create; what makes them sweat is rather their coining of the idea of loving one's enemy).

For Socrates, vision is both the medium of illusion and the medium for its overcoming; the way to realize that we have been taking shadows for reality is first to be turned around so that we can see the fire and the objects that produce those shadows, and second, to leave the cave for the domain of daylight and the initially blinding perception of the solar source of that illumination. And of course, Socrates' interpretation of that final reorientation depends upon identifying direct perception of the sun with ascent to the intelligible region, accessible only to the eye of the mind. Hence, the Socratic emphasis on vision has repeatedly been castigated as isolating the perceptual sense whose mode of action at a distance most easily lends itself to a kind of self-etherealization or self-subliming, no sooner registering the body than facilitating its denial in favour of a purely intellectual species of sight.

In Nietzsche, by contrast, the medium of illusion and of its overcoming is the production and reception of acts of speech. The false reality of our everyday existence is fabricated from malicious whispering; its true value is revealed only when we open our ears, smell the bad air expelled by the breath and sweat of the whisperers, and taste the delirious sweetness of the vengeance that hides behind the sweet sound of their terminological perversions; and the liberating effect of these revelations is achieved via a chain of testimony, as Mr Rash and Curious reports on what he overhears to a listening narrator. It is quite as if emancipatory philosophizing on Nietzsche's conception of the matter requires what contemporary medicine would call an expertise in ENT (ear, nose, and throat)—as if the bodily emphases of the tale in section 14 prefigure the claim he advances in the note appended to the first essay, encouraging the disciplines of philosophy, physiology, and medicine to transform their mutual reserve and suspicion into 'a cordial and fruitful exchange'.

Why this aversion from vision in the name of hearing—this favouring of the ear over the eye? Still thinking in physiological terms, it might be interpreted as a preference for the more archaic (hence subterranean) levels of human embodiment, quite as if vision addresses an aspect of ourselves that is at best shallowly rooted in our nature. And this preference generates a perception of words as not merely vehicles of intellectual content, but as having a vividly material reality of a kind that asks to be heard, smelt, and tasted—modes of rumination. One might also think here of Wittgenstein's late airing of the thought that words have a physiognomy—their physical features expressive of every last connotation or association they have acquired in their employment. Physiognomy would here stand for an interest in the physiological that is not opposed to an interest in the psychological but is rather a mode of it.

Suppose we take up this invitation to ruminate on Nietzsche's words, by asking how far the theme of words as whispered, echoed, and perverted ties section 14 to the sections which precede and succeed it in the *Genealogy*. There are at least two moments or places in which the employment of specific terms in section 14 might be read as deliberate turnings of earlier uses of them—that is, as intended to betray or declare something of significance that goes beyond their immediate intellectual content, and that depends upon specific uses to which Nietzsche has previously put just those words. The moments I have in mind are the way in which the subterranean fabricators are reported to be turning weakness into an accomplishment, and as making a perverted use of 'faith, hope and love'.

The idea that it is central to slave morality to treat natural endowments as subject to the will, and hence as open to praise and blame, is the central theme of section 13, which famously contrasts the birds of prey with the lambs, and argues that a certain ascetic interpretation of the subject as agent is designed to fabricate the existence of a subject (existing behind or beyond the doing of a deed) who is possessed of freedom of choice, which thereby permits the condemnation of the strong for not refraining from exercising their strength and the praise of the weak for manifesting restraint. Sure enough, Mr Rash and Curious discovers early on in section 14 that 'lies are turning weakness into an accomplishment—it's just as you said'. But a difficulty surely arises here: for is not turning weakness into an accomplishment itself an accomplishment? Indeed, if our witness is right to describe what the rumour-mongers are doing as telling lies in a way which effects a creative revaluation of values, is he not crediting them with accomplishing something stupendous?

Should we perhaps distinguish the thought that weakness is an accomplishment from the thought that weak people can accomplish things? One might, after all, think that Nietzsche's argument in section 13 is designed not to deconstruct the very idea of voluntary action, but merely the idea that a person's nature or character is something for which they can be held responsible. But even if we respect this restriction of focus, it would still follow that the weak are not free to do anything other than to act in accordance with their weakness. How, then, can their feeble whisperings have accomplished such a world-historical shift in our sense of ourselves (a shift that includes the reconstruction of weakness itself as an accomplishment)? Such a thoroughgoing remaking of the world in their own image would rather suggest that these lambs are wolves in sheep's clothing, close kin to the birds of prey that they mean to condemn to self-condemnation.

Hence, because of his way of witnessing to the truth of his narrator's immediately preceding claims about the slavish, Mr Rash and Curious seems to make himself and his creator vulnerable to a dilemma. Either his condemnation of their rumour-mongering presupposes the very fabrication of which they stand accused, or it misdirects the contempt of a predator for its prey upon creatures whose actions reveal themselves to be predators of a uniquely successful kind. The first interpretation would register an instinctive endorsement of the very ideal he wishes to condemn; the second would reveal an instinctive revulsion towards an accomplishment of strength. Either way, we confront a gesture expressive of slavishness in someone who claims to find slavishness offensive to ear, nose, and tongue.

What, then, of faith, hope, and love? Mr Rash and Curious' testimony about the slave's rumour-mongering climaxes with the revelation that the true meaning of their invocation of these virtues is vengeance and hatred. For the object of their faith, hope, and love is the kingdom of God—an imagined consolation for all their sufferings in this world that is also a perspective from which they can take pleasure in the imaginary sufferings that will at the same time be meted out to their enemies (section 15 lays out some powerful textual evidence for the sadistic dimension of this fabrication). And at this point, even the narrator of section 14 cannot bear the reports of his intermediary: for it is he (not, as Janaway states, Mr Rash and Curious) who concludes the section by shouting 'Enough! Enough!'—quite as if this aspect of the rumour-mongering brings its malevolence to an unprecedented pitch, or strikes a particularly sensitive nerve in the narrator's ear.

It is therefore noteworthy that this same triad of terms has already been at work in section 12 of the essay, in which Nietzsche turns aside from his analysis in order to pray for a glimpse of a man 'who makes up for and redeems man, and enables us to retain our *faith in mankind!*', in the light of what he sees as the threat of losing 'our love for him, our hope in him and even our will to be man' (GM, section 12). In other words, Nietzsche finds that the most intimate and powerful way in which to express his ideal for mankind involves precisely the terms whose presence in the mouths of Christians drives him to block his ears. He must turn the words of Christianity against themselves in order to liberate himself, and us, from it.

Putting together these two moments of linguistic perversion, one of which opens the little drama and the other of which closes it, we have a portrait of a divided diagnostician. On the one hand, the narrator and his volunteer find themselves unwittingly subject to the influence of that which they condemn; on the other, they discover that the only way to overcome that influence is (not to dispense with the words employed by their enemies but rather) to employ them otherwise—to find their liberation through specific reorientations of exactly that vocabulary. In short, either the slave ideal exploits our ignorance of its true value, and so exploits us; or we overcome that ignorance, and exploit an emancipatory potential that lies hidden within the linguistic fabric of that ideal—hence one that can be achieved only by going through and beyond its underlying valuation of the world, not by its simple denial or by any kind of rebalancing of our existing impulses for and against both ideals. Something more radically transformative seems to be envisioned: but exactly how is that transformation to be imagined?

Mr Rash and Curious is shown first to betray a certain unconscious indebtedness to the slavishness he means to condemn, and then to reveal the painful struggles of his narrator and interlocutor to turn slavish words to emancipatory purposes. But it also matters that each of these revelatory moments corresponds to a distinct phase in the diagnostic process into which the narrator has invited his volunteer. For the first phase of testimony from Mr Rash and Curious primarily concerns the attempted transformation of weakness into virtue, whereas the second phase concerns the attempt to present vengeful hate as a kind of brotherly love.

With respect to the first, the narrator is ahead of his volunteer, expressing serene confidence about what exactly a careful attention will reveal, and repeatedly asking him to continue his reports. With respect to the second, however, his volunteer eventually ends up ahead of the narrator; for although the narrator initiates that second series by discouraging Mr Rash and Curious from re-emerging from the workshop after his confirmatory testimony, suggesting instead that he attend to a further aspect of the rumour-mongering, his volunteer's willingness to accede to that suggestion quickly brings him to a point of diagnostic revelation that leads the narrator to countermand his original command to explore further—to demand that he stop his testimony.

If Mr Rash and Curious represents Nietzsche's reader, and the narrator of section 14 (whose linguistic fabric is, after all, interwoven with elements drawn from earlier and later sections) represents the author of the *Genealogy*, then this dialectic of the willing volunteer eventually exceeding the endurance of his recruiter suggests that Nietzsche envisions his relation with his readers as one which, if successfully managed, will ensure that the student can teach his teacher. Whereas Socrates envisions the emancipatory philosopher as having to coerce individual prisoners first to turn their heads and then to leave the cave, and so envisions the philosopher as not only forcibly authoritative but always ahead of his student, Nietzsche presents himself as someone whose leaps of insight function most successfully when they function for those to whom he offers them as a basis upon which to leap beyond even him. Nietzsche's readers thereby appear as retaining their autonomy in a way that Socrates' prisoners appear never to recover; and they do so by discovering a mode of internalization that resists mere reduplication. Once again, the idea of transfiguration rather than denial or rejection is at work; Mr Rash and Curious' progress embodies an image of transcending an ideal precisely by going more deeply into and through it. But how is such a discovery of the beyond within that which it exceeds to be properly understood?

Further guidance here comes from the earlier suggestion that Nietzsche's dark workshop is a counter-image to Socrates' cave. After all, Socrates explicitly identifies his ideal republic as a 'city of words' (*Republic*, Book IX, 592)—meaning first that the city he and his interlocutors have been founding and describing does not exist anywhere except in heaven, as an ideal; but surely meaning also that the dialogue in which it is described—the *Republic*—embodies that ideal, and hence gives it earthly habitation of a kind, the kind that might be used as a standard against which to criticize existing cities, prevailing modes of human communal life. Either way, however, the myth of the cave contained within that dialogue should be

understood as a contribution to this greater city of words, and so as contributing to the assumption that such linguistic fabrications are in the service of
realizing what will otherwise remain ideal. By contrast, Nietzche's myth of
the workshop emphasizes that our present, supposedly ideal reality is itself
always already a city of words, established and sustained by a discreditable
trafficking in rumours and forgeries. Perhaps this is why only a polemic (as
the author of the *Genealogy* subtitles his efforts) against that reality—that is,
an essentially linguistic mode of warfare—can hope to overcome its falsity.
Then again, how are we to judge whether the reports Mr Rash and Curious
delivers to his narrator are instances of the genuine other to rumours and
forgeries (a small community of genuine knowledge, in which testimony
merits the authority it claims) or simply one more simulacrum of words in
which one can truly place one's trust? It is, after all, a fictional exchange—or
more precisely, one author's attempt to conjure up the reader he hopes for
and desires: is this permissible?

But it is not just that these contrasting cities are constructed from words;
it is also that a key word in both constructions is the word 'city' itself—
indeed, that word above all links section 14 to the sections that succeed it.
The key section here is section 16, in which Nietzsche tells a highly
compressed tale of the millennia-long battle between the two opposed
moral codes in terms of a war between Rome and Judaea, a war which
itself crystallizes into a fight for the soul of the city of Rome itself—a fight
between the values of its founders and the values of the Papacy that
presently resides in it, with each attempting to turn the other into a city
of tombs, as if its vitality depended on that other's death. More specifically,
according to Nietzsche, 'Rome saw the Jew as something contrary to
nature, as though he were its polar opposite, a monster; in Rome, the Jew
was looked upon as *convicted* of hatred against the whole of mankind' (GM,
16—Nietzsche's source here is Tacitus). And he claims that we can see what
the Jews felt about Rome in the Book of the Apocalypse—whose author
testifies to the advent of the City of God (some of whose lineaments are
tellingly specified in the citations in section 15), but only on the understanding that the city of Babylon, the inhabitation of the great beast, is first set
aflame and razed to the ground. Rome is, therefore, the exemplary City of
Man, the realization of a form of life whose nature systematically orients us
away from goodness and truth.

Nietzsche takes it to be self-evident that Judaea has triumphed over Rome—that it has succeeded in overcoming every attempt by that ancient conception of the human good to reassert itself, even if it has never succeeded in founding the new Jerusalem. And since he will go on (in the second essay) to present the kinds of drive-inhibition which slave morality brings to an extreme as a precondition for any form of communal human life, call it the inhabitation of a city, one might think that the symbolic medium for this warfare has rather slanted the odds towards a Judaic victory. But Nietzsche does note in conclusion a recent, wholly unexpected and unprecedentedly splendid bodily appearance of the ancient ideal, a stronger, simpler and more penetrating answer to the *ressentiment* unleashed by the French Revolution: 'Like a last signpost to the *other* path, Napoleon appeared as a man more unique and late-born for his times than ever a man had been before, and in him, the problem of the *noble ideal itself* was made flesh—just think *what* a problem that is: Napoleon, this synthesis of *monster* [*Unmensch*] and *Übermensch*' (GM, 1.16). And in section 17, with which the first essay literally or in fact concludes, Nietzsche prophesies a further flaring up of this old flame, which presumably means a new Napoleon, a new signpost and synthesis.

Section 16's tale of a long fight between cities over a city is thus as starkly allegorical, and in exactly the same way, as Plato's *Republic*, in which the structure of the psyche and the structure of the city housing it famously mirror one another; Nietzsche does, after all, declare that 'there is today, perhaps no more distinguishing feature of the "*higher nature*", the intellectual nature, than to be divided in this sense, and really and truly a battleground for these opposites' (GM, 1.16), thereby identifying we men of knowledge as having internalized that conflict. Moreover, he thinks of Napoleon, and hence of his prophesied successors, as a synthesis—and more specifically, as a synthesis of the monstrous and the more-than-human. He has just established the term 'monster' as Rome's word for the Jew, thereby emphasizing the fact that Napoleon was the warrior-emperor of the revolutionary hordes rather than of the *ancien régime* they subverted; so if we take 'Übermensch' as Nietzsche's term for Rome itself and what it represents, it follows that Nietzsche sees the human future as residing not in the absolute triumph of one ideal over the other, as if Rome could simply re-find itself by denying the traces of Judaic civilization on which it would necessarily have to re-found itself, but rather in the internalization and re-interpretation of the contradiction that has hitherto dominated our history, at the level of both individual and culture.

The first of these two stages is, after all, what Nietzsche has just specified as the most distinctive intellectual condition of our present times; so the future must presumably involve a step beyond simple internal division or conflict (or rebalancing). Nietzsche warns us in the final sentence of section 17 that the dangerous slogan on the spine of his last book, *Beyond Good and Evil*, at least does not mean 'Beyond Good and Bad'; but that warning leaves it open to us to ask whether the slogan even means 'Beyond Good and Evil'—that is, whether it means 'leaving utterly behind any conception of "Good and Evil"', or rather 'leaving utterly behind any conception of "Good and Evil" that denies its aversive but constitutive relation to "Good and Bad"'.

That interpretative difference could, after all, make all the difference. It might, for example, suggest that one way of overcoming the opposition between masters and slaves is to internalize it in such a way as to achieve self-mastery in the form of endless self-denial, where self-denial means not so much the once-for-all denial of self and life as such, but rather the denial of every attained or actualized (call it mastered) state of the self in the name of another, unattained but attainable state of that self—an aspiration to the realization of which one willingly enslaves oneself, in the knowledge that once attained, each such state will reveal another, unattained but attainable state that neighbours it.

5) The Promise of Knowledge: Giving, Taking, and Turning One's Word

If the third essay interprets an aphorism, and the first solves a riddle, the second essay confronts a paradox:

> To breed an animal *which is able to make promises*—is that not precisely the paradoxical task which nature has set herself with regard to humankind? Is it not the real problem *of* humankind? (GM, 2.1)

The problem, in other words, is that of the origins of moral responsibility: the ability to make promises is exemplary of rendering oneself accountable for one's actions, which involves the construction or development of what philosophers would call freedom of the will—the elaboration and maintenance of whatever is needed 'so that a world of strange new things, circumstances and even acts of will may be placed quite safely in between the original "I will", "I shall do" and the actual discharge of the will, its *act*, without breaking this long chain' (GM, 2.1). But the ability to make promises is also, and equally, exemplary of the more general ability to give one's word:

The 'free' man, the possessor of a durable, unbreakable will ... will necessarily respect his peers, the strong and the reliable (those *with the right* to give their word) ... [and] gives his word as something which can be relied on, because he is strong enough to remain upright in the face of mishap or even 'in the face of fate'. (GM, 2.2)

In short, to contemplate our acquisition of the right to make promises is to contemplate our accession to the realm of language as such, the domain in which one gives and takes words from one's fellow language-users, the sharers of the form of animal life that is informed by the circulation of words; it is our accession to humanity, the becoming human of the human. And to present the making of promises as exemplary of that distinctively human capacity is to imply that there is no use of language that is not possessed of a distinctively ethical dimension; it invites us to think of any and all acts of speech as exercises of personal responsibility—as ways in which we commit ourselves, laying ourselves open to evaluation.

What is paradoxical about the emergence of the ability under question here is precisely that it emerges from nature: the domain of causal law and determination manages to engender a creature capable of achieving freedom from such determination.[5] If the reality of that capacity is not to constitute an irrefutable argument for supernaturalism, and so for the very religious conception of humanity that Nietzsche is concerned to criticize, he must take the responsibility for providing a wholly natural accounting of it—call it a genealogy. And it turns out that the key elements of that genealogy will emerge from the very mechanisms and processes upon which the English psychologists lay such emphasis: the business of memory and forgetting, and its companion pair of habit and novelty.

---

[5] A point made by Stanley Cavell, in a paper entitled 'On Nietzschean Perfectionism', delivered to the APA meeting in Philadelphia, December 2008: this section of my essay is pervasively indebted to the way Cavell there aligns Nietzsche and Austin with respect to their ways of aligning promises and claims to knowledge.

Nietzsche's first essay reported that, according to these psychologists, although the original connection between 'goodness' and altruism was forged in recognition of the usefulness of such acts to their recipients, this connection became so routine and repetitive that its real origin was forgotten, and altruism began thereby to appear intrinsically good. In his second essay, he turns these explanatory concepts against their employers by turning them against themselves: he argues that forgetfulness is not a passive but an active phenomenon, and that habit or routine is not an alternative to creativity or originality but rather a precondition for it.

On Nietzsche's account, forgetfulness is a strength rather than a weakness or a malfunction, because it is an activity essential to life—'like a doorkeeper or guardian of mental order, rest and etiquette' (GM, 2.1); without it, every single thing that a creature lives through or experiences, together with every phase of the process of internal absorption to which it is then subject, would be routed through its consciousness, and it simply could not cope with the overwhelming, chaotic immensity of what was going on around and inside it. In short, 'there could be no happiness, cheerfulness, hope, pride, *immediacy* without forgetfulness . . . that apparatus of suppression' (GM, 2.1). Forgetfulness is thus the default position, the starting point of any healthy animal; but for the human animal, a counter-device is needed to that repression mechanism; for if promises are to be made, remembering must be possible. But this kind of memory is no passive inability to be rid of an impression; it, too, must be understood as active and engaged, as 'an active *desire* not to let go, a desiring to keep on desiring what has been, on some occasion, desired, really it is the *will's memory*' (GM, 2.1). To remember is thus an achievement rather than an automatic effect of experience; more precisely, it is a counter-achievement, a form of self-overcoming, the creation within the self of a continuity (between past and present) that is also a discontinuity (between the merely actual and the previously envisaged or desired or willed present)—a resistance to what is in itself an achievement of robust animal health. An animal with the right to give its word is thus an animal that must overcome its animality, transcending it from within in order to fulfil its unnatural nature.

And what are the conditions for the possibility of such self-overcoming?

In order to have that degree of control over the future, man must first have learnt to distinguish between what happens by accident and what by design, to think causally, to view the future as the present and anticipate it, to grasp with certainty what is end and what is means, in all, to be able to calculate, compute—and before he can do this, man himself will really have to become *reliable, regular, automatic,* even in his own self-image, so that he, as someone making a promise is, is answerable for his own future! (GM, 2.1)

It is vital to note that regularity or habituation, which finds its cultural expression in what Nietzsche calls 'the morality of custom', is not the end of nature's project but rather one of its most demanding and time-consuming preconditions: the ultimate point of making man truly predictable is to engender the sovereign individual, an autonomous creature like only to himself, the one not only able to make a promise but possessed of the right to do so, because possessed of the individuality without which the word he gives to others cannot truly be regarded as his own to give. But it is equally vital to note what is involved in establishing the automaticity or herd-identity from which such self-sovereignty can alone grow: for Nietzsche's list of preconditions amounts to a synthesis of two types of category—those internal to understanding action as that for which the agent is responsible, and those comprising the armature or skeleton of human cognition. The former type includes the distinction between accident and design, and the idea of ends as opposed to means (call this the field of practical reason), and more specifically the preconditions for excusing or otherwise accounting for one's deeds; the latter type includes the notion of causal relations, predictions of the future on the basis of the past (induction), and the practice of computation or calculation (epitomized by the certainty attainable by logical calculi)—call this the field of theoretical reason.

From the outset, therefore, Nietzsche's account of responsibility presents pure cognition as something whose primary function is to make possible the creation of the genuinely creative human being: theoretical reason is not just internally related to the domain of practical reason (as the blending of types of category in the cited list already implies), but is a human organ whose basic structure can facilitate the emergence of the sovereign individual. In other words, properly evaluated, knowledge subserves the ability to give one's word: cognition is always already imprinted by the practical, moral, and existential concerns from which it aspires to abstract itself.

Two possibilities immediately arise. The first is engendered by the fact that pure cognition is a precondition for enforcing the predictability of human beings, rather than directly facilitating their creativity or originality. For that lack of immediacy raises the possibility that its essentially instrumental function will become detached from the end which accounts for it, and instead be regarded as (and so become) an end in itself (just as, according to the preface, we knowers come to value collecting over what is collected). In such circumstances, men and women of knowledge will constitute an obstacle to the creation of fully human beings, rather than a means towards their emergence; the plurality and indirectness of these processes of becoming human—call it the fluidity of their form and meaning (GM, 2.12)— threatens to loosen our grip on the distinction between end and means. The second possibility depends upon taking seriously the fact that knowledge itself finds expression in language—knowledge is something claimed, hence given, taken, and contested in acts of speech. But if, as Nietzsche thinks, the use of language as such can be epitomized in the speech act of promising, he thereby invites us to consider claims to knowledge as a (perhaps radical) variation on that way of giving one's word. It would then follow that claims to knowledge are not only to be understood as speech acts, but as possessing an ineliminable moral dimension; knowing is not an alternative to, but a particular way of, taking a stand in the distinctively linguistic space of cares and commitments. Accordingly, Nietzsche's ensuing account of the conditions for the possibility of giving one's word ought to be regarded not as an account of promising (and so morality) as opposed to knowing, but rather as an account of the root from which both ways of becoming humanly accountable grow, each in its own way.

The story Nietzsche goes on to tell has three main stages. First, the counter-achievement of memory is established and maintained by the infliction of pain deployed as a mnemonic technique. Forgetfulness is overcome by branding what must be remembered into the physiology of the not-yet-human animal—by systems of blood-letting, torments, sacrifices, and forfeits; and these systems are primarily designed to impress upon their recipients a range of their most important pre-social responsibilities— their answerability to those with whom they stand in primitive relationships of credit and debt (barter, buying and selling, and trading more generally). Punishment for reneging on a debt establishes an equivalence between the value of the debt and the pleasure the creditor can take in the infliction of suffering on the debtor; it amounts to an extension of economic thinking from objects to experiences, and thereby to the subjects of experience. Indeed, Nietzsche goes further:

Fixing prices, setting values, working out equivalents, exchanging—this preoccupied man's first thoughts to such a degree that in a certain sense it *constitutes* thought: the most primitive kind of cunning was bred here...man designated himself as the being who measures values, who values and measures, as 'the calculating animal as such'. (GM, 2.8)

If, as we have seen, the calculating animal is the knowing animal, then knowing as such carries traces of specifically economic evaluation: its categories carry with them a conception of things and persons as elements in a system of exchange-value, access to which requires a willingness to regard one's own suffering (as well as that of others), together with the pleasure to be derived from either, as further elements in that system. This is a vision of economics and thought (and so the capacity for speech they depend upon and help constitute) as sadomasochism.

The second stage of the story concerns the transition from pre-social and pre-historical practices to collective or genuinely communal life. On the one hand, the demands of shared existence compel techniques of punishment to moderate themselves, so that wrongdoing can be entirely paid off and so the doer separated from the deed: once the debt is settled, the one in debt can slough off the imputation of being a debtor, and thereby maintain a sense of his punishment as akin to a visitation of fate or a natural disaster, rather than the external sign of intrinsic personal failure. On the other hand, even moderate versions of these penal practices encourage those subject to them to moderate their desires, thus exemplifying the ways in which social life forces the repression of one's instincts and impulses, and thus the internalization of punishment:

All instincts which are not discharged outwardly *turn inwards*—this is what I call the *internalization* of man: with it there now evolves in man what will later be called his 'soul'. The whole inner world, originally stretched thinly as though between two layers of skin, was expanded and extended itself and gained depth, breadth and height in proportion to the degree that the external discharge of man's instincts was *obstructed*. (GM, 2.16)

This process amounts to the systematic infliction of cruelty by the individual on the individual, and so to a form of self-hatred or self-abuse; but without that internalization of punishment, there could be nothing resembling an individual in the first place, since the idea of human individuality presupposes the idea of a distinction or division between the interior world of the self and the external world it inhabits. What Nietzsche's account makes clear is that the existence of that division is inseparable from the enforcement of a division within the self: if an interior impulse fails to find expression in action, that can be so only if another aspect of the self opposes that impulse. Individuality and self-division thus come into being together (call it selfhood as non-self-identity). And this double creation is also the creation of the human being as an interesting animal:

[T]he prospect of an animal soul turning against itself, taking a part against itself, was something so new, profound, unheard-of, puzzling, contradictory and *momentous* on earth that the whole character of the world changed in an essential way . . . Since that time, man . . . arouses interest, tension, hope, almost certainty for himself, as though something were being announced through him, were being prepared, as though man were not an end but just a path, an episode, a bridge, a great promise. (GM, 2.16)

This is the creation of conscience in the form of bad conscience: but this kind of bad conscience is also good—in part because from this desire 'to give form to oneself as a piece of difficult, resisting, suffering matter . . . a wealth of novel, disconcerting beauty [comes] to light' (nothing less than all the creativeness and originality of Western culture); but most importantly because the creation of such bad conscience is the creation of the human, of the animal capable of giving his word. And here, being an animal with the right to make a promise is explicitly equated with being a promising animal—an animal whose existence takes the form of being promising. To make a promise is to anticipate the future, and to take responsibility for how it will be; to be promising is to be more or other than one presently is, to relate to oneself as being not-yet-realized, constantly open to the future, and taking one's bearings for that future state of oneself from the state one currently instantiates.

But promises can be broken as well as fulfilled, and a promising animal can have its anticipatory relation to the future foreclosed by its relation to the past; one need only think of Wotan, and the extent to which the terms of the contract marked on his spear constrain his room for manoeuvre from the outset of the *Ring* narrative to fateful effect. The third stage of Nietzsche's narrative tells how Christianity exploited and inflected this possibility at the cultural level—when the relationship between creditor and debtor, having first been extended to the community's relationship to its forebears, was then absolutized by the substitution of God for the tribe's actual and mythological ancestors. For how, in the first place, can we be sure that we have properly repaid our debt to our actual forefathers? How much sacrifice is enough to satisfy an ever-increasing body of those without whom we would not exist at all? But when our ultimate father is God, then our debt becomes crushing beyond measurement; and when God's Son gratuitously takes the burden of that debt upon himself, He only intensifies the burden. The religious narrative of original sinfulness and its overcoming thus intensifies the sadomasochism of bad conscience to the point at which human existence appears cursed rather than promising, essentially incapable of escaping its past and hence essentially closed to the future. The human promise becomes not so much unfulfillable as invisible; the morality of custom becomes an end in itself rather than a means to sovereign individuality.

What remains importantly unclear (even deliberately unsettled) in this narrative is the structure of its second stage. We are never entirely sure whether the interiorization of man is established solely by the demands of social life and the natural amelioration of pre-social punishment regimes, and so by shifts that need not be tainted by specifically ascetic or priestly motives; or whether the self's decisive turning upon itself is necessarily cruel and self-lacerating in the ways distinctive of slave morality (dependent, for instance, upon practices of confession, with their disciplines of interior scrutiny and scouring). The problem is encapsulated in Nietzsche's ambivalence about the priests, whom he describes from the outset as both a branch of the nobility and the prime movers of the slave revolt; does their revolution construct a counter-civilization to that of the masters, or does it rather create the conditions for the possibility of civilization as such? Would masters who had already turned their natural cruelty upon themselves (and thereby given themselves the interior room for dissembling, reflection, and cleverness) still be masters, or would they rather be suffering the onset of the revaluation of values that their priestly brothers have encouraged (or even be beginning to become priests themselves)? Perhaps this ambivalence is one more way in which Nietzsche acknowledges his awareness that recovery from the ascetic ideal will involve finding the necessary resources for that emancipatory transformation within our currently unredeemed condition.

Regardless of whether we judge the ascetic revaluation process to begin at the second or the third stage of this narrative, however, the outcome seems clear. The interlinked enterprises of cultivating a will to remember and a willingness to become predictable have been (re)shaped in such a way as to occlude the possibility for which they could be preconditions. Instead of functioning as the background of regularity or routinization against which the sovereign individual becomes a single, coherent being of the kind who might achieve freedom, they come to figure as ends in themselves, in the form of a morality of custom or conformity that is constitutionally averse to individuality, in which everyone does only and always what everyone else does (GM, 2.24). Instead of allowing painful self-discipline to open up the possibility of taking pleasure in the endless re-achievement of self-mastery, our culture prefers us to take pleasure in the infliction of pain upon ourselves as an end in itself, thereby closing ourselves off within a vicious circle of reiterated, endlessly intensifying cruelty. And insofar as this evisceration of our right to make promises exemplifies our current nature as language users, it is figured by our willingness to use words as if their rates of exchange (both with one another and with whatever they represent) were fixed, as if fated to reiteration—to the repetition of inherently impersonal patterns of use inherited from our ancestors and passed on to our descendents, without ever realizing their potential to make something new of our experience of the world, and thereby to renew both their own intelligibility and that of their users.

In effect, then, the current realization of our (birth)right to make promises is the interiorized inflection of a regime in which pleasure is taken from the infliction of pain, and in which evaluation is a matter of seeking equivalence rather than celebrating singularity—call them the customary morality and economics of speech, hence of humanity and selfhood. Since there cannot be genuine individuality without some version of these preconditions, its achievement must involve their being inflected otherwise—perhaps by suffering the world's capacity (or that of another within it) to inflict pleasure on us (call it a willingness to be delighted by what wounds us), perhaps by seeing the equality of all in each human being's capacity for singularity. After all, When Nietzsche asks: 'What is more deeply offensive to others and separates us most profoundly from them than allowing them to realize something of the severity and high-mindedness with which we treat ourselves?' (GM, 2.24), he need not simply be indicting his others for lacking something he possesses; he may rather be pointing out that realizing that his way of living exemplifies such self-mastery may inspire them to realize it in their own cases, which would mean genuinely realizing their own individuality—something which would require that they be repelled rather than attracted by him, since it could hardly avoid enforcing their separateness from their exemplar.

Recalling Nietzsche's invitation to see the making of promises as exemplary of speech as such, we might accordingly take particular aversive, emancipatory delight in the way Nietzsche's tentative visions of human redemption are saturated in economic terms—credit and debt, interest, exchange value, contracts, even redemption itself (figured as the self's indebtedness to itself, taken together with its willingness to credit the possibility of a future of its own)—that have been reversed, inverted, turned against themselves. In this way, our culture's apparently inveterate tendency to conceive things in terms of evaluative equivalence has been turned back on itself; its evaluative terms have been redeemed by being spiritualized and interiorized.

What, then, of knowledge? Its nature is such that it helps at once to compose a picture of the world as essentially predictable (necessarily subject to causal determination, and to inductive and deductive calculation), and to occlude the self altogether (insofar as the will to truth is an offshoot of the ascetic ideal, and so is a mode of self-denial that is also a mode of self-ignorance). One might say that it aspires to abolish the openness of the future, to discredit the idea of novelty in the world and our experience of it. And in so doing, it resonates with the broader cultural world whose group portrait Nietzsche paints in his third essay—one whose apparently various and vital inhabitants ultimately appear to be mere instantiations of a single, life-occluding and self-denying ethos, with each reflecting the others' orientation, and thereby reinforcing its hegemony to the point at which even the possibility of original thought, speech, and experience goes missing.

At the same time, however, this mode in which knowledge currently manifests itself actually occludes its own nature as an aspect of the distinctively human, talking form of life: for claiming to know something is before all else a speech act, hence one way in which the promising animal gives its word—a way in which one speaker gives others his authority for believing that things are as he says they are, which means authorizing them too to claim that things are that way. In short, when a speaker gives his word in this way, others may take it, and then give it to others in their turn—putting that claim into circulation. One might say that the one who claims to know places others in his debt, but only insofar as they credit what he says, which means accepting his credentials as an authority on the matter at hand. In short, knowledge takes on the aspect of testimony—this is, after all, the burden of Nietzsche's creation of Mr Rash and Curious, the emissary who bears witness to the reality of our world's construction, and so functions both as Nietzsche's proxy or servant and (insofar as his final testimonial outrages even his author) his master or over-masterer. Claiming to know is a way of inviting others to credit assertions that rightly aspire to objectivity, but are nonetheless rooted in evaluations of the credibility of the one who claims knowledge (of whether he is really in a position to know, whether it is within his cognizance).[6]

And what, finally, of the one who claims to know about knowledge—to know of its indebtedness to the ascetic ideal, and so to know that we knowers are unknown to ourselves, hence unaware of our specific position in the world, hence to that extent not properly authorized to make any claims to know, that is to say, uncomprehendingly suffering an injury to our cognitive status (not so much philosophical kingfishers as fisher kings)? What exactly is the basis of his claims to know these things about know-ledge, and about us knowers; how should we go about evaluating his testimony?

To do so, we must recall that the one advancing these claims explicitly includes himself within their range of application (if, as his prefatory remarks declare, 'we' are unknown to ourselves, then so too is he—he is one of us, and so what he says of us declares how things stand, or partly stand, or used to stand, with him: he is baring his own soul). We should also recollect that (at the beginning of his first essay, when resisting

---

[6] Cf. J.L. Austin, 'Other Minds', in the third edition of his *Philosophical Papers*, ed. J. O. Urmson and G. Warnock (Oxford: Oxford University Press, 1979).

commonly-accepted claims about the character of the English psychologists) he all-but-explicitly identifies the terrain his cognitive claims occupy as equally open to the demands of desire and the aspirations of hope. If we further assume Nietzsche's continued willingness to turn the terms of religion against themselves, we might conclude that this amounts to saying that Nietzschean knowledge claims are at once modes of confession and modes of prophecy.

This places them fully in the stream of time: what might otherwise appear solely to aim at the representation of what is the case now appears to look at once backwards (identifying wounding errors that inform the present) and forwards (calling for a future that will look otherwise than the present from which it emerges). For taken seriously, confession and prophecy do not ignore the present in favour of attending exclusively to the past and the future respectively; Augustine's radical and scathing confession of his past errors is something he takes to be required of him in order to re-ground and re-orient himself at the moment of confession, just as the Biblical prophets do not claim divinely-underwritten knowledge of what is yet-to-come so much as invite us to make something of our unwritten future by acknowledging their radical and scathing critiques of the present to be divinely underwritten. Nietzsche's use of Zarathustra to bridge his second and third essays certainly implies a sense on his part that the furthest reaches of his current thinking go beyond what his not-very-much-earlier self could have managed; but after all, Zarathustra himself was always only the over-man's prophet, so to get further than Zarathustra need only involve attaining a better critical perspective on the present, and so a clearer prophetic vision of the possibility and necessity of that over-man. It certainly need carry no claim to have attained that status, except insofar as such an exercise in self-overcoming amounts to an instance of the generic human capacity for existing in and as a transition, for being underway.

What, then, should be our criteria for evaluating the credibility of words offered to us as knowledge claims that are both confessional and prophetic? According to Nietzsche himself, we should ask ourselves how far those claims wound and delight us, and delight us because they wound us; and we should further ask what the relation between pain and pleasure here really is—which means asking how far they contribute to the vicious circle of delighting in self-inflicted pain (pain inflicted by another knower), and how far they break that circle by envisioning and internalizing a way of achieving self-mastery, and so self-abasement, that leaves room for hope for the human future. But if we are to achieve this kind of self-knowledge about our experience of this book, of these words in these orderings, we must first credit ourselves with the capacity to do so.

The Decipherment of Signs

Sartrean Scenes IV
(*Existentialism As A Humanism*)

1. The Father's Anguish

Sunlight came slanting through the windows of the kitchen and illuminated every scar and ridge in the scrubbed surface of the table. He folded up the letter, taking care not to crease or smudge the pencil-sketched map it enclosed, and returned it to its envelope, which he tossed to one side before picking up the slim book that he'd abandoned to answer the postman's knock. He turned the page, first glancing at the untidy pile of lecture notes on which the book had been lying to remind himself of what particular mystery in this particularly mysterious book he had been trying to grapple with.

To be honest, he hadn't understood at first why his teacher had wanted them all to spend so much time—indeed, any time at all—on this book. They'd signed up for a class on philosophy and politics, from a teacher who was rumoured to be as deeply committed to atheism as to the new phenomenological methods first developed in Germany long before the war; and so far they'd spent all their time working their way through a Danish philosopher's pseudonymous reflections on the Old Testament story of Abraham's willingness to sacrifice his son Isaac at God's command. But he had to admit that Kierkegaard's—or, as his teacher kept on insisting, Johannes de Silentio's—writing style was extremely effective in conjuring up an atmosphere of hysterical intensity, a passionate identification with this father of faith and his fearful, trembling devotion to a course of action that threatened to destroy the foundations of his own existence as well as that of his family. The student—along with most of his fellow-students, all of them consumed by hatred of the soldiers occupying their country and of those collaborating with them, and all claiming allegiance to the Resistance, to the Free French forces in London, and in particular to de Gaulle—could certainly identify with de Silentio's bewildered and bewildering devotion to Abraham.

But their teacher had said something very peculiar about Abraham in the last class—something about a question of identity posed by the divine command's being addressed to him. He looked again through his notes: 'An angel commanded Abraham to sacrifice his son: and obedience was obligatory, if it really was an angel who had appeared and said: "Thou, Abraham, shalt sacrifice thy son". But anyone in such a case would wonder, first, whether it was indeed an angel, and secondly, whether I am really Abraham.'[1]

Forget for a moment the introduction of an angelic intermediary, of which the book of Genesis (he had checked this in his mother's battered family bible) makes no mention, stating rather that Abraham is directly addressed by God. The first issue of identity his teacher was raising seemed straightforward enough: hearing a voice in one's head left entirely undetermined its origin or owner—why not conclude that its sheer existence indicated mental imbalance, or that the specific content of its utterance indicated a demonic rather than a divine source? But the second issue was rather more puzzling: what exactly did his teacher mean by suggesting that anyone in Abraham's position would wonder, in the light of this putatively divine address, whether he was really Abraham?

To be sure, even if someone else really were in Abraham's position, then he wouldn't as a matter of fact be Abraham (he'd be that someone else); although of course that utterly truistic point might seem hardly worth making, except that one did sometimes wonder whether de Silentio—whose commemorative paroxysms enact an endless cycle of intense attraction and despairing repulsion—is ultimately willing to acknowledge the limits it imposes (to acknowledge that he is not, and cannot ever be, the object—or rather the subject—of his groping admiration). And of course, if he remembered rightly (here, the student went over to retrieve the family bible), Abraham himself might wonder whether he really was Abraham at

---

[1] Jean-Paul Sartre, *Existentialism and Humanism*, trans. P. Mairet (London: Methuen, 1973), p. 31—hereafter EH.

the point at which God's command about Isaac is issued to him. After all, his name at the beginning of the story of his relationship with God was in fact Abram; indeed, God only decreed that his name be changed to 'Abraham' at precisely the point at which He promised to make him the father of many nations—the very covenant that His present decree threatens to render null and void (by requiring him to prepare for the annihilation of his only son). So one could say that the reception of that decree precisely puts Abraham's self-identity in question; for he could not comprehend the content of such a demand at all without comprehending it as making an issue of his own identity (am I one and the same person as the one addressed by God as the father of many nations?) and that of his interlocutor (is this the voice of the God who renamed me as the father of many nations?).

But there might be another way of taking his teacher's suggestion, one which depended on taking seriously de Silentio's most common way of referring to Abraham—namely, as a father of faith. Suppose, then, we imagine the question reposed or transfigured in these terms: 'Am I really Abraham?' would become, 'Am I really a father of faith?'. To answer this question, one would have to know what it means to be a father of faith; and this, of course, is the topic of de Silentio's three problemata—those stretches of his book in which he argues that Abraham can only be regarded as a father of faith if there can be a teleological suspension of the ethical (if, that is, ethical demands can coherently become a temptation to disobey God), if one's duties to God are absolute (and hence one's ethical duties are relative), and if one can find oneself to be beyond the demands of intelligibility altogether (incapable of providing an ethically or rationally coherent account of one's motives). In short, in order to think of himself as a father of faith, Abraham must be able to regard the situation in which he finds himself as one in which his ethical responsibilities (to his son, his family, and the ethical community at large) have suffered a teleological suspension. Could he think such a thing? Could anyone? What is involved in thinking it?

The student quickly turned the pages of de Silentio's text, looking for two passages that he recalled from an earlier reading about the features that might allow one to regard a situation as one in which ethical demands have become a temptation (as opposed to being part of a spiritual trial—that is, in which one is being tempted to take ethical demands with insufficient seriousness). The first was relatively early in the book:

If it fell to my lot to speak about him, I would begin by showing what a devout and God-fearing man Abraham was, worthy of being called God's chosen one. Only a person of that kind is put to such a test, but who is such a person? Next I would describe how Abraham loved Isaac. For that purpose I would call upon all the good spirits to stand by me so that what I said would have the glow of fatherly love. I hope to describe it in such a way that there would not be many a father in the realms and lands of the king who would dare to maintain that he loved in this way. But if he did not love as Abraham loved, then any thought of sacrificing Isaac would surely be a spiritual trial. (FT[2], 31)

And the other was rather later—yes, this is it:

The absolute duty can lead one to do what ethics would forbid, but it can never lead the knight of faith to stop loving. Abraham demonstrates this. In the moment he is about to sacrifice Isaac, the ethical expression for what he is doing is: he hates Isaac. But if he actually hates Isaac, he can rest assured that God does not demand this of him, for Cain and Abraham are not identical. He must love Isaac with his whole soul. Since God claims Isaac, he must, if possible, love him even more, and only then can he *sacrifice* him, for it is indeed this love for Isaac that makes his act a sacrifice by its paradoxical contrast to his love for God. (FT, 74)

The second passage declares what the first implies: that a voice in your head inciting you to kill your son can only be the voice of God if your love for your son is perfect. Any imperfection, the slightest grain of impurity in your attachment to the Isaac in your life, and your attempts to carry out that command would identify you with Cain rather than with Abraham; and that would remain true even if you were Abraham himself. That is, the moment the voice in Abraham's head addresses him, he must confront the possibility that he is not Abraham but Cain—not a father of faith but a spiller of blood, the blood of his kin and of ethical community as such.

De Silentio seems to believe that Abraham himself can dismiss this charge of non-self-identity. In other words, he seems to think that Abraham is in a position to assure himself that he is an ethically perfect being—one who lives out the demands of the ethical realm without exception, one whose soul is permeated and informed by the ethical. This already strains credulity— certainly for anyone trying to imagine themselves (inhabitants of the here

---

[2] Kierkegaard, *Fear and Trembling & Repetition*, trans. H.V. and E.H. Hong (Princeton: Princeton University Press, 1983)—hereafter FT.

and now, a world of renewed global warfare, permeated by rumours of genocide on an industrial scale) in Abraham's position. And surely—here the student begins once more, with increasing excitement, to search the pages of the text in front of him—surely de Silentio also says somewhere that events in the spiritual realm after Abraham's time make such a claim to greatness no longer conceivable. Here it is—an interruption in his discussion of the third problema, concerning a father of faith's inability to render himself intelligible:

> An ethics that ignores sin is a completely futile discipline, but if it affirms sin, then it has *eo ipso* exceeded itself... As long as I move around in these spheres, everything is easy, but nothing of what is said here explains Abraham, for Abraham did not become the single individual by way of sin—on the contrary, he was a righteous man, God's chosen one...
>
> Up until now I have assiduously avoided any reference to the question of sin and its reality. The whole work is centred on Abraham, and I can still encompass him in immediate categories—that is, insofar as I can understand him. As soon as sin emerges, ethics founders precisely on repentance; for repentance is the highest ethical expression, but precisely as such it is the deepest ethical self-contradiction. (FT, 98–9)

If we begin to think of our lives in terms of sinfulness, the very idea of human ethical perfection is utterly lost: repentance is not capable of entirely eradicating the stain of past wrongdoing because even the smallest misdemeanour reveals our absolute difference from Absolute Goodness, and hence our inability to save ourselves by our own powers (thereby simultaneously opening us to the possibility and the necessity of redemption). And of course, the notion of sinfulness—in particular the notion of original sinfulness, that apotheosis of the idea of the sins of the fathers being visited on the sons beyond any particular wrongdoing on their part—is introduced to us not before or through Abraham but after him: through Christ's Incarnation.

So the advent of Christianity entails the dissolution of the possibility of ethical perfection, and so dissolves the possibility of the ethical functioning as a temptation, as it might have functioned (at least in principle) for a pre-Christian version of the God-relation such as Abraham's. Whereas Abraham did not become the single individual by way of sin, Christianity teaches that the only way to God is through sin—through recognizing our sinfulness and our inability to overcome it through our own resources. The Atonement is precisely God's response to our neediness, his loving sacrifice of Himself to redeem our sins. It's this shift in religious sensibility that Abraham's prophetic utterance on Mount Moriah (his vision of the Lord as providing a lamb for the sacrifice—a vision unfulfilled by the ram who actually appears on that peak) foretells; and according to such a sensibility, the teleological suspension of the ethical is not so much inoperative as transfigured—for in excluding the possibility of the ethical appearing as a temptation to disobey God, Christian religious belief suspends us teleologically *in* the ethical, requiring us always to live within its parameters, even if we reconceive them as dependent upon an external, absolute, divine point of reference and thereby radically intensify the demands they make upon us by asking us to make room for the idea of sacrificing oneself rather than something other than oneself (whether something we have or some other self).

But what about those who think of themselves as having gone beyond Christianity and its conception of the ethical as teleologically transfigured? Unless they somehow remain indebted to the perspective they claim to have transcended, surely they can no longer exclude the possibility of ethical perfection—that is, of ethical demands as something we can in principle imagine ourselves as meeting in full. So when the post-Christian asks himself, 'Am I Abraham? Am I capable of being a father of faith, that is, an exemplar of ethical life?', he must regard this as a genuine question; and in this sense, he occupies Abraham's position, since Abraham is distinguishable from those who situate themselves in relation to Christ in that he is someone for whom that question was genuinely open. Thus, all genuine post-Christians are indeed Abrahams, open to hearing a voice in the head that discloses them as capable of ethical purity or authenticity, with neither the possibility nor the necessity of a Christ-relation to supply the necessary resources. They can, and so must, demand authentically ethical existence—genuine individuality—from themselves, however hard it may be to comprehend even the bare possibility of such good faith; and insofar as they fail to meet that demand, they have no one but themselves to blame. What de Silentio claims that Abraham achieved is thus what every post-Christian must aspire to achieve; and insofar as they fail to achieve it, they must condemn themselves. In effect, then, the only ethical question in a genuinely post-Christian world is, 'Am I Abraham?'

So that's why the teacher made that other bizarre claim—here, the student leafs back through his notes—yes, he said that, 'There is nothing to show that I am Abraham; nevertheless I also am obliged at every instant to perform actions that are examples. Everything happens to every man as though the whole human race had its eyes fixed upon what he is doing and regulated its conduct accordingly. So every man ought to say, "Am I really a man who has the right to act in such a manner that humanity regulates itself by what I do?" If a man does not say that, he is dissembling his anguish' (EH, 31–2). After Christ, it is as if every human being is his own Abraham, the voice of each person's conscience is a divine utterance, and every individual must live as if under the gaze of his own de Silentio.

Can that really be true? Can I, for example (the student thinks), really confront the choice that this letter puts before me in these terms? He reaches for the envelope, unfolds the letter, and extracts the map—with its hastily-drawn route from northern France over the Pyrenees, through Spain, and then by boat to England. It lies there, next to his mother's Bible, with its family-tree frontispiece—one branch carrying the all-too-recent date of his brother's death, another bearing the name of the father who was now dead to him. Could an atheist de Silentio disclose this ethical dilemma as being (no more and no less than any other dilemma) a matter of fear and trembling?

2. The Son's Abandonment

The lecturer is looking over his text one more time: he is due to deliver it at the Club Maintenant the next day, but there's plenty of time to revise it, even to make radical changes to its basic argument. Not that he wants to disavow its deliberately provocative conjunction of concepts: why should his philosophical and political enemies have any particular claim on the humanist ideal? Nor is he unhappy with the underlying structure or gestalt of the lecture, the quasi-geometrical intuition that guided its composition from the outset; the question was rather how well he had managed to embody it.

He'd long seen the issue between the existentialists and their opponents as a matter of the relative priority of essence and existence with respect to human being; but here, he'd chosen to present these competing assignments of priority as opposing ways of conceiving of the relation between the individual and that which lies outside, beyond, or prior to him—between the particular and the general, the token and the type. Think first of those whose commitment to the priority of essence over existence takes the form of a belief in God as the creator of mankind: God makes man in accordance with a procedure and a conception, just as a human artisan makes a paperknife; each individual man is the realization of a certain conception or idea of man as such that resides in the divine mind. And this priority of the type over the token is retained even when God is dismissed, insofar as one continues to regard individual men as realizing 'human nature' as such, each instantiating that general kind of creaturehood. Either way, the individual is essentially a specimen: the shape or form of his particular existence is the wholly determinate expression of a prior, general form that is written into the fabric of the universe (whether by its Author, or by no author at all—it's hard to say which would be worse, that is to say, most conducive to despair: being God's instrument or the outcome of a mindless process). His reality as a human being is the reality of the idea of 'being human' writ small, the particularity of its actualization as nothing in comparison with what is thereby actualized: to be is to be the realization of a general type, hence to be essentially indistinguishable from all other such realizations and from that general type—to be essentially typical or generic. One might say (in fact I think I do say somewhere, don't I?—yes, here it is) that such a conception of human beings also makes them indistinguishable from material objects, regarding them as sets of predetermined reactions in no way different from the patterns of properties that constitute a table or a stone as the thing it is (things whose modes of behaviour and response are scientifically explicable as ultimately dependent on the kinds of thing they are) (EH, 45). In other words, giving essence priority over human existence amounts to annihilating human freedom.

If, by contrast, one begins from the reality of human freedom, and so prioritizes existence over essence, one reverses all of these related polarities: the flow of energy switches direction, so that now it is the concrete actuality of individual human being that determines the genus or genre or type of human reality as such, making it the creation of particular human creatures and their concrete choices. Think of the matter in three steps. First, there can be no choice that does not betray the standards or hierarchies of values by which the chooser guides his choices, and no such standards that are not themselves part of a broader vision of what it is to live well or flourish as a human being, hence of what it is to be human. If I choose to join a Christian rather than a Communist trade union, then

I make manifest my belief that resignation is preferable to revolution, which amounts to believing that resignation better becomes a man than revolution; and so I commit myself to a vision of what is best for human beings as such, not just for me. If I decide to marry and have children, I may do so only because of the particularities of my situation and desires; but I thereby declare that anyone in such a situation ought to practice monogamy as opposed to polygamy or infidelity, and that evaluation of monogamy will in turn depend on my convictions about how human beings are best able to find love and satisfaction. Second, insofar as I live out my life in accordance with my values, I realize or actualize them, and thereby create myself in their image; I become the kind of creature who flourishes in a life of resignation or monogamy, the kind of creature that I believe human beings as such really are. And (third) I thereby weave myself into the fabric of the human community as a concrete example of what I regard as the essence of humanity; I become an exemplar rather than a specimen, illuminating or illustrious rather than illustrative, some-one whose self-fashioning invites all other human beings to realize in their own particular way the vision of humanity as such that my individual existence embodies.

These, then (the lecturer thinks) are the three steps I mean to summarize when I say: 'I am thus responsible for myself and for all men, and I am creating a certain image of man as I would have him to be. In fashioning myself, I fashion man' (EH, 30). Have I left the relationship between this idea of exemplary self-fashioning and Abraham's exemplarity as a father of faith a little too obscure? Surely no more so than its relation to art, insofar as both involve ideas of invention or creation in the absence of predetermined and predetermining ideals; after all, I wouldn't want to prevent my hearers from going to the trouble of thinking for themselves. Nevertheless, there do seem to be some potential misunderstandings that it might be worth trying to avert—particularly for such a general audience. For it wouldn't be hard to regard my emphasis on freedom as itself a choice, hence merely expressive of my own vision of the world, and so an emphasis that others might reasonably reject; and even if this emphasis on freedom weren't itself arbitrary, it appears to license arbitrariness, in that it appears to entail that any concrete choice anyone makes is no more and no less legitimate (hence, immune from evaluation or criticism) than any other.

If I'm going to address the first worry, I should probably make use of Descartes. Suppose (he thinks, as his pen moves rapidly over a clean sheet of paper) I acknowledge that existentialism grounds itself in individual subjectivity, but that in so doing it seeks and finds a starting point that no human individual can coherently contest. For what the Cartesian meditations disclose is that what no subject can deny—the absolute truth of consciousness as it attains to itself—is 'cogito ergo sum': I think, therefore I am. In short, to exist as an individual consciousness is to apprehend oneself as conscious (of the world) and so as intellectually active (as intentional consciousness and as apprehender of oneself as such a consciousness). What Descartes shows is that one cannot so apprehend oneself without apprehending the reality of one's existence: and since the latter apprehension is logically related to the former, it amounts to an apprehension of oneself as thinking. But (as Kant later confirmed and exploited) thinking presupposes freedom: to be a thinker is to be subject to critical evaluation against the standards of logic ('Is this course of reasoning valid or invalid?'), which presupposes that the thinker might have done otherwise, and so that he is free. And to say that one might merely be thinking (erroneously) that one is thinking is simply to confirm the necessity of that presupposition—for to think of oneself as being in error is precisely to think of oneself as critically evaluable by the standards of logic, hence as a thinker, hence as free. So: the idea of one's consciousness as determined could not gain any purchase on one's existence and the choices that constitute it, for even those impossibly convinced of its truth must live as if it is false (because they must choose how to respond to the world as they find it). In short, any subject in a position to apprehend himself as a subject of consciousness cannot avoid regarding himself as free; freedom is an objective condition of subjectivity.

If so, then one judgement of value inherits that objective status—the positive valuation of freedom. For if freedom is a condition of the possibility of any evaluation whatever, then anyone who exercises their freedom in evaluative choice of any kind is implicitly committed to valuing the freedom they thereby exercise. But the value of that freedom does not reside in its being my freedom as opposed to someone else's, but rather in its being freedom (as opposed to determination): if its value derives from its being what makes it possible for value to exist in the world, then another's freedom is just as valuable as one's own. Doesn't Mill make a parallel (and much misunderstood) point, in that otherwise misbegotten essay of his on utilitarianism? If one comes to acknowledge happiness as something worth pursuing on the basis of reflective consideration of one's own unreflecting tendency to pursue it when given the opportunity, what one thereby apprehends is the pursuit-worthiness (the desirability) of happiness as such, not of one's own happiness alone; for whatever it is that I value about happiness, it does not reside in its being mine (as opposed to yours) but in its being happiness (as opposed to unhappiness). I may only be in a position directly to apprehend its desirability in my own case: but what I thereby apprehend is equally apprehensible by others from their own experience of being happy, and what is thereby apprehended (the value of being happy) is equally valuable whoever is fortunate enough to be the one experiencing it.

On second thoughts (the lecturer reflects), it might not help to make this point clearer by invoking an equally vexed and contentious parallel case. Kant's way of putting things might be more useful, since his concern is with freedom understood as practical rationality, and it's surely self-evident that rationality's value (if it has any at all) is essentially impersonal; so if being rational is of value, it is equally valuable whichever individual succeeds in realizing it in his existence. But the key point remains, whether understood in Kantian or Millian terms: if I am committed to valuing freedom, then I am committed to valuing it wherever it occurs, which means valuing the freedom of others as much as my own. And that point is made here as clearly as it could be: 'when I recognize . . . that man is a being whose existence precedes his essence, and that he is a free being who cannot, in any circumstances, but will his freedom, at the same time I realize that I cannot not will the freedom of others' (EH, 52).

So far, so good: but that analogy with Kant might lead people to think that I share his sense that a substantial moral code or system might be deduced from this formal obligation to will the liberty of others at the same time as mine. Whereas something like the opposite is true: for if my view of existence as preceding essence really does entail that any general conception of human nature or humanity as such is made real by the imagination and action of individual human beings, then the legitimate content of these conceptions is limited only by our need to presuppose the value of freedom in our relation to it. And this limitation needn't mean that every such conception must contain a central or even a positive place for freedom as a principle or value: it means rather that we can commit ourselves to that conception only as something whose authority over us is necessarily mediated by our free acknowledgement of it. In other words, to present any vision of human flourishing or human nature to others as if it were somehow written into the fabric of the universe—as if its application to us were determined prior to and independent of our relating ourselves to it—would be to situate them (and so oneself) as specimens rather than exemplars, as tokens of a given type, hence as a species of material object.

We might think of this as a practical or existential self-contradiction; it's another way of characterizing inauthenticity or bad faith. And what that shows is that it's only judgements of authenticity or inauthenticity that are licensed by my vision of human existence as preceding human essence: such judgements are not nothing, but they certainly don't amount to an endorsement of a Kantian vision of human beings as rational animals (any more than they underwrite a Millian vision of us as desiring animals, or an Aristotelian vision of us as political animals). Suppose I say (his pen races again across another clean page): 'Thus, in the name of that will to freedom which is implied in freedom itself, I can form judgements upon those who seek to hide from themselves the wholly voluntary nature of their existence and its complete freedom. Those who hide from this total freedom, in a guise of solemnity or with deterministic excuses, I shall call cowards. Others, who try to show that their existence is necessary, when it is merely an accident of the appearance of the human race on earth—I shall call scum. But neither coward nor scum can be identified except upon the plane of strict authenticity' (EH, 52). So any moral philosopher who attempts to justify his values by presenting them as the inevitable conclusion to be drawn from any objective assessment of the way things are (whether as a matter of natural fact, or of metaphysical necessity) is a coward: whereas those who do so by invoking their identification of and with necessitarian historical processes rather than structures or states of affairs—the Hegels and Marxs of the philosophical world—are scum (for if they were right, they would be nothing more than the inert and superficial product of oceanic energies).

But isn't this criticism of abstract or general modes of philosophical claims to authority a little too general and abstract itself? If I'm to give this claim a properly phenomenological grounding, I need a concrete example of the way in which any such vision of human nature or moral reality or practical reason founders when it comes into contact with the reality of any concrete choice-situation. The lecturer paused for a moment—then reached again for the sheet of paper. He had remembered an incident many years ago, when he had been teaching a clandestine class on 'philosophy and politics' to a group of young men involved in the Resistance; hadn't one of those students come to him with a problem of exactly the kind he now needed?

His brother had been killed by the German invaders in 1940; his mother was endlessly quarrelling with his father, who was inclined to collaborate with the occupiers, and endlessly anxious about her remaining son, whose desire to avenge his brother had led him to contemplate joining the Free French in England, but who worried that his absence would threaten his mother's sanity and perhaps her life. Looking back on it, it was as if the world had conspired to present the lecturer with a perfect gift for the future, for this present moment: a rich, over-determined family drama in which the concrete consequences for one individual had to be weighed against a far less certain contribution to larger social goals, in which a morality of personal sympathy stood in tension with one of social obligation. No moral philosophy could determine how to balance these competing considerations: Kant might tell him always to treat people as ends, but each available course of action involves treating some as ends and others as means. The student himself had acknowledged this (the lecturer recalled), and drew from it the conclusion that he should simply act on whichever instinct or feeling (for his mother, or for the cause) was strongest; but it did not take much discussion for him to realize that this approach was no more decisive than the previous one. For how was he to judge which feeling was the stronger except by discovering which course of action he finally chose to take? If so, to cite the greater strength of that feeling is not to locate an independent basis for the choice; on the contrary, it's rather more likely that it's precisely the pursuit of the course of action the feeling inclined us towards that renders it stronger in its reality than the other feeling. No: whatever indication or inclination the student might cite, it requires interpretation (as either decisive or not); and that simply means that its relation to action always goes through the agent's interpretative choice. The gap—however infinitesimal—between the signpost and its application is always only closed by his individual choice, hence is always ineliminably his responsibility, an expression of his freedom.

His pen raced on . . .

3. The Ghost's Despair

It took a long time for the crowded auditorium to empty, as some of the audience stayed to argue with one another, and others waited hoping to begin or continue an argument with the lecturer, until they realized that he intended to stay on the dais with the chairman for as long as it took to escape any such confrontations. So the lecturer was more than a little irritated to discover, as he eventually pushed through the main doors of the club after parting from his hosts, that one audience member had waited patiently on the steps for his emergence. Then he properly took in the appearance of his obdurate would-be interlocutor, and the blood drained from his own features.

'I wondered whether you'd recognize me after all these years; but then again, you've just been talking about me to all these people, so perhaps it isn't surprising that you made the connection so quickly. I always remembered your classes with pleasure—they really engaged my attention; and I wanted to let you know that I soon got over my sense of offense—of abandonment, really—at our final exchange, the one you recounted today. At the time, I really couldn't understand why you responded to my request for advice in that way—how did you summarize it in the lecture? 'You are free, therefore choose—that is to say, invent . . . no signs are vouchsafed in this world' (EH, 38). Not exactly helpful, on the face of it: verging on the insulting, really—as if you meant not so much to answer my question as to reject it. But it didn't take me long to see your point—your pedagogical purpose, if you like; you thought that I was treating the business of asking for advice about my dilemma as if it were not itself a choice or decision for which I had to assume responsibility, even a part of my chosen way of responding to that dilemma. Why come to you, rather than a priest with collaborative inclinations, or one inclined towards the Resistance, or even one inclined to go with the tide of events whatever turn they appeared to be taking?

'What else, after all, could I have expected from you—the philosopher of human freedom—if not the suggestion that I exercise my freedom to choose? And I did understand, even at the time, that this wasn't as empty a piece of advice as it looked. To begin with, your refusing to advise me was a refusal to accommodate any assumption I might still be making about a philosopher or a teacher (or indeed anyone with that kind of status) having some species of authoritative insight into ethical choices that mere students or ordinary men and women lacked. If I'd spent a little more time reflecting on the Kierkegaard text we'd been studying together, I might have seen that you were finding your own way of making the point that Kierkegaard himself made by his use of pseudonyms; everything we learnt about Abraham in that text was filtered through de Silentio's relationship to him, and by mediating our relation to this father of faith in that way, Kierkegaard makes it possible for us to put de Silentio's perspective on Abraham, and so his own, in question—and so to make unavoidable our responsibility for interpreting his example in any particular way.

'But there was more to it than that, wasn't there? For your refusal to advise me was, in another way, a concrete piece of advice (just as what de Silentio describes as Abraham's beyondness to language in fact consists in a number of concrete remarks, carefully recorded in the Genesis account). The truth is that you said exactly what I must already have been expecting to hear (why else would I have chosen to ask you for advice?); and by making this expectation explicit, you forced me to confront the fact that I had already decided *not* to ask for advice from someone who would have told me to choose one course of action rather than another, and so that my strongest instinct or feeling about my dilemma was to refuse to confront it— to defer or delay my exquisitely painful choice. By asking for advice from you, I not only delayed the moment of choice (which would have been true of any request for advice from anyone), I did so in such a way that I left myself exactly where I had been before asking for it.

'That much I understood pretty quickly after our last meeting; and it helped me to see not only that my range of choices was wider than I'd previously taken it to be, but to see which of those choices I wasn't willing to take responsibility for. But after today's lecture, I can see that your advice had a further dimension to it. For if you're right in thinking that one cannot choose without willing one's own freedom, and one cannot will one's own freedom without willing the freedom of others, then telling me to choose amounts to advising me to regard my choice as the creation of a certain image of man as I would have him be. It means advising me that in fashioning myself, I fashion mankind; it means inviting me to think of myself in this situation as if the whole human race had its eyes fixed upon what I do, and regulated its own conduct by mine. It means inviting me to consider myself (just like any other human being) as exemplary, as Abraham is taken (by whom?) as the father of faith, the exemplar of devotion to God.'

'Interpreting the choice I had to make between my mother and the Allied cause in terms of which course of action most fully wills the freedom of all would certainly have cast a rather different light upon it than the one it had for me when I had to confront that choice (even if not exactly the same light in which it might have appeared to you); but I can't ask you to take responsibility for my not seeing that this was part of what you were advising me all those years ago. For just that reason, however, I not only can but must ask you to take responsibility for what you did with this incident from our past just now, in that hall—to hold yourself accountable for the relation in which you placed yourself and your audience, here and now, to the relation in which we placed ourselves to each other in the past.

'Kant might say that you used me as a means rather than an end; I would say that you used me as an example rather than an exemplar, as a specimen or a token of a type—the type of bad faith or inauthenticity, someone from whose anguished abandonment to existence you drew a general philosophical moral. But when you recount our encounter in a way that reduces me to an illustrative instance of bad faith, it simultaneously reduces you to an illustrious instance of omniscient, authoritative philosophical wisdom—a father of intellectual faith in precisely the wrong sense; and this inauthenticity is reinforced by your present recounting of it—presenting yourself as dispensing to that audience exactly the authoritative wisdom that you dispensed to me long ago. For that amounts to presenting yourself as essentially continuous with that earlier self, and so as precisely not the self-surpassing being that you end the lecture by claiming that all human beings are (EH, 55). I don't see how you can treat your past as phenomenologically usable in this way without falsifying it, and so falsifying yourself.

'Can you really claim so fully to understand me and my situation without situating yourself in relation to me, and so in relation to yourself, in a manner that your own account of human intersubjectivity must condemn as inauthentic? If human beings are essentially self-surpassing, necessarily projecting themselves beyond themselves and so incapable of grasping themselves as a whole, how can you claim that it's always possible to understand anyone given sufficient information (EH, 47), let alone give an account of particular episodes in which you encounter others as if from a God's-eye perspective on the utterly transparent and self-identical consciousnesses of both? By your own lights, such methods of teaching can only be attempts to reduce others to objects, to slaves of your own intellectual and literary mastery, and so to philosophize in bad faith.

'Think of this as my attempt to repay my debt to you.'

The student turned his back on the lecturer and walked briskly off into the teeming streets. The lecturer stood there for a long moment; then he shouted at the retreating back:

'Did you stay with your mother?'

Quartet

Wallace's Wittgenstein, Moran's Amis

David Foster Wallace is the author of the novels *The Broom of the System* and *Infinite Jest*, the story collections *Girl with Curious Hair*, *Brief Interviews with Hideous Men*, and *Oblivion*, the essay collections *A Supposedly Fun Thing I'll Never Do Again* and *Consider the Lobster*, and an unfinished novel *The Pale King*. His writings have appeared in *Esquire*, *Harper's*, *The New Republic*, the *New Yorker*, *The Paris Review*, and other magazines. He was the recipient of a MacArthur Fellowship, the Lannan Award for Fiction, the *Paris Review*'s Aga Khan Prize and John Train Prize for Humour, and the O. Henry Award. David Foster Wallace died in 2008.

1. Gramma's Disappearance

David Foster Wallace's first novel, *The Broom of the System*,[1] begins with the disappearance of Lenore Stonecipher Beadsman's great-grandmother (since she shares Lenore's name, Lenore refers to her as 'Gramma') from the nursing home in which she has resided for years, and tracks its consequences for the various members of their extended family and interlinked network of colleagues and friends. Gramma was once a student of Ludwig Wittgenstein's during her time in Cambridge, England; her most valuable possession is an autographed copy of the *Philosophical Investigations*; and over the years, she has attempted to pass on to the Beadsman family in general, and to Lenore in particular, her understanding of the nature and significance of

---

[1] New York: Viking Penguin, 1987—hereafter 'BS'.

Wittgenstein's later conception of the relationship between language and reality, as encapsulated in the slogan 'meaning is use'.

So it isn't surprising to find a literary critic such as Marshall Boswell[2] claiming that 'Wittgenstein's *Philosophical Investigations*...is the key to understanding Wallace's audacious first novel' (UDW, 23). Of course, what this claim really means is that *The Broom of the System* is informed by *a particular reading* of Wittgenstein's masterpiece—that of the novel's author (who as it happens spent many years studying philosophy, and has elsewhere spoken of his deep admiration for Wittgenstein's writings); and that seems eminently plausible, although it would surely be foolhardy to assume that Wallace's understanding of Wittgenstein can simply be identified with that evinced by one of his characters—even the one whose defining feature is her having been a student of Wittgenstein himself. But even if one did make that assumption, matters would not be straightforward: for since the main business of the novel begins with Gramma's disappearance and ends only with the discovery of her hiding place, we are never given unmediated access to her understanding of her Cambridge teacher—there are no scenes in which she speaks directly to others (and so to us) about what she has learnt from him. Rather, we hear various other characters articulate to one another their interpretation of Gramma's various attempts to impart that understanding to them over the years: Lenore's father recalls how Gramma tried to teach him about Wittgenstein's vision, Lenore's would-be-lover Rick Vigorous recalls Lenore's own attempts to explain what she took away from her conversations with Gramma, Lenore's younger brother LaVache expresses his sense of the evil those 'indoctrination sessions' effected, and so on.

One might think of this as Wallace's novelistic embodiment of another famous Wittgensteinian emphasis—his sense of the inner life as essentially tellable or utterable, say oriented towards the outer (a point that Lenore reports Gramma as emphasizing to her). Pretty much every section of the novel primarily focuses on rendering, in very various ways, the speech or writing of some character or set of characters (whether by transcriptions of therapy sessions, gubernatorial administrative meetings and hospital trauma room exchanges, interior monologues and one-sided telephone conversations,

---

[2] *Understanding David Foster Wallace* (Columbia, SC: University of South Carolina Press, 2003)—hereafter 'UDW'.

or explicitly fictional prose composed by characters in the fiction), with only very occasional outbreaks of authorial description of the individual faces, bodies, and worldly contexts in and through which these torrents of words are enunciated. However that may be, experiencing the elusive recession of Gramma's own voice behind or within such complex orchestrations of multiply-refracted and mutually-contesting other voices might well lead any reader to conclude that the business of establishing exactly what Wallace's understanding of Wittgenstein might be, and exactly how it informs his novel, will be an exceedingly delicate one.

Q: What is the broom of Wallace's Wittgenstein's system?

Marshall Boswell finds little difficulty in delineating the Wittgensteinian vision that he takes to be central to the novel's work, largely because he takes the relevance of Wittgenstein to Wallace to be primarily determined by Wallace's desire to find a way of avoiding the dead end into which he believes that his postmodern metafictionalist predecessors (such as John Barth) have led those interested in the practice of serious literary fiction in the USA.

According to Boswell's Barth, postmodernist fiction inherits a context in which the modernist attempt to recover literature's engagement with human reality (by rejecting the tired conventions of objective Victorian realism in favour of an emphasis upon the structures of subjective experience) had resulted only in the generation of new literary conventions (stream of consciousness, disruptive spatial form) that themselves interposed between reader and reality, and that could claim no deeper correspondence with that reality than those they had replaced. The postmodernist response depends upon a thoroughgoing attempt to acknowledge this defeat and its full consequences: by employing literary conventions with self-conscious irony, it aims to explode the hypocrisy of those who wrote and read as if literary language could ever directly connect with reality.

But of course, even the ironic deployment of conventions is itself bound to become one more set of literary conventions; so the postmodernist project not only risks seducing its protagonists into reinforcing the same illusions as their unwitting literary forebears (with reality purportedly being disclosed once again, this time by irony or parody), but also makes their strategies more broadly available for co-option by contemporary cultural powers. And indeed, American mass culture was very quick to employ irony and parody in order to reinforce the very patterns of gratifying consumption and unquestioning spectation that the postmodernists originally aspired to skewer (in knowing forms of advertising and television—as when David Letterman created a successful television chat show by ironically deploying the conventions of television chat shows). In these ways, what was meant to be an honest revelation of our imprisonment, and so a pointer towards possible emancipation from it, quickly became one more way of imprisoning us—a funfair or playground in which it seemed that no linguistic convention (that is, no use of language at all) could be deployed at once straightforwardly and honestly. To deploy it without acknowledging its conventionality would be dishonest; but to deploy it whilst acknowledging it to be mere convention would seem at once to risk hypocrisy (as if one thought it possible to avow something whilst simultaneously disavowing that which made the avowal possible, as if aspiring to enunciate a self-disavowing avowal), to verge upon meaninglessness (for when one's words are no sooner uttered than ironized, one never means anything one says, which amounts to never saying anything at all), and to implicate the utterer in the broader commercial hypocrisies of the mass media. How, then, could anyone re-inherit the project of serious literary fiction without entanglement in either dishonesty or despair?

Derridean theories of language partly fuelled the development of postmodernism and its ensuing double bind, in Boswell's view; but they also amount to a reinforcement of its perspective on the world, because they are taken to mirror the postmodernist perception of language as interposing between us and reality rather than facilitating any connection between the two—language replaces reality rather than effecting any direct relationship between words and what they purport to name. The key advantage of the Wittgensteinian vision of language is that it, by contrast, allows Wallace to defuse the threats to human community and meaningfulness posed by the kinds of theory of language associated (rightly or wrongly) with Derrida's name, and exploited (rightly or wrongly) by the poststructuralist writers of metafiction by whom Wallace has been decisively influenced but from whom he in the last instance wishes to dissociate himself.

Seen through the lens of these concerns, Wittgenstein's later conception of language resolves itself into a small number of principles or insights. First, it foregrounds the bewildering heterogeneity of our life with words: 'a language is not built around some core or essence nestled in its interior like a peach pit . . . the multiple aspects of language might best be imagined as a "complicated network of similarities overlapping and criss-crossing: sometimes overall similarities, sometimes similarities of detail" . . . all the uses of language are linked the same way continuously overlapping fibres form a thread' (UDW, 24–5). Second, it suggests 'that we cease thinking of words as having meanings in and of themselves, and begin to conceive of them as having functions in various real-life situations, which he liked to call ["language-]games". The meaning of a word is therefore determined by its use in a given situation' (UDW, 25). Third, grasping the use of a given word is a matter of knowing the rules of the language-game being played: 'Grammar is one component, but so is the real-life situation in which the sentence is being uttered, the sociohistorical moment, the country and so on' (UDW, 26). And fourth, 'language can *mean* only when the rules are agreed upon by more than one person . . . language cannot be separated from the real world in which it is used, because it is inextricably bound up with what Wittgenstein calls the "forms of life". And without a community in which the rules are generally known, there can be no meaning, no communication at all' (UDW, 26).

Boswell takes it that Wallace is interested in Wittgenstein because the latter's account of language contests that of Derrida and Barth, but without denying their insights. For like Derrida, Wallace's Wittgenstein views the meaning of a word not as some extralinguistic 'thing' to which it refers, but as its function in a language-game; but unlike Derrida's vision of language as a self-referential system within which the play of meaning flickers and plays undecidably along and between chains of signifiers, the playing of Wittgensteinian language-games does not displace us from the world (entailing that there is nothing outside the text) but rather places us 'in' that world, and even more specifically in relations with other language-users:

Hence, for Wallace, the job of the post-Barth novelist is to honour the master's insights into the inherent artificiality of novelistic conventions, but to overturn the related insistence that texts are 'closed systems' that produce their own meaning through endless self-reference. Rather, the self-conscious meta-fictional novel, in David Foster Wallace's hands, becomes an open system of communication—an elaborate and entertaining game—between author and reader. (UDW, 31)

How, then, do these matters of strategic linguistic and literary-theoretical concern work themselves out in *The Broom of the System*? According to

Boswell, their primary functionary is Gramma, or more precisely the emancipatory relation in which Gramma aspires to stand to Lenore, whose progress in working herself free of her initial problems and recovering her own sense of identity is to be conceived of as her moving from a 'closed system' to an 'open system' model of language, life, and reality. Boswell traces Lenore's initial problems to three interlinked causes: her sense of the insubstantiality or unreality of her existence, her feeling of being used or controlled from without, and her anxiety about the fact that her name is shared with her Gramma. The first pair of these perceptions Lenore explains both to her therapist and to Rick Vigorous as deriving from her conversations with Gramma, and in particular from Gramma's claim that 'all that really exists of my life is what can be said about it . . . it's not really like a life that's told, not lived; it's just that the living is the telling, . . . there's nothing going on with me that isn't either told or tellable, and . . . if there's nothing about me but what can be said about me, what separates me from [a] lady in [a] story?' (BS, 119). Since tales have tellers, call them authors, Lenore's inability to distinguish her life from that of a fictional character naturally leads her to 'an intuition that her own personal perceptions and actions and volitions were not under her control. . . . [She felt] as though she were being used . . . as if what she did and said and perceived and thought were having some sort of . . . function beyond herself' (BS, 66).

Both perceptions are Lenore's way of drawing conclusions from two of what she presents as her Gramma's fundamental claims: first 'that there's no such thing as extra-linguistic efficacy, extra-linguistic *anything*' (BS, 121), and second 'that any telling automatically becomes a kind of system, that controls everybody involved' (BS, 122). And for Boswell, both of these claims accurately reflect Wallace's Wittgenstein's understanding of the role of the rules of language-games in the constitution of meaning: '[in] the wide-open spaces of Wittgenstein's language-game . . . meaning is achieved through functional and constructive interaction with others rather than the referential connecting of words to their objects' (UDW, 34); 'Lenore is "controlled" from without by the language-games she inhabits, like it or not' (UDW, 32). For Wittgenstein as much as Derrida, then, language creates 'a self-referencing web . . . over the reality it would seek to illuminate' (UDW, 29), and individual speakers are subordinate to the pre-existing rules of the language-games they inhabit. Boswell therefore takes Lenore's crippling anxiety about the reality of her own existence to be an accurate reflection (as far as it goes) of the way both Wittgenstein and Wallace think things really are between speakers, language, and the world.

The third cause of Lenore's difficulties is, however, essentially un-Wittgensteinian: according to Boswell (although he never provides a single quotation from the novel to establish its presence or significance), 'Lenore's identity problems stem from the fact that her name, the foremost signifier of who she is, points to someone else . . . Lenore does not know what to do with herself; she does not know, to use Wittgenstein's term, what her *function* should be, largely because she feels that her primary function has already been pre-empted by Gramma Beadsman' (UDW, 33). In so thinking, Lenore commits the primal logocentric, anti-Wittgensteinian sin of imagining that the meaning of her name and her life is founded on outside referents rather than on its own function within a system. And Boswell understands Gramma's disappearance, together with the complex plot management that she and her assistants effect during their withdrawal (manipulating Lenore's father, therapist, siblings, friends, and boyfriends in a variety of sophisticated but concealed ways) as her attempt to correct Lenore's error—first by removing the false outside referent (i.e. Gramma herself), and second by encouraging her to find a partner who is truly capable of participating in a genuinely open communicative system (i.e. rejecting Rick Vigorous, whose unceasing storytelling is all centred on his own desires and in particular the desire to subordinate Lenore to those desires, in favour of Andrew Sealander Lang, with whom she flees the scene at the novel's end). Furthermore, by committing herself to this emancipatory project, Gramma brings about her own emancipation from the nursing home, in which (her grandson reports) she felt her existence to be entirely lacking in usefulness, hence in meaning; for the space of the novel's sequence of carefully-engineered events, she finds a new function and so a new meaning in life—that of helping her great-granddaughter to locate the meaning of her own life within an open system of linguistic relations.

According to Boswell, then, Wallace's Wittgenstein accepts the inevitable recession of the real world behind the veil of language, but offers us the compensation of conceiving of that language as a field in which speakers might (contra Derrida and Barth) come into genuine contact with one another: in order to come into such 'constructive interaction with others', one must give up on the idea of 'the referential connecting of words to their objects'. But he also claims that this supposedly open and non-alienating field of constructive linguistic interaction is one in which individual speakers are controlled by the rules of the language-games they are inhabiting. If this is a form of human community, it is not one in which individual autonomy or self-expression has any apparent room to breathe: on the contrary, as Lenore accurately perceives it, it amounts to eviscerating the lives of speakers of any genuinely individual substance or meaning. So the very thing that is supposed to compensate us for our loss of referential connection with the world of objects—a new possibility of connection with other people, and so with ourselves—is in fact one more mode of our subordination to impersonal forces outside our control. And Gramma's supposedly emancipatory role is simply one further confirmation of Lenore's worst fears: her supposed progress towards individual meaning and liberty is in fact one more way in which her existence is reduced to its function in a larger system—in this case, Gramma's omnipotent plotting and manipulation, the true teller of the tale in which she remains enmeshed until the very last pages (and probably beyond, since her new boyfriend is the one whose sexually-abusive frater- nity initiation traumatized her in the novel's prologue, and that boyfriend's abandoned wife, Mindy Metalman, ends the novel by vowing to pursue them both wherever they might go).

Since Wittgenstein's term for the meaning-constituting rules (say, the normative articulation) of language-games is 'grammar', we might say that Boswell's Gramma(r) is a paranoid reading of Wittgensteinian grammar. It is certainly not the only available reading of Wittgenstein: and it patently rests on two false choices or oppositions. The first is the assumption that acknowledging the communal nature of language entails giving up on its referential function: but one might perfectly well accept that words attain meaning only in the communal context of a practice of employing them in a rule-governed way, whilst simultaneously claiming that these words thereby acquire the capacity to refer to objects in the real world. Those objects may not be the meanings of the words—that is, merely associating signs with objects will not transform them into meaningful linguistic units; but once signs acquire meaning by acquiring a use in a language-game, one of the things that they thereby acquire is the power to refer successfully to non-linguistic items. (The basic but crucial philosophical distinction here is that between sense or meaning, on the one hand, and reference on the other.) The second false opposition or choice is between rules and individual autonomy. Boswell assumes that to accept the rules of a language-game is to accept subordination to a power outside one's control; but a linguistic rule doesn't force anyone to do anything. Linguistic rules are conditionals: to define an 'umiak' as 'an Eskimo boat' is simply to say that if one encounters an Eskimo boat, it is correct to call it an 'umiak'. This doesn't involving dictating to reality (since one may never come across any such boat, the world might simply fail to contain one) or dictating to a speaker (since the rule licences a linguistic transformation rather than ordering us either to make a remark to which it applies, or to apply it even if one does make such a remark). On the contrary, the rules of Wittgensteinian language-games simply articulate a medium in which people can say things to one another about the world they have in common: they neither compel them to say anything at all, nor dictate what particular things they might have it at heart to say.

Of course, showing that Boswell's reading of Wittgenstein is not only non-compulsory but riddled with confusion and paranoia does not establish that it is not also Wallace's reading of Wittgenstein. Perhaps this exceptionally able student of philosophy misunderstood the *Investigations* in exactly these rather unsophisticated ways, and incorporated those misunderstandings into his novel; there are, after all, contexts external to the novel in which Wallace makes remarks that might be construed in a Boswellian way.[3] But even if we do so construe them, if we were able to establish that a paranoid reading of Wallace's Gramma is itself non-compulsory—that she can be read otherwise, and so his novel can be understood as embodying a non-paranoid reading of Wittgenstein's grammar—then we would have good reason to consider the possibility that the reach of Wallace the novelist exceeded the grasp of Wallace the commentator on his own novels. In my view, such a non-Boswellian reading of *The Broom of the System* is indeed available; and the best way of locating it is to ask what the title of that novel really refers to.

---

[3] Although many of those remarks are themselves open to alternative construals—so that, for example, Wallace's later description of his novel as having a 'Derridean-Wittgensteinian logic' will only count as support for a Boswellian reading if one assumes that Wallace understands Derrida as being committed to a species of linguistic idealism, in which there is nothing outside the text. Many Derrideans seem to read Derrida in that way (as does Boswell): but many others would regard such a reading as being exactly as paranoid and as inaccurate as the analogous reading of Wittgenstein appears to many Wittgensteinians. Why assume that Wallace's conjunction of the two proper names places him on one side of that interpretative divide rather than the other?

Here is Lenore's father, talking to her on the phone about her Gramma and his memories of her ways of explaining Wittgenstein to him:

Has she done the thing with the broom with you? No?...What she did with me—I must have been eight or twelve, who remembers—was to sit me down in the kitchen and take a straw broom and start furiously sweeping the floor, and she asked me which part of the broom was more elemental, more *fundamental*, in my opinion, the bristles or the handle. The bristles or the handle. And I hemmed and hawed, and she swept more and more violently, and I got nervous, and finally when I said I supposed the bristles, because you could after a fashion sweep without the handle, by just holding on to the bristles, but you couldn't sweep with just the handle, she tackled me, and knocked me out of my chair, and yelled into my ear something like 'A*ha*, that's because you want to *sweep* with the broom isn't it? It's because of what you want the broom *for*, isn't it?' Et cetera. And that if what we wanted a broom for was to break windows, then the *handle* was clearly the funda-mental essence of the broom, and she illustrated with the kitchen window, and a crowd of domestics gathered; but that if we wanted the broom to sweep with, see for example the broken glass, sweep sweep, the bristles were the thing's essence... Meaning as fundamentalness. Fundamentalness as use. Meaning as use. (BS, 149–50)

Despite Stonecipher Beadsman's concluding introduction of the idea of meaning, this teaching vignette in fact only concerns the relationship between essence (or fundamentalness) and use, and it operates not in the realm of language, but in that of reality; in short, it concerns not the meaning of the word 'broom' but the essential nature of brooms. On Boswell's reading of Wittgensteinian grammar, one would expect Gramma to emphasize that the grammatical rules for the use of the word 'broom' determine what we will take to be its essential nature, prior to any individual language-user's interpretation of it; but in fact, her lesson emphasizes the extent to which the individual user of a broom is capable of determining what is essential to it by choosing for himself what he wishes to use it for. In other words, Wallace's Wittgensteinian Gramma(r) does not veil us from reality but places us within it, as users of the objects to which our words refer; and it does not control our modes of interaction with those objects, but rather creates a space within which each individual can define what is truly fundamental about those objects for himself, constrained only by the limits of his imagination. Nor does the shaping or informing function of our choice of language-game deprive us of direct contact with extralinguistic reality; on the contrary, the broom's handle really breaks the kitchen window, and its bristles really do sweep up the shattered glass that really results. What this lesson conveys is thus a vision of reality as ours to inhabit, and a vision of ourselves as imaginative, improvisatory creative inhabitants of it (rather than mere functionaries of a language system, however open).

It's worth emphasizing how faithfully this fictional scene appropriates its philosophical original in the *Investigations* (in a sequence of early passages I touched upon in the first essay in this book); for in those passages, Wittgenstein also makes use of the example of a broom, whose significance is best appreciated if we acknowledge its emergence after his employment of another of the objects populating Stonecipher's recollection of Gramma's teaching—a chair:

But what are the constituent simple parts of which reality is composed?—What are the simple constituent parts of a chair?—The pieces of wood from which it is assembled? Or the molecules, or the atoms?—'Simple' means: not composite. And here the point is: in what sense 'composite'? It makes no sense at all to speak absolutely of the 'simple parts of a chair'.

[D]oes my visual image of this . . . chair consist of parts? And what are its simple constituent parts? Multi-colouredness is *one* kind of compositeness; another is, for example, that of an open curve composed of straight bits. And a continuous curve may be said to be composed of an ascending and a descending segment.

If I tell someone without any further explanation, 'What I see before me now is composite', he will legitimately ask, 'What do you mean by "composite"? For there are all sorts of things it may mean!' The question . . . makes good sense if it is already established what kind of compositeness—that is, which particular use of this word—is in question.

When I say, 'My broom is in the corner', is this really a statement about the broomstick and the brush? Well, it could at any rate be replaced by a statement giving the position of the stick and the position of the brush. And this statement is surely a further analysed form of the first one.—But why do I call it 'further analysed'?—[D]oes someone who says that the broom is in the corner really mean: the broomstick is there, and so is the brush, and the broomstick is fixed in the brush? – If we were to ask anyone if he meant this, he would probably say that he had not specifically thought of either the broomstick or the brush. And that would be the *right* answer, for he did not mean to speak either of the stick or of the brush in particular. Suppose that, instead of telling someone to, 'Bring me the broom!', you said, 'Bring me the broomstick and the brush which is fitted on to it!'—Isn't the answer: 'Do you want the broom? Why do you put it so oddly?' . . . Imagine a language-game in which someone is ordered to bring certain objects which are composed of several parts . . . [a]nd two ways of playing it: in one (a) the composite objects (brooms, chairs . . . etc) have names . . . ; in the other (b) only the parts are given names, and the wholes are described by means of them.—In what sense is an order in the second game an analysed form of an order in the first? Does the former lie concealed in the latter, and is it now brought out by analysis? True, the broom is taken to pieces when one separates broomstick and brush; but does it follow that the order to bring the broom also consists of corresponding parts? (PI, 47, 60)

In one way, Gramma's lesson is a less radical or far-reaching (although entirely authentic) version of that taught by Wittgenstein: where she merely demonstrates that the significance or importance of a part is determined by the use to which the composite object is to be put, Wittgenstein further invites us to see that the specific parts into which an object might be deemed to decompose, as well as its status as composite as opposed to simple, is a function of the language-games in which it is to be employed. But both, in their different ways, work to disabuse us of the notion that this vision subordinates the language-user and their modes of access to reality to the predetermined grammar of language-games. Wittgenstein does so by stressing that the composition or grammatical structure of linguistic phenomena (both utterances and language-games) is no more predetermined than is the composition of the objects to which those phenomena refer; for whether or not his two imagined versions of the order to bring the broom amount to one and the same order is entirely dependent on context, having to do with such factors as whether one is currently more interested in the practical outcome of the order's being carried out (which would foreground their common point), or rather in the ease with which it will be understood (which would foreground their relative oddness). Gramma does so by stressing that neither the broom nor our familiar ways of referring to it determine what counts as its fundamental or essential parts; that is rather determined by the creative imagination of the person interested in using it. In effect, then, both Gramma and Wittgenstein use their brooms to represent the grammar of language-games as translucent to reality and as ultimately determined by rather than determinative of the autonomous choices of language-users. For them, participation in language-games requires neither the sacrifice of contact with non-human reality nor the subordination of interpersonal communication to the external, impersonal control of predetermined grammatical rules.

This critical scene in the novel thus creates an opportunity for us to exercise our own creative imaginations in relation to Gramma's broom. For once we register that the meaning of its use in Gramma's teaching appears to exceed or run directly counter to the moral that Lenore's father draws from that teaching, we might thereby be encouraged to consider that Lenore's own interpretation of Gramma's Wittgensteinian teaching may be far from accurate to its primary emphasis or impetus—perhaps not surprisingly, given her description of herself as 'not being an especially verbal person in a family that tends to see life as more or less a verbal phenomenon' (BS, 398). To believe that there is nothing extralinguistic is something like the reverse of the evident moral of Gramma's broom; to believe that one's own existence is indistinguishable from that of a fictional character is precisely to overlook Gramma's emphasis on the distinction between world and words, between various ways of using the word 'broom' and various ways of using the broom; and to believe that one is being controlled from without is to mistake the structure of a pre-given space for individual speech with a script that all inhabitants of that space might be compelled to follow.

What Stonecipher's recounting of this pedagogical moment actually demonstrates is that even such a ferociously committed educator as Gramma working in a tightly-policed family context cannot control whether and how her meaning is transmitted or taken up. The tale itself thereby subverts the moral its teller erroneously draws from it; for it shows that even in a best-case scenario for the paranoid reading (a scenario of the kind Wittgenstein explicitly envisaged when introducing the concept of a 'language-game'—namely, that of a simple game that is played solely in order to teach a child about the meaning of something[4]), the structures of language-games do not control their own outcomes or dictate the responses of everyone involved. But it also shows that the scene of instruction it recounts contains a moral for the teacher as well as the student, insofar as it makes manifest a certain tension between that teacher's intended message (of individual imaginative freedom) and her (furiously coercive) way of attempting to convey it. And in so doing, it raises the possibility that Gramma's current ways of attempting to educate or edify her grand-daughter show that she is at least attempting to learn from those earlier pedagogical misfires.

---

[4] Cf. PI, 7.

On this reading, LaVache's sense of the evil inflicted on Lenore by Gramma's teaching can still be taken as an understandable response to its impact on his sister; but it can't be seen as legitimating his (or our) dismissal of the teacher or her teaching. By contrast, their father's depiction of this primal teaching scene is distorted only by his misleading concluding gloss on its significance; but that gloss connects his misapprehension to Lenore's, because it leads him to accede to a crippling idea that Lenore shares—that of transposing Wittgenstein's slogan 'meaning is use' to the domain of human lives. Wittgenstein never says that the meaning of a human being's existence is a matter of her function or usefulness; indeed, to make such a transposition from the realm of language and tools is precisely to treat real people as if they were fictional creations, made for an authorial purpose. And if we understand Wallace's Wittgenstein in the terms provided by Gramma's words and deeds in this primal scene, rather than the ways in which they have been taken by her family, then we are not compelled to assume that he means to endorse any such transposition. Indeed, the fact that Lenore's therapist (Dr Jay) persistently criticizes and mocks Lenore's attempts to express this Gramma-derived anxiety about the indistinguishability of real and fictional people in their sessions (e.g. BS, 116–22), when his every therapeutic move is later revealed as being under Gramma's surveillance and control (cf. BS, 309–11), suggests that Gramma wants Lenore to free herself from any such anxiety, and so should positively encourage us to distinguish Gramma's actual views on the matter from those Lenore imputes to her (and from those apparently widely held in, and pervasively elicited by, their world and its peculiar ways).

If we do read Gramma in the terms that this teaching vignette with the broom provides, we can still agree with Boswell that she is the broom of the novel's system; but then she need not be interpreted as 'the ghost of this book's plot machinery' (UDW, 32), at least not if this means (as it means for Boswell) the absent but omnipotent authorial controller of all that goes on in the novel's narrative. For the real point of the book's title might then rather be that the idea of this or any book as being a controlling system or a piece of perfectly-crafted totalitarian machinery is as inapposite as the idea of its author as an omnipotent, absent controller; more precisely, this essentially paranoid understanding of literature and reality would then be the book's critical target rather than its *raison d'être*—the bait, not the hook.

Certain of Gramma's other strategies might then be taken to express an aversion to that paranoid stance. For example, she decides to communicate with Lenore and her brother LaVache by sending them two drawings, the first of which (the barber with the exploding head) illustrates a famous logical paradox standardly taken to demonstrate truth's capacity to exceed or outrun the expressive powers of formal languages, and the second of which (the man on a slope) illustrates the inherent openness of representations to multiple interpretations. Her mode of embodiment in the world is also worth considering more closely: for Gramma's body lacks any kind of internal heat regulation, but rather takes on the temperature of her environment (this is why her room in the nursing home is maintained at 98.6 degrees). We ought not to ignore the fact that this feature of her mode of being makes her literally cold-blooded—a term of criticism that her initial teaching methods (even in the novel's primal scene of instruction) would already have amply invited, and that acquires particular gravity and penetration when the philosopher whose teachings she aspires to impart made so much of the traumatic consequences of coercive teaching methods in his various invocations of children as pupils in the *Investigations*. But neither should we ignore other aspects of its figurative significance—aspects that relate Gramma (and her current modes of pedagogy) rather more positively to the real spirit of her teacher and his works.

To begin with, such unconditioned openness of inner to outer has a certain Wittgensteinian flavour to it; and it might also be seen as embodying Wittgenstein's sense that to imagine a language is to imagine a form of life— that is, that the meaning of things is internally related to (not so much facilitated as constituted by) the contexts in which one encounters them. Most importantly, however, having one's internal temperature entirely dependent on the external temperature also amounts to a basic incapacity to control one's own bodily being, and so hardly suggests a capacity to control the environment of others, let alone the whole ambient landscape of the novel in which she lives. If anything, it suggests a pure form of receptivity—an inherent tendency to suffer or submit to the circumstances in which one finds oneself rather than to manipulate or alter them.

There is something deeply Wittgensteinian about this kind of receptivity: for it is central to his understanding of philosophical method that the philosopher should merely describe what is actually in front of her eyes, rather than imposing any theoretical preconceptions on what is there to be seen (assuming that reality must be a certain way, and looking to reinterpret it in accordance with those preconceptions when it stubbornly fails to match up to one's expectations). The ideal philosopher is therefore someone who utterly withdraws herself from the scene—someone whose representations of our life with words merely register what presents itself to her, so that her prose is utterly impressed or imprinted with it, in all its indeterminacy, open-endedness, ragged edges, and blurred contours. Her absence is not a means of self-imposition, a withdrawal in order better to exercise control over the landscape she surveys (although establishing and maintaining that absence may involve demanding and elaborate modes of control over herself and others); it rather reflects a refusal to interpose her subjectivity between that landscape and her interlocutors or readers, in the hope that they might come to see it as it really is.

Gramma's self-withdrawal might accordingly be taken as an acceptance of impotence, not a means of attaining omnipotence; and its self-abnegating motive would then be crystallized in the novel's clear implication (noted by Boswell) that she dies at the climax of the central plot, when the artificially-overheated telephone tunnels in which she has been concealing herself are breached (cf. BS, 463). After all, if absolutely effective manipulation of all the other people in the world of the novel had been her goal, she would have signally failed to achieve it; for Lenore is not at all slow to realize that the intersecting plans of her father, Rick Vigorous, and her therapist are as if designed to invite her to a certain location (The Great Ohio Desert); and although she does go there, she goes because that is what she decides to do, not because she is being controlled by forces unknown and external to her. Such an exercise of autonomy on Lenore's part is surely what any genuinely therapeutic engagement with her would aspire to provide. And not only is that what Gramma's subversion of Dr Jay's perversion of his sessions with Lenore in fact achieves; she does so in a manner that effectively acknow-ledges the mismatch between form and content in her earlier teaching practices—for now her formidable pedagogical powers are no longer exer-cised in order to coerce others into accepting the necessity to transcend coercion, but solely in order to negate the coercive impulses of another.

Insofar as *The Broom of the System* has or is a system, then, it is indeed a Wittgensteinian system—but that means that it is systematically committed to the unsystematic, to the limits of any predeterminate system, to the primacy of the heterogenous: committed, that is, to language's capacity to be carried by the irreducible variety of individual voices and their unpredictable, improvised interactions and contradictions in directions that the grammar of words neither dictates nor prohibits, from starting points which always have a prior history to end points that are always open to continuation (as the emancipatory mood of Lenore's escape with Andrew Lang never shakes off the traumatic traces of their first encounter or of his brutal freeing of himself from his wife, who reveals the non-terminal nature of the book's conclusion by declaring there her adamant intention to follow them both).

Gramma's absence and end may thus amount to an initial incarnation of Wallace's persisting Wittgensteinian conviction that a way can be found out of the writerly dead end of postmodernist metafiction only if one is willing to divest oneself of any ambition towards closure and control, as if arrogating to oneself a position entirely outside the tangled contexts within which alone the possibility of authentically and sincerely articulating what one has it at heart to say can be realized. The authentic author is not a *deus ex machina*, protected from everyday human failures of attentiveness and honesty by the systematic application of irony, parody, and pastiche; he is a *deus absconditus*, to be found nowhere in particular in the world of his creation because everything in it speaks of him (since its createdness points towards a creator), and is in fact a mode of his speech—an utterance from him to us, his hypocritical readers and siblings. With the early Wallace, absence is the mode of his presence.

2. The Self-Censurer

J.L. is a married librarian in the Welsh town of Aberdarcy, who becomes involved in an affair with the wife of one of Aberdarcy's more influential town councillors—an affair much complicated by differences of temperament, class, and wealth, not to mention very different levels of guilt and anxiety about its possible consequences. At the beginning of their relationship, after visiting a nightclub together and kissing for the first time, J.L. returns home to his wife and two young children and reports the following train of thought:

Feeling a tremendous rakehell, and not liking myself much for it, and feeling rather a good chap for not liking myself much, and not liking myself at all for feeling rather a good chap, I got indoors, vigorously rubbing lipstick off my mouth with my handkerchief.[5]

> Q: Is J.L. a good chap? (Marks will be awarded for how you arrived at your answer, even if it is incorrect; so show your working out.)

Richard Moran provides an answer to this question in his excellent study of self-knowledge, *Authority and Estrangement*,[6] in which he cites the protagonist of Kingsley Amis' second novel (John Lewis, although Moran never names him) in order further to explore the ways in which a human being might suffer the conflicting demands of realism about oneself and responsibility for oneself—an exploration in which Moran draws upon both Wittgenstein and Sartre.

The Wittgensteinian element is rooted in his famous response to what is known as Moore's paradox—why does it make no sense to say, 'It's raining and I don't believe it'? The first clause makes a claim about the world independent of the subject, whereas the second says something about how it is with that subject; and yet combining these two clauses with their two apparently different subject matters engenders something paradoxical. Why is this?

Wittgenstein's answer, according to Moran, depends upon seeing that expressions of belief are expressions of what the subject takes to be true (hence, in many cases, true of the world existing independently of the subject). Typically, the point of saying that I believe that it's raining is not to describe a feature of my psychological state but to describe how I take things to be in the world: it gives expression to a conclusion I have reached (perhaps by looking, perhaps by listening to others), and so amounts to a commitment or resolution—the utterance declares that and how I have exercised my rational judgement. At the same time, however, I recognize that it is one thing for it to be raining, and another for me to believe that it's raining: as a finite being, one fallible person in the world amongst others, I cannot avoid acknowledging that my believing something is hardly equivalent to its being true, hence that my believing that it's raining is something additional to the fact towards which it is directed or transparent—the fact of precipitation.

---

[5] Kingsley Amis, *That Uncertain Feeling* (London: Panther, 1955), p. 81—hereafter UF.
[6] Princeton: Princeton University Press, 2001—hereafter AE.

The contrast with the third-person case may help to clarify matters here. Another person's beliefs represent (psychological) facts on the basis of which one may make up one's mind about some matter (say, the weather); whereas one's own beliefs just are the extent to which one's own mind *is* (already) made up. The beliefs of another person can represent indicators of the truth, evidence on the basis of which I draw conclusions; but with respect to my own beliefs, there is no distance between them and how the facts present themselves to me, and hence no going from one to the other. I may either trust or mistrust another's beliefs, but I can neither trust nor mistrust my own; for to speak of my beliefs just is to speak of my convictions about the facts, and not of some additional thing by which I might be convinced. Even though I recognize that my beliefs are empirical facts about me, I don't primarily relate to them, as I do the beliefs of others, *as* empirical facts or data; the critical difference here is between the sort of thing one may treat as evidence on which to base one's judgements about how things are, and the judgement itself.

As an empirical matter, the fact of anyone's believing P leaves open the question of the truth of P itself, although another person may close this opening by inferring from a psychological fact to a non-psychological fact. But for the person herself, if her belief that it is raining does not constitute the question's being settled for her, then nothing does. To have beliefs at all is for various questions to be settled in this way ... to be a believer at all is to be committed to the truth of various propositions. (AE, 76–7)

Sartre joins forces with Wittgenstein when he invokes his example of the gambler (already touched on in this book), which Moran regards as comprehensible only if understood as illustrating in the domain of action what Wittgenstein's treatment of Moore's paradox discloses in the domain of cognition—namely, the distinction between commitment of oneself and theoretical knowledge about oneself. If the gambler has resolved to stop gambling, then he has made a decision—he has committed himself in a certain way, committed himself to avoid the gaming tables; so for him, his decision is not just empirical evidence about what he will do, but a resolution of which he is the author and which he is responsible for carrying through. Nevertheless, he does know himself empirically; he knows his akratic history, and from this point of view on himself, his 'resolution' is a psychological fact about himself, the strength of which provides whatever justification he might have for the theoretical expectation that he will avoid the gaming tables. And from this perspective (that of facticity rather than transcendence, in Sartrean terms), it appears to him as an ungrounded, inconstant thing on which to repose any confidence about what he will do. And he is right about this: from within this theoretical perspective no additional strength can be disclosed, since all of it is borrowed from the strength of the resolution itself, which is accessible only from the perspective of commitment or resolution. Having diverted himself from the practical reasons that issued in the commitment in the first place—having displaced the resolution from the realm of rational decision-making—he can only view it as a psychological phenomenon in himself, as which it appears far from compelling.

But if this utter submersion of oneself in facticity is a kind of evasion (an evasion of one's existence as transcendence, as a being capable of commitment or responsibility), it is equally an evasion absolutely to deny one's facticity—as if saying, 'Don't worry about my actual history of letting you down, for I hereby renounce and transcend all that.' I shouldn't ignore that history, because my practical perspective has no automatic trumping power over my character flaws or proneness to backsliding (another mark of my finitude); and even if I am confident about my ability to avoid such backsliding, the key point about a resolution is that it is mine to keep or to break at any time. My resolution exists as a fact on which others might base their predictions about me only insofar as I continue to endorse it, which means only insofar as the reasons in favour of acting in one way continue to seem sufficient to me. And if they come to seem insufficient, then I come to be unresolved, and I cannot even (inauthentically) relate to my resolution as an empirical fact, since it no longer is one.

Now back to John Lewis, who appears in Moran's account as exemplifying a paradox of self-censure. Something has plainly gone wrong in the case of John's course of reflection; it appears both self-undermining and morally dubious. Something in the spectator's stance he takes towards his original self-censure creates the illusion that he can bootstrap himself out of that initial judgement; what would be unproblematic if he were reflecting on another person here launches him on an apparently unending recursive chain of reversals of judgement. There is nothing wrong in itself in someone's reflecting on one of his beliefs about himself as a psychological fact about him, hence as something from which certain conclusions about himself may be drawn (after all, it is). But any such expressive interpretation of John's shame depends on his endorsing the judgement it embodies, actually committing himself to it; whereas his committing himself to the commendatory self-evaluation that results from that expressive interpretation amounts to his withdrawing that initial endorsement. His initial sense of shame can only be the basis for his belief that he is rather a good chap if it does actually manifest what he takes to be true of himself, if it expresses his conviction about himself (as having behaved shamefully, as being a disgrace); but to commit himself to the belief that he is a good chap is precisely to decide that he is not a disgrace, and so must require the withdrawal of his initial judgement about himself. However, since it is only his commitment to the initial judgement that gives him any reason to endorse the second-order judgement, its withdrawal would entail that he must withdraw that second-order judgement. Ultimately, John has to stop with his initial sense of shame; for the second-order evaluation that is the only candidate basis for his retracting that original evaluation can only provide such a basis if he continues to endorse the original evaluation.

That initial self-evaluation is not just a belief—something that manifests a conviction about its object (in this case, his moral character); shame is a general moral attitude, with characteristic feelings and moods—it is something close to a total orientation of the self, the inhabiting of a particular perspective. This means that one *can* jettison the total orientation of shame without ever losing one's belief that what one did was shameful; the passage of time might rescue someone from constantly feeling again his utter worthlessness, and allow him to look back on his earlier behaviour with a cooler, more affectless but still negative appraisal, as if thinking that the shameful actions of this earlier self no longer shame *him*. And this might allow him to say that he can retain his initial condemnatory belief about himself whilst abandoning his original shamefaced attitude. But to exactly that extent, that earlier undergoing of shame and self-disgust would no longer provide a basis for a positive current self-appraisal—it would no longer give him reason to endorse the belief that he is (as opposed to was) rather a good chap.

The first step in John's chain of reversals of judgement thus attempts to exploit a conflation between the stance of commitment and the stance of theoretical knowledge, by regarding his first-order judgement as both a commitment and a psychological fact:

He wants to be permitted to incorporate his current shame into the total evidence base for determining what sort of person this shows him to be . . . [But] if he's asking himself a question which he's appealing to certain evidence to settle, then the sense of this activity presumes both that this question is indeed open for him, and that it is one that is properly settled by the evidence (rather than by, e.g. a decision or resolution). If he is appealing to his own shame as evidence for something, we must ask, 'Evidence for what?', and the answer is clearly: evidence for what sort of person he has shown himself to be, evidence for settling the question of how he is to feel about himself. But supposedly, he has just answered this question for himself; that's precisely what the shame itself is a response to. He thus would need some *reason* to reopen that question, something grounded in some dissatisfaction with his original *answer* to that question, which is his response of shame. Yet nothing in his reflections displays any reason for such dissatisfaction—reasons . . . that are internal to the justification of a response like shame (as opposed to pragmatic reasons for avoiding its discomforts) . . . And even granting some reason to reopen the question, the deeper problem remains . . . for the very [expressive, exculpatory] conclusion he is now attempting to draw is *based on* the fact of his having settled that question, and . . . in a particular way . . .

He wants to take *credit* for his feeling ashamed, and invest that credit in a renewed deliberation about how to feel about himself . . . But reopening the question of how he is to feel undoes the creditworthy aspect of his shame as his settled attitude. (AE, 185–6)

So, Moran's answer to the Q with which we began would be: Yes and No. 'What he comes to see and what he expresses in the judgement he breaks off with . . . is that what presents itself at first as an inquiry into his character is in fact a continual shifting between two perspectives on the self in order to continually reopen the question, defer closure, keep the answer in suspense for as long as it takes to keep a "redeeming interpretation" in play' (AE, 187). So John Lewis rightly ends his chain of thought by not liking himself at all, and so judging himself to be not at all a good chap; but his decision to break off his potentially indefinite, recursive chain of reversals of judgement at such a self-critical point gives others a reason to account him a good chap after all.

This is not to recreate the paradox of self-censure: for the chain of recursive reversals with which Moran is concerned is paradoxical only when initiated and followed through entirely within the first-person perspective; there is nothing paradoxical in John judging himself to be dislikeable, whilst other people judge him to be a good chap precisely because he

judges himself to be the reverse (and does so in part because he began by
attempting to evade a condemnatory judgement of himself by means of the
morally dubious conflation or deferral of closure whose [il]logic Moran so
nicely delineates). Of course, in order for any of his friends or acquaintances
in Aberdarcy to gain access to his own ultimate self-evaluation, together
with the process by means of which he arrived at it, he would have to tell
them; and that would raise the question of whether and how his decision to
do so should affect the credit he would otherwise accrue if the necessary
information had been acquired by others without his intervention. Would
not such a decision be open to sharply critical expressive interpretation—
along the lines of, 'This is just a transparent attempt to gain credit in the eyes
of others for something for which you can't honestly take credit yourself'?
Here, we have something like a mirror-image of the paradox of self-
censure: for now, although the empirical fact of John's recursive self-
censure might legitimately function for others as a basis for commending
him (or at least thinking better of him), it can only be made available for that
role in a way which would deprive its subject of the credit he would
otherwise acquire. In effect, then, although John's (initial) shame and
(third-order) self-disgust are to his credit, they cannot function as a legitimate basis for assigning that credit to him either through the first-person
perspective or through its (second- and) third-person counterparts. Might
we call this a paradox of the self-exposure of self-censure?

Perhaps not. After all, John's initial critical self-evaluation takes the form
of feeling ashamed; and if he does indeed arrive at a sense of the even greater
shamefulness of his attempt to evade commitment to that initial evaluation,
then shame ought to be even more thoroughgoingly determinative of his
total orientation to himself and the world. And the one thing shame
canonically seeks is privacy or concealment—it is an emotion that shuns
the gaze of others. Why, then, would he even contemplate disclosing this
whole shameful process of self-evaluation to others—particularly to his
friends? It could only redouble his sense of shamefulness, by suggesting
that he was attempting once more to evade his initial evaluation (this time
by attempting to evade his concluding, third-order self-evaluation).

However, even if exposing one's self-censure is not paradoxical in the
way that engaging in the form of self-censure it would expose may be, it
nevertheless leaves the self-censurer in a peculiar position—credit is due,
but it cannot possibly be given. To put matters the other way around:

morally decent behaviour here compels self-concealment, and so demands the sacrifice of what one is owed, morally speaking. And of course, it further compels the self-concealing self-censurer to sacrifice any credit accruing to him for concealing his self-censure: he cannot permit himself to give himself credit for it (due to the paradoxical nature of self-censure), and he cannot permit himself to do the only thing that would permit others to give him credit for it (due to the credit-subverting shamefulness of the necessary self-exposure). And the same would hold for the credit due to him for sacrificing the credit due to him for his initial self-concealment, and for the credit due to him for concealing that second-order sacrifice; and so on.

Indefinitely increasing amounts of genuine but essentially inaccessible moral credit? Unstoppably recurring acts of moral self-sacrifice set in train the moment one judges oneself to be shameful? Something is going wrong here.

2 (A). The Tremendous Rakehell

Try it again. 'Not liking himself much' is John's initial, and relatively moderate, mode of self-censure; but what he doesn't like himself much *for* is 'feeling a tremendous rakehell'. That's an interesting turn of phrase: according to the OED, 'rakehell' gave up the linguistic ghost in the sixteenth century, being supplanted by its own abbreviation, viz. 'rake', which itself carries an air of nostalgia, conjuring up a mode of dissolute behaviour (together with a mode of evaluating it) that probably lost its cultural grip well before the end of the nineteenth century. So John's feeling this way is not just a matter of his taking pleasure in the intensely pleasurable beginnings of a sexual relationship with a beautiful woman, or even of his taking pleasure in what the general population of Aberdarcy (including himself, in certain moods or at certain moments) would regard as deeply immoral behaviour; in so describing his feeling, he is also putting into his own mouth a characterization of his adulterous affair that suggests a massively overblown conception of it—implying that this ordinary-verging-on-sordid venture is something of Byronic stature and transgressive significance, the exploit of a Don Giovanni. To describe himself as feeling a tremendous rakehell after one furtive kiss is to express his own view of himself in a way that ironizes, and so savagely criticizes, it long before he gets to the first, explicitly self-critical stage of not liking himself much for having the feeling. Or perhaps one should rather say that a fundamental part of why he doesn't like himself much for having the feeling is that how he experiences it amounts to a way of misleading himself about its real nature— it is a mode of self-interpretation that amounts to a mode of self-deception.

John's dislike of himself is thus rooted not (or not only) in a sense of shame about his adulterous activities, but also in a sense of shame about his tendency to romanticize their nature. But as his choice of self-description implies, he no sooner romanticizes himself than he is aware that he has done so: the ironic excess of the description inserts a gap or distance between his interpretation of what he is up to and what he is really up to, and because that description comes from him—because the novel is a first-person narrative—its inordinateness registers his unwillingness or inability simply to identify himself with his own initial self-interpretation. In this respect, John's description of himself as a tremendous rakehell exemplifies some-thing absolutely fundamental to his character—his incessant attempts at (or at least, his incessant inability to avoid) establishing ironic distance from any and every description of himself that might be thought to capture his identity. He is a librarian—but he is a librarian in the way Sartre's waiter is a waiter: it is a pure performance, a perfect following-out of the script that role thrusts upon him, usually to great comic effect. He really believes that he loves his wife and children, but he struggles to realize or enact that belief in his dealings with them. He regards himself as a savage critic of bourgeois pretensions in those who claim superior social status in Aberdarcy; but he cannot carry out this role without extreme self-consciousness, he is infuri-ated by his tendency to recognize admirable human qualities in those he should be criticizing, and he eventually finds himself conducting a deeply unsatisfactory affair with one of the most shamelessly self-serving, egotis-tical, and unkind members of that group. The structure of ironic self-distancing that generates the process of recursive reversals of judgement exemplified in the passage upon which Moran fastens is thus not only already at work in the very phrasing upon which the recursive process operates; it is at work, implicitly or explicitly, in a variety of ways through-out the language of the novel. It is, one might say, the signature of its narrative voice—the interior monologue of a subject who no sooner feels something than he questions its sincerity or justice, who oscillates unpre-dictably between performing pitch-perfect parodies of what others expect him to say or do and really saying what he thinks (typically in tones of savage sarcasm), who no sooner resolves to do something than he eagerly does the opposite. This is someone who is not so much governed by an uncertain feeling as he is constituted by feeling uncertain, someone who truly is not what he is and is what he is not—the Existentialist individual as Angry (and ferociously funny) Young Man.

So we find ourselves once more brought back to the fact that Moran's paradoxical self-censurer has not only a name and a highly specific character, but also a particular status: he is both a highly specific character in a fiction, and the narrator of that fiction. It is only because it is John himself who describes himself as a tremendous rakehell that we can be confident that ironic self-distancing does not merely come in at a relatively late or isolated stage in his thinking (and so opens itself to interpretation as instantiating a very specific form of moral weakness), but goes all the way down into the most basic or immediate forms of his experience—call it his orientation to the world. And to be reminded that our access to John's story is always through his consciousness is to be provided with a hint as to where things went wrong in section 2, when I seemed to confront a bewildering diffi-culty with respect to whether anyone else might gain access to the infor-mation needed in order to appreciate the moral credit John deserved for stopping his recursive reversals of self-judgement at the particular critical (rather than admiring) point that proved to be its terminus. For in puzzling over what ought to stop him from revealing this aspect of his interior life to those around him, I omitted to recall that we were only in a position to be confronted by that puzzle because we had already been given access to his interior life; we are reading the novel in which he appears, and more specifically reading his account of the events it narrates. Access to his interior life is thus not something we have to achieve—it is not something of which he might even in principle deprive us altogether, since his mode of fictional being is such that it is automatically bestowed on anyone who makes his literary acquaintance.

So what is beginning to emerge is that our evaluation of John Lewis has so far been conducted as if (with Moran) his key relationship is with himself, or (with me) as if his relationship with the other inhabitants of Aberdarcy is at least equally important; but what both approaches occlude is his relationship with those who are reading about him, and so the significance of the possibility that the themes of sincerity and irony that dominate the world of the fiction might also have a bearing upon the relationship between that world's author, its inhabitants, and its readers—the very territory staked out by David Foster Wallace's attempts to find a way out from postmodernism and its dangerous, despairing predilection for irony, parody, and pastiche in the face of the perceived impossibility of sincerity.

Thus re-oriented, suppose we go back to the problem in which we became entangled at the end of section 2. I got into the indefinitely recursive anxiety about John Lewis' inability to disclose matters redounding to his moral credit by glossing over a certain ambiguity in my reference to the 'others' to whom such disclosure might or might not be effected. But the moral imperative not to disclose the basis of his claim to be considered a (relatively) good chap applies only with respect to his fellow fictional inhabitants of Aberdarcy; it cannot apply to those others whose existence and relationship to him are presupposed and to some extent determined by his status as a fictional narrator—his readers, me, and (ideally) you. For John has no choice to make about whether or not he discloses himself to us: insofar as his existence is that of a fictional narrator of a fiction about himself, disclosure is a consequence of his mode of being, or rather of his existing as opposed to not existing as a fictional character. As his readers, accordingly, we are automatically given the necessary access to the grounds for judging him to be a good chap that he cannot in good conscience provide to anyone inhabiting his fictional world; we cannot relate to him at all except as someone to whom moral credit is owed (insofar as it is owed)—someone who deserves our approbation to at least this extent, and who does not risk that credit by creating the conditions under which we can recognize its reality.

That would seem to get John Lewis off the 'self-exposure as self-condemnation' hook on which we left him in section 2. But if we truly take seriously his status as fictional, then we need to consider the implications of the fact that he is a fictional creation, and ask ourselves how these considerations affect the moral credit of his creator; in other words, we need to consider not just the character-reader relationship but the author (-character)-reader relationship. For suppose, as most literary critical readers (and no doubt many readers *simpliciter*) have certainly done, that *That Uncertain Feeling* has a strong autobiographical element—putting it crudely (but not in terms of any simple identity relation), that John Lewis is a powerful synthesis of some of the characteristic thoughts, feelings, and situations of Kingsley Amis with those of his closest friend Philip Larkin in the mid-1950s (not to mention the succeeding decades). What, then, are we as readers to make of the fact that someone whose incessant self-ironizing has very likely incorporated the paradox of self-censure, and who has accordingly encountered the problem of self-condemning self-exposure, should decide to write a novel in which the central character undergoes the paradox but (by virtue of his status as narrator of the fiction) automatically escapes the problem of self-exposure? John Lewis thereby gets all the moral credit owing to him for being a (relatively) good chap; but since the only people in a position to accredit him with it do not inhabit his world, it hardly improves his standing within it. But if those same readers are inclined to see an internal relation between John Lewis and his creator, then they will similarly be inclined to give Kingsley Amis the credit that he shows to be due to his creation—and Amis inhabits one and the same world as his readers (doesn't he?), hence a world in which those lines of credit can be established and maintained (perhaps over a whole career).

Q: (A) Is John Lewis Kingsley Amis' way of gaining credit for being a (relatively) good chap?

Q: (B) What would John Lewis think of such a strategy?

3. The Death of the Author

At the centre of his 1999 collection *Brief Interviews with Hideous Men*,[7] David Foster Wallace placed a piece called 'Octet'. It is divided into five sections, each of which adopts the formal structure of a 'pop quiz'—the kind of unannounced tests by means of which high school teachers commonly evaluate their students; the format involves first outlining a highly schematic scenario, and then posing a question about it directed at the reader. 'Octet' contains five such pop quizzes, numbered 4, 6, 7, 6(A), and 9, and arranged in that order; numbers 4 and 7 are half-a-page in length, number 6 is two pages, number 6(A) eight pages, and number 9 is around thirteen pages,[8] as long as the first four put together.

---

[7] London: Abacus, 2000—hereafter HM.
[8] Including its footnotes.

'Pop Quiz 4' imagines two late-stage terminal drug addicts out on a freezing winter's night, one wearing a coat, the other (burning up with a fever) lacking even that protection; the first takes off his coat and lays it over the other. Q: 'Which one lived'?

'Pop Quiz 6' imagines two male friends who have a serious disagreement at work: Y refuses to do something dishonourable in order to protect X, but X feels deeply betrayed by Y. Y nevertheless continues with his practice of regularly visiting X's family, seemingly oblivious to the general discomfort and X's increasingly offensive reaction to his presence, culminating in a half-slap that damages Y's spectacles. But without ever determining exactly how the narrative will continue (will X forgive Y, or will Y stop visiting, or will the whole situation simply continue), it is abandoned, on the grounds that 'the whole *mise en scene* here seems too shot through with ambiguity to make a very good Pop Quiz, it turns out' (HM, 113).

'Pop Quiz 7' imagines a woman who, after her divorce, fights her ex-husband for custody of their baby; but his extremely wealthy family line up behind him, on the grounds that any member of this family should get whatever he wants, and they threaten to deprive the baby of the hefty trust fund set up in its name unless the husband gets custody. So the mother walks away from the battle, leaving the child to its father. Q: (A): Is she a good mother? Q: (B)—optional: explain whether and how receipt of the information that the woman had grown up in dire poverty would affect your response to (A).

'Pop Quiz 6(A)' Returns to the X of 'Pop Quiz 6'. Now, however, the focus is on his father-in-law, who has never liked X, has in fact urged his daughter to divorce X when they were going through a rocky patch, and is now dying of inoperable brain cancer. X's wife and her whole, close-knit family are deeply upset; and although X continues to feel disliked by the father and alienated from the whole family, he resolves to keep his feelings to himself, and support his wife in any way he can. So he keeps her company during hospital visits, and castigates himself privately, not only for his hatred of a sick old man (hatred that leads him to view his visits as supportive of the cancer rather than the patient), but also for being obsessed with his own feelings rather than focusing on his wife and her sense of devastation, which of course makes him worry that his shame and self-doubt about his self-involvement are themselves just another form of self-involvement. Eventually, he confesses his problems to Y, who advises him simply to continue with his supportive stance, and regard the self-loathing it involves as penance for his loathsome feelings; and X follows this advice, feigning concern so convincingly that, when the old man finally dies, the rest of his wife's family invite him to a private, inner-circle ritual of remembrance, in which everyone takes turns to expatiate upon their most treasured memories of that wonderful old man. As the time for him to speak comes rapidly closer, X finds that he has less and less idea what to say. Q: (A): Self-evident. Q: (B): X has found that his decision to conceal his true feelings from his wife has made him feel not only alienated from but angry with her over an ignorance he has made every effort to cultivate and sustain. Evaluate.

'Pop Quiz 9' directly asks its reader to imagine that she is, 'unfortunately', a fiction writer:

You are attempting a[n eight-part] cycle of very short belletristic pieces, pieces which as it happens are not *contes philosophique* and not vignettes or scenarios or allegories or fables, exactly, though neither are they really qualifiable as 'short stories' . . . [T]hey're supposed to compose a certain sort of '*interrogation*' of the person reading them, somehow—i.e. palpations, feelers into the interstices of something, etc . . . though what that 'something' is remains maddeningly hard to pin down . . . You know for sure, though, that the narrative pieces really are just 'pieces' and nothing more, i.e. that it is the way they fit together into the larger cycle that comprises them that is crucial to whatever 'something' you want to 'interrogate' a human 'sense of', and so on. (HM, 123)

But the whole thing turns into a total fiasco. Five of the eight pieces don't work at all;[9] if the sixth works at all, it does so only after a complete

---

[9] In a footnote designed to bolster this claim, two examples of failed Pop Quizzes are given, together with reasons for their rejection. The first asks us to imagine a psychopharmacologist who invents an incredibly effective broad-spectrum antidepressant, and who is then besieged in his own home by hordes of grateful patients, whose overbearing attentions reduce him to the point of contemplating shimmying up his chimney and expressing via a megaphone his incandescent hate-filled rage for those he helped; its culminating questions concerned whether and why he might deserve what happened to him, and whether any positive shift in the happiness/misery ratio in the world must always be compensated for. This was rejected because it was too long, and at once too obvious and too obscure; and most importantly, its cartoonishness gave the impression of being merely grotesquely funny, rather than simultaneously grotesquely funny and grotesquely serious, 'such that any real human urgency in the Quiz's scenario and palpations is obscured by what appears to be just more of the cynical, amusing-ourselves-to-death-type commercial comedy that's already sucked up so much felt urgency out of contemporary life in the first place' (HM, 127, fn 3). The second example asks us to imagine a group of early twentieth-century immigrants to the USA, to whom a sadistic processing officer on Ellis Island assigned the most obscene, ridiculous, and undignified English-language equivalent of their original

rewriting, and only if its unsuccessful earlier version precedes it—matters that can be mitigated aesthetically only by embedding acknowledgements of them into the Pop Quizzes themselves, thereby flirting with meta-textuality of a kind that will seem facile and will risk compromising the urgency of the whole project. You originally hoped to counteract the pervasive and ineliminable risk that the 'Pop Quiz' structure itself might make the project seem to be a mere formal exercise in readerly interrogation by fitting them into one another so tightly that their overall organic unity would allow the urgency of your concerns to come through; it would in fact interrogate 'the reader's initial inclination to dismiss the pieces as shallow formal exercises simply on the basis of their shared formal features [by] forcing the reader to see that such a dismissal would be based on precisely the same sorts of shallow formalistic concerns she was (at least at first) inclined to accuse the octet of' (HM, 128–9). But now your best attempts to rescue or reconceive that overall unity have generated pieces that only court more intensively that initial charge of shallow formalism.

So, imagine further that now you're trying to read your remaining pieces objectively—trying to work out whether they individually and collectively convey the redemptive urgency that inspired you to begin and to revise them, by imagining how they might appear to the person for whom they're intended, i.e. to your envisaged reader. This is a truly terrible position to be in as a writer:

There are right and fruitful ways to try to 'empathize' with the reader, but having to try to imagine yourself *as* the reader is not one of them; in fact it's perilously close to the dreaded trap of trying to anticipate whether the reader will '*like*' something you're working on, and . . . there is no quicker way to tie yourself in knots and kill any human urgency in the thing you're working on than to try to calculate ahead of time whether that thing will be '*liked*'. (HM, 129)

---

names that he could come up with. After a lifetime spent suffering the consequences, these immigrants end up in a nursing home to which the officer himself is ultimately consigned, in a paralysed, mute, and emphysematic state of utter helplessness; and they have to decide whether or not to exact revenge upon him. This Quiz did have the necessary grotesque/redemptive urgency; but it was rejected nevertheless, in part because all the key concluding, reader-interrogating questions are necessarily already thrashed out in the final stages of the piece's narrative, and in part because 'this piece didn't fit with the octet's other, more "workable" pieces to form the sort of plicated-yet-still-urgently-unified whole that'd make the cycle a real piece of bellestristic art instead of just a trendy, wink-nudge pseudo-avant-garde exercise' (HM, 128, fn 3).

Q: So does 'Octet' contain these two rejected Pop Quizzes?

But then you realize that your 'Pop Quiz'-style interrogative structure, with its added meta-textual flirtations, might give you a way out of the conundrum it is causing: 'you could poke your nose out of the mural hole that "Isn't working as a Pop Quiz" and "Here's another shot at it" etc. have already made, and address the reader directly and ask her straight out whether she's feeling anything like what you feel' (HM, 131).

You realize that this will only work if you are 100 per cent honest; anything less than completely naked, defenceless, helpless sincerity (with all its risks of appearing pathetic and/or manipulative and/or desperate to please) will just land you back in the same conundrum. But there is a way to achieve this: you can construct a ninth Pop Quiz, (one which will further intensify your meta-textual flirtation since it will be in effect a meta-Quiz, but nevertheless) one in which you will describe the situation in which you find yourself (the fiasco, the conundrum, the feeling that what originally drove you to start the project still survives in its reconceived remains), and in which you will simply puncture the fourth wall, completely naked, cap in hand, and flat-out ask the reader whether she feels what you feel.

The 'interrogation' structure will then no longer be a mere formal device; you will really be bothering the reader in just the way that a chef would be bothering someone if he chose to ring her just as she was sitting down to eat a take-away meal from his restaurant in order to ask whether she's enjoying it and whether it works as a dinner. It will make you seem like someone attending a party who is not only obsessed about whether or not the other partygoers like him, but spends the whole party going up to people and asking them directly whether or not they like him. Take the time to imagine the expressions on these people's faces, and to imagine those expressions directed at you. If you take this route, you risk looking desperate and pathetic; you will certainly not look wise, or serene, or authoritative, but rather lost and confused and uncertain about the validity of even your most pressing impulses and intuitions. 'So decide' (HM, 136).

Q: (A): What is the 'something' that the fiction writer in 'Pop Quiz 9' wants to interrogate or palpate or feel his way into his reader's human sense of, and that he hopes is conveyed by the other Pop Quizzes?

Suppose we begin to answer this by separating the sheep from the goats— the pieces that merit inclusion in the writer's envisaged cycle from those that he rejects; and suppose further (in good Wittgensteinian style) that we avoid presuming that such unity as the sheep may exhibit must take the form of a single common feature (or even a set of them), as opposed to a variety of overlapping similarities (call this a family resemblance model of unity). Leaving the claims of Pop Quiz 9 to one side for the moment, this would mean that we regard Pop Quizzes 4 and 7 as primary or central cases; Pop Quiz 6-and-6(A) would be a less central case (at the very best, given its desperately jerry-rigged engendering); and the second failed Pop Quiz (call it number '2') would be a peripheral but nevertheless serious candidate for inclusion (since, unlike the first failed Pop Quiz, its author feels that it carries significant traces of the urgency he wanted to convey). What, if anything, holds this quartet together?

The first two cases are virtual transcription of Biblical scenarios. PQ 7 reworks the tale of Solomon having to decide between two women each of whom claims to be the mother of the same baby; he discovers which is telling the truth by seeing which refuses his offer to settle the dispute by literally dividing the baby between them. And PQ 4 takes its central image of a coat from one of the Beatitudes invoked in Christ's Sermon on the Mount:

Ye have heard that it hath been said, An eye for an eye, and a tooth for a tooth; But I say unto you, That ye resist not evil; but whosoever should smite thee on thy right cheek, turn to him the other also.

And if any man will sue thee at the law, and take away thy coat, let him have thy cloak also.

And whosoever compel thee to go a mile, go with him twain.
Give to him that asketh thee, and from him that would borrow of thee turn thou not away.

Ye have heard that it hath been said, Thou shalt love thy neighbour, and hate thine enemy. But I say unto you, Love your enemies. Bless them that curse you, do good to them that hate you, and pray for them which despitefully use and persecute you; That you may be the children of your father who is in heaven. (Matthew, 5: 3842)

Seen against this background, the core of PQ 6(A)-with-(6) would be the willingness of X to love his enemy, and the self-sacrificial consequences of his doing so—the need to sacrifice not only his closeness to his wife, and his prideful disdain for Y, but also his image of himself as compassionate, decent, and (ultimately) truthful. And PQ 2 would plainly fit perfectly into the same self-sacrificial, loving-one's-enemy framework—perhaps a little too perfectly or at least too explicitly for its author's purposes, since its sheer obviousness would make the concluding question virtually redundant as an invitation to genuine interrogation on the part of the reader.

We can, then, take the Pop Quiz 9 fiction writer's belated and hesitant specification of this 'something' as accurate to the texts it follows:

> [T]he surviving semiworkable pieces all seem to be trying to demonstrate some sort of weird ambient *sameness* in different kinds of human relationships, some nameless but inescapable '*price*' that all human beings are faced with having to pay at some point if they ever want truly 'to be with' another person instead of just using that person somehow . . . , a weird and nameless but apparently unavoidable 'price' that can actually sometimes equal death itself, or at least usually equals your giving up something (either a thing or a person or a precious long-held 'feeling' or some certain idea of yourself and your own virtue/worth/identity) whose loss will feel, in a true and urgent way, like a kind of death, and to say that there could be (you feel) such an overwhelming and elemental *sameness* to such totally different situations and *mise en scenes* and conundra . . . seems to you urgent, truly urgent, something almost worth shimmying up chimneys and shouting from roofs about. (HM, 133)

Q: (B): Does the author of 'Octet' puncture the fourth wall?

It really does feel like it. As you gradually begin to figure out exactly what is going on in Pop Quiz 9, it really does feel as if the author of the previous three (or four) Pop Quizzes is stepping out from the fictional machinery, utterly naked, cap in hand, attempting with 100 per cent honesty (and with full awareness of how pathetic or desperate he will seem) simply to describe the difficult situation in which he has found himself as a writer, and thereby to contextualize and motivate his attempt to ask the reader (each and every reader) whether he or she feels what he is feeling.

But he isn't. First of all, the fiction writer delineated in Pop Quiz 9 never actually straight-out asks his readers whether or not they feel what he feels; rather, he presents himself as realizing that he can do so, and realizing the risks and costs attached to doing so—but the piece ends before or without his ever actually doing so. Second, the delineation of this critically incomplete, evaluative contemplation of the possibility of authorial coming-on-stage is itself a part of 'Octet'; it is another of that piece's pieces—one more Pop Quiz. This means that the fiction writer it describes is himself a fictional character—one more authorial creation (like the generous terminal drug addict, like X and Y, like the mother) rather than the author who created him (even if he resembles that author very closely in certain pertinent respects); these fictional characters are created solely as a means of posing a question to the readers of the Pop Quiz, but they don't themselves ask the questions that their actions are designed to invite or provoke. And with good reason: for any question directly asked by a fictional character can only be a fictional question—that is, a question asked by the character, not the author, and asked of his fellow fictional characters, not of their reader. If the author of 'Octet' really were the fiction writer of Pop Quiz 9, then he couldn't ask the readers of 'Octet' anything at all.

However, even if the fourth wall of 'Octet' can't possibly be directly punctured, it doesn't follow that its author can't ask his readers the relevant question in another way. After all, something resembling a question really is posed by Pop Quiz 9; but it is one that is doubly distinct from any of those posed by the other Pop Quizzes in 'Octet'. As we have already noted, it doesn't have the grammatical form of a question as such (certainly not one whose presence is signalled with the archetypal 'Q' prefix, as is every other Pop Quiz question in 'Octet'), but rather with something between an order and a reminder: 'So decide'; and this in turn reminds us that Pop Quiz 9 begins with the following sentence: 'You are, unfortunately, a fiction writer.' In other words, this Pop Quiz doesn't just offer its readers one more imaginary scenario containing characters whose thoughts and actions we are asked to evaluate from the outside, as it were—from what one might call the logical space of the test-setter or test-taker; it specifically invites us to imagine ourselves to be one of those characters. The invitation posed by Pop Quiz 9 is not (or not simply) to imagine others to whom one remains other (evaluative spectators of their deeds), but to imagine oneself *as* this particular other. Consequently, Pop Quiz 9 turns out not to be a means by which the author of 'Octet' asks his reader to evaluate something; it is a means by which the author of 'Octet' asks the reader to imagine being the author of (something very like, even indistinguishable in all the respects which matter to us, here and now, from) 'Octet'—an author who must decide whether or not to ask his readers to evaluate something. Why?

Here, we need to recall that the author of 'Octet' includes Pop Quiz 9 within 'Octet', and hence implies that (meta-Quiz though it may appear to be) it succeeds in contributing to the organic unity to which he thinks the other three (or four) successful Pop Quizzes also contribute. That would mean that it supplies another instance of the ways in which our attempts to be with another human being might involve risking either our literal death or the death of something we take to be central to our psychological identity and existence. Now, let's listen again to the concluding sentences of Pop Quiz 9, and so of 'Octet':

[Asking the reader directly whether she feels what you feel is] *not* going to make you look wise or secure or accomplished or any of the things readers usually want to pretend they believe the literary artist who wrote what they're reading is when they sit down to try to escape the insoluble flux of themselves and enter a world of prearranged meaning. Rather it's going to make you look fundamentally lost and confused and frightened and unsure about whether to trust even your most fundamental intuitions about urgency and sameness and whether other people deep inside experience things in anything like the same way you do . . . more like a reader, in other words, down here quivering in the mud of the trench with the rest of us, instead of a *Writer*, whom we imagine [fn: at least I sure do . . .] to be clean and dry and radiant of command presence and unwavering conviction as he coordinates the whole campaign from back at some gleaming abstract Olympian HQ.

So decide. (HM, 135–6)

Two constitutive and interlinked self-images are being diagnosed here: the idea of the author as Authority (omniscient, omnipotent, and radiant with conviction), and the idea of the reader as seeking in fiction a relationship in which she escapes from the insoluble flux that characterizes her relationship with herself and with the other real people she meets in her non-reading life. The author of 'Octet' believes that the relationship between reader and writer is in fact just one more kind of troubled and troubling relationship between human beings; it is one more place in which we encounter the insoluble flux of ourselves and others rather than an escape from it (which is why Pop Quiz 9 only appears to be meta-textual). He aspires to write in such a way as to 'be with' his readers, to meet them as equals on the common ground of their lostness and confusion and self-doubt; and the idea of the Authoritative author (by removing him as writer from the trenches to an Olympian realm of clarity and control) makes this impossible. Hence, he aspires to write in such a way as to do without—to disavow or sacrifice—this immensely comforting self-image, and thereby to encourage his readers to do without its foundational role in their self-image as well; for both parties, this will amount to a radical kind of dying to the self (as that self is presently constituted). But he cannot coherently do so by exercising that magical Authority, or even by appearing to believe that he can exercise it, on pain of self-subversion; so, for example, he cannot either directly say that he is, or directly present himself as, such a self-sacrificing person in his fiction (since either move would amount to an—incoherent—attempt to violate the necessary conditions of the author-reader relationship, as if he took himself to possess power that was at once genuinely authorial and utterly without limits). Instead, he invites his reader to imagine herself as that reader's author, as himself: he thereby invites her to acknowledge the mere humanity of the author, to rid herself of the idea of the Authoritative author by admitting his essential accessibility to her imagination, hence his no more (but no less) than equal standing with her. But he doesn't then tell her how the problems that the author of 'Octet' is facing are to be dealt with—for example, by elaborating the imaginary author of (something very like) 'Octet' to the point at which that author actually makes the decision that confronts him; for then the creator of the fiction would be dictating the reader's course of imaginative action whilst purporting to be respecting their essential equality, their shared, quivering, improvisatory, and risky occupation of the muddy trenches of human relationships. Instead, he leaves his imaginary counterpart's decision entirely in his reader's hands; he hands over the decision-making authority finally and entirely to her.

Will she dismiss this as one more shallow, dissembling, and hypocritical meta-textual exercise—one more way in which a postmodern author feigns a full acknowledgement of his status as the humble creator of mere illusions, whilst continuing to exercise all the creative power in that relationship, and so actually maintaining his superiority vis-à-vis his reader? Or will she recognize it rather as an unprecedentedly explicit, pervasive, and sophisticated way of acknowledging the primacy of his reader's imagination (as the domain in which alone his characters, and so himself as their creator, can alone come fully alive)? When a hyperbolically talented author devotes all his creative genius to crafting a text whose involutions and reflexivities ultimately deliver decision-making power to his reader, does that show the extent to which an author really can die to the idea of his Authority, or is it rather one more devious way in which he in fact preserves it? What matters more—what he delivers, or the fact that (when all is said and done) he delivered it?

You decide.

Bibliography

Amis, K., *That Uncertain Feeling* (London: Panther, 1955).

Austin, J.L., 'Other Minds', in *Philosophical Papers*, ed. J.O. Urmson and G. Warnock (Oxford: Oxford University Press, 1979).

Baker, G.P. and Hacker, P.M.S., *Wittgenstein: Understanding and Meaning*, 2nd edition (Oxford: Blackwell, 2005).

Bauer, N., *Simone de Beauvoir, Philosophy and Feminism* (New York: Columbia University Press, 2001).

Boswell, M., *Understanding David Foster Wallace* (Columbia, SC: University of South Carolina Press, 2003).

Cavell, S., *The World Viewed: Expanded Edition* (Cambridge, MA: Harvard University Press, 1979).

——*Pursuits of Happiness* (Cambridge, MA: Harvard University Press, 1981).

——*Conditions Handsome and Unhandsome* (Chicago: Chicago University Press, 1990).

——*A Pitch of Philosophy* (Cambridge, MA: Harvard University Press, 1994).

——*Contesting Tears* (Chicago and London: Chicago University Press, 1996).

——'Old and New in Emerson and Nietzsche', in Stanley Cavell, *Emerson's Transcendental Etudes*, ed. D.J. Hodge (Stanford, CA: Stanford University Press, 2003).

——'Companionable Thinking', in Cavell et al. *Philosophy and Animal Life* (New York: Columbia University Press, 2008).

——'The Touch of Words', in W. Day and V. Krebs (eds), *Seeing Wittgenstein Anew* (Cambridge: Cambridge University Press, 2010).

——'On Nietzschean Perfectionism', in M. Baghramian (ed.) *Reading Putnam* (London: Routledge, 2013).

Coetzee, J. M., *The Lives of Animals* (Princeton: Princeton University Press, 1999).

——*Elizabeth Costello* (London: Secker and Warburg, 2003).

Cohen-Solal, A., *Sartre: A Life* (London: Heinemann, 1987).

Conant, J., 'Nietzsche's Perfectionism: A Reading of *Schopenhauer as Educator*', in R. Schacht (ed.), *Nietzsche's Postmoralism* (Cambridge: Cambridge University Press, 2001).

Descartes, R., *Meditations on First Philosophy*, in *Descartes: Selected Philosophical Writings*, trans. J. Cottingham, R. Stoothoff, and D. Murdoch (Cambridge: Cambridge University Press, 1998).

Diamond, C., 'Wittgenstein on Religious Belief: the gulfs between us', in D.Z. Phillips and M. von der Ruhr (eds), *Religion and Wittgenstein's Legacy* (London: Ashgate, 2005).

—— 'The Difficulty of Reality and the Difficulty of Philosophy', in Stanley Cavell et al., *Philosophy and Animal Life* (New York: Columbia University Press, 2008).

Dostoevsky, F., *Notes from Underground* and *The Gambler*, trans. J. Kentish (Oxford: Oxford University Press, 1991).

Fincher, D., *The Curious Case of Benjamin Button: The Making of a Film* (New York: Rizzoli International Publications, 2008).

Fitzgerald, F. Scott, *The Curious Case of Benjamin Button and Six Other Stories* (London: Penguin, 2008).

Frank, J., *Dostoevsky: A Writer in His Time*, ed. M. Petrusewicz (Princeton and Oxford: Princeton University Press, 2010).

Freud, S., 'Moses and Monotheism', trans. L. Strachey; in Vol. 13 of the Penguin Freud Library, *The Origins of Religion* (London: Penguin, 1985).

Gardner, S., *Sartre's* Being and Nothingness (London: Continuum, 2009).

Grayling, A. C., *Descartes: The Life of René Descartes and its Place in His Times* (London: Free Press, 2005).

Greenblatt, S., 'The Lonely Gods', *New York Review of Books* (23 June 2011).

Hall, A., *The Quiller Memorandum* (London: Fontana, 1965).

—— *The Ninth Directive* (London: Fontana, 1966).

—— *The Striker Portfolio* (London: Fontana, 1969).

—— *The Warsaw Document* (London: Fontana, 1971).

—— *The Pekin Target* (London: Collins, 1981).

—— *Northlight: A Quiller Mission* (London: W.H. Allen, 1985).

—— *Quiller's Run* (London: W.H. Allen, 1988).

—— *Quiller Barracuda* (New York: William Morrow, 1990).

—— *Quiller Balalaika* (London: Headline, 1996).

Higham, N.J., *King Arthur: Myth-Making and History* (London: Routledge, 2002).

Hughes, T. 'Six Young Men', in *Collected Poems*, ed. P. Keegan (London: Faber, 2003).

Janaway, C., *Beyond Selflessness* (Oxford: Oxford University Press, 2007).

Kafka, F., *The Trial*, trans. W. and E. Muir (London: Vintage, 1983).

Kierkegaard, S., *Fear and Trembling & Repetition*, trans. H.V. and E.H. Hong (Princeton: Princeton University Press, 1983).

Malory, T., *Le Morte Darthur*, ed. H. Cooper (Oxford: Oxford University Press, 1998).

Moran, R., *Authority and Estrangement* (Princeton: Princeton University Press, 2001).

Mulhall, S., *Stanley Cavell: Philosophy's Recounting of the Ordinary* (Oxford: Oxford University Press, 1994).

——*Heidegger and* Being and Time, 2nd edition (London: Routledge, 2005).

——*Philosophical Myths of the Fall* (Oxford: Princeton University Press, 2005).

——*The Conversation of Humanity* (Charlottesville and London: University of Virginia Press, 2007).

——*On Film: 2nd Edition* (London: Routledge, 2008).

——*The Wounded Animal* (Princeton and Oxford: Princeton University Press, 2009).

Nietzsche, F., *Thus Spake Zarathustra*, trans. R. Hollingdale (London: Penguin, 1969).

——*On the Genealogy of Morality*, trans. C. Diethe, ed. K. Ansell-Pearson (Cambridge: Cambridge University Press, 1994).

——*Human, All Too Human*, trans. R.J. Hollingdale (Cambridge: Cambridge University Press, 1996).

——*The Birth of Tragedy*, ed. R. Geuss and R. Speirs, trans. R. Speirs (Cambridge: Cambridge University Press, 1999).

Sartre, J-P., *Being and Nothingness*, trans. H. Barnes (London: Routledge, 1958).

——*Existentialism and Humanism*, trans. P. Mairet (London: Methuen, 1973).

Silk, M.S. and Stern, J.P., *Nietzsche on Tragedy* (Cambridge: Cambridge University Press, 1981).

Wagner, R., *The Valkyrie*, ed. N. John, trans. A. Porter (London: Calder Publications, 1983).

——*Siegfried*, trans. R. Sabor (London: Phaidon, 1997).

Wallace, D. Foster, *The Broom of the System* (New York: Viking Penguin, 1987).

——*Brief Interviews With Hideous Men* (London: Abacus, 2000).

Wittgenstein, L., *Philosophical Investigations*, trans. G.E.M. Anscombe (Oxford: Blackwell, 1953); revised fourth edition by P.M.S. Hacker and J. Schulte (Oxford: Blackwell, 2009).

Filmography

Alien³ (1992: dir. David Fincher).

The Bourne Identity (2002: dir. Doug Liman).

The Bourne Supremacy (2004: dir. Paul Greengrass).

The Bourne Ultimatum (2007: dir. Paul Greengrass).

Casino Royale (2006: dir. Martin Campbell).

The Curious Case of Benjamin Button (2008: dir. David Fincher).

Die Another Day (2002: dir. Lee Tamahori).

District 13 (2004: dir. Pierre Morel).

Forrest Gump (1994: dir. Robert Zemeckis).

The Game (1997: dir. David Fincher).

Gaslight (1944: dir. George Cukor).

Letter From an Unknown Woman (1948: dir. Max Ophuls).

Now, Voyager (1942: dir. Irving Rapper).

Panic Room (2002: dir. David Fincher).

Quantum of Solace (2008: dir. Marc Forster).

The Quiller Memorandum (1966: dir. Michael Anderson).

Stella Dallas (1937: dir. King Vidor).

Se7en (1995: dir. David Fincher).

Zodiac (2007: dir. David Fincher).

Index

Printed and bound by CPI Group (UK) Ltd, Croydon, CR0 4YY